D0173012

K

DATE DUE

Brodart Co.   Cat. # 55 137 001   Printed in USA

DIKE

N. DIKE

Community Organizing and
Community Building for Health

N. DIKE

OKANAGAN COLLEGE
LIBRARY
BRITISH COLUMBIA

Community Organizing and Community Building for Health

EDITED BY MEREDITH MINKLER

RUTGERS UNIVERSITY PRESS
New Brunswick, New Jersey, and London

Third paperback printing, 1999

Library of Congress Cataloging-in-Publication data

Community organizing and community building for health / edited by Meredith
   Minkler.
         p.   cm.
      Includes bibliographical references and index.
      ISBN 0-8135-2435-0 (cloth : alk. paper). — ISBN 0-8135-2436-9 (paper : alk.
   paper)
      1. Health promotion.   2. Community health services—Citizen participation.
   3. Community organization.   4. Community development.   I. Minkler,
   Meredith.
   RA427.8.C64   1997
   362.1'2—dc21   96-49716
                                                                                    CIP

British Cataloging-in-Publication information available

This collection copyright © 1997 by Rutgers, The State University

All rights reserved

No part of this book may be reproduced or utilized in any form or by any means,
electronic or mechanical, or by any information storage and retrieval system, without
written permission from the publisher. Please contact Rutgers University Press,
Livingston Campus, Bldg. 4161, P.O. Box 5062, New Brunswick, New Jersey 08903.
The only exception to this prohibition is "fair use" as defined by U.S. copyright law.

Manufactured in the United States of America

Contents

Part VII   Building and Maintaining Effective Coalitions

Part VIII   Measuring Community Empowerment

Part IX   New Tools for Community Organizing and Community Building into the Twenty-first Century

Appendixes

Acknowledgments

An edited volume is, by definition, the work of many people. I am deeply indebted to my coauthors for believing in this book enough to put other tasks aside so that it could become a reality. Each of them writes from the heart, and their combination of passion and professionalism has contributed much to the final product.

Many other colleagues, practitioners, and activists have shared with us case studies and examples, ethical dilemmas faced in practice, and new ways of conceptualizing key aspects of community organizing and community building. Although too numerous to mention here by name, their contributions are cited throughout the book, and they are deserving of special thanks and recognition.

Like many of my coauthors, I have been blessed in the choice of a profession that places a strong emphasis on the centrality of empowerment and social justice for health and well-being. Numerous public health leaders and activists have inspired me in their unstinting efforts to live up to the profession's mission, but three in particular—Henrick Blum, Joyce Lashof, and Dorothy Nyswander—have been special mentors and role models to whom I am deeply grateful.

My colleagues at the School of Public Health have been a tremendous source of support and encouragement, and I wish to acknowledge especially my other community health education and behavioral sciences faculty members, Denise Herd, Mia Luluquisen, Patricia Morgan, Cheri Pies, William Vega, and Lawrence Wallack. I also owe a very deep debt of gratitude to my current and former students, who have taught me far more about community organizing than I could ever have hoped to teach them.

Many of my best teachers and mentors in community organizing and community building have been people on the front lines, and I wish to acknowledge, above all, the men and women of the Tenderloin. Through their tireless efforts with the Tenderloin Senior Organizing Project, they demonstrated over sixteen years what courage, power, and community are all about. The many staff and volunteers of the project deserve my very deep thanks, particularly cofounders Sheryl Kramer and Robin Weschler, former directors Diana Miller and Lydia Ferrante, and longtime project adviser and friend Mike Miller.

Acknowledgment of my special mentors and role models in organizing would be incomplete without mention of my dear friend Lillian Rabinowitz, whose leadership and unflagging efforts with the Gray Panthers nationally and locally have been a source of special inspiration. Together with such other "aging activists" as friends Ethyl Molo and the late Maggie Kuhn and Celestine Greene, Lillian Rabinowitz has beautifully demonstrated that there are no age limits on effective community organizing and community building.

This project came to fruition thanks in part to the stimulation and support of my family and friends. My parents have been lifelong supporters and role models, providing encouragement and love beyond measure. My siblings, Donna, Jay, Chris, and Joan, and friends Diane Driver, Larry Wallack, Frances Saunders, Beverly Ovrebo, Linda Nettekoven, Rena Pasick, Kathleen Roe, and Rose Marie Springer have, each in her or his own way, contributed to this project. My friend, colleague, and former student Nina Wallerstein is owed a special debt of thanks for her belief in and encouragement of this project and for her countless contributions since its inception.

The sheer mechanics of a project like this one can be overwhelming, and I am very grateful to Susan Alward, Debora DeNaro, Diane Driver, Janey Skinner, Tom Alexander, and the library research staff at the School of Public Health for their willing help and support. Karen Reeds, Martha Heller, and Marilyn Campbell at Rutgers University Press and copy editor Jess Lionheart played a key role in helping this book become a reality, and I am very grateful for their belief in and contributions to this project. Finally, this book could never have been completed on schedule without the tireless efforts of my research assistant Patsy Wakimoto. I am deeply indebted not only for the organizational abilities and other talents she so generously shared but also for her sincere caring and commitment.

This project sometimes spilled over into family time, and I am grateful, above all, to my husband, Jerry Peters, and our son Jason for their patience, love, and support throughout. Together with my parents and siblings, they have been a constant reminder that real "family values" are embedded, in large part, in the support and love that families, however they are defined, give to and receive from their members.

Part I Introduction

Chapter 1   Introduction and Overview

MEREDITH MINKLER

As we approach the twenty-first century, health educators, social workers, and other professionals who work at the interface of health systems and communities face unprecedented new challenges and opportunities. On the positive side, the importance of broadening our gaze beyond the individual to the community and broader systems levels is increasingly being appreciated. *Community based, community empowerment, community participation,* and *community partnerships* are among a litany of terms used with greater frequency by health agencies, outside funders, and policymakers alike. Although the reality of the accent on community has not begun to match the rhetoric (Green and Frankish in press; Labonte 1990; Robertson and Minkler 1994), clear movement in this direction is evident on a number of fronts.

In the United States, a plethora of new community-based organizations and coalitions have sprung up in the last two decades, and through these, local communities have mobilized to fight the environmental racism reflected in the location of toxic waste dumps (Avila 1992; Freudenberg 1984; Rivera and Erlich 1995); the closing of public hospitals (Brown 1983–1984); the increased targeting of young people and people of color in cigarette and alcohol advertisements (Ellis, Reed, and Scheider 1995); and continued discrimination against people with human immunodeficiency virus/acquired immune deficiency syndrome (HIV/AIDS) and other disabilities (Freudenberg and Zimmerman 1995; Lehr 1993; McQuire 1994).

On a global scale, the Healthy Cities Movement counts among its members more than forty-five hundred communities worldwide that are using intersectoral cooperation and high-level public participation to assess their health and mobilize their resources to create healthy cities and communities (Duhl 1993, 1996). The concepts of empowerment and community participation, defined as the "twin pillars" of the new health promotion movement (Robertson and Minkler 1994), are reflected in the World Health Organization's (WHO) (1986, 1) definition of health promotion as "a process of enabling people to increase control over and to improve their health." And that definition is replacing older conceptualizations of health promotion that focused on "individual responsibility for health" without attending to the equally important need for increasing individual and community "response-ability"(Zimmerman 1980), in part through healthy environments and healthy public policies. The availability of powerful new organizing tools, such as media advocacy and online computer networks, have further enhanced the prospects for effective community building and community organizing for health and welfare, and health promotion professionals have been in the forefront of developing, disseminating, and utilizing these potent new resources (see chapters 20 and 21).

Such encouraging developments, however, have been accompanied by troubling ones. Economic inequalities in the United States have reached unprecedented levels, with just 20 percent of the population now controlling 85 percent of the wealth and almost 67 percent of the earnings gains of males in the last decade going to the top 1 percent (Feenberg and Poterba 1992). As Lester Thurow (1996, 2) asks, "How far can inequality rise before the system cracks?" Inequities by race and gender also remain pronounced, with women who worked full time in 1994 paid just 76 percent of what men were paid and African-American families having a median income less than 55 percent of that of white families (U.S. Bureau of the Census 1995). The health implications of these continuing inequities are profound. People who are disadvantaged by "systems of inequality" (Stoller and Gibson 1994) have more acute and more chronic health problems, and poverty is widely recognized as a, if not the, major risk factor for disability and premature death (Alder 1994; House, Landis, and Umberson 1988).

Individual and institutionalized racism and the undercurrent of racial and ethnic tensions in our society also remain an American tragedy. The acquittal of four white police officers who had been videotaped beating African-American Rodney King, the bloody aftermath of the verdict, and the sharp and painful racial divide in public opinion following the acquittal of football hero O. J. Simpson on murder charges remind us, yet again, that the "problem of the color line" articulated by W.E.B. Du Bois almost one hundred years ago remains very much a part of our reality.

To the problems posed by continuing race, class, and gender inequities and tensions, Harvard's Robert Putnam (1996, 34) has added "the strange disappearance of civic America." Putnam laments the loss of our social capital—such "features of social life" as our norms, our networks, and our trust—and the loss of "civic engagement," defined as "people's connections with the life of their communities." He offers a stark picture of an America where television "privatizes our leisure time"

(1996, 48) and supplants our connections with communities. Although Putnam's analysis can be justifiably criticized as overly simplistic, the heart of his message resonates with many who feel increasingly disconnected and disenfranchised in a land where ever more sophisticated technology and an impoverished sense of individual and community embeddedness often lie side by side.

Finally, as this book goes to press, a continuing conservative political climate is enabling even mainstream politicians in the United States and elsewhere to advocate openly for drastic cutbacks in government commitments to health care, public health programs, and entitlements for the poor and other vulnerable groups. In the United States, calls for increased health access and equity, as part of a failed health care reform effort, have been all but buried beneath the quest for cost containment through strategies such as managed care. And while AIDS, violence, teen pregnancy, tuberculosis, and a host of chronic illnesses and disabilities continue to affect growing numbers of Americans, the pool of available dollars for core public health functions falls ever further behind the need. Within such a climate, where is the place for community organizing and community building in our professional practice? And how relevant are these approaches in today's world?

This book is premised on the belief that community organizing and community building must occupy a central place in community health education, health promotion, and related fields into the next century. With Lawrence Wallack and his colleagues (1993, 5), the book argues that "contemporary public health is as much about facilitating a process whereby communities use their voice to define and make their health concerns known as it is about providing prevention and treatment." As professionals concerned with helping communities have their voices heard and their strengths realized and nurtured, health educators and their allies in fields such as health planning and social welfare have a critical role to play.

This book advocates for the adaptation and use of community organizing principles and methods in response to a whole host of public health issues, such as HIV/AIDS, violence, and legal and illegal substance abuse. But it also advocates for a "purer" approach to community organizing, which is "a process through which communities are helped to identify common problems or goals, mobilize resources, and in other ways develop and implement strategies for reaching the goals they collectively have set" (chapter 3). In this latter process, the professional's role is one of helping to create the conditions in which community groups, rather than outside experts, can determine and set the health agenda and then act effectively to help transform their lives and the life of their community.

Although this book is primarily concerned with community *organizing,* a case is also made for health educators and other professionals to use their skills and resources in helping promote community *building.* As described in chapter 3, community building is an orientation to community that is strength based rather than need based and stresses the identification, nurturing, and celebration of community assets.

Increased attention to community building, and not merely community organizing around health issues, is well justified from a public health perspective. As Marc Pilisuk and his colleagues argue in chapter 7, we confront daily the "threadbare social fabric" of our postindustrial society, where individuals often lack secure embeddedness in a family, a workplace, a neighborhood, or a community of common interest. This lack of embeddedness represents not only a social hazard but also a public health hazard, as alienation and lack of a sense of connection to others have long been associated with heart disease, depression, risky health behaviors, and a variety of other adverse health outcomes (Bloomberg, Meyers, and Braverman 1994; Cohen and Syme 1985). Health professionals who draw upon their resources to support community building can make a real contribution to improving the public's health.

Health Educators and Other Social Change Professionals as "Conscious Contrarians"

Jacqueline Mondros and Scott Wilson (1994, 14–15) have described community organizers as conscious contrarians. They delineate three components of conscious contrarianism: a particular *worldview* or set of beliefs and values about people and society, a *power analysis* that rejects the dominant ways of thinking about power and how power is distributed, and a *deliberate selection of work* (community organizing) that is consistent with the other two. I would argue that community health educators, social workers, and other social change professionals may also be described as conscious contrarians along these three dimensions, but I would add a forth dimension as well. Borrowed from the old Native American tradition of the Heyoehkakhs, or "sacred clowns," this last dimension involves the social change professional's role in *doing things differently* and in the process challenging traditional ways of thinking (Tilleras 1988).

WORLDVIEW
Like professional organizers, health educators, social workers, and other social change professionals engaged in community organizing tend to share a worldview characterized by "a strong sense of what is just in and for the world" (Mondros and Wilson 1994, 15; Lippman 1937). Concerns with justice, fairness, the application of democratic principles, and a sense of collective responsibility thus can be seen to characterize the worldview reflected in such fields as public health and social welfare. Indeed, public health leader Dan Beauchamp (1976) has argued that social justice is the very *foundation* of public health and is an ethic that contrasts sharply with the dominant American worldview, which is characterized

by a market-justice orientation. "Under the norms of market justice," Beauchamp (1976, 4) points out, "people are entitled only to those valued ends such as status, income happiness, etc. that they have acquired . . . by their own individual efforts, actions or abilities. Market justice emphasizes individual responsibility, minimal collective action, and freedom from collective responsibility, except to respect other persons' fundamental rights."

This market-justice ethic in turn underlies the strong American tendency to frame and view problems, including health problems and their solutions, in individual terms (Wallack and Montgomery 1992). As applied to health, the market-justice ethic thus is clearly reflected in the words of John K. Iglehart (1990, 4), editor of the journal *Health Affairs*, when he writes, "Most illnesses and premature death are caused by human habits of living *that people choose for themselves*" (emphasis added).

The major role that individuals can play in improving their health through smoking cessation, diet and exercise, and other lifestyle modifications has, of course, been well demonstrated (McGinnis and Foege 1993). And health educators and other health professionals often play an important role in helping to create programs through which individuals can be enabled to change unhealthy habits and in other ways improve their own and their families' health status. But without discounting the importance of such work, the worldview of community health educators and other public health professionals recognizes its limitations. This alternative worldview sees health as intimately tied to social and environmental conditions and suggests that the primary focus of intervention be at the community and policy levels rather than at the level of the individual (Epp 1986; Freudenberg 1984; Hancock 1993; Minkler 1994; Wallack and Montgomery 1992).

The dimension of the public health and social change worldview that sees health and social problems as deeply grounded in a broader social context is very much in keeping with a power analysis that departs from mainstream ways of thinking about how and why societal resources are allocated as they are. But another critical dimension of the worldview of health educators, social workers, and other social change professionals deserves mention as well, and that involves their embracing of diversity and multiculturalism not as a problem or obstacle to be dealt with but as a rich resource and opportunity to be seized. In a nation such as the United States, where politicians can make political hay through their promotion of "English-only ballots," border patrols, and a clamping down on the rights of gays and lesbians, there is increasing need for professionals who can emphasize the many ways in which society benefits from its growing heterogeneity. The "respect for diversity" that health education leader Dorothy Nyswander (1967) laid out thirty years ago as a central criterion against which to measure our professional work has only increased in significance in the intervening decades. Its importance, moreover, will reach new heights in the twenty-first century, whose halfway mark is projected to see almost half of the U.S. population made up of African Americans, Hispanics, Asian/Pacific Islanders, and Native Americans. The value of inclusion rather than exclusion and the embracing of diversity as a means of enriching the social fabric are central to the worldview of practitioners in community health education, social work, and the other social change professions.

POWER ANALYSIS

Closely intertwined with the worldview just described is a power analysis that differs sharply from the dominant ideology. As Mondros and Wilson (1994, 15) have pointed out, "Mainstream definitions of who benefits in society and why are questioned along class, racial, ethnic, gender and other lines."

While typically not articulated as such, the power analysis of social change professionals often is rooted in political economy. This theoretical framework accepts Max Weber's (1978) classic definition of power as the probability that an individual or a group will have its will win out despite the resistance of others. A power analysis rooted in political economy argues that resources are allocated not on the basis of relative merit or efficiency but on the basis of power (O'Connor 1976; Navarro 1993). The unequal distribution of wealth, health, and life chances in a society is seen in this analysis as heavily determined by the interaction of political, economic, and sociocultural factors (Minkler, Wallace, and MacDonald 1994-1995; Walton 1979). The dynamics of race, class, and gender and the role of broad social influences in determining "what gets defined or undefined, treated or untreated" as a health or social problem are among the central issues with which political economy is concerned (Miller 1976, 1), and each has a great deal to say about the nature of power in society.

As suggested in subsequent chapters, feminist perspectives on community organizing and community practice (Bradshaw, Soifer, and Gutierrez 1994; Hyde 1989; Weil 1986) and newer community building perspectives (Himmelman 1992: McKnight 1987) often contain an alternative power analysis that stresses "power with" and "power to" (French 1986) rather than more traditional and hierarchical notions of "power over." As Bradshaw et al. (1994, 29) have suggested, within such perspectives "the target of change, that is, the power structure, is not seen as the enemy but rather as a potential collaborator toward a win-win situation."

Although the contributors to this book offer a number of perspectives on power, their power analyses have in common a rejection of the dominant notion that power accrues to individuals and groups on the basis of merit and "deservingness" (Katz 1995). Further, and whether visualized primarily in terms of power over or power to and power with, the role of factors such as race, class, gender, and sexual orientation in influencing power and access to societal resources is a critical component of the power analysis of contributors to this volume.

Of equal importance as the authors' power analyses, however, are their conceptualizations of empowerment. As Nina Wallerstein (1992, 198) has pointed out, "In the public health field, empowerment has traditionally been defined by its absence, as powerlessness." More recently, however, far more careful attention has been paid to this multilevel construct, which Julian Rappaport (1984) defines as an enabling process through which individuals and communities take control over their lives and their environment. In Wallerstein's (1992, 198) words, empowerment is "a social-action process that promotes participation of people, organizations, and communities toward the goals of increased individual and community control, political efficacy, improved quality of community life, and social justice."

Such a perspective figures prominently in the power analysis of many community organizers, health educators, social workers, and other social change professionals for whom facilitating individual and community empowerment is a central goal. Yet as discussed in subsequent chapters, a cautionary attitude toward the rhetoric of empowerment also is important. For particularly in these times of fiscal retrenchment, the language of individual and community empowerment and self-reliance frequently is being invoked by conservative policymakers to justify cutbacks in entitlement programs and health and social services. Indeed, as Ronald Labonte (in Bernstein et al. 1994, 287) points out, "Divorced of its historical contingency, empowerment is more a sop than a challenge to the status quo." While embracing authentic notions of empowerment, then, part of the worldview of health educators and other social change professionals involves a rejection of the argument that individual and community empowerment can take the place of a broader societal-level commitment to creating the conditions in which people and communities can be healthy.

DELIBERATE CAREER CHOICE

The third component of Mondros and Wilson's (1994, 16) conscious contrarianism involves the deliberate seeking out of jobs "that at least appear to contain the possibility to promote change." As suggested previously, the promotion of change that organizers embrace is most heavily concentrated on the community and broader institutional and societal levels.

Fields such as public health bring little fame, glory, or money to those who select them. In Dan Callahan's (1995, 2) words, disease prevention and health promotion "still remain the step-children of the American health care system: accepted but not well fed, praised but not always allowed in the living room, beloved unless they start making real financial demands." For health educators, moreover, the goal of facilitating empowerment can be particularly hard to live up to when funding is not only grossly inadequate but also is often "from categorical sources requiring us . . . to reduce cholesterol levels among people who cannot find employment, or to develop smoking cessation methods for communities who are despairing over the drug wars being fought on their children's playgrounds" (Pasick 1987).

Yet the increasing emphasis being placed by funders, health departments, and policymakers on health promotion and on strategies such as community participation, partnerships, and coalition building offers unique opportunities to help broaden still further the scope of our professional contributions to improving the public's health. In the United States, the massive shift to managed care and similar upheavals provide both new and fertile grounds for an increased emphasis on community building as a vital and health-promoting part of the health educator's role. In short, and even (and perhaps especially) at this critical juncture in our history, the choice of a career in fields such as community health education and health promotion can offer real opportunities for helping to create the conditions in which healthier communities and societies can emerge. As Barbara Kingsolver (1990) reminds us in her novel *Animal Dreams*, "The very least you can do with your life is to figure out what to hope for. And the most you can do is to live inside that hope. Not admire it from a distance but live right in it, under its roof." In choosing a career in community organizing, health education, or social welfare, we are in a very real sense choosing to live inside the hope we share for a healthier society and a healthier world.

DOING THINGS DIFFERENTLY

A fourth dimension of conscious contrarianism may be found in the Native American tradition of the Heyoehkahs—those people in the tribe who challenged people's thinking and shook them up. As Perry Tilleras (1988, viii) explains, the function of the sacred clowns, who were also known as contraries, "was to keep people from getting stuck in rigid ways of thinking and living." And so these tribal members, who were often gay, "lived backward," walking and dancing backward and doing everything contrary to the norm. Tilleras (1988, viii) describes the gay community's response to AIDS as in keeping with the Heyoehkah tradition: "When the normal response was to react with fear and panic, there were people dancing backwards, responding with love and confidence. . . . When the normal reaction to a diagnosis was isolation, the Heyoehkahs dragged us into community."

For organizers, community health educators, and other social change professionals, the Heyoehkah tradition of doing things differently is a familiar one. Whereas traditional medicine looks for pathogens and other agents of disease causation, health educators, for example, look for the strengths on which people and communities can build in achieving and maintaining health. And whereas in business and many other professions "getting ahead" means pushing one's self and one's achievements, the good community organizer, health educator, or social worker typically remains in the background so that achievements and victories are seen as being of and by people and communities rather than of and by outside professionals. In these and other ways, community health educators and other social change professionals are indeed contraries. As such, they play a role that is highly consistent with the philosophy and methods of community organizing and community building.

Purposes and Organization of the Book

This book has three purposes. First, it attempts to put together in one place, for students of health education and other social change professions, some of the critical recent thinking in community organizing and community building theory and practice. These contributions address both long valued aspects of organizing, such as issue selection and participation, and more recently applied perspectives, such as Brazilian educator Paulo Freire's (1973) "education for critical consciousness" and the approaches to "healthy community assessment" (chapter 9) and "mapping of community capacity" (chapter 10) that have emerged in the last decade.

Second, the book attempts to demonstrate, through a series of case studies, the concrete application of many of the concepts and methods discussed in real-world organizing and community building settings. Most of these case studies demonstrate the adaptation and use of community organizing and community building strategies by health educators and other social change professionals as part of their efforts to address such public health problems as substance abuse, HIV/AIDS, and lead paint poisoning. In other case examples, however, the health educator engages in a purer approach to organizing, creating the conditions in which communities can identify and address their own health and social issues. The frequent use of such analytical case studies and illustrations is designed to help bridge the still sizable gap between theory and practice in community organizing and community building.

A third and final purpose of the book is to make explicit the kinds of hard questions and ethical challenges that should be reflected upon continually by those of us who engage in community organizing or community building as part of our professional practice. Questions of the appropriate role of people in positions of privilege vis-à-vis community empowerment; the problem of conflicting loyalties between one's agency and the community; competing visions of "the community"; potential unanticipated consequences of an organizing intervention; issues of working across boundaries in terms of race, class, or other dividing lines; and questions of how to develop empowering, rather than disempowering, approaches to community health assessment and the evaluation of community health initiatives are among the types of questions with which we grapple. By raising these questions rather than providing pat answers, the book attempts to foster an approach to community organizing and community building that is, above all, self-critical, reflective, and respectful of the diverse communities with which health professionals are engaged.

Before providing an overview of what this volume contains, I want to state up front what it does not contain. First, the book does not provide a step-by-step approach to community organizing or community building. Excellent manuals are available elsewhere for this purpose (cf. Bobo, Kendall, and Max 1996), and interested readers are encouraged to peruse several of them to get a sense of the differences in style and approach they represent. Second, this volume is not intended as a comprehensive casebook, and consequently it cannot begin to do justice to the myriad exciting community organizing and community building efforts taking place among and with different racial/ethnic communities in both urban and rural areas or in communities based on shared interests locally or internationally. Once again, the interested reader is directed to other volumes, such as Felix Rivera and John Erlich's (1995) *Community Organizing in a Diverse Society* and Robert Fisher and Joseph Kling's (1993) *Mobilizing the Community*, that provide useful collections of such case studies.

Third, a distinction is made in this book between community-*based* interventions (e.g., the Community Intervention Trial for Smoking Cessation [COMMIT] tobacco control program [Thompson et al. 1990-1991]), the Centers for Disease Control's [CDC] Planned Approach to Community Health [PATCH] programs [Kreuter 1992], and numerous smaller-scale social planning interventions) and true *community organizing* and *community building* efforts in which community empowerment is a—and often *the*—central feature of the project itself. Although interventions like PATCH and COMMIT are discussed briefly in some of the chapters, they do not form a central focus of the book. Indeed, only one social planning effort (the CDC's HIV Prevention Planning Councils, which attempt to place a heavy emphasis on community empowerment) is discussed in some detail (chapter 19).

Fourth, this volume does not attempt to cover the voluminous body of literature on social movements. Although some discussion is provided (e.g., in chapters 4 and 7) on the importance of linking community organizing efforts whose joint actions eventually may constitute a social movement, such movements themselves are the topic of a number of comprehensive volumes. Again, the reader is directed to other sources, such as Steven Buechler and Frank Kurt Cylke Jr.'s *Social Movements: Perspectives and Issues* (1996), for a fuller discussion of this subject.

In making these omissions, I in no way mean to downplay the importance of social movements in bringing about change or the role of social planning interventions in health education and related fields. Similarly, the inability of this book to address in detail the impressive community organizing efforts that are taking place in areas such as antitobacco organizing, aging and disability rights, and homelessness, as well as among many diverse racial/ethnic and other communities, reflects solely limitations of space. Given these limitations, it is hoped that this book enables the reader to think critically about community organizing and community building for health, asking hard questions and exploring their relevance in practice settings.

In chapter 2, John McKnight sets a provocative tone for this volume, discussing the increasing professional use of the term *community* without adequate appreciation of its meaning. He argues that "associative communities" are more important than health and medical systems in terms of their impacts on the public's health, and he introduces several themes for community building professionals that are returned to and expanded upon in subsequent chapters.

The next three chapters together provide several conceptual frameworks and models within which community organizing and community building for health can be understood. Meredith Minkler and Nina Wallerstein begin, in chapter 3, by providing a theoretical and historical introduction to community organizing and community building and introducing several key themes (e.g., power and empowerment, community competence, and the principle of participation) to set the stage for their more detailed examination in later chapters. In chapter 4, Robert Fisher provides a more in-depth look at grassroots social action as a distinct and widespread model of community organizing worldwide. The ideological and historical roots of social action organizing are discussed, and its concerns with such issues as capacity building and culture and social identity are explored. Fisher raises a number of implications for practice, among them the need to combine postmodern demands for autonomy and identity with the older "modern" emphasis on social justice and connectedness between people.

In chapter 5, Cheryl Walter shifts our focus from community organizing to community, arguing that in our preoccupation with *the* community, we as social change professionals sometimes have lost sight of the broader concept of community and what it symbolizes. Viewing community as "an inclusive, complex, and dynamic system *of which we are a part*" rather than as an entity *with which we as outsiders interact*, Walter proposes a way of framing community practice that differs from that of most of the other contributors. Although not all readers will agree with this conceptualization, it is consonant with a number of important skills for social change professionals and is offered here as a means of stimulating fresh thinking and challenging us to reflect more critically about our roles in community.

In chapters 6, 7, and 8, we turn our attention to the challenging and often difficult role of health educators and other social change professionals as community organizers. Ronald Labonte begins, in chapter 6, by questioning some of the prevailing wisdom about community and raising a number of cautions for health workers who engage in community development toward the end of building authentic partnerships. Stressing the difference between community-based and true community development approaches, he provides a number of criteria to be met if authentic partnerships between health agencies and communities are to be realized. In chapter 7, Marc Pilisuk, JoAnn McAllister, and Jack Rothman then highlight the geopolitical contexts of current community organizing and use these as a context within which to examine the functions and dilemmas of the organizer. The problem of expert knowledge, identity politics, and the pros and cons of linking with larger public interest groups are among the topics explored. Several of the hard questions and issues raised in chapters 6 and 7 are examined in greater detail in chapter 8, as Meredith Minkler and Cheri Pies provide case examples of the ethical dilemmas frequently faced by health educators and other professionals in their roles as community organizers. Problems such as conflicting loyalties between the community and one's agency and the potential for negative unanticipated consequences of our organizing efforts are considered. Questions are posed for health educators and other social change professionals to ask themselves in an effort to make more explicit the difficult ethical terrain in which we operate.

One of the most important—and neglected—aspects of the health or social change professional's role as organizer involves his or her involvement in the process of community assessment. Chapters 9 and 10 are based on the premise that such assessments need to stress community strengths and assets rather than merely needs or perceived problems and that such assessments should truly be "of, by, and for" the community. In chapter 9, Trevor Hancock and Meredith Minkler introduce this perspective and challenge the reader to think not in terms of a community health assessment but in terms of a broader, healthy community assessment. In chapter 10, this approach is translated into practice in the form of John McKnight and John Kretzmann's classic piece, "Mapping Community Capacity." The reader is provided with a simple, yet effective tool that can help communities—and the professionals who work with or as part of them—find and map the building blocks or strengths and assets that can in turn be called upon in the building of healthier communities.

Chapters 11 and 12 turn our attention to two areas that are critical to effective professional involvement in community work. In chapter 11, Lee Staples discusses selecting the issue and "cutting" the issue in community organizing. Frequently drawing upon case studies and examples, Staples lays out the criteria for a "good issue," as well as the factors to be considered in cutting the issue as part of a strategic analysis. In chapter 12, Nina Wallerstein, Victoria Sanchez-Merki, and Lily Dow build on a theme introduced in chapters 1 and 3, laying out in more detail Freire's (1973) philosophy and methods of "empowerment education" and demonstrating their application through a case study. The New Mexico–based Adolescent Social Action Program, which addresses substance abuse and related problems on multiple levels, is described and analyzed, and implications are discussed for practitioners interested in adapting and replicating this model.

A major theme running through much of this book involves the role of community organizing and community building in and across diverse groups. In chapter 13, Lorraine Gutierrez and Edith Lewis describe their approach to organizing with women of color through the application of an empowerment framework stressing principles of education, participation, and capacity building. Arguing that existing models of community organizing fail to adequately address the strengths, needs, and concerns of women of color, Gutierrez and Lewis present a feminist perspective on organizing that specifically addresses problems and issues for organizing by and with this population. In chapter 14, Dan Wohlfeiler provides a case study of the development, by members of San Francisco's gay and bisexual community, of a nationally recognized grassroots AIDS prevention program. Social psychologist Kurt Lewin's (1947) "force field analysis" is used to demonstrate the factors working for and against the changes Stop AIDS wished to introduce and how the project has worked to address these through community building and community organizing efforts. Chapter 15, by Meredith Minkler, provides a case study of the Tenderloin Senior Organizing Project, a sixteen-year effort to facilitate community building and community organizing among low-income elders. The project's evolution from an outreach to an organizing project is described, as is its grounding in the philosophy and methods of organizers Saul Alinsky (1972) and Michael Miller (1993) and adult educator Paulo Freire (1973) and the community building orientation of John McKnight (1987).

Building and maintaining effective coalitions have increasingly been recognized as vital components of much effective community organizing and community building. In chapter 16, Abraham Wandersman, Robert Goodman, and Frances Butterfoss look carefully at coalitions, their unique capabilities, and how they operate. Using as a conceptual model an open systems framework from organizational development theory, this chapter examines coalition viability along several key dimensions and explores both the benefits and drawbacks of these popular organizing vehicles. In chapter 17, Daniel Kass and Nicholas Freudenberg draw on several of Wandersman et al.'s observations to describe and analyze a New York City–based effort at coalition building to prevent childhood lead poisoning. Following a brief look at lead poisoning as a public health problem, the authors describe the formation and evolution of a citywide coalition whose activities have included bringing a major lawsuit against the city. The victories achieved and barriers and dilemmas faced in this case study are examined, the coalition's structure critically analyzed, and lessons drawn for health educators and other social change professionals.

A central dilemma faced by professionals as organizers is how to facilitate the evaluation of organizing and community building efforts in ways that do not disempower communities in the process. In chapter 18, Chris Coombe describes how the process of evaluation can be used as a capacity building tool in community organizing, as well as a source of knowledge about a project's value and effectiveness. Empowerment evaluation is described and compared to traditional evaluation approaches, and David Fetterman, Shakeh Kaftarian, and Abraham Wandersman's (1996) four steps for conducting an empowerment evaluation are presented. Particular attention is paid to how these steps can be adapted specifically to the evaluation of community organizing efforts. The utility of this approach is demonstrated in chapter 19, as Kathleen Roe, Cindy Berenstein, Christina Goette, and Kevin Roe describe and analyze an innovative effort to facilitate empowerment through the evaluation of HIV Prevention Planning Councils on the city, regional, and state levels. As noted earlier, their analysis represents the only detailed look in this volume at a social planning, rather than social action or community building, approach to practice. It is included, however, because this new national experiment in empowering community planning is important and because the case study itself demonstrates many of the challenges, dilemmas, and rewards involved in an empowerment approach to evaluation.

The volume ends with a discussion of the new tools available for community organizing and building. Although any number of promising new approaches could be discussed, two have been selected for special attention. In chapter 20, Courtney Uhler Cart explores the use of online networks both as virtual communities and as tools for health educators, social workers, and other professionals engaged in community organizing and community building for health. Grounded in a conceptual framework that draws on Alinsky's (1972) social action organizing, Alexis de Tocqueville's (1835) community associations, and newer notions of community building, the chapter includes current examples of online organizing and community building for health and explores the ethical dilemmas that have emerged and their implications for practitioners. In chapter 21, the final chapter, Lawrence Wallack discusses the increasingly popular technique known as media advocacy, or "the strategic use of mass media to advance public policy initiatives." Media advocacy is described in this chapter as a potent community tool that is being used to get the media to reframe local and national problems and change the ways in which they are presented and viewed. An approach that seeks to enhance community groups' visibility, legitimacy, and power, media advocacy is a critical tool for building healthier communities through advocacy for healthy public policy.

The volume ends with appendixes designed to provide the reader with concrete tools and applications that correspond to a number of the chapter themes and issues raised. Ranging from an action-oriented community assessment technique to a coalition checklist and some helpful tips on fostering leadership and participation, the appendixes are designed to help practitioners put into practice some of the messages central to this volume and to community organizing and community building.

Although this book is written primarily for students and practitioners in fields such as community health education, health planning, and social welfare, it should be of interest as well to activists and others concerned with the many hard questions and realities that surround community building and community organizing for health at the dawn of the twenty-first century. The contributors to this volume have attempted to write provocatively and critically, challenging the reader—and each other—to ask hard questions and to rethink some of our most basic assumptions. We ask you, the reader, to join us in this process of critical questioning and dialogue as you seek to apply theory to practice, and practice to the rethinking of theory, toward the end of helping build healthier communities and more caring and humane societies.

References

Alder, N. E., T. Boyce, M. A. Chesney, S. Cohen, S. Folkman, R. L. Kahn, and S. L. Syme 1994. Socioeconomic status and health: The challenge of the gradient. *American Psychologist* 49:15–24.

Alinsky, S. D. 1972. *Rules for radicals*. New York: Random House.

Avila, M. 1992. Environmental racism and issues of social justice. Keynote address to the University of Michigan Law School, Ann Arbor, Michigan, January 23.

Beauchamp, D. 1976. Public health as social justice. *Inquiry* 12:3–14.

Bernstein, E., N. Wallerstein, R. Braithwaite et al. 1994. Empowerment forum: A dialogue between guest editorial board members. *Health Education Quarterly* 21 (3):281–294.

Bloomberg, L., J. Meyers, and M. T. Braverman. 1994. The importance of social interaction: A new perspective on social epidemiology, social risk factors, and health. *Health Education Quarterly* 21 (4):447–463.

Bobo, K., J. Kendall, and S. Max. 1996. *Organizing for social change*. 2d ed. Santa Ana, Calif.: Seven Locks Press.

Bradshaw, C., S. Soifer, and L. Gutierrez. 1994. Toward a hybrid model for effective organizing in communities of color. *Journal of Community Practice* 1 (1):25–41.

Brown, E. R. 1983-1984. Roles for health educators in a time of health care cutbacks: Preventive and ameliorative approaches. *International Quarterly of Community Health Education* 4 (4):293–302.

Buechler, S. M., and F. K. Cylke Jr. 1996. *Social movements: Perspectives and issues*. Mountain View, Calif.: Mayfield.

Callahan, D. 1995. Issues in health promotion and disease prevention. Hastings on the Hudson, N.Y.: Hastings Center. Unpublished proposal.

Cohen, S., and S. L. Syme. 1985. *Social Support and Health*. New York: Academic Books.

Duhl, L. 1993. Conditions for healthy cities: Diversity, gameboards, and social entrepreneurs. *Environment and Urbanization* 5 (2):112–124.

———. 1996. Personal communication, August 26.

Ellis, G. A., D. F. Reed, and H. Scheider. 1995. Mobilizing a low-income African-American community around tobacco control: A force field analysis. *Health Education Quarterly* 22 (4):443–457.

Epp, J. 1986. Achieving health for all: A framework for health promotion. *Canadian Journal of Public Health* 77 (6):393–408.

Feenberg, D. R., and J. Poterba. 1992. *Income inequality and the incomes of very-high-income taxpayers*. Working Paper 4229. Cambridge, Mass.: National Bureau of Economic Research.

Fetterman, D. M., S. J. Kaftarian, and A. Wandersman. 1966. *Empowerment evaluation: Knowledge and tools for self-assessment and accountability*. Newbury Park, Calif.: Sage.

Fisher, R., and J. Kling. 1993. *Mobilizing the community: Local politics in a global era*. Newbury Park, Calif.: Sage.

Freire, P. 1973. *Education for critical consciousness*. New York: Seabury Press.

French, M. 1986. *Beyond power: On women, men, and morals*. London: Abacus.

Freudenberg, N. 1984. *Not in our backyards! Community action for health and the environment*. New York: Monthly Review Press.

————. 1984-1985. Training health educators for social change. *International Quarterly of Community Health Education* 5 (1):37–52.

Freudenberg, N., and M. Zimmerman, eds. 1995. The role of community organizations in public health practice: The lessons from AIDS prevention. In *AIDS prevention in the Community: Lessons from the first decade*. Washington, D.C: American Public Health Association.

Green, L. W., and C. J. Frankish. In press. Finding the right mix of personal, organizational, decentralized, and centralized planning for health promotion. In *Community Health Promotion*, ed. B. Berry, E. Wagner, and A. Cheadle. Seattle: University of Washington Press.

Hancock, T. 1993. Seeing the vision, defining your role. *Healthcare Reform Journal* (May-June):30–36.

Himmelman, A. 1992. Communities working collaboratively for a change. Minneapolis: Himmelman Consulting Group. Unpublished paper.

House, J. S., K. R. Landis, and D. Umberson. 1988. Social relationships and health. *Science* 241:540–545.

Hyde, C. 1989. A feminist model for macro practice: Promises and problems. *Administration in Social Work* 13:145–182.

Iglehart, J. K. 1990. From the editor: Special issue on promoting health. *Health Affairs* 9 (2):4–5.

Katz, M. 1995. *Improving poor people*. New York: Pantheon Books.

Kingsolver, B. 1990. *Animal dreams*. New York: Perennial Books.

Kreuter, M. 1992. PATCH: Its origins, basic concepts, and links to contemporary public health policy. *Journal of Health Education* 23 (3):135–139.

Labonte, R. 1990. Empowerment: Notes on professional and community dimensions. *Canadian Review of Social Policy* 26:1–12.

Lehr, V. 1993. The difficulty of leaving "home": Gay and lesbian organizing to confront AIDS. In *Mobilizing the Community*, ed. R. Fisher and J. Kling. Newbury Park, Calif.: Sage.

Lewin, K. 1947. Quasi-stationary social equilibria and the problem of social change. In *Readings in Social Psychology*, ed. T. M. Newcomb and E. L. Hartley. New York: Holt, Rinehart and Winston.

Lippman, W. 1937. *An inquiry into the principles of good society*. Boston: Little Brown.

McGinnis, J. M., and W. H. Foege. 1993. Actual causes of death in the United States. *Journal of the American Medical Association* 270:2207–2212.

McKnight, J. 1987. Regenerating community. *Social Policy* (Winter):54–58.

McQuire, J. F. 1994. Organizing from diversity in the name of community: Lessons from disability civil right movement. *Policy Studies Journal* 22 (1):112–122.

Miller, M. 1993. Community organizing. In *A journey to justice*. Louisville, Ky.: Presbyterian Committee on the Self-development of People.

Miller, S. M. 1976. Themes for the 1976 SSSP meetings: Official program. Paper presented at the twenty-sixth meeting of the Society for the Study of Social Problems.

Minkler, M. 1994. Ethical challenges for health promotion in the 1990s. *American Journal of Health Promotion* 8 (6):403–413.

Minkler, M., S. P. Wallace, and M. MacDonald. 1994–1995. The political economy of health: A useful theoretical tool for health education practice. *International Quarterly of Community Health Education* 15 (2):111–125.

Mondros, J. B., and S. M. Wilson. 1994. *Organizing for power and empowerment*. New York: Columbia University Press.

Navarro, V. 1993. *Dangerous to your health: Capitalism in health care*. New York: Monthly Review Press.

Nyswander, D. 1967. The open society: Its implications for health educators. *Health Education Monographs* 1 (1):3–13.

O'Connor, J. 1976. What is political economy? In *Economics: Mainstream readings and radical critiques*, ed. D. Mermelstein. New York: Random House.

Pasick, R. J. 1987. *Health promotion for minorities in California*. Report to the East Bay Health Education Center. Berkeley: School of Public Health, University of California.

Putnam, R.1996. The strange disappearance of civic America. *American Prospect* (Winter):24, 34–48.

Rappaport, J. 1984. Studies in empowerment: Introduction to the issue. *Prevention in Human Services* 32 (3):1–7.

Rivera, F., and J. Erlich, eds. 1995. *Community organizing in a diverse society*. 2d ed. Boston: Allyn and Bacon.

Robertson, A., and M. Minkler. 1994. The new health promotion movement: A critical examination. *Health Education Quarterly* 21 (3):295–312.

Stoller, E. P., and R. Gibson. 1994. *Worlds of difference: Inequalities in the aging experience*. Thousand Oaks, Calif.: Pine Forge Press.

Thompson, B., L. Wallack, E. Lichtenstein, and T. Pechacek. 1990–1991. Principles of community organizing and partnership for smoking cessation in the Community Intervention Trial for Smoking Cessation (COMMIT). *International Quarterly of Community Health Education* 11 (3):182–203.

Thurow, L. 1996. *The future of capitalism*. New York: William Morrow.

Tilleras, P. 1988. *The color of light: Meditations for all of us living with AIDS*. San Francisco: Harper and Row.

Tocqueville, A. de. [1835] 1945. *Democracy in America*. New York: Harper and Row.

U.S. Bureau of the Census. 1995. *Statistical abstract of the United States*. Washington, D.C.: GPO, Table 732.

Wallack, L., L. Dorfman, D. Jernigan, and M. Themba. 1993. *Media advocacy and public health: Power for prevention*. Newbury Park, Calif.: Sage.

Wallack, L., and K. Montgomery. 1992. Advertising for all by the year 2000: Public health implications for less developed countries. *American Journal of Public Health Policy* 13 (2):76–100.

Wallerstein, N. 1992. Powerlessness, empowerment, and health: Implications for health promotion programs. *American Journal of Health Promotion* (6):197–205.

Walton, J. 1979. Urban political economy: An overview. *Comparative Urban Research* (7):5–17.

Weber, M. 1978. *Economy and society*. Berkeley and Los Angeles: University of California Press.

Weil, M. 1986. Women, community, and organizing. In *Feminist visions for social work*, ed. N. V. DenBergh and L. Cooper. Silver Spring, Md.: National Association of Social Workers.

World Health Organization. 1986. Ottawa charter for health promotion. *Canadian Journal of Public Health* 77 (6):425–430.

Zimmerman, E. 1980. Personal communication, October 16.

Chapter 2   Two Tools for Well-Being

JOHN L. McKNIGHT   *Health Systems and*
Communities

We HAVE CLEARLY entered a new era in popular conceptions of health. Whereas once people perceived health as a commodity produced by medical systems, today people recognize that health is also a capacity that ordinary citizens can maintain or enhance. Under the new era's banners of prevention and health promotion, health clubs multiply, health foods proliferate, corporate well-being programs appear, and consciousness of health grows among Americans of all ages.

The new prohealth consciousness has created a hidden dilemma for health professions and professionals, most clearly manifested in the increasing professional use of the term *community*. Under prevention and promotion rubrics, we hear of community education, community programs, community participation. However, the meaning of a community focus is less clear. At the very least, community usually means not in a hospital, clinic, or doctor's office. Community is the great "out-thereness" beyond the doors of professional offices and facilities—the social space beyond the edges of our professional systems.

The dilemma we face is lack of familiarity with the real community. We have great professional skills in managing and working within our systems, but our skills are much less developed once we leave the system's space and cross over the frontier into the community. Indeed, many professionals are confused and frustrated when they attempt to work in community space, which seems very complex, disordered, unstructured, and uncontrollable. And many health professionals begin to discover that their powerful tools and techniques seem weaker, less effective, and even inappropriate in the community.

Because of this dilemma, thoughtful health professionals have begun to

Reprinted from *American Journal of Preventive Medicine* 10 (3) (1994):23–25, by permission of Oxford University Press.

think more carefully about this social space called the community. They have attempted to better understand how their profession and tools can work effectively in community space. The most obvious finding of these professionals is best summarized by Mark Twain's maxim "If your only tool is a hammer, all problems look like nails." If your only tools are based upon medical models and systems, the community must be a nail. However, the community is not a nail; rather, it is a tool as distinctive and useful as the medical system tool.

To understand these distinctive tools called health system and community, we must look at their designs, capacities, and appropriate uses. Just as we can readily distinguish the different shape and use of a hammer from those of a saw, we can discern the distinctive shape and usefulness of a medical/health system and a community. The design or shape of a system is best exemplified by an organizational chart, a pyramid of boxes connected by lines of authority and responsibility. This pictography of our medical, prevention, and health promotion systems should clarify the nature of the tool professionals use, of which they are also a part. The system tool allows a few people to control the work of many other people. It enables a manager or an administrator to design and assure a standard output from the work of diverse professionals and workers. Therefore, it is clearly a tool designed to control and to produce standardized practices and outcomes. As an example, think about the production of an automobile. Here a pyramidal system transfers a design from the minds of the designers and administrators to the hands of the technicians and workers, who create a uniformly repetitive commodity called a Chevrolet. The auto company, like our medical system, is a system designed to control in order to assure uniform quality.

Systems also depend upon another element of social organization: a consumer or a client. The frequent use of the words *consumer* and *client* is a product of modern system development and proliferation. Indeed, only in the last twenty-five years have medical systems created a previously unknown label: the health consumer. Our grandparents could not have imagined such a being since they thought health was a condition, not a commodity. However, our powerful new systems have needed and thus created a class of people called consumers and clients. Therefore, the tool we use called a system is designed to control people, to produce uniform goods and services of quality, and to expand the number of people who act as consumers and clients.

What kind of tool is the community? It is obviously not a nail to be hammered by the health and medical systems. However, our answer must be vague because no widely accepted definition of the community focuses upon a uniquely North American social tool first described and analyzed by Alexis de Tocqueville, a brilliant young Frenchman. In his monumental work *Democracy in America*, Tocqueville ([1835] 1945) observed that Americans had created a new social tool, the association, a self-generated gathering of common people, or citizens, who assumed the power to decide what was a problem and how to solve it and could then act to carry out the solution. According to Tocqueville, these self-appointed, self-defining assemblies of nonexpert citizens were, in their local aggregate, the new community of the new world—a universe of associated citizens. And through mutually supportive associations, he saw the creation of a citizen power that led to a powerful new form of democracy.

If we examine the nature of our current community of associations, we see that they are tools with a special shape, design, and use unlike those of systems. First, associations depend upon the active consent of people. Unlike a system, the associational structure is not designed for the control of people. Systems ultimately depend upon people bending their uniqueness to a professional vision in exchange for money and security. However, associations depend upon the consent of free individuals to join equally in expressing their creative and common visions.

Second, associations provide a context in which care can be expressed, unlike a system, in which standardized outcomes are the principal expression. Thus, at a gathering of an association of citizens, we see a social form that depends on consent, creativity, and care, a social tool distinct from systems, with different capacities. Third, associations require citizens rather than clients or consumers. *Citizen* is a political term that describes the most powerful person in a democracy. An association is a tool to magnify the power of citizens. System tools create and magnify clients. The Greek root of the word *client* is "one who is controlled." This is, of course, the opposite of a citizen, "one who holds power."

A community of associations, then, is a social tool designed to operate through consent, combining the creative uniqueness of the participants into a more powerful form of expression. Put simply, the unique American community is an assembly of associations that is the vital center of our democracy, our creativity, and our capacity to solve everyday problems.

However, this vital center has been weakened since Tocqueville's observations of American social structure in 1831. Today, the poverty of American associations in community is less visible. The reason for the apparent decline of our community of associations is not very obvious to most of us, even though it has been clearly defined by such brilliant social historians as Ivan Illich (1976), Jacques Ellul (1965), and Robert Bellah and his colleagues (1985). Their work demonstrates that the weakening of the tools of community results directly from the increasing power of the tools of systems. Indeed, they suggest a paradox—a zero-sum game. As the power of system tools grows, the power of community tools declines. As control magnifies, consent fades. As standardization is implemented, creativity disappears. As consumers and clients multiply, citizens lose power.

The implications of this analysis are provocative. For if our health promotion tool is a system, we can achieve only a particular and limited set of goals. We cannot perform the necessary functions and achieve the goals of the tools of community.

And yet the work of a public health mission of promotion and prevention must be done in and by communities.

Some modern health professionals, recognizing this necessity, have begun to design complex programs said to interface with, involve, or use the community. As noble as the intentions of these professionals may be, they fail to recognize the historical evidence demonstrating that as systems grow in capacity, influence, and power, communities and their associations lose capacity, influence, and power (Polanyi 1944). As systems expand, communities contract. As systems invade, associations retreat.

As we enter an era that seeks healthy communities, we face four hard realities. First, systems and communities are different tools designed to do different work. Second, systems can never replace the work of communities. Third, system growth and outreach can diminish and erode the power of the community's tools. Fourth, when systems growth erodes community associations, the system itself causes community weakness and disempowerment, creating a local environment for ill health, unwellness, and dis-ease. Put simply, powerful, pervasive health systems can create unhealthy communities by replacing consent with control and active citizens with compliant clients.

No easy trick or technical gimmicks can overcome either the limits or the potential counterproductivity of health system tools. However, in some hopeful experiments and initiatives, health professionals and their powers have enhanced the strength of communities and their associations. My analysis of these cooperative initiatives suggests that they reflect at least four values.

First, the professionals respect the wisdom of citizens in association. These professionals do not speak of training or paying citizens or associations to do the system's work. Rather, they realize they are citizens each with one symbolic vote to cast in association with other citizens. Although they are not a part of the community, they walk with the community in its journey. They are neither making the path nor leading the group.

Second, community building professionals often have useful health information for local folks. They share that information in understandable forms. For example, they might prepare a map that shows where the neighborhood auto accidents occurred last year. They ask local citizens in their associations why the accidents occurred and how the local citizens' association can help. They are not the source of analysis or solutions; rather, they are the source of information not easily discovered by local citizens. They provide information that mobilizes the power of local citizen associations to develop and implement solutions (McKnight 1978).

Third, these professionals use their capacities, skills, contacts, and resources to strengthen the power of local associations. They listen for opportunities to enhance local leadership, strengthen local associations, and magnify community commitments. Instead of trying to gain space, influence, credit, or resources for their system, they ask how the system's resources might enhance the problem-solving capacities of local groups.

Finally, the new community building professionals escape the ideology of the medical model. For all its utility, the medical model always bears a hidden negative assumption that what is important about a person is his or her injury, disease, deficiency, problem, need, empty half. The able, gifted, skilled, capable, and full part of a person is not the focus of the medical model. And yet communities are built upon the capacities of people, not their deficiencies. Communities are built by one-legged carpenters. Medical systems are built on the missing leg. For this reason, community building health promotion professionals inevitably find that they must invert the medical model and focus on capacities rather than needs and deficiencies (McKnight and Kretzmann 1990).

Initiatives that enhance healthy associative communities necessarily build upon the identification and expression of the gifts, skills, capacities, and associations of citizens. And so it is that community building professionals focus not on how many young women are "parents-too-soon" but on what these same young women can contribute to the community. How are they connected to local associations to express their gifts? What existing groups will give them a new source of power and identity? What can I, and the resources of my system, do to join the effort to answer these questions without overwhelming or coopting local citizen efforts?

In summary, to build a healthful society, we need two tools. One is a system. The other is a community. Neither can substitute for the other, but systems can displace communities or enhance them. To enhance community health, we need a new breed of modest health professionals, people who respect the integrity and wisdom of citizens and their associations. They will understand the kinds of information that will enable citizens to design and solve problems. They will direct some system resources to enhancing associational powers. And, above all, they will focus upon magnifying the gifts, capacities, and assets of local citizens and their associations.

Health is not an input. Health is not a commodity. Health cannot be consumed. Health is a condition. Health is the by-product of strong associative communities. Health is the unintended side effect of citizens acting powerfully in association. Without that citizen power in associative relationships, we will be reduced to a nation of clients— impotent consumers feeling the unhealthful disease from the manipulation of our lives as they are managed and controlled by hierarchical systems.

Alexis de Tocqueville had it right in 1831. He saw vital, creative, vigorous, lively, inventive, healthful people who were neither slaves nor clients, serfs nor consumers. Instead, they were citizens, and that fact was the source of their health and their healthful communities. Although Tocqueville thought he was a reporter, he was instead a prophet who understood that the basic source of health is powerful citizens and vigorous associations. The name he gave to that health-giving condition was not system. It was democracy.

References

Bellah, R., R. Madsen, W. Sullivan, A. Swidler, and S. M. Tipton. 1985. *Habits of the heart: Individualism and commitment in American life*. Berkeley and Los Angeles: University of California Press.

Ellul, J. 1965. *The technological society*. New York: Knopf.

Illich, I. 1976. *Medical nemesis: The expropriation of health*. New York: Pantheon Books.

McKnight, J. 1978. Politicizing health care. *Social Policy* 9 (November–December):36–39.

McKnight, J., and J. Kretzmann. 1990. *Mapping community capacity*. Center for Urban Affairs and Policy Research Report. Evanston, Ill.: Northwestern University.

Polanyi, K. 1944. *The great transformation*. New York: Farrar and Rinehart.

Tocqueville, A. de. [1835] 1945. *Democracy in America*. New York: Harper and Row.

Part II

Contextual Frameworks and Models

Pᴏʟɪᴛɪᴄᴀʟ sᴄɪᴇɴᴛɪsᴛ Richard Couto (1990, 144) argues that "because Americans have so little sense of community, we pay a great deal of attention to it." He suggests that "our rose-tainted view of community and the processes we describe as empowerment, community development, and community organizing" have led to considerable conceptual confusion. That confusion in turn has enabled both political liberals and conservatives to claim these concepts and to use the term *grass roots* "as if it were herbal medicine for current public problems and to renew American social health."

The contributors to this part attempt to move us beyond the prevailing confusion by creating conceptual frameworks and models within which community, community organizing, and community building can be better understood. Although additional perspectives on these concepts are offered throughout the book, this initial section seeks to lay a foundation for their subsequent exploration.

In chapter 3, Meredith Minkler and Nina Wallerstein offer initial definitions of community organizing and community building and underscore the centrality of the notion of empowerment to both of these processes. Introducing a theme that appears throughout much of the book, they suggest that real community organizing must begin with a group or community's identification of its issues and goals, rather than with the goals or concerns of a health department, social service organization, or outside organizer.

Following a brief historical overview, Minkler and Wallerstein introduce the best-known typology of community organization, Jack Rothman's (1995) locality development, social planning, and social action. Newer alternative and complementary models also are explored, including collaborative empowerment, community building, and those approaches, such as Ronald Braithwaite, Cynthia

Bianchi, and Sandra Taylor's (1994) Community Organization and Development (COD) model, that borrow from both community organizing and community building but put their greatest accent on culturally relevant practice.

The heart of this chapter is the discussion of several key concepts in community organizing and community building that are central to effecting change on the community level. Empowerment and critical consciousness, community competence or problem-solving ability, the principles of participation and "starting where the people are," and issue selection are each examined briefly, as is the often neglected area of measurement and evaluation in community organizing. Although this chapter covers a wide terrain, it necessarily does so "once over lightly," as a prelude to the more in-depth discussion of many of the issues and topics raised in subsequent chapters.

The next two chapters in this part each look in more detail at one of the major approaches to community organizing and community building practice introduced in chapter 3. Robert Fisher takes a closer look at the social action organizing approach most closely identified with Saul Alinsky and Cesar Chávez, which continues to play a vital role in organizing and the development of social movements worldwide as we approach the twenty-first century. Fisher presents social action as a dynamic organizing model that uses both conflict and consensus strategies in the quest to redress power imbalances and promote social justice. Key characteristics of social action efforts worldwide are described, as are such antecedents of present-day social action organizing as the seminal work of Alinsky, the liberation struggles of people of color, the increased accent on community participation of the 1960s and beyond, and the social movements of the 1960s through the 1980s.

Building on a wealth of experience and expertise in this field, Fisher presents a number of implications for practice. Prominent among these are the need for coalition building across diverse constituencies, the need to make government or the state the focus of organizing efforts, and the importance of combining post-modernist demands for autonomy and identity with the older modern emphasis on social justice and connectedness between people. Fisher's chapter provides much food for thought and an important introduction to many of the themes and issues examined in greater detail by Marc Pilisuk and his colleagues (chapter 7) and others later in the book.

In chapter 5, Cheryl Walter shifts our focus from community organizing to community, arguing that in our attention to "*the* community," we as social change professionals sometimes have lost sight of the broader concept of community and what it symbolizes. Walter envisions communities not as geographic or other units that we, as outside professionals, interact with but as inclusive and dynamic systems to which we belong. The various dimensions or attributes of community, including vertical and horizontal relationships to other units and the larger society or culture, and the dimensions of action and of consciousness are described as giving breadth and depth to our understanding of the communities of which we are apart. Walter lays out the various dimensions of community building practice and uses an AIDS WALK to illustrate how such a practice orientation might guide health educators or other social change professionals involved in the creation and implementation of such an event.

The approach to community building offered by Walter differs from that of a number of other contributors to this book in its emphasis on the professional as part of community rather than as an outsider looking in and working with the community. Yet the skills for community building practice that she elaborates, including awareness of the dynamic quality of community and an ability to articulate and foster a discussion of process, have great relevance for health educators and other social change professionals who work on the community level. Walter's conceptualization of community building presents an important new way of thinking about our roles in community and both complements and challenges more traditional approaches offered elsewhere in this volume.

References

Braithwaite, R. L., C. Bianchi, and S. E. Taylor. 1994. Ethnographic approach to community organization and health empowerment. *Health Education Quarterly* 21 (3):407–416.

Couto, R. A. 1990. Promoting health at the grass roots. *Health Affairs* 9 (2):144–151.

Rothman, J. 1995. Approaches to community intervention. In *Strategies of community intervention*, ed. J. Rothman, J. L. Erlich, and J. E. Tropman. 5th ed. Itasca, Ill.: Peacock.

Chapter 3

Improving Health through Community Organization and Community Building

MEREDITH MINKLER
NINA WALLERSTEIN

A Health Education Perspective

ALTHOUGH A NUMBER of new approaches and change strategies have been developed and adapted by health education professionals in recent years, the principles and methods loosely referred to as community organization remain a central method of practice. For the purposes of this book, community organization is the process by which community groups are helped to identify common problems or goals, mobilize resources, and in other ways develop and implement strategies for reaching the goals they collectively have set. The newer and related concept of community building, as Cheryl Walter suggests in chapter 5, is not a method so much as an orientation to the ways in which people who identify as members of a shared community engage together in the process of community change.

Implicit in both of these definitions is the concept of empowerment—an enabling process through which individuals or communities take control over their lives and their environment (Rappaport 1984). Indeed, Murray Ross (1955), widely regarded as the father of community organizing practice, argued early on that community organization could not be said to have taken place unless community problem-solving ability had been increased in the process.

Strict definitions of community organization also suggest that the needs or problems around which community groups are organized must of necessity be identified by the community itself, not by an outside organization or change agent. Thus, even though a health education professional may borrow some principles and methods from community organization to help mount an AIDS organizing

Portions of this chapter are based on "Improving Health through Community Organizing and Community Building," in *Health Behavior and Health Education: Theory, Research, and Practice*, ed. K. Glantz, F. M. Lewis, and B. K. Rimer (San Francisco: Jossey-Bass, 1996). Adapted and reprinted by permission of the publhsher.

effort in the community, he or she cannot be said to be doing community organization in the pure sense unless the community itself has identified AIDS as the problem area it wishes to address.

Community organization is important in health education in part because it reflects one of the field's most fundamental principles, that of starting where the people are. But community building and organizing are also important in light of the evidence that social involvement and participation can themselves be significant psychosocial factors in improving perceived control, individual coping capacity, health behaviors, and health status (Cohen and Syme 1985; Eng and Cunningham 1990). Finally, as suggested in chapter 1, the "rediscovery" of community and the heavy accent being placed on community partnerships and community-based health initiatives by government agencies, foundations, and the like suggest the need for a further refinement of theory, methods, and measurement techniques in this area. In this chapter, key concepts and principles of community organization and community building are examined for their relevance for health education professionals and others working at the interface of health systems and communities. After a brief historical look at the field and process of community organization and the emergence of community building practice, the concept of community is examined, and several models of community organization and community building are presented. Key theoretical and conceptual bases of community organization and community building are then explored and a basis laid for their further development and use in subsequent chapters.

Community Organization and Community Building in Historical Perspective

The term *community organization* was coined by American social workers in the late 1800s to describe their efforts to coordinate services for newly arrived immigrants and the poor. As Charles Garvin and Fred Cox (1995) have pointed out, however, although community organization is typically portrayed as having been born of the settlement house movement, several important milestones that took place outside of social work should by rights be included in any history of community organization practice. Prominent among these are (1) the organizing by African Americans during the post-Reconstruction period to try salvaging newly won rights that were rapidly slipping away; (2) the Populist movement, which began as an agrarian revolution and became a multisectoral coalition and a major political force; and (3) the labor movement of the 1930s and 1940s, which taught the value of coalition formation around issues, the importance of full-time professional organizers, and the use of conflict as a means of bringing about change.

Within the field of social work, early approaches to community organization stressed collaboration and the use of consensus and cooperation as communities were helped to self-identify and to increase their problem-solving ability (Garvin and Cox 1995; Ross 1955). By the 1950s, however, a new brand of community organization was gaining popularity that also stressed confrontation and conflict strategies for social change. Most closely identified with Saul Alinsky (1969, 1972), social action organizing stressed redressing power imbalances by having outside organizers help to create dissatisfaction with the status quo among the disfranchised, build communitywide identification, and assist members in devising winnable goals and nonviolent conflict strategies and other means to bring about change.

From the late 1950s onward, as Robert Fisher describes in chapter 4, strategies and tactics of community organization were increasingly being applied to the achievement of broader social change objectives through the civil rights movement, followed by the women's movement, the gay rights movement, anti–Vietnam War organizing, the disability rights movement, and increased organizing among people of color worldwide. The 1980s and 1990s witnessed the adaptation and development of new community organization tactics and strategies in areas as diverse as the AIDS crisis and the New Right's efforts to have abortion banned in the United States. In addition, the effective use of personal computer technology has greatly increased, with groups across the political spectrum going online to build community and to identify and organize supporters on a mass scale (see chapter 20).

In the health field, a major new emphasis on community participation beginning in the 1970s culminated in the World Health Organization's adoption in 1986 of a new approach to health promotion that stressed increasing people's control over the determinants of their health, high-level public participation, and intersectoral cooperation (World Health Organization 1986). As noted in chapter 1, the WHO-initiated Healthy Cities Movement emerged as a prominent reflection of this new approach and quickly grew to involve more than forty-five hundred healthy cities and communities worldwide (Duhl 1996). Its aims were to create sustainable environments and processes through which governmental and nongovernmental sectors could work in partnership to create healthy public policies, achieve high-level participation in community-driven projects, and, ultimately, reduce inequities and disparities between groups (Duhl 1993; Tsouros 1995).

Finally, alongside these developments has been a growing appreciation of the importance of organizers facilitating *community building*, a process that people in a community engage in themselves, rather than being concerned solely with *community organizing*, a process in which the outside organizer typically plays a key role (see chapter 5). The community building orientation is reflected in efforts such as the Black Women's Health Project, a network of close to one hundred groups in the United States and in several Third World countries that stresses empowerment through self-help and consciousness-raising for social change (Avery 1990). As Walter suggests in chapter 5, community building projects like this one are strength based and grounded in feminist notions of power to and power with rather than the more masculine concept of power over frequently encountered in traditional organizing (French 1986). These efforts further borrow from feminist organizing an accent on the process of practice (Hyde 1990) and on organizing as holistic, involving both rational and nonrational elements of human experience (Gutierrez and Lewis 1995). Although theoretical work and practical applications and research in the area of community building remain in their infancy, community building practice may become an increasingly important complement to more traditional notions of community organization in the years ahead.

The Concept of Community

Integral to a discussion of community organization and community building practice is an examination of the underlying concept of community. Although typically thought of in geographic terms, communities may also be non–locality identified and based instead on shared interests or characteristics, such as ethnicity, sexual orientation, or occupation (Fellin 1995). Communities indeed have been defined as (1) functional spatial units meeting basic needs for sustenance, (2) units of patterned social interaction, and/or (3) symbolic units of collective identity (Hunter 1975). Eugenia Eng and Edith Parker (1994) add a fourth political definition to community as a social unit, that is, people coming together to act politically to make changes.

Two sets of theories are relevant for understanding the concept of community. The first of these, the ecological system perspective, is particularly useful in the study of autonomous geographic communities, focusing as it does on population characteristics such as size, density, and heterogeneity; the physical environment; the social organization or structure of the community; and the technological forces affecting it. In contrast, the social systems perspective focuses primarily on the formal organizations that operate within a given community, exploring the interactions of community subsystems (economic, political, etc.) both horizontally within the community and vertically as they relate to other, extracommunity systems (Fellin 1995). Roland Warren's (1963) classic approach to community clearly fits within the latter perspective, envisioning communities as entities that change their structure and function to accommodate various social, political, and economic developments. Similarly, Alinsky's view of communities as reflecting the social problems and processes of an urban society (Reitzes and Reitzes 1980, 40) provides a good example of a social systems perspective.

Clearly, the perspective on community that one adopts will influence one's view of the appropriate domains and functions of community organization process. Community development specialists (e.g., agricultural extension workers and Peace Corps volunteers) thus have tended to focus over the years on helping people identify with and bring about changes within their own geographic community, implicitly defining the latter as a unit unto itself (Khinduka 1975). By contrast, proponents of a broader approach, typified by Alinsky (1972) and other social action organizers, have encouraged organization around issues such as public housing and unemployment in recognition of the tremendous impact those larger socioeconomic issues have on local communities. Similarly, though communities are rich in diversity, with multiple interacting subcommunities, whether one views the community as more or less heterogeneous will determine the strategies one employs and often the types of organizing goals one pursues.

Finally, as Felix Rivera and John Erlich (1995) have suggested, an appreciation of the unique characteristics of communities of color should be a major consideration in any thinking about organizing within such communities. These investigators argue that many communities of color may be characterized as neogemeinschaft, exhibiting some of the characteristics of gemeinschaft social systems in having strong social support systems and relationships that are personal, informal, and sentiment based rather than formal, specialized, and utilitarian (see chapter 13). The "neo" aspect of Rivera and Erlich's (1995, 97) designation, however, refers to the fact that "these communities' life experience takes place within a causal, deterministic reality, based on racism and exploitation." In African-American communities, for example, market exploitation, argues Cornel West (1993), has led to a shattering of the religious and civic organizations that have historically buffered these communities against hopelessness and nihilism. He calls for community change through a re-creation of a sense of agency and political resistance based on "subversive memory—the best of one's past without romantic nostalgia" (19). A view of community that incorporates such a perspective would support building on preexisting social networks rather than creating new structures and would emphasize self-determination and empowerment (Rivera and Erlich 1995). The different models of community organization and community building described here illustrate how alternative assumptions about the nature and meaning of community heavily shape and determine how community organization and community building are conceptualized and practiced.

Models of Community Organization

Although community organization is frequently treated as though it were a singular model of practice, several typologies of community organization have been developed on the premise that this phenomenon comprises various alternative change models. The best known of these typologies is Jack Rothman's (Rothman and Tropman 1987) categorization of community organization as consisting of three distinct models of practice: locality development, social planning, and social action. Briefly, locality development is heavily process oriented, stressing consensus and cooperation and aimed at building group identity and a sense of community. By contrast, social planning is heavily task oriented, stressing rational-empirical problem-solving—usually by an outside expert. Social action is both task and process oriented. It is concerned with increasing the problem-solving ability of the community and with achieving concrete changes to redress imbalances of power and privilege between an oppressed or a disadvantaged group and the larger society. Originally arguing that most community organizing efforts tended to fall in one or the other of these categories, Rothman more recently has suggested that many professionals use a "mixing and phasing" of two or more of the models (Rothman and Tropman 1987) rather than relying solely or principally on any one. The heart health community trials and PATCH interventions have mixed social planning with elements of locality development (Farquhar et al. 1994; "PATCH" 1992; Bracht and Kingsbury 1990), whereas organizers in the Alinsky tradition have mixed social action and locality development in their community actions (Marquez 1990; Wechsler 1990; Guillory, Willie, and Duran 1988).

Rothman's typology has remained, for more than twenty years, the dominant framework within which community organization has been examined and understood, and as such, it has had a significant impact on practice. Despite continued widespread application, however, the typology and its underlying assumptions have a number of important limitations. First, use of the term *locality development* may be unnecessarily restrictive, discouraging a consideration of organizing along nongeographic lines. Second, inclusion of a model (social planning) that often relies heavily on outside technical experts and does not necessarily increase the problem-solving ability of the community appears to contradict one of the most basic criteria of effective organizing. Third, as Walter suggests in chapter 5, the fact that this typology is problem based and organizer centered, rather than strength based and community centered, constitutes a philosophical and practical limitation that may be particularly problematic as organizing increasingly occurs in multicultural contexts.

Partly in reaction to the perceived limitations of the Rothman typology, Walter (chapter 5) and others (Gardner 1991; Himmelman 1992; Labonte 1994; Wallerstein and Sanchez-Merki 1994; Kaye and Wolff 1995) have suggested newer models of collaborative empowerment and community building practice that provide important alternative approaches. These models are, in part, descendants of the community development model in their emphases on self-help and collaboration. Yet they extend beyond the tradition within community development that is externally driven and may implicitly accept the status quo. They take their parentage from community-driven development, where community concerns direct the organizing in a process that creates healthy and more equal power relations (Labonte 1994; Purdey et al. 1994).

The newer community building model emphasizes community strengths not as nostalgia for the "good old days," but as a diversity of groups and systems that can identify shared values and nurture the development of shared goals (Gardner 1991). Arthur Himmelman's (1992) collaborative empowerment model, for example, includes many of the steps or activities stressed in more traditional organizing (e.g., clarifying a community's purpose and vision, examining what others have done, building a community's power base) but puts its heaviest accent on enabling communities to play the lead role so that real empowerment, rather than merely "community betterment," is achieved. John McKnight's (1987) notion of community regeneration has at its heart enabling people to recognize and contribute their "gifts," the totality of which represents the building blocks or assets of a community that enable it to care for its members (see chapter 10).

Along similar lines, Walter's community building practice approach is described in chapter 5 not as a method but as a way of orienting one's self in community that places community "at the center of practice." Walter's concept of community building attempts to "balance and blend" such elements of community as historicity, identity, and autonomy with the dimensions of community development, community planning, community action, community consciousness, and "the commons" (where the latter encompasses the relationship between the community and its broader environment). As such, the community building approach contrasts significantly with more traditional notions of community organization practice that are community based but not necessarily of and by community (Wolfe 1993; see also chapters 5 and 6).

Lying midway between older models of community organizing and newer conceptualizations of community building are models that incorporate some elements of each, while putting the greatest accent on culturally relevant practice. As Rivera and Erlich (1995) have pointed out, the preferred models and ideologies of organizers from the dominant white culture frequently are ill-suited to addressing issues of race and culture that often represent the most urgent concerns within communities of color. As a counter to what Rivera and Erlich describe as "organizers' myopia" (from Horwitt 1989), newer models for community organizing in a multicultural society are needed. Prominent among these models is the feminist approach to community organizing with women of color developed by Lorraine Gutierrez and Edith Lewis (1995) and described in detail in chapter 13. The model borrows a number of salient principles from feminist organizing, among them the use of a "gender lens" to analyze the causes and solutions of community problems, a heavy accent on process and empowerment, and application of the feminist principle "the personal is political" to organizing with and by women. But Gutierrez and Lewis's model is critical of feminist organizing for its failure to adequately address racism, to focus on issues of salience in communities of color, and to "acknowledge the other 'lenses' or 'voices,'" such as race and ethnicity, through which much of the experience of women also must be understood (1994, 23). Gutierrez and Lewis's model is based on practice principles that would have the outside organizer "learn about, understand and participate in the women's ethnic community, . . . recognize and build upon the ways in which women of color have worked effectively in their own communities, . . . and recognize and embrace the conflict that characterizes cross cultural work" (34).

Another community organizing model that puts its heaviest accent on culturally relevant practice is Ronald Braithwaite and colleagues' (1989; Braithwaite, Bianchi, and Taylor 1994) Community Organization and Development model for health promotion in communities of color. Although written from the perspective of the outside organizer and admonishing him or her to engage in such initial steps as getting to know the community and its ecology through participatory ethnography, and gaining entrée and credibility, the central thrust of the COD model involves facilitating the development and effective functioning of a community-dominated and -controlled coalition board. The latter in turn undertakes its own community assessment, sets policy, facilitates leadership development, and, on the basis of bottom-up planning and community problem-solving, designs culturally relevant interventions. The COD model, in short, appears to move from initial reliance on more traditional community organizing to an incorporation of many of the principles of community building practice, while stressing throughout the cultural context within which both organizing and community building take place.

Finally, alternately defined as a model of community organization practice and as a strategy or method used across models is coalition building. Increasingly popular in the health field in areas as diverse as chronic disease, drugs and alcohol, violence, and the fight against budget cuts (Goodman, Burdine et al. 1993; Kaye and Wolff 1995), coalitions have attracted heavy public and private sector funding but have only begun to be studied in a systematic fashion (see Goodman, Burdine et al. 1993; and Goodman, Wandersman et al. 1996, for important recent exceptions). Coalitions have spanned the continuum from locality development to social action models, and from community organizing to community building, and have been both needs based and strengths based. In theory, if not always in reality, they are well suited to the new emphasis on collaboration and partnership in community practice. At the same time, the inevitability of hidden agendas and the need to understand conflict and negotiate differences (Gardner 1991; Kaye and Wolff 1995) may make effective coalition building a difficult undertaking (see chapters 16 and 17).

Thus, several models of community organizing and community building have surfaced within the last decade to complement a long history of earlier organizing approaches. Figure 3.1 attempts to integrate new perspectives with the older models, presenting a typology that incorporates both needs- and strengths-based approaches. Along the needs-based continuum, "community development," primarily a consensus model, is contrasted with Alinsky's "social action," primarily a conflict-based model. The newer strengths-based models contrast a community building capacity approach with an empowerment-oriented social action approach. Several concepts span these two strengths-based approaches, such as community competence, leadership development, and the multiple perspectives on gaining power. Empowerment, though a separate quadrant in the figure, is also a concept that ideally can be realized within the three other models of organizing. Collaboration straddles the needs- and strengths-based quadrants as primarily a consensus strategy, with advocacy primarily a conflict strategy.

In the middle circle of the figure are several strategies of organizing, such as grassroots organizing and coalition building. None of these falls into one quadrant; rather, each may incorporate multiple tendencies or models depending on the starting place and the dynamics of an ever-changing social context.

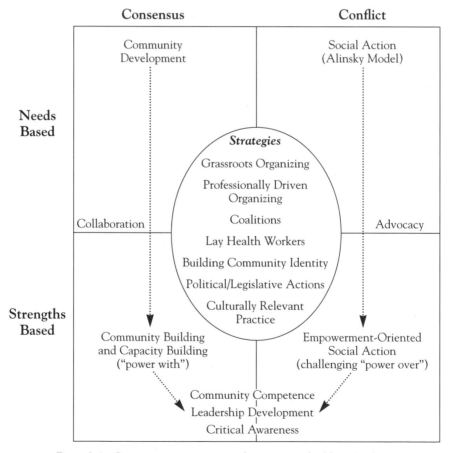

Figure 3.1. Community organizing and community building typology.

Key Concepts in Community Organization and Community Building Practice

Although no single unified model of community organization or community building exists, several key concepts are central to affecting and measuring change on the community level.

POWER, EMPOWERMENT, AND CRITICAL CONSCIOUSNESS

As noted in chapter 1, power is central to community organizing, particularly in the social action tradition of Saul Alinsky (1969, 1972). Indeed, Alinsky argued that organizing and power are almost synonymous, and he defined power (1969) as the ability to bring about decisions that shape and determine outcomes.

Steven Lukes's (1974) conceptualization of power as occurring on several levels is helpful for understanding power and its relationship to community organizing. At the level of the individual, power refers to the ability to make decisions within the existing rules of the game, such as by voting on a health care reform or antismoking initiative. At the level of the organization, power involves the ability to define the rules of the game, as when elites and powerful organizations determine what issues become "hot topics" of debate. As Meredith Minkler, Steven Wallace, and Marian McDonald (1994–1995, 115) point out, "The ability of the 'new right' to repeatedly make abortion an election issue, and the ability of the tobacco industry to pour millions of dollars into fighting (albeit sometimes unsuccessfully) laws that would prohibit smoking in public places, are illustrative of organizational power." At the level of the system, power involves the ways in which the structure of the economic and political systems favor certain interests without any conscious decisionmaking, agenda setting, or manipulation of public policy. The fact that actions that would improve the environment and/or promote the public's health tend not be taken if they would restrict corporate profits is an example of such systemic or structural power (Minkler et al. 1994–1995; see also chapter 7). Antonio Gramsci's notion of hegemony (Simon 1991), which involves people actively accepting values that are against their best interests, is one reason that structural power is reproduced.

As noted in chapter 1, feminist perspectives on organizing (Hyde 1990; Bradshaw, Soifer, and Gutierrez 1994; Weil 1986) and newer conceptualizations of community building (McKnight 1987; Himmelman 1992; see also chapter 5) have added depth and breadth to our understanding of power as it relates to community practice. Feminist perspectives, for example, view power not as a "finite resource that must be gained from the other" (Bradshaw et al. 1994, 31) but as an essentially limitless resource "rooted in energy, strength and effective communication" (Bricker-Jenkins and Hooyman 1986, 12). Ronald Labonte addresses power as a social relationship with contradictory elements (in Bernstein et al. 1994;

Labonte 1990). Borrowing from Marilyn French (1986), Labonte suggests that power from within and power with (the collective aspect of power from within) are moral, spiritual sources of power that can constantly expand as people empower themselves. It may be necessary, however, to use power to influence and challenge oppressive power over relationships, which have a material base of domination through force or ideological hegemony, in order to create change on personal, interpersonal, and political levels (Gutierrez and Lewis 1995; Hawks 1991; Labonte 1990).

Just as there a number of perspectives on power, numerous perspectives now exist on the notion of empowerment. Although the term itself has been justifiably criticized as a "catchall phrase" in social science (Rappaport 1984), empowerment nevertheless represents a central tenet of community organization and community building practice. Within public health, empowerment or community empowerment has been variously defined, from communities achieving equity (Katz 1984) or having the capacity to identify problems and solutions (Braithwaite et al. 1989; Cottrell 1976), to communities possessing participatory self-competence in their political life (Florin and Wandersman 1990; Kieffer 1983–1984). Though many limit their definition to a narrow individual focus similar to self-esteem or self-confidence, community organizing needs a broader definition: empowerment is a social action process by which individuals, communities, and organizations gain mastery over their lives in the context of changing their social and political environment to improve equity and quality of life (Rappaport 1984; Wallerstein 1992).

For health educators and other social change professionals, these contradictory elements raise issues of our own practice. Many of us have higher-status positions than community members. Can people in positions of dominance or privilege derived from culture, gender, race, or class empower others, or must people empower themselves? If empowerment includes the dimension of transferring power to others, professionals may need to let go of their own power to make it more available to others. In Labonte's words, "Empowerment . . . is a fascinating dynamic of power given and taken all at once, a dialectical dance between consensus and conflict, professional expertise and lay wisdom, hierarchic institutions and community circles" (in Bernstein et al. 1994, 285).

The processes and outcomes of empowerment need to accommodate a view of a change process that includes the interaction of individuals, the interaction of individuals and communities, and changes in the social structure itself. For individuals, empowerment challenges the perceived or real "powerlessness" that comes from the health injuries of poverty, chronic stressors, lack of control, and few resources, or what Len Syme (1988) has termed lack of "control over destiny." Individuals may experience enhanced psychological empowerment, which includes increased political efficacy and motivation to act (Zimmerman 1990) and enhanced social support.

As individuals engage in community organizing efforts and community build-ing, community empowerment outcomes can include increased sense of commu-nity, greater participatory processes and community competence, and outcomes of actual changes in policies, transformed conditions, or increased resources that may reduce inequities. As communities become empowered and better able to engage in collective problem-solving, key health and social indicators may reflect this, with rates of alcoholism, divorce, suicide, and other social problems beginning to decline. Moreover, the empowered community that works effectively for change can bring about changes in some of the very problems that contributed to its ill-health in the first place (Israel 1985; Minkler 1992).

The link between individual- and community-level empowerment is strength-ened through the development of critical consciousness, or "conscientization," a concept that comes from Brazilian educator Paulo Freire (1970, 1973). Freire devel-oped a methodology for teaching illiterate peasants to read by teaching them to "read" their political and social reality. His work has been a catalyst worldwide in the last three decades for programs in adult education, health, and community devel-opment (Hope and Timmel 1984; Minkler and Cox 1980; Wallerstein and Bern-stein 1994; Wallerstein and Weinger 1992).

As discussed in chapter 12, Freire's central premise is that the purpose of edu-cation should be liberatory: to transform the status quo in the classroom and in people's lives. He questions whether education reinforces powerlessness by treating people as objects who receive knowledge or whether education enables people to engage in active dialogue and to challenge the conditions that keep them powerless. Freire proposes a dialogic problem-posing process, with equality and mutual respect between learner-teachers and teacher-learners. Problem-posing contains a cycle of listening-dialogue-action that enables all participants to engage in continual reflection and action. Through structured dialogue, group participants listen for the issues contained in their own experiences, discuss common problems, look for root causes and the interconnections between the "problems behind the problem-as-symptom," and devise strategies to help transform their reality (Freire 1970, 1973).

Conscientization is the consciousness that comes through the social analysis of conditions and people's role in changing those conditions. This awareness enables community groups to analyze moments and open spaces to enact change or to under-stand those "limit-situations" that may prohibit change (Barndt 1989). Conscienti-zation is a key ingredient in maintaining a broader vision and sustaining community organizing efforts over time and is one of the links between individual psychological and community empowerment.

COMMUNITY COMPETENCE
Closely related to the concept of empowerment is the notion of community com-petence or problem-solving ability as a central goal and outcome of community

organization practice. The competent community is defined by Leonard Cottrell (1976, 403) as "one in which the various component parts of the community are able to collaborate effectively on identifying the problems and needs of the community; can achieve a working consensus on goals and priorities; can agree on ways and means to implement the agreed upon goals; can collaborate effectively in the required actions." Important recent refinements in our thinking about community competence have come with lay health worker programs that have incorporated community development and an emphasis on lay health workers themselves, instead of assessing only their impact on clients (Eng and Parker 1994; Ovrebo et al. 1994). A major challenge has been to find measurement variables that encompass community competence and capacity changes and are not simply aggregates of measures of individuals or service providers (see chapters 18 and 19).

Leadership development also represents a key aspect of development of competent communities. In particular, the development of leaders able to fulfill the roles of animator (stimulating people to think critically and to identify problems and new solutions) and facilitator (providing a process through which the group can discuss its own content in the most productive possible way) is key to building group competence and effectiveness (Hope and Timmel 1984). (See appendixes 7 and 8.)

Although Cottrell (1983) and others (Eng and Parker 1994; Fellin 1995) have tended to apply the concept of community competence primarily to geographic communities, its relevance to nongeographic communities is apparent. Indeed, whether the community is a neighborhood in the South Bronx, a union local in Ohio, or people with HIV/AIDS working together for change, increasing the community's capacity for collective problem identification and problem-solving is of paramount importance if the community is to effectively reach both its current and future goals.

Many principles and concepts basic to health education have relevance for achieving an increase in community competence. In addition to the concept of empowerment, Barbara Israel (1985) notes that key approaches within social network theory and social support may be usefully applied in the development of competent communities. Social network techniques by which one can "map" the web of social ties in which individuals are embedded may be employed to help identify natural helpers or leaders within a community, to help these natural leaders in turn identify their own networks, to identify high-risk groups within the community, and to involve network members in undertaking their own community assessment and actions necessary to strengthen networks within the community. A number of network assessment tools are available for mapping personal and/or community networks (McCallister and Fischer 1978; Heitzmann and Kaplan 1988) and other community assets (McKnight and Kretzmann 1992) and may be usefully employed by health education professionals.

THE PRINCIPLES OF PARTICIPATION AND RELEVANCE

Two principles central to community organization practice are participation and relevance, or starting where the people are (Nyswander 1956). Even though these precepts have been "rediscovered" in recent decades, both have early conceptual roots in social learning theory and in the field of adult education.

Fundamental to learning theory, for example, is the realization that individuals must experience a felt need to change or to learn before change can take place. German social psychologist Kurt Lewin (1958) postulated in the mid-1940s that individuals must experience an "unfreezing" of old attitudes and beliefs before they can consider and try out new ones. In the field of social action organizing, unfreezing is reflected in Alinsky's (1972) articulation of the need to "disorganize" communities (stirring frustration, creating dissatisfaction with the status quo) before they can be organized, or, more accurately, reorganized. Change is thus not a one-step occurrence but a complex process in which old attitudes and practices must be opened to reexamination (unfrozen) before change can take place (Lewin 1958).

Health education leader Dorothy Nyswander (1956) built on this perspective when she articulated the principle of relevance, or "starting where the people are," as perhaps the most fundamental tenet of health education practice. The health education professional who begins with the individual or community's felt needs and concerns, rather than with a personal or agency-dictated agenda, will be far more likely to experience community ownership and success in the change process than if he or she were to impose an agenda from the outside (Bracht and Tsouros 1990). As important as this tenet is in theory, however, its implementation in practice settings is fraught with difficulties (see chapters 6 and 8). As John McKinlay is fond of saying, professionals frequently suffer from an unfortunate malady known as "terminal hardening of the categories." They often seek information in ways that identify those community health issues that they, the experts, have already determined to be the most important (see chapter 8).

Even if organizers genuinely attempt to start where the people are, they may lack access to the "hidden discourse" in a community and may therefore misinterpret an apparent community apathy because of their own lack of cultural competence, access to key stakeholders or cultural translators, or self-reflection on the problematic nature of power dynamics between themselves and community members (Scott 1990). Organizers who do have access to community discourse may nevertheless find that the community's identification of goals and selection of organizing strategies challenge their own level of comfort or reflect values such as racism, sexism, or homophobia (see chapters 6 and 8). In the latter instance, the health educator's commitment to starting where the people are and to community self-determination must be tempered with the paramount principle of social justice in the larger community, whose interests would not be served by the parochial and prejudicial concerns and actions of one subgroup (Minkler 1994; see also chapter 8).

Closely related to the principle of relevance, the principle of participation has its roots in social psychology theories of learning and adult education (Dewey 1946). Indeed, the very notion of adult education as a process of creating situations in which learners, or in Freire's (1973) terminology, learner-teachers, can develop their own understandings and make and act on their own decisions is highly congruent with the community organization principle of facilitating high-level participation by community members at all stages of the organizing process. For Neil Bracht and Agis Tsouros (1990, 201), "citizen participation" refers to "the social process of taking part (voluntarily) in either formal or informal activities, programs and/or discussions to bring about planned change or improvement in community life, services and/or resources." For the World Health Organization (and UNICEF), as defined in the Alma Ata Declaration (1978), "Community participation is the process by which individuals and families assume responsibility for their own health and welfare and for those of the community, and develop the capacity to contribute to their and the community's development."

As noted earlier, the principle of participation has indeed been a hallmark of the recent WHO vision of health promotion, which stresses high-level participation as one of its principle components, and of empowerment education for health (see chapter 12) and the Healthy Cities Movement. In Canada, the new model of health promotion adopted in the mid-1980s was centered around a broadly defined concept of citizen participation, along with the concepts of self-help and mutual aid (Epp 1986). In the United States, the development of the CDC's PATCH program was heavily influenced by the community organization literature on participation and local ownership (Kreuter 1992). Indeed, active participation by a wide range of community members is described by PATCH (1992) architects as the first of five elements critical to the success of PATCH projects. Multisite community-based efforts such as the eight-year, $45 million COMMIT project have stressed community participation through the development of community boards and task forces (Thompson et al. 1990–1991). Embedded in each of these is a conviction that effective participation means sharing power and responsibility. Yet as both the PATCH and COMMIT projects have demonstrated, competing goals (e.g., meeting the scientific goals of a research study or assigning highest priority to health department, rather than community, definitions of need) may severely restrict the degree to which high-level community participation can be achieved (see chapter 8).

Such problems are largely overcome when we move from efforts at incorporating principles of participation in health education program development to purer forms of community organizing and to community building practice. In the latter regard, as Walter explains in chapter 5, participation is almost synonymous with community building itself: "With community at the center, a broad and inclusive continuum of community participants and stakeholders is encompassed in a way that extends to each power and recognition of its contribution to building and shaping community." (See appendix 6.)

ISSUE SELECTION

One of the most important steps in community organization practice involves the effective differentiation between problems, or things that are troubling, and issues or problems the community feels strongly about. As Michael Miller (1986) and Lee Staples (chapter 11) suggest, a good issue must meet several important criteria. First, it must be winnable, to ensure that work on the campaign does not simply reinforce fatalistic attitudes and beliefs. Second, it must unite members of the group and must involve them in a meaningful way in achieving problem resolution. Third, it should affect lots of people and build up the community or organization (giving leadership experience, increased visibility, etc.). Fourth, it should be part of a larger plan or strategy (see chapter 11 for a detailed discussion of these criteria). A variety of methods familiar to health educators and other social change professionals can be used to help a community group acquire the data needed for issue selection. Among those most popular currently is the focus group, through which a moderator, using a predetermined discussion guide or series of questions, elicits input from a small group of community members to determine their qualitative perceptions of key issues or concerns facing the community (Stewart and Shamdasani 1990). Focus groups, door-to-door surveys, and other data collection instruments can be useful in assessing felt needs while increasing a sense of participation. Too often, however, community members are merely invited to express their relative agreement with the outside professionals' preconceived notion of what the problems of significance in the community really are. As discussed in chapter 11, surveys, focus groups, and other methods are useful for issue selection only to the extent that they enable the discovery of the real issues of concern to the community.

As noted earlier, the facilitation of authentic community selection of issues involves taking significant risks, for the group or its leaders may choose issues that are too broad to be winnable or that reflect underlying discriminatory values and attitudes that the organizer cannot ethically endorse (see chapters 6 and 8). An approach to issue selection that has proved especially helpful in confronting and overcoming some of these difficulties involves the use of Freire's (1970, 1973) dialogic problem-posing method. As noted previously, part of a Freirian approach involves engaging participants in identifying their core generative themes— those themes that elicit social and emotional involvement and therefore high-level motivation to participate. Community development approaches worldwide have adopted Freire's educational strategies to identify the core issues for starting organizing efforts (Arnold et al. 1991; Hope and Timmel 1984).

Community organizers in the United States have adopted strategies from organizational development in creating strategic action plans to prioritize issues by available resources, appropriate time lines, and barriers to reaching goals (French and Bell 1990). In choosing an issue that may be feasible to win, politically minded organizers have included an analysis of power brokers, allies, and resisters (Feldblum et al. 1994; see also chapter 11).

Thoughtfully undertaken issue selection processes can contribute to community empowerment and serve as a positive force for social change. However, calls have increasingly been made for "a new process of community organizing—one relying less on issue based mobilization and more on community education, leadership development and support, and building local sustainable organizations" (Traynor 1993, 7). Community building practice is being looked to as this new process, one that is less concerned with community issue selection as with the identification, nurturing, and celebration of community strengths and the creation of a context, by people in community, for the sharing of those strengths (McKnight 1987; see also chapter 5).

MEASUREMENT AND EVALUATION ISSUES

A major limitation of most community organizing efforts to date has been their failure to adequately address evaluation processes and outcomes (see chapter 18). This failure typically stems from several sources, among them severe funding constraints and lack of knowledge concerning how to build a meaningful evaluation component into the organizing effort. As John Connell and others (1995) have pointed out, the continually evolving nature of community organizing and community-based initiatives, complex contextual issues, and the fact that these projects often seek change on multiple levels make many traditional evaluative approaches inappropriate or ill-suited to such organizing endeavors. Similarly, the focus of many standard evaluation approaches on long-term change in health and social indicators may miss the shorter-term system-level impacts with which community organizing is heavily concerned. Among the latter are improvements in organizational collaboration, increased levels of community involvement and action, and the promotion of healthier public policies or environmental conditions (Maldrud, Polacsek, and Wallerstein in press).

The lack of formal evaluations of most community organizing efforts, coupled with the failure of many engaged in these projects to write up and publish their results, has made it difficult for scholars or practitioners to amass a literature of "successful" and "unsuccessful" organizing efforts and the hallmarks of each. Although some characteristics of successful community collaborations have been identified (e.g., shared vision, strong leadership, and an accent on process and not merely task achievement) (Connell et al. 1995), much remains to be examined and assessed. The careful evaluation and documentation of both successful and unsuccessful community organizing projects must be a vital part of this new database.

Fortunately, the late 1980s and the first half of the 1990s saw important steps forward in empowerment education and related areas with direct applicability to community organizing. Key among these were the convening of a "round-table" on community initiatives for children and families and its development of *New Approaches to Evaluating Community Initiatives* (Connell et al. 1995). This edited volume explores dilemmas commonly faced in the design, measurement, and interpretation of community initiatives, as well as a variety of options and strategies for evaluators working with such projects. A special issue of *Health Education Research* (Goodman, Burdine et al. 1993) on community coalitions includes several articles that address measurement and evaluation issues. A two-part issue of *Health Education Quarterly* (Wallerstein and Bernstein 1994) further adds to the literature in this area, including both concepts and case studies that deal, in part, with issues of evaluation and measurement.

Within the latter collection, Eng and Parker's (1994) development and testing of a scale for measuring community competence represent a particularly important contribution, offering readers an effective new tool for measuring a key dimension of community organizing efforts. Similarly, Israel et al.'s (1994) development, validation, and application of a scale for measuring perceptions of individual, organizational, and community control (presented in appendix 9) provides a critical missing piece in the evaluation literature to date and one well suited to evaluating community organization outcomes.

Still another useful evaluation resource can be found in the self-reflection workbook developed in New Mexico to evaluate community organizing and community building in the context of creating healthier communities (Maldrud et al. in press). The workbook focuses on changes in community processes, such as grassroots participation, and changes in short-term system-level outcomes, such as the development of new programs, as a result of the organizing experience. It is these middle-level outcomes, rather than long-term changes in self-rated health and other health or social indicators, that are often most important in documenting community competence and empowerment.

A final recent contribution to the literature in this area is the publication of *Empowerment Evaluation* (Fetterman, Kaftarian, and Wandersman 1996). Empowerment evaluation is defined as "an interactive and iterative process by which the community, in collaboration with the support team, identifies its own health issues, decides how to address them, monitors progress toward its goals and uses the information to adapt and sustain the initiative" (Fawcett et al. 1996, 169). Although some of the evaluation approaches described in this book fit more a social planning, than a true organizing, approach to practice, most have immediate relevance for health educators and other social change professionals concerned with the evaluation of community organizing efforts (see chapters 18 and 19 for a fuller discussion of empowerment evaluation and its applications).

The availability of new theoretical contributions and practical tools that lend themselves to evaluation of community organizing fails, of course, to solve the problem of insufficient funding and/or commitment to carrying out high-quality evaluative research. Yet the increased attention of both foundation and government funders to evaluation and measurement issues in community organizing and community-based initiatives is encouraging. If translated into increased funding, this increased attention, together with the availability of new measurement tools and processes, could help spur major advances in the evaluation and documentation of community organizing in the years ahead.

Conclusion

The continued pivotal role of community organization in health education and related disciplines reflects not only its time-tested efficacy but also its high degree of philosophical fit with the most fundamental principles of effective community health education and other social change approaches. Community organization thus stresses the principle of relevance, the principle of participation, and the importance of creating environments in which individuals and communities can become empowered as they increase their community competence or problem-solving ability. Similarly, newer conceptualizations of community building stress many of these same principles within an overall approach that focuses on community growth and change from the inside through increased group identification; the discovery, nurturing, and mapping of community assets; and the creation of critical consciousness, all toward the end of building stronger and more caring communities. Using community organizing and community building skills and approaches, health educators and other social change professionals can help communities identify and build on their strengths, select the issues they feel are of greatest relevance, and work together in mobilizing their resources and in other ways addressing the goals they collectively have set.

Of at least equal importance, however, professionals can challenge themselves to examine their own dynamic of power, with their professional colleagues and members of the community, to understand the complexities of working in partnership toward the goals of community ownership of the projects undertaken and increased empowerment and community competence. In sum, both community organization and newer conceptualizations of community building practice have essential messages for health educators and other social change professionals in a wide variety of settings and may hold particular relevance in the changing sociopolitical climate at the dawn of the twenty-first century.

References

Alinsky, S. D. 1969. *Reveille for radicals*. Chicago: University of Chicago Press, 1969.
————. 1972. *Rules for radicals*. New York: Random House, 1972.
Arnold, R. et al. 1991. *Educating for a change*. Toronto: Between the Lines and Doris Marshall Institute for Education and Action.
Avery, B. 1990. Breathing life into ourselves: The evolution of the Black Women's Health Project. In *The black women's health book*, ed. E. White. Seattle: Seal Press.
Barndt, D. 1989. *Naming the moment: Political analysis for action*. Toronto: Jesuit Center for Social Faith and Justice.
Bernstein, E. et al. 1994. Empowerment Forum: A Dialogue Between Guest Editorial Board Members. *Health Education Quarterly* 21 (3):281–294.
Bracht, N., and L. Kingsbury. 1990. Community organization principles in health promotion: A five-stage model. In *Health promotion at the community level*, ed. N. Bracht. Newbury Park, Calif.: Sage.
Bracht, N., and N. Tsouros. 1990. Principles and strategies of effective community participation. *Health Promotion International* 5 (3):199–208.
Bradshaw, C., S. Soifer, and L. Gutierrez. 1994. Toward a hybrid model for effective organizing in communities of color. *Journal of Community Practice* 1 (1):25–41.
Braithwaite, R. L., C. Bianchi, and S. E. Taylor. 1994. Ethnographic approach to community organization and health empowerment. *Health Education Quarterly* 21 (3) (Fall):407–416.
Braithwaite, R. L. et al. 1989. Community organization and development for health promotion within an urban black community: A conceptual model. *Health Education* 2 (5):56–60.
Bricker-Jenkins, M., and N. Hooyman. 1986. A feminist world view: ideological themes from the feminist movement. In *Not for women only: Social work practice for a feminist future*, ed. M. Bricker-Jenkins and N. Hooyman. Springfield, Mass.: National Association of Social Workers.
Cohen, S., and S. L. Syme, 1985. *Social support and health*. New York: Academic Press.
Connell, J. P., A. C. Kabisch, L. B. Schorr, and C. H. Weiss, eds. 1995. *New approaches to evaluating community initiatives: concepts, methods, and contexts*. Washington, D.C.: Aspen Institute.
Cottrell, L. S. Jr. 1976. The competent community. In *Further explorations in social psychiatry*, ed. B. H. Kaplan, R. N. Wilson, and A. A. Leighton. New York: Basic Books.
————. 1983. The competent community. In *New perspectives on the American community*, ed. R. Warren and L. Lyon. Homewood, Ill.: Dorsey Press.
Dewey, J. 1946. *The public and its problems: An essay in political inquiry*. Chicago: Gateway Books.
Duhl, L. 1993. Conditions for healthy cities: Diversity, game boards, and social entrepreneurs. *Environment and Urbanization* 5 (2):112–124.
————. 1996. Personal communication, May 3.
Eng, E., J. Briscoe, and A. Cunningham. 1990. The effect of participation in water projects on immunization. *Social Science and Medicine* 30 (12):1349–1358.
Eng, E., and E. Parker. 1994. Measuring community competence in the Mississippi Delta: The interface between program evaluation and empowerment. *Health Education Quarterly* 21 (2):199–220.
Farquhar, J. et al. 1984. The Stanford five-city project: An overview. In *Behavioral health: A handbook of health enhancement and disease prevention*, ed. J. D. Matarazzo, N. E. Miller, S. M. Weiss, and J. A. Herd. Silver Spring, Md.: John Wiley.
Fawcett, S. B., A. Paine-Andrews, V. Francisco, J. Schultz et al. 1996. Empowering community health initiatives through evaluation. In *Empowerment evaluation: Knowledge and tools for self-assessment and accountability*, ed. D. Fetterman, S. Kaftarian, and A. Wandersman. Thousand Oaks, Calif.: Sage.

Feldblum, M., N. Wallerstein, F. Varela, and G. Collins, eds. 1994. *Community organizing: An experience for building healthier communities*. 3d ed. Albuquerque: New Mexico Department of Health, Public Health Division.

Fellin, P. 1995. Understanding American communities. In *Strategies of community intervention*, ed. J. Rothman, J. Erlich, and J. Tropman. 5th ed. Itasca, Ill.: Peacock.

Fetterman, D., S. Kaftarian, and A. Wandersman, eds. *Empowerment evaluation: Knowledge and tools for self-assessment and accountability*. Thousand Oaks, Calif.: Sage.

Florin, P., and A. Wandersman. 1990. An introduction to citizen participation, voluntary organizations, and community development: Insights for empowerment through research. *American Journal of Community Psychology* 18 (1):41–54.

Freire, P. 1970. *Pedagogy of the oppressed*. New York: Seabury Press.

————. 1973. *Education for critical consciousness*. New York: Seabury Press.

French, M. 1986. *Beyond power: On women, men, and morals*. London: Abacus.

French, W., and C. Bell. 1990. *Organization development: Behavioral science interventions for organization improvement*. 2d ed. Englewood Cliffs, N.J.: Prentice-Hall.

Gardner, J. 1991. *Building community*. Washington, D.C.: Independent Sector Leadership Studies Program.

Garvin, C. D., and F. M. Cox. 1995. A history of community organizing since the Civil War, with special reference to oppressed communities. In *Strategies of community intervention*, ed. J. Rothman, J. Erlich, and J. Tropman. 5th ed. Itasca, Ill.: Peacock.

Goodman, R., J. Burdine, E. Meehan, and K. McLeroy. 1993. Coalitions. *Health Education Research* 8 (3):313–314.

Goodman, R. M., A. Wandersman, M. J. Chinman, P. S. Imm, and E. Morrissey. 1996. An ecological assessment of community coalitions: Approaches to measuring community-based interventions for prevention and health promotion. *American Journal of Community Psychology* 24:33–61.

Guillory, B., E. Willie Jr., and E. Duran. 1988. Analysis of a community organizing case study: Alkali Lake. *Journal of Rural Community Psychology* 9 (1):27–35.

Gutierrez, L., and E. Lewis. 1994. Community organizing with women of color. A feminist approach. *Journal of Community Practice* 1 (2):23–43.

————. 1995. A feminist perspective on organizing with women of color. In *Community organizing in a diverse society*, ed. F. Rivera and J. Erlich. 2d ed. Boston: Allyn and Bacon.

Hawks, J. H. 1991. Power: A concept analysis. *Journal of Nursing* 16:754–762.

Heitzmann, C. A., and Kaplan, R. M. 1988. Assessment of methods for measuring social support. *Health Psychology* 7 (1):75–109.

Himmelman, A. 1992. Communities working collaboratively for a change. July. Minneapolis: Himmelman Consulting group. Unpublished paper.

Hope, A., and S. Timmel. 1984. *Training for transformation: a handbook for community workers*. Gweru, Zimbabwe: Mambo Press.

Horwitt, S. D. 1989. *Let them call me rebel: Saul Alinsky, his life and legacy*. New York: Knopf.

Hunter, A. 1975. The loss of community: An empirical test through replication. *American Sociology Review* 40 (5):537–552.

Hyde, C. 1990. A feminist model for macro practice. *Administration in Social Work* 13:145–181.

Israel, B. 1985. Social networks and social support: Implications for natural helper and community-level interventions. *Health Education Quarterly* 12 (1):66–80.

Israel, B., B. Checkoway, A. Schulz, and M. Zimmerman. 1994. Health education and community empowerment: Conceptualizing and measuring perceptions of individual, organizational, and community control. *Health Education Quarterly* 21 (2):149–170.

Katz, R. 1984. Empowerment and synergy: Expanding the community's healing resources. *Prevention in Human Services* 3:201–226.

Kaye, G., and T. Wolff, eds. 1995. From the ground up: A workbook on coalition building and community development. Amherst, Mass.: Area Health Education Center/Community Partners.

Kieffer, C. 1984. Citizen empowerment: A developmental perspective. *Prevention in Human Services* 3:9–36.

Khinduka, S. K. 1975. Community development: Potentials and limitations. In *Readings in community organization practice*, ed. R. M. Kramer and J. Specht. 2d ed. Englewood Cliffs, N. J.: Prentice-Hall.

Kieffer, C. 1984. Citizen empowerment: A developmental perspective. *Prevention in Human Services* 3 (2–3):9–36.

Kreuter, M. 1992. PATCH: Its origins, basic concepts, and links to contemporary public health policy. *Journal of Health Education* 23 (3):135–139.

Labonte, R. 1990. Empowerment: Notes on professional and community dimensions. *Canadian Review of Social Policy* 26:1–12.

———. 1994. Health promotion and empowerment: Reflections on professional practice. *Health Education Quarterly* 21 (2):253–268.

Lewin, K. 1958. Group decision and social change. In *Readings in social psychology*, ed. E. Maccoby, T. Newcombe, and E. Hartley. 3d ed. New York: Henry Holt.

Lukes, S. 1974. *Power: A radical view*. London: Macmillan.

Maldrud, K., M. Polacsek, and N. Wallerstein. In press. *A workbook for participatory evaluation of coalitions*. Albuquerque: University of New Mexico and New Mexico Partnership for Healthier Communities.

Marquez, B. 1990. Organizing the Mexican-American community in Texas: The legacy of Saul Alinsky. *Policy Studies Review* (Winter):355–373.

McCallister, L., and C. S. Fischer. 1978. A procedure for surveying personal networks. *Sociological Methods and Research* 7:131–148.

McKnight, J. 1987. Regenerating community. *Social Policy* (Winter):54–58.

McKnight, J. L., and J. P. Kretzmann. 1992. *Mapping community capacity*. Evanston, Ill.: Center for Urban Affairs and Policy, Northwestern University.

Miller, M. 1986. The Tenderloin Senior Organizing Project. In *A journey to justice*. Louisville, Ky.: Presbyterian Committee on the Self-development of People.

Minkler, M. 1992. Community organizing among the elderly poor in the U.S.: A case study. *International Journal of Health Services* 22 (1):303–316.

———. 1994. Ten commitments for community health education. *Health Education Research* 9 (4):527–534.

Minkler, M., and K. Cox. 1980. Creating critical consciousness in health: Applications of Freire's philosophy and methods to the health care setting. *International Journal of Health Services* 10 (2):311–322.

Minkler, M., S. P. Wallace, and M. McDonald. 1994–1995. The political economy of health: A useful theoretical tool for health education practice. *International Quarterly of Community Health Education* 15 (2):111–125.

Nyswander, D. 1956. Education for health: Some principles and their applications. *Health Education Monographs* 14:65–70.

Ovrebo, B., M. Ryan, K. Jackson, and K. Hutchinson, K. 1994. The homeless prenatal program: A model for empowering homeless pregnant women. *Health Education Quarterly* 21 (2):187–198.

PATCH. 1992. *Journal of Health Education* 23 (3).

Purdey, A., G. Adhikari, S. Robinson, and P. Cox. 1994. Participatory health development in rural Nepal: Clarifying the process of community empowerment. *Health Education Quarterly* 21 (3):329–344.

Rappaport, J. 1984. Studies in empowerment: Introduction to the issue. *Prevention in Human Services* 3 (2–3):1–7.

Reitzes, D. C., and D. C. Reitzes. 1980. Saul Alinsky's contribution to community development. *Journal of the Community Development Society* 11 (2):39–52.

Rivera, F., and J. Erlich. 1995. An option assessment framework for organizing in emerging minority communities. In *Tactics and techniques of community intervention*, ed. J. Tropman, J. Erlich, and J. Rothman. 3d ed. Itasca, Ill.: Peacock.

Ross, M. 1955. *Community organization: Theory and principles*. New York: Harper and Brothers.

Rothman, J., and J. E. Tropman. 1987. Models of community organization and macro practice: Their mixing and phasing. In *Strategies of community organization*, ed. F. M. Cox, J. L. Erlich, J. Rothman, and J. E. Tropman. 4th ed. Itasca, Ill.: Peacock.

Scott, J. 1990. *Domination and the arts of resistance: Hidden transcripts*. New Haven: Yale University Press.

Simon, R. 1991. *Gramsci's political thought: An introduction*. London: Wishart.

Stewart, D., and P. Shamdasani. 1990. *Focus groups: Theory and practice*. Newbury Park, Calif.: Sage.

Syme, S. 1988. Social epidemiology and the work environment. *International Journal of Health Services* 18 (4):635–645.

Thompson, B., L. Wallack, E. Lichtenstein, and T. Pechacek. 1990–1991. Principles of community organization and partnership for smoking cessation in the Community Intervention Trial for Smoking Cessation (COMMIT). *International Quarterly of Community Health Education* 11 (3):187–203.

Traynor, B. 1993. Community development and community organizing. *Shelterforce* (March-April).

Tsouros, A. 1995. The WHO healthy cities project: State of the art and future plans. *Health Promotion International* 10 (2):133–141.

Wallerstein, N. 1992. Powerlessness, empowerment, and health: Implications for health promotion programs. *American Journal of Health Promotion* 6:197–205.

Wallerstein, N., and E. Bernstein, eds. 1994. *Health Education Quarterly* 21 (2–3).

Wallerstein, N., and V. Sanchez-Merki. 1994. Freirian praxis in health education: Research results from an adolescent prevention program. *Health Education Research* 9 (1):105–118.

Wallerstein, N., and M. Weinger, eds. 1992. *American Journal of Industrial Medicine* 22 (5).

Warren, R. 1963. *The community in America*. Chicago: Rand McNally.

Wechsler, R. 1990. Harnessing people power: A community-based approach to preventing alcohol and drug abuse. *Western City* (June):1–4.

Weil, M. 1986. Women, community, and organizing. In *Feminist visions for social work*, ed. N. Van DenBergh and L. Cooper. Silver Spring, Md.: National Association of Social Workers.

West, C. 1993. *Race matters*. Boston: Beacon Press.

World Health Organization. 1986. *Ottawa charter for health promotion*. Copenhagen: WHO Europe.

World Health Organization/United Nations International Children's Emergency Fund. 1978. International conference on primary health care. Alma Ata, USSR.

Zimmerman, M. 1990. Taking aim on empowerment research: On the distinction between individual and psychological conceptions. *American Journal of Community Psychology* 18 (1):169–177.

Chapter 4

Social Action Community Organization

ROBERT FISHER

Proliferation, Persistence, Roots, and Prospects

SOCIAL ACTION is a distinctive type of community organization practice (Burghardt 1987). As articulated by Rothman (1968), in a seminal essay that provides the framework for much work in the field, it is different in a number of critical respects from other forms of community intervention, such as community locality development and community social planning. The "classic" social action effort is grassroots based, conflict oriented, with a focus on direct action, and geared to organizing the disadvantaged or aggrieved to take action on their own behalf. It has a long and important history, including, for example, such practitioners and efforts as Saul Alinsky and the numerous Industrial Areas Foundation projects associated with the "Alinsky method" since the late 1930s; Communist Party community organizing in the 1930s and 1940s; civil rights efforts in the 1950s and 1960s; the work of Cesar Chávez and the United Farm Workers; Community Action Programs and the confrontational organizing of SDS, SNCC, the Black Panthers, the Brown Berets, and La Raza Unida in the 1960s; and the wave of community-based social action since the 1970s organized around identity groups based on gender, sexual orientation, ethnicity, race, or neighborhood (Fisher 1994; Fisher and Kling 1993). Unlike community development and social planning efforts, social action focuses on power, pursues conflict strategies, and challenges the structures that oppress and disempower constituents. It is the type of community intervention that most lives up to the

Reprinted from *Strategies of Community Interventions*, 5th ed., ed. J. Rothman, J. L. Erlich, J. E. Tropman, and F. M. Cox, 327–340 (Itasca, Ill.: F. E. Peacock, 1995) by permission of the publisher. Copyright © 1995 F. E. Peacock Publishers Inc., Itasca, Illinois. Parts of the chapter appeared earlier as "Community Organizing Worldwide," in *Mobilizing the Community*, ed. R. Fisher and J. Kling (Newbury Park, Calif.: Sage, 1993).

social justice and social change mission of social work, and yet, because of its oppositional politics, tends to be the least practiced within social work institutions and social service agencies.

Community-based social action, however, is not a static phenomenon. Social action is always changing in response to the conditions and opportunity structures in which it operates. In the 1980s, for example, one hallmark of community-based social action, as practiced by Alinsky groups and many others, was its withdrawal from a singular emphasis on conflict theory and confrontational politics. Involved in developing housing projects, organizing community development projects, and handling job training grants, these efforts, the heirs to classic social action community organization, now look more like a blending of social action with community development and social planning (Fisher 1994).

This essay seeks to contribute to the expanding knowledge of community-based social action by making four essential points. First, because community-based social action is an evolving and ever-changing phenomenon, we must now view it beyond our national borders, as a global phenomenon. The community development literature has done this for more than a generation. Moreover, unlike in the past, when social action efforts were said to last no more than six years, current efforts persist much longer and often become important community institutions. Second, these social action community organizations share common characteristics, reflective of what some observers call the new social movements. Third, new social theory and histories of social action efforts have reconceptualized contemporary community-based social action as primarily a product of post-1945 social movement organizing. These movement roots help further distinguish community-based social action from other forms of community organization and help explain why Rothman's model of social action continues to have salience for the study of grassroots oppositional movement efforts. Fourth, like all eras, but perhaps even more so for the current one, our contemporary context poses both significant opportunities and immense barriers to effective community-based social action and practice. It is these changing conditions and the responses of organizers and organizations to them that are significantly expanding and altering our knowledge and understanding of social action.

Proliferation and Persistence

Two things are certain about contemporary community-based social action organizing. It is both a widespread and a long-term phonomenon. Once thought of as confined to narrow geographic areas (like New York City or Chicago) or to a specific historical era (like the late 1960s and early 1970s), proliferation and persistence, not provincialism and short-term existence, are the hallmarks of contemporary efforts. Without doubt, community-based social action has a long history in both social work practice and social work education (Burghardt 1987; Fisher 1994). Most social action, however, occurs outside of social work. That has always been the case. Since the 1960s, when the social work profession first began to take a very strong interest in social action approaches to community organization, grassroots organizing has become the dominant form of popular resistance and social change worldwide. Instead of not "enjoy[ing] the currency it once had" (Rothman with Tropman 1987, 7), these efforts have proliferated widely outside the social work profession, and within as well as outside of the United States.

Jeff Drumtra (1991–1992) recently provided sketches of citizen action in thirty-eight countries. His research emphasized how recent political reform in twenty-five countries in Asia, Africa, and Latin America now allowed for wide voter participation in free elections with multiple candidates. Durning (1989, 5) goes further. In a comparable comparative study he argues that people are coming together "in villages, neighborhoods, and shantytowns around the world," in response to the forces which endanger their communities and planet. Paget (1990) estimates two million grassroots social action groups in the United States alone. Lowe (1986) sees a similar upsurge of activity in the United Kingdom. The same is true for most of Western Europe. Grassroots social action organizing and urban protest have been key elements of politics in the West since the late 1960s. But community-based social action is not limited to Western industrial states. What happened in the West is only part of a widespread escalation of urban resistance throughout the world. The picture shows "an expanding lattice-work covering the globe," Durning (1989, 6–7) continues. "At the local level, particularly among the close to 4 billion humans in developing lands, it appears that the world's people are better organized in 1989 than they have been since European colonialism disrupted traditional societies centuries ago." Community organizing efforts, with hundreds of millions of members, have proliferated worldwide in the past 20 years, extending from nations in the West to those in the South, and, most recently, with extraordinary results, to those in the East (Frank and Fuentes 1990, 163).

Similarly, the persistence of grassroots social action, as well as their proliferation, is another hallmark of our contemporary era. Many efforts have come and gone in the past decade. But the old rule of thumb that social action community organizing, like that pioneered by Saul Alinsky, lasts no more than six years, is no longer valid. ACORN celebrated its twentieth anniversary in 1990, National People's Action (NPA) did so two years later, and COPS soon thereafter. Citizen Action, TMO in Houston, the New Jersey Tenants Union (NJTU), and many others recently passed the ten-year mark, with no signs of declining despite having to organize in very adverse conditions. Grassroots efforts tied to national issues, such as pro-choice, gay rights, and the environmental movement, not only persist but continue to grow.

The Nature of Contemporary Social Action

But what is the nature of contemporary, community-based, social action organizing? Are these comunity-based social action efforts all of the same piece? Do prior models (Rothman 1968; Fisher 1994) capture the complexity of current efforts? If a global proliferation exists, what are the shared, essential characteristics of contemporary, community-based, social action organizing? Building on the insights from new social movement theory (Epstein 1990; Melucci 1989), contemporary social organizing worldwide shares the following characteristics.

First, the efforts are community based, that is, organized around communities of interest or geography, not at the site of production (the factory) or against the principal owners of capital as was the case of most pre-1960s organizing (Offe 1987).

Second, the organizations are transclass groupings of constituencies and cultural identities such as blacks, ethnics, women, gay men, neighborhood residents, students, ecologists, and peace activists. Labor becomes one, not *the*, constituency group. Class becomes part of, not *the*, identity (Brecher and Costello 1990; Fisher 1992).

Third, the ideological glue is a neopopulist vision of democracy. The groups reject authoritarianism: in the state, leadership, party, organization, and relationships (Amin 1990). Their organizational form is most often sufficiently small, loose, and open to be able to "tap local knowledge and resources, to respond to problems rapidly and creatively, and to maintain the flexibility needed in changing circumstances" (Durning 1989, 6–7). Some see contemporary social action as "non-ideological," because the organizations dismiss the old ideologies of capitalism, communism, and nationalism and because they tend to be without a clear critique of the dominant system. But others argue that ideological congruence is their essence. Their "neopopulist" principles and beliefs are what make them so important and filled with potential (Dalton and Kuechler 1990; Offe 1987; Boyte and Riessman 1986; Fisher and Kling 1988; Boyte, Booth, and Max 1986).

Fourth, struggle over culture and social identity play a greater role in these community-based efforts, especially when compared to the workplace-based organizing of the past, which focused more on economic and political issues. "After the great working class parties surrendered their remaining sense of radical political purpose with the onset of the cold war," Bronner (1990, 161) writes, "new social movements emerged to reformulate the spirit of resistance in broader cultural terms." Feminism. Black Power. Sexual identity. Ethnic nationalism. Victim's rights. Of course, culture and identity—grounded in historical experience, values, social networks, and collective solidarity—have always been central to citizen social action (Gutman 1977). And, of course, identity and constituency efforts include economic and political issues. But as class becomes increasingly fragmented in the postindustrial city and as the locus of workplace organizing declines in significance, resistances that emerge increasingly do so at the community level around cultural issues and identity bases (Touraine 1985; Fisher and Kling 1991).

Fifth, strategies include elements of locality development self-help and empowerment. An aim is building community capacity, especially in an era hostile to social change efforts and unwilling to support them. Some of the more effective efforts go beyond community capacity building to target and make claims against the public sector. They see the future of community-based social action as interdependent with political and economic changes outside their communities. They understand that the state is the entity potentially most responsible and vulnerable to social action claims and constituencies (Piven and Cloward 1982; Fisher 1992). But most contemporary community-based organizing seeks independence from the state rather than state power. As Midgley (1986, 4) points out, central to the rationale of community participation "is a reaction against the centralization, bureaucratization, rigidity, and remoteness of the state. The ideology of community participation is sustained by the belief that the power of the state has extended too far, diminishing the freedoms of ordinary people and their rights to control their own affairs." Community capacity building becomes a natural focus, reflecting antistatist strategies and decentralization trends of the postindustrial political economy.

Historical Antecedents:
The Roots of Ideologies and Strategies

One of the key causes for this common form of social action organization is the common heritage of citizen resistance since the end of World War II. It is this common heritage that continues to structure and inform contemporary efforts. For our purposes I emphasize five major historical roots: the (1) community-based resistance of Saul Alinsky, (2) liberation struggles of people of color, (3) urban decentralization and citizen participation programs, (4) New Left movement, and (5) new social movements. Of course, this is not to suggest that the heritage of community resistance does not include efforts prior to 1945 (Fisher 1992). Nor is it to suggest that all contemporary community mobilization efforts build on each of these antecedents or that these are the only sources. Admittedly, roots are more numerous and entangled than here suggested, but the following five are essential to contemporary community-based social action.

COMMUNITY-BASED RESISTANCE OF SAUL ALINSKY
While the organizing projects of Saul Alinsky during his lifetime never amounted to much in terms of material victories and while his projects only took off when the southern civil rights movement shifted to northern cities in the 1960s, the community-based, constituency-oriented, urban populist, confrontational politics

developed by Alinsky in the United States provides one of the earliest models of
the community-based social action form (Fisher and Kling 1988). Beginning just
before World War II, Alinsky's work in Chicago built on the older, union-based
models of social action, such as the Congress of Industrial Organizations and
Communist Party United States of America (Horwitt 1989; Fisher 1984). From
these it drew its labor organizing style, conflict strategies, direct-action politics,
and the idea of grounding organizing in the everyday lives and traditions of working people. But Alinsky's model added something new: a kind of labor organizing
in the social factory (Boyte 1981). The community organizer was the catalyst for
change. The task was to build democratic, community-based organizations. The
goal was to empower neighborhood residents by teaching them basic political and
organizing skills and getting them or their representatives to the urban bargaining table (Fisher 1994; Boyte 1981). Both the site of production (supporting labor
demands) and the public sector (making City Hall more accountable) served as
the primary targets of Alinsky organizing.

     This was an insurgent consciousness of "urban populism," based in neighborhood
"people's organizations," oriented to building community power, discovering
indigenous leaders, providing training in democratic participation, and proving
that ordinary people could challenge and beat City Hall (Boyte, Booth, and Max
1986; Swanstrom 1985; Horwitt 1989). At their weakest, Alinsky efforts sought
to replace the political program and ideology of the old social action efforts with
the skills of democratic grassroots participation, the abilities of professionally trained
organizers, a faith in the democratic tendencies of working people to guide organizations toward progressive ends, and a reformist vision of grassroots pluralistic
politics. At their best, however, Alinsky efforts continue to empower lower- and
working-class, black and Latino community residents to demand expanded
public sector accountability and public participation in an increasingly privatized
political context (Fisher 1994; Horwitt 1989; Rogers 1990; Delgado 1986; Kahn
1970). Alinsky may not be the "father of community organizing," but, especially
in the United States, his work and the work of his successors have been seminal
to social action community organizing (Boyte 1981).

LIBERATION STRUGGLES OF PEOPLE OF COLOR
Much more significant in terms of impact are the liberation struggles of people
of color throughout the world since the 1950s. The civil rights movement in the
United States and the national liberation struggles in the southern hemisphere
served as important models for a community-based, ethnic/nationalist politics
oriented to self-determination and sharing the political liberties and material afflu-
ence of the societies that exploited people of color. As a model for grassroots direct
action and insurgent consciousness, the southern civil rights movement spawned
most of what was to follow in the United States and established important

precedents for others throughout the world (Branch 1988; Morris 1984; Reagon 1979). The liberation struggles in Africa, Asia, Latin America, and the Middle East, as well as specifically early efforts in Ghana, Vietnam, Iran, Guatemala, and Cuba, not only provided models for people worldwide, including activists in the civil rights movement in the United States, but symbolized the mobilization of a worldwide liberation struggle for people of color. The demand for national self-determination for all people (not just those of European descent), the opposition to policies of racism and imperialism, and the plea of the civil rights movement for "beloved community" helped pierce the consensus politics of the 1950s and early 1960s. More recent liberation struggles in Nicaragua, El Salvador, and South Africa, to name but a few, continued to challenge conservative, racist, and imperialist paradigms in the 1980s and 1990s.

The continuous liberation struggles of people of color emphasize three lessons critical to the insurgent consciousness of contemporary community activism. First, citizen insurgency is not a political aberration. It is a legitimate and important, informal part of the political process to which all those without access to power can turn. Second, if oppressed people—often illiterate, rural peasants with few resources—could mobilize, take risks, and make history, then people of other oppressed or threatened constituencies can, with sufficient organization and leadership, do the same. Third, strategy must include both community self-help and constituency empowerment, on the one hand, and the struggle for state power, or at least the targeting of the public sector as the site of grievances and as a potential source of support, on the other. This dual quality of building community capacity and targeting the state, though not always in equal balance and often in tension, as exemplified in struggles between the Southern Christian Leadership Conference (SCLC) and the Student Nonviolent Coordinating Committee (SNCC), was as true for the civil rights movement in the United States as it was for the liberation struggles in the Third World (Carson 1982).

URBAN DECENTRALIZATION AND CITIZEN PARTICIPATION

The struggles of people in the southern hemisphere dramatized the exploitative nature of the imperial postwar political economy at the very moment in the 1960s that some progressive capitalists, political leaders, and planners in both the public and voluntary sectors found themselves unable to address mounting urban problems at home. From 1960 onward, as liberal leaders such as presidents Kennedy and Johnson in the United States advocated for modest social reforms and a more democratized public sector, pressure mounted for urban decentralization and citizen participation. The Community Action Program of the 1960s in the United States and the Urban Programme of the late 1960s in Britain were among the most noted of public projects seeking "maximum feasible participation" at the grassroots level. But such programs proliferated widely, making state-sponsored municipal decentralization and community participation an international phenomenon (Kjellberg 1979; Blair 1983; Midgley 1986; Chekki 1979).

Of course, such postwar programs differ dramatically from Alinsky and liberation movement efforts in their origins and problem analysis. They are initiated largely by reformers in the public and voluntary sectors—professionals such as urban planners and social workers who either seek modest structural change or find themselves too constrained on the job to do much more in their agencies than deliver needed services at the grassroots level. As such, these initiatives represent a more institutionalized, more formalized wing of the community-based social action phenomenon. They tend, as well, to implement decentralized structure and democratic participation into public agencies without a sense for the contradictions inherent in doing so, but with a knowledge of the importance of linking the state and grassroots activism. The state becomes not the target of democratic insurgency but the employer and supporter of citizen initiatives (Merkl 1985). At their worst, these measures defuse and coopt insurgency. At their best, contemporary organizing draws from this legacy a commitment to serving the people, to advocacy, and to citizen participation: (a) Deliver services at a grassroots level where people will have better access. (b) Include more people, even lay people, in the decision-making process at a more decentralized level. (c) Make sure they have real power to make decisions and control resources. (d) Struggle from within the state bureaucracies and agencies to achieve economic and participatory democracy for the greatest number of urban dwellers.

THE NEW LEFT MOVEMENT

Despite the efforts noted so far, urban problems and tensions continued to escalate in the late 1960s. In response, direct-action movements mounted, especially in the United States. Early SDS (Students for a Democratic Society) and SNCC (Student Nonviolent Coordinating Committee) community organizing projects focused on "participatory democracy" and "letting the people decide," seeking not only to pressure local and national policy but to create "prefigurative," that is alternative, social groups (Breines 1982; Evans 1979). They also developed a critique of American policy abroad and the liberal consensus at home. They built a movement in opposition to the politics of both corporate capital and the old social movement. After 1965, organizing adopted more nationalist and Marxist perspectives; Black Power efforts, for example, were less concerned with participatory democracy and more interested in challenging imperialism abroad and at home, winning "community control," and building black identity (Jennings 1990).

Such efforts in the United States were part of an insurgent trend in the West. Massive peace protests in the United Kingdom registered strong disapproval of Cold War policies, directly challenging social democratic regimes. These early efforts, among others, initiated a widespread "New Left" movement throughout the

West, one which was soon to expand beyond university sites and student constituencies to develop, according to Ceccarelli (1982, 263), into "an unprecedented outburst of urban movements": Paris and West German cities in the spring of 1968; Prague, Chicago, and Monterrey, Mexico, during that summer; in Italy the "hot autumn" of 1969 and the urban conflicts of the early 1970s; squatters in Portugese cities after the April Revolution; and urban social movements in Madrid and other Spanish cities after Franco. All testify to a massive grassroots mobilization which developed rapidly, and perhaps even unprecedentedly, throughout Europe, the United States, and parts of the Third World (Ceccarelli 1982; Teodori 1969).

Concern for and experimentation with participatory democracy, nonhierarchical decision making, prefigurative cultural politics, linking the personal with the political, direct-action tactics, and constituency-based organizing (students, the poor, etc.) characterized New Left insurgent consciousness (Jacobs and Landau 1966; Breines 1982). Unlike the new social movement resistances to follow, the New Left emphasized the formation of coalitions or political parties tied to national revolutionary/emancipatory struggles. There was a sense in the late 1960s, in cities as disparate as Paris, Berlin, Berkeley, and Monterrey, that "successful and autonomous urban movements are not a real alternative outside the context of a revolutionary national movement (Walton 1979, 12). The struggle over state power, over who should make public policy, fueled local organizing efforts. Grassroots efforts were for most activists a democratic means to larger objectives which transcended the local community. This strategy persists, in a more reformist form, in certain notable national efforts since then, such as the Green parties in Europe, the Workers Party in Brazil, and the Rainbow Coalition idea in the United States (Spretnak and Capra 1985; Alvarez 1993; Collins 1986).

Community-based social action efforts which followed tended to borrow more heavily from the "newer" side of the New Left. These activists saw community organizing, alternative groupings, and grassroots efforts as at least the primary focus, if not the sole end. They emphasized democratic organizational structure, the politics of identity and culture, existential values of personal freedom and authenticity, and the development of "free spaces" where people could learn the theory and practice of political insurgency while engaging in it. So did much of the New Left, but the other, more Marxist segments, closer in style and politics to the old labor-based social action, adhered strongly to older concerns with public policy and winning state power (Evans 1979; Evans and Boyte 1986; Carson 1982).

NEW SOCIAL MOVEMENTS

Despite a marked backlash worldwide against the radical activism of the late 1960s, the 1970s and 1980s witnessed not the end of community-based activism but the proliferation of grassroots activism and insurgency into highly diversified, single-issue or identity-oriented, community-based efforts. These efforts, the subject of this essay, include women's shelters and feminist organizations; efforts in defense of the rights and the communities of oppressed people of color; struggles around housing, ecology, and peace issues; gay and lesbian rights and identity groups; and thousands of neighborhood and issue-based citizen initiatives, complete with organizer training centers. While these organizing efforts vary from one national and local context to another, they share a common form and movement heritage. Based in geographic communities or communities of interest, decentralized according to constituencies and identity groups, democratic in process and goals, and funded most often by voluntary sources, they serve as the archetype for contemporary social action.

The roots of their insurgent consciousness, while not always direct, can be found in the ideals discussed thus far: (1) that ordinary and previously oppressed people should have a voice and can make history; (2) that citizen and community participation, which gives "voice" to people previously silent in public discourse, is needed to improve decision making, address a wide range of problems, and democratize society; (3) that "by any means necessary" covers the gamut of strategies and tactics from revolutionary to interest-group politics; (4) that culture, whether found in a traditional ethnic neighborhood, battered women's shelter, counterculture collective, or gay men's organization, must be blended with the quest for "empowerment" into an identity- or constituency-oriented politics; and (5) that "the personal is political," articulated first by radical feminists in the late 1960s, guides people to organize around aspects of daily life most central to them, while keeping in mind that struggles over personal issues and relationships—personal choice, autonomy, commitment, and fulfillment—are inextricably tied to collective ones of the constituency group and the larger society.

Most commentators tend to see the focus on democracy as the essence of new social movement insurgent consciousness and the source of its potential. As Frank and Fuentes (1990, 142) put it, the new social movements "are the most important agents of social transformation in that their praxis promotes particpatory democracy in civil society." Pitkin and Shumer (1982, 43) go further, declaring that "of all the dangerous thoughts and explosive ideas abroad in the world today, by far the most subversive is that of democracy. . . . [It] is the cutting edge of radical criticism, the best inspiration for change toward a more humane world, the revolutionary idea of our time." And these democratic projects have had profound impact: empowering participants, teaching democratic skills, transforming notions of political life, expanding political boundaries, returning politics to civic self-activity, strengthening a sense of public activism, raising new social and political issues, struggling against new forms of subordination and oppression, and even advancing agendas of the middle class to which formal, institutional politics remain closed (Roth 1991; Slater 1985).

But while the emphasis on democracy unites these efforts, it also helps detach them in the Western industrialized nations from the material needs of the poor, and it contributes to their fragmentation into a plethora of diverse, decentralized community organizations. The pursuit of democracy, without sufficient concern for equality, has resulted in the failure of the new social movements to address the material needs of the most disadvantaged. Moreover, the new social movement origins in culturally oriented, identity-based efforts tend to fragment social change efforts in general (Fisher and Kling 1993). For example, the diversity and flexibility that theorists of postmodernity attribute to contemporary society are nowhere more evident than in the variety of these new social movement efforts. A commitment to diversity embodies their emphasis on democratic politics. It encourages each constituency or identity group to name its own struggles, develop its own voice, and engage in its own empowerment. This may be the future of politics, a "postmodernization of public life," with its "proliferation of multiple publics [and] breaking down of rigid barriers between political and private life" (Kaufmann 1990, 10). But the central challenges to these efforts require more immediate and realistic strategies. How do they encourage diversity *and* counteract fragmentation? How do they influence or get power at levels—the city, state, and nation—beyond their own limited universes *and* at the same time build community capacity? How do we organize grassroots social action efforts *and* at the same time build a larger social change movement or political party, the size of which can only accomplish the needed, large structural changes?

Practice Implications

Without question, the fragmentation of contemporary social action weakens the possibility for coherently imagined challenges to current problems. To address this problem of contemporary organizing, the historical dialectic of domination and resistance must be understood and fashioned in terms of the *interplay* between class, community, and the search for new cultural orientations. In this regard Kling and I have offered elsewhere the following sets of strategies (Fisher and Kling 1991).

First, mobilization in the fragmented metropolis demands that broad coalitions be sought between various constituency groups, and that community politics be more cohesively integrated with electoral activity. Single community-based efforts are not large enough to challenge the enormous power of corporate capital or centralized government. Because community problems almost always originate beyond local borders, the ability to affect change depends to a great extend upon coalition building. The success of coalition building, however, ultimately will be based upon whether specific ways can be found to break down the racial and cultural barriers that are so entrenched in the United States and growing again in Western Europe.

Pressure group politics, even through powerful coalitions, is not enough;

movements must also struggle to win and hold power, not simply to influence it. The electoral arena must become a prime target for social movement mobilizing while, at some later point, political parties serve the critical role of formalizing and structuring relationships between loosely formed coalitions and constituency-based groups (Boyte et al. 1986; Delgado 1986; Spretnak and Capra 1985). We offer such advice knowing how coalition and electoral efforts draw already scarce resources away from the fundamental task of grassroots organizing. But the local and the global are equally necessary, and numerous models of such dually focused practice have emerged over time. The experience of leading organizing effots in the United States, such as IAF, ACORN and Citizen Action, and in Western Europe, such as the Green parties, illustrates how, while still focusing on the grassroots, they recognized the importance of coalition building and electoral activity.

Second, as others argue (Evans et al. 1985), we need to bring back in, and use legislative policy to challenge the ideology of privatization and free enterprise that meets so well the needs of international capital. The state, of course, is not inherently an ally of low- and moderate-income people. But in the late twentieth century, where private sector targets disappear in the electronic global economy, and where, in a new social movement context, the community replaces the workplace as the locus of organizing, a legitimized and expanded public sector becomes a critical ingredient for continued citizen action. Without it public life cannot even begin to be restored; without it grassroots mobilization devolves into self-help strategies which further fragmentation and perpetuate the use of private, voluntary solutions to massive, public problems (Fisher 1993).

For example, take the worldwide push for privatization (Barnekov, Boyle, and Rich 1989). By undermining government legitimacy and responsibility, it results not only in a declining public life and fewer public services, but also in loss of access to a potentially accountable and responsible public sector, *the* major victory of pre-1945 social movements and a crucial target of some of the earlier antecedents to current social action efforts (Fisher 1988, 1992; Piven and Cloward 1982). Increasingly, in our current context, as the public sector declines as a source of grievances or solutions, citizen action is undercut. Contemporary resistance focuses its attention on community-based self-help and empowerment partly because the state—one of the primary arenas and targets for antecedents such as Alinsky, the civil rights movement, national liberation efforts, and the New Left—has been delegitimized. But contemporary social action community organization requires a public-sector arena and target because, unlike union organizing, which had some power at the site of production, in our current era of high-velocity global capital and declining labor activism, where it is much more difficult for workers and citizens to affect the private sector, community-based social action efforts have the state as the entity most responsible and vulnerable to their constituencies (Fisher 1992; Piven and Cloward 1982).

Third, we must move to a more consciously ideological politics. We must seek new, centering narratives, or, at least, more common programs that can draw the decentered narratives of our time toward a focal point. New formations and groupings will make mobilization on local levels more potent, perhaps, but they will not resolve the fundamental divisions that plague the effort to challenge broad, culturally entrenched structures of domination, prejudice, and exploitation.

Organizers must continue to teach the techniques of organization—the kowledge of how to bring people together to identify common grievances; to get them to communicate with each other accross differing and even conflicting agendas; to enable them to run effective meetings; and to empower them to recognize what sorts of strategies are most suitable for particular contexts, and identify those points in the political regime most vulnerable to the pressures of collective action. But among the organizer's most valuable skills remains the ability to challenge the accepted vision of things and to develop ideological congruence with other oppositional efforts. Good organizational leadership—and good community practice—lies with understanding what is involved in moving people beyond their received notions of how they are related to other cultural and identity-based groups. An authentic commitment to "human solidarity, mutual responsibility, and social justice" demands that people engage in a profound reexamination of the values on which their society and way of life are based. Such transformations of consciousness do not emerge without intervention and engagement.

An organizing ideology for our times needs to combine the new postmodern demands for autonomy and identity with older, modernist ones for social justice, production for human needs, rather than profit, and the spirit of connectedness and solidarity among people, rather than competition. Day-to-day organizing, if it is to move beyond fragmented values and cultures, still needs to be informed by this sort of centering, oppositional ideology. To continue to open activists and constituencies to broader conceptions of social action and social change remains the primary responsibility of the organizer in the 1990s.

References

Alvarez, S. 1993. Deepening democracy: Social movement networks, constitutional reform, and radical urban regimes in contemporary Brazil. In *Mobilizing the community: Local politics in a global era*, ed. R. Fisher and J. Kling. Newbury Park, Calif.: Sage.

Amin, S. et al. 1990. *Transforming the revolution*. New York: Monthly Review Press.

Barnekov. T., R. Boyle, and D. Rich. 1989. *Privatism and urban policy in Britain and the United States*. Oxford: Oxford University Press.

Blair, H. W. 1983. Comparing development programs. *Journal of Community Action* 1.

Boyte, H. 1981. *The backyard revolution*. Philadelphia: Temple University Press.

Boyte, H., and F. Riessman. 1986. *The new populism*. Philadelphia: Temple University Press.

Boyte, H., H. Booth, and S. Max. 1986. *Citizen action and the new American populism*. Philadelphia: Temple University Press.

Branch, T. 1988. *Parting the waters: America in the King years, 1954–1963*. New York: Simon and Schuster.

Brecher, J., and T. Costello. 1990. *Building bridges: The emerging grassroots coalition of labor and community*. New York: Monthly Review Press.

Breines, W. 1982. *Community and organization in the new left, 1962–1968: The great refusal*. New York: Praeger.

Bronner, S. E. 1990. *Socialism unbound*. New York: Routledge.

Burghardt, S. 1987. Community-based social action. In *Encyclopedia of social work*, 18th ed. New York: NASW.

Carson, C., Jr. 1982. *In struggle: SNCC and the black awakening of the 1960s*. Cambridge, Mass.: Harvard University Press.

Ceccarelli, P. 1982. Politics, parties, and urban movements: Western Europe. In *Urban policy under capitalism*, ed. N. Fainstein and S. Fainstein. Beverly Hills, Calif.: Sage.

Chekki, D. 1979. *Community development: Theory and method of planned change*. New Delhi: Vikas Publishing House.

Collins, S. 1986. *The rainbow challenge*. New York: Monthly Review Press.

Dalton, R., and M. Kuechler, eds. 1990. *Challenging the political order: New social and political movements in western democracies*. New York: Oxford University Press.

Delgado, G. 1986. *Organizing the movement: The roots and growth of ACORN*. Philadelphia: Temple University Press.

Drumtra, J. 1991–1992. Power to the people. *World View* 4 (Winter): 8–13.

Durning, A. B. 1989. Action at the grassroots: Fighting poverty and environmental decline. *Worldwatch Paper* 88 (January): 1–70.

Epstein, B. 1990. Rethinking social movement theory. *Socialist Review* 90 (January-March).

Evans, P., et al., eds. 1985. *Bringing the state back in*. New York: Cambridge University Press.

Evans, S. 1979. *Personal politics: The roots of women's liberation in the civil rights movements and the new left*. New York: Vintage Books.

Evans, S., and H. Boyte. 1986. *Free spaces: The sources of democratic change in America*. New York: Harper and Row.

Fisher, R. 1988. Where seldom is heard a discouraging word: The political economy of Houston, Texas. *Amerika-studien* 33 (Winter): 73–91.

———. 1992. Organizing in the modern metropolis. *Journal of Urban History* 18: 222–237.

———. 1993. Grassroots organizing worldwide. In *Mobilizing the community: Local politics in a global era*, ed. R. Fisher and J. Kling. Newbury Park, Calif.: Sage.

———. 1994. *Let the people decide: Neighborhood organizing in America*. rev. ed. Boston: Twayne.

Fisher, R., and J. Kling. 1988. Leading the people: Two approaches to the role of ideology in community organizing. *Radical America* 21 (1): 31–46.

———. 1991. Popular mobilization in the 1990s: Prospects for the new social movements. *New Politics* 3: 71–84.

———, eds. 1993. *Mobilizing the community: Local politics in a global era*. Newbury Park, Calif: Sage.

Frank, A. G., and M. Fuentes. 1990. Civil democracy: Social movements in recent world history. In *Transforming the revolution: Social movements and the world-system*, ed. S. Amin et al. New York: Monthly Review Press.

Gutman, H. G. 1977. *Work, culture, and society in industrializing America*. New York: Vintage Books.

Horwitt, S. 1989. *Let them call me rebel: Saul Alinsky, his life and legacy*. New York: Knopf.

Jacobs, P., and S. Landau. 1966. *The new radicals: A report with documents*. New York: Vintage Books.

Jennings, J. 1990. The politics of black empowerment in urban America: Reflections on race, class, and community. In *Mobilizing the community: Local politics in a global era*, ed. R. Fisher and J. Kling.

Kahn, S. 1970. *How people get power: Organizing oppressed communities for action.* New York: McGraw-Hill.

Kaufmann, L. A. 1990. Democracy in a postmodern world. In *Social Policy* (Fall): 6–11.

Kjellberg, F. 1979. A comparative view of municipal decentralization: Neighborhood democracy in Oslo and Bologna. In *Decentralist trends in western democracies,* ed. L. J. Sharpe. London: Sage.

Lowe, S. 1986. *Urban social movements: The city after Castells.* London: Macmillan.

Merkl, P. 1985. *New local centers in centralized states.* Berkeley, Calif.: University Press of America.

Melucci, A. 1989. *Nomads of the present: Social movements and individual needs in contemporary society.* Philadelphia: Temple University Press.

Midgley, J. 1986. *Community participation, social development, and the state.* London: Methuen.

Morris, A. 1984. The *origins of the civil rights movement: Black communities organizing for change.* New York: Free press.

Offe, C. 1987. Challenging the boundaries of institutional politics: Social movements since the 1960s. In *Changing boundaries of the political: Essays on the evolving balance between the state and society, public and private in Europe,* ed. C. Maier. Cambridge: Cambridge University Press.

Paget, K. 1990. Citizen organizing: Many movements, no majority. *American Prospect* (Summer).

Piven, F., and R. Cloward. 1982. *The new class war: Reagan's attack on the welfare state and its consequences.* New York: Pantheon Books.

Pitkin, H., and S. Shumer. 1982. On participation. *Democracy* 2 (Fall): 43–54.

Reagon, B. 1979. The borning struggle: The civil rights movement. In *They should have served that cup of coffee,* ed. D. Cutler. Boston: South End Press.

Rogers, M. B. 1990. *Cold anger: A story of faith and power politics.* Denton: University of North Texas Press.

Roth, R. 1991. Local green politics in West German cities. *International Journal of Urban and Regional Research* 15. 75–89.

Rothman, J. 1968. Three models of community organization practice. In *National conference on social welfare, social work practice 1968.* New York: Columbia University Press.

Rothman, J., with J. Tropman. 1987. Models of community organization and macro practice perspectives: Their mixing and phasing. In *Strategies of community organization,* ed. F. Cox et al. 4th ed. Itasca, Ill.: Peacock.

Slater, D., ed. 1985. *Social movements and the state in Latin America.* Holland: Foris Publications.

Spretnak, C., and F. Capra. 1985. *Green politics.* London: Grafton.

Swanstrom, T. 1985. *The crisis of growth politics: Cleveland, Kucinich, and the challenge of urban populism.* Philadelphia: Temple University Press.

Teodori, M. 1969. *The new left: A documentary hsitory.* New York: Bobbs-Merrill.

Touraine, A. 1985. An introduction to the study of social movements. *Social Research* 52 (Winter): 749–787.

Walton, J. 1979. Urban political movements and revolutionary change in the third world. *Urban Affairs Quarterly* 15 (September): 3–22.

Chapter 5

Community Building Practice

CHERYL L. WALTER

A Conceptual Framework

Cᴏᴍᴍᴜɴɪᴛʏ ʙᴜɪʟᴅɪɴɢ is a term that is often used but rarely defined. This may have to do with the fact that community building involves practice elements and dimensions that we are not used to talking about; we lack the vocabulary and conceptual framework within which to articulate our experience. Yet if we are to effectively engage in, teach, and learn community building practice, we must begin the process of describing what it is. Toward creating a conceptual framework for community building practice, I (1) critically examine the conceptualization of "the community" that underlies community organization strategies; (2) suggest a shift in perspective that expands our conception of what "community" is to include practitioners, broader partnerships, and the extent to which those involved actually experience being in community; and then (3) develop a model for community building practice rooted in this new conceptualization of community. In this model, I identify the elements of community, the dimensions of community building practice, and the kind of skills that are drawn upon and developed in building community.

The Essence of Community Building Practice

How we conceptualize community powerfully influences what we see and what we do in community practice. We draw upon theories of community, and models of community practice rooted in those theories, to orient ourselves, to assess what is going on, and to help us make decisions concerning what to do, why, and how. Operating from the base of this body of knowledge is one of the key factors that distinguishes us as professionals.

As suggested in chapter 3, community practice has been defined and categorized primarily according to various strategies and methods of practice, such as Jack Rothman's (1995) "three strategies of community organization"—locality development, social planning and social action (Taylor and Roberts 1985). Community organization strategies operate from the assumption that problems in society can be addressed by the community becoming better or differently "organized," with each strategy perceiving the problems and how or whom to organize in order to address them somewhat differently. The concept of community as a social unit with which we as outsiders interact underlies this way of framing community practice.

In contrast, the essence of a community building orientation to practice lies in conceptualizing and relating to community as an inclusive, complex, and dynamic system, *of which we are a part*. Such an orientation envisions community as a system that is multidimensional, involving people and organizations at many levels engaged in relationships with one another that are manifested in both actions and consciousness. Community building practice seeks to engage with these multiple dimensions of community, recognizing the range of perspectives and relationships that exist and integrating diverse strategies and methods of practice. The goal is to build the capacity of the entire system, and all of its participants, to operate as community. Such an orientation has special relevance for the increasing numbers of us who, by virtue of our race, gender, or sexual orientation, consciously identify as part of the community in which we are working. But even those not so identified can benefit from this broader reconceptualization of community because it enlarges what we take into account when orienting ourselves in practice and thereby reveals additional avenues for practice activity.

The Community

In practice, we are generally taught to conceive of the community as being a neighborhood of people with whom we work, the people within a city or county dealing with a particular issue or problem to which our organization provides services, or people with a shared racial, ethnic, gender, or sexual orientation identity. The community, in this sense, is a fairly boundaried social or demographic unit involving a neighborhood or people who share a common issue or interest with which practitioners interact to bring about change (Warren 1963).

But this conceptualization of the community does not provide as complete a picture as could be useful to us in our thinking and acting in practice, and thus it may at times limit the usefulness of our existing models for guiding community practice. Within this limited frame of reference of the community, we may neglect to adequately take into account, for example, the influence of our role as community practitioners, the organization we work with and its agenda, or the objectives of the sources that fund our work. Similarly, we may overlook how the consciousness in the broader culture around a particular issue influences the experiences and priorities of those involved with that issue at the community level. By not explicitly acknowledging the multiple constituencies and interests that are engaged with, and exist within the community, as an integral part of the community, we run the risk of oversimplifying issues, of seeing and attempting to address problems only at the community level, and of being self- and society- serving, as opposed to community serving, with our interventions (Rivera and Erlich 1992; McKnight 1987). Although the imperative "Start where the people are" is familiar to most health educators and other social change practitioners, more often than not we start where we are funded to start, which has powerful ramifications for how we interact with the community, the strategies we employ, and what priorities or needs of the community will be elicited, supported, and sustained (see chapter 8).

Community as a Multidimensional System

The new way of conceptualizing community that I am proposing involves making a shift in perspective regarding what community is, a shift that expands the frame of what is included in community and reexamines how what is included is related. This shift in perspective changes our focus from the community as a social/demographic entity or unit with which we interact, to community as a multidimensional/dynamic whole or system of which we are a part.

I refer to community as multidimensional to describe the way in which the various dimensions that characterize community—such as people and organizations, consciousness, actions, and context—are integrally related with one another, forming the whole that is community. To develop an understanding of community, then, we need to articulate, visualize, and examine the unique qualities exhibited by each of these dimensions and how these dimensions come together to make up the complex and dynamic "system" of community.

Roland Warren (1963, ix) identifies two dimensions of community involving the interrelations of units (whether individuals, groups, or organizations). The horizontal dimension involves "the relation of local units to one another"; this is what we think of as the community. The vertical dimension involves "the relation of local units to extracommunity systems" in the larger society and culture. This dimension might include, for example, the relationship between a national organization and its local chapters. Clearly, Warren does not perceive relationships with more remote organizations to involve community, calling them "extra-community systems."

In contrast, I am suggesting that by virtue of involvement in relationships with one another, every organization and every person at every level within both the horizontal and vertical dimensions is potentially a part of community. The people and organizations included in this new conceptualization of community represent multiple stakeholders with diverse interests, those referred to as the community in all their diversity, as well as those formerly considered to be outside the community that have been missing from the perceptual mix. As indicated earlier, the latter include the organizations for which we work, the funders of our work and of services for the community, and us as practitioners. Those residing in the neighborhood or those closest to the issue in terms of experience may be seen as being local or intimately involved. Those farther removed who influence the issue or locality because they control resources could be said to be more remote. But all are integral to community.

For community to exist, there must be relationships between the people and organizations in these horizontal and vertical dimensions. These relationships involve actions and consciousness, which can be conceived of as dimensions of community as well. Warren (1963) has an interesting theory on community action. He hypothesizes that there is no preexisting community that takes action; rather, for each episode of action an ad hoc body emerges or is formed. Looked at in this way, community can be described as dynamic and emergent in that it is continually being created and re-created, its parameters and relationships taking shape and changing shape, through the actions and interactions of people and organizations.

That those of us engaged in community occupy a variety of positions in relation to the issue or locality around which community is defined suggests that we will often have different interests, experiences, levels of power, and perspectives. These differences are reflected in our consciousness, which is manifested in the identities and values we hold, the language we use to name and label, and the themes of the "stories" we tell regarding ourselves and our role, each other, and how we are related. Here and now, we decide what voices will be heard, what truths will be legitimated, and thus what story of community will be told. Interestingly, with the notable exception of Paulo Freire's (1973) work, this dimension of community is generally not addressed in theories of community practice. This is particularly ironic in a society such as the United States in which we are bombarded each day with thousands of images, stories, and slogans designed to influence our thoughts and actions.

The inclusion of consciousness in our conceptualization of community is fundamental to this shift from the community to community and therefore deserves further elaboration. In the view of the community as a functional unit, consciousness has no central role, which may lead us in practice to overlook the impact of the consciousness around the issue in the broader culture and in the community effort at every level. For example, beliefs around whether people who are poor "deserve" assistance have a direct impact on what kind of social and health policies and services are implemented, on what barriers to access to these services are erected, and on how people feel who are recipients of those services. Because organizations and institutions are not machines but are made up of people, they "are conscious entities, possessing many of the properties of living systems" (Wheatley 1994, 13). If we view community as a multidimensional system, consciousness becomes one of the important dimensions to consider in community practice. Consciousness is the mesh that joins us in community, the full spectrum of perceptions, cultural constructs, and frameworks through which interaction with one another and our environment is filtered and shared. In our actions, this consciousness and these relationships are played out and emerge as the substance of what community is.

Finally, all of this takes place in the context of the larger society and cultures, our place in history's unfolding, and the physical environment of geographic regions and the planet. This dimension is the atmosphere in which community lives and breathes; it is one of the principle resources and shapers of community.

Conceptualizing community in this way enables us to see ourselves and each other as part of a dynamic system that is continually being created and re-created and that affects and is affected by our consciousness and actions. Everything within the dimensions is related, influenced by and influencing all of the dimensions, and coming together to make a complex and inextricable whole. This is one of the qualities that makes community a system.

Another quality of community as a multidimensional system is the permeability of its boundaries. Taken together, what is within the dimensions at any given moment could be said to constitute the "field" of community. Yet what the community is, or who and what are perceived to be inside or outside the community, involves an ongoing process of negotiation. And different systems display different degrees of openness and closeness (Tappen 1995). Are people of mixed racial heritage considered to be a part of a specific racial community? Are bisexual people included in the gay and lesbian communities? Are practitioners outsiders in the communities in which they work? Does an organization see the people it works with or serves as a part of its community? These are difficult questions and are handled differently in different communities and at different times. How they are answered has profound and far-reaching ramifications for the character of community. How they are answered also has to do with the perspective from which they are answered. What community is can look very different depending on where one is sitting.

Elements within the Dimensions of Community

The preceding description provides a good beginning in reconceptualizing community. Yet as we have all likely experienced, the word *community* is often used even where little true community can be found. An organization, for example, may create token "community involvement" to satisfy a funding mandate and/or may use precious community resources of time and energy without ever intending to actually share power or seriously consider recommendations. Similarly, a few community members seeking power may represent themselves as "community leaders" and for their own political gain wreak havoc with local organizations (see chapter 6). In such instances, the community can be a less than community-like place. It is no wonder that we as community practitioners are often met with suspicion and resistance in our attempts to engage with the oppressed or to encourage our organizations to work in partnership.

Community has to do not just with engagement in relationship but with the quality of the relationship. Calling something community does not necessarily make it so. There can be greater or lesser degrees of "communityness." As Philip Selznick (1992) aptly points out, simply because community is often found in common residence, for example, does not make common residence an essential or defining feature of community. This is increasingly clear in an era when many of us do not even know the names of our closest neighbors (see chapter 7). Selznick further suggests that "a group is a community to the extent that it encompasses a broad range of activities and interests, and to the extent that participation implicates whole persons rather than segmental interests or activities. Thus understood, *community can be treated as a variable aspect of group experience*" (358). Selznick goes on to argue that "a framework of shared beliefs, interests, and commitments unites a set of varied groups and activities. Some are central, others peripheral, but all are connected by bonds that establish a common faith or fate, a personal identity, a sense of belonging, and a supportive structure of activities and relationships. The more pathways are provided for participation in diverse ways and touching multiple interests . . . the richer is the experience of community" (358–359).

Community as variable provides an intriguing alternative conception of community in that it simultaneously acknowledges the dynamic nature of community and community as a quality of experience, of which there can be more or less. Selznick refers to the indicators of communityness as the elements of community. These elements are historicity, identity, mutuality, plurality, autonomy, participation, and integration. The presence of these elements and their mix are what make for community. Although different communities will have different mixes, "a fully realized community will have a rich and *balanced* mixture of all of these seven elements" (364).

Along the same lines, John Gardner (1991) has written about the ingredients of community. These include shared vision, sense of purpose and values, wholeness incorporating diversity, caring, trust, teamwork, respect and recognition, communication, participation, affirmation, links beyond the community, development of new members, conflict resolution, investment in community, and community resources. There is a remarkable similarity in the qualities of community of which Selznick and Gardner write, indicating that as elusive as "community" might seem, perhaps we do know what makes for community.

Community Building Practice

The shift to a new way of conceptualizing community has important implications for community practice. First, *it places community, not the community and not the community organizer, at the center of practice.* Rather than being the social unit with which practitioners interact as various strategies are employed, community becomes the milieu in which we as community practitioners interact with people and organizations and of which we are an integral part. With community at the center, a broad and inclusive continuum of community participants and stakeholders is encompassed in a way that extends to each power and recognition of its contribution to building and shaping community. This means that regardless of the context or level we occupy—whether as a person facing an issue, a resident in a neighborhood, a volunteer, a professional providing services, an administrator, a student, or a high-level official—we can be practicing community.

Second, *thinking of community as multidimensional, involving people and organizations at many levels, consciousness, actions, and context, allows us to model greater complexity.* By perceiving community as a complex whole, we develop our ability to perceive and work with the actual complexity that exists. This enables us to take more information and relationships into account when orienting ourselves in practice; suggests many possible levels and areas with which to engage and in which to work; and by highlighting the interrelatedness of the dimensions, shows us how we might have an impact on multiple dimensions simultaneously with our efforts.

Third, *if we perceive community not as an existing unit that needs to be organized differently but as a dynamic and emergent whole embodying varying degrees of community-ness that is continually being built or created, then the building of community will be one of the central concerns and activities of community practice.* Community is created or built, or not, with each of our actions; with our consciousness concerning ourselves, others, and the issues; and with our relationships, whatever the task. "Process and content are inseparable" (Senge 1995, 52). Congruence between what we do and how we do it, a joining of ends and means, is essential if we aim to foster communication, participation, diversity, identity, a shared vision, and the other elements and ingredients of community. Opportunities for building and practicing community are continually available, whether in communicative/expressive events or functional activities, such as meetings, document writing, telephone calls, theater productions, picnics and parties, marches/rallies, program operations, legislation, policy implementation, or budgeting.

Fourth, *community practice then becomes less an intervention or coming between and more an interchange, where each of us is changed through coming together.* Learning to engage with one another with respect and trust, developing partnerships, and attending to our consciousness and actions call upon us as whole persons, necessitating that we be open to learning and change within ourselves and not just trying to create change outside ourselves in the community or in institutions. This change can involve conflict, emotion, identity crises, and ethical dilemmas; and it may require that we confront racism, classism, sexism, handicappism, "professionalism," and homophobia in ourselves, in others, and in institutions as we struggle for "wholeness incorporating diversity."

The essence of a community building orientation to practice is in how we conceptualize and relate to community. It is not a practice orientation that employs a particular strategy for intervening in the community. Rather, it is a theoretical orientation that begins from a theory of community as a multidimensional, dynamic, and emergent whole of which we are a part. This whole includes people, organizations, consciousness, actions, and context; and it can exhibit greater or lesser degrees of communityness. The theoretical orientation proposed here seeks to build community through fostering the elements and ingredients of community and engaging with the multiple dimensions of community both as an approach to doing things and as a desired outcome.

Community Building: A Case Example

To illustrate how a community building orientation might guide practice, I use the example of an AIDS organization in a midsized county that produced an AIDSWALK. The purpose or need that inspired the idea for the event was to raise funds, but the "success" of the event within a community building orientation was linked to its effectiveness in building community through the blending and balancing of the elements and dimensions of community. Thus, the purposes of the event from a community building perspective were to increase awareness of HIV, have an event in which people could participate, involve business and the media, develop credibility with funding sources and the larger society, increase the number of people actively involved in and having a stake in the issues and the organization, expand the capacity of the organization to be a resource and provide services for people with HIV and their loved ones, express and affirm values, recruit and involve volunteers, tell stories, celebrate working together, and remember.

Holding an awareness of all these facets while planning and developing an event is a skill involved in community building. It is helpful to have words and/or an image that expresses and represents the multifaceted nature of the process and event in order to guide and shape the experience and all those involved as they work together. In this case, Heart and Sole AIDSWALK was used as the theme of the event, which spoke to the activity of walking, articulated values and consciousness, served as a hook for both media and business sponsorship, mentioned AIDS as the issue, and grounded the ceremonial and identity aspects with rich imagery.

In every aspect, the elements of community were attended to and nurtured. *Historicity* was developed by the AIDS organization making the event annual and was honored by the telling of the story of those who had passed and how the people involved and the organization had all changed over the years. *Identity* was fostered by the theme found on T-shirts and buttons, by teams that participated in the walk, and by the involvement of people in activities with meaningful roles. *Mutuality* was expressed through the involvement of volunteers (including people with HIV who would benefit from the money raised) and the opportunities available to learn new skills and to take leadership. *Plurality* was displayed and witnessed through the participation of diverse teams, walkers, speakers, and volunteers and through materials that spoke directly to diverse audiences (including people of color, non-English speakers, women, gays and lesbians, and heterosexuals). *Autonomy* was manifested in the choice of whether and how to participate and in the opportunities available to the task area teams to be creative in how they went about their tasks. *Participation* was open, involved multiple opportunities for participation at varying levels of commitment, and was acknowledged and welcomed. *Integration* was created through the bringing together of the diverse participants, groups, and businesses to do something meaningful that involved everyone actively.

Each of the dimensions was engaged with and drawn from in this community building process as well. *People and organizations* worked together in new ways in planning the event and in developing skills and relationships. A lead team of staff and volunteers was assembled to develop the event in every aspect, including publicity and media, walk logistics, registration, communications, obtaining of sponsors, and coordination of walk day volunteers. And many more volunteers were involved in each of the task area groups. The lead team developed ways of communicating and coordinating its efforts as a group that group members carried with them into the leadership of their task area groups. Finally, intensive volunteer trainings were conducted. Each person involved learned new skills and had a chance to build on existing ones by taking leadership and responsibility in a task area and facilitating the participation of others. Many of the people involved in this project have gone on to leadership roles in event and program planning and implementation in the organization and the larger community, and they are widely recognized as skilled leaders. Thank-you letters were sent to all of the people and organizations that participated, even as walkers and pledgers, to acknowledge the important role that everyone played in making the event successful on so many levels.

Another outgrowth of the event was that individuals, local groups and organizations, businesses, and the media developed a greater awareness of one another, of HIV in their community, and of their interrelatedness. The AIDS organization demonstrated its competence in planning and implementation of a large-scale event. The organization also showed that it had the support and involvement of the community it served, which enhanced its opportunities to be selected for funding, to be trusted to influence policy, and to be respected by others and used as a model for building community.

Action was taken by hundreds of people who volunteered, gathered pledges and walked, and sponsored walkers or the event. By taking action on their values in this way, these people and organizations became more involved and invested in the issue, were more likely to talk with others about their experiences and to educate others about HIV, and discovered that there were others who shared their concerns. Many became ongoing volunteers and supporters of the organization. Not only were funds raised, but also something was accomplished that extended the boundaries of community and was an expression of caring and a celebration of the power of taking action.

In the realm of *consciousness*, awareness around HIV was raised, values were established and reaffirmed, and communication was increased. This event, all of the preparations that went into it, and all of what followed from it influenced how the issues around HIV and AIDS were seen and framed. And the Heart and Sole theme and all that it connoted carried on throughout the year as people referred to the event and wore their T-shirts and buttons, becoming part of the language and imagery of the community. In *the commons*, the HIV community and organization developed a greater presence in the larger community and were able to garner broader participation in the event the following year.

Even though it rained the day of the event, and three other walks were held that same day, people came and walked in the rain, and this walk was the one that received the media coverage. People continually remarked on how good it felt to be a part of the walk and how smoothly everything went. What people talked about was how magical it was. The attention given in every detail to humanness infused the event with an aliveness that was the expression of caring in action, of the power of heart and sole.

This approach and event were successful precisely because all of the elements and dimensions were valued and engaged. The event was also successful in raising money for the services provided by the organization, over $60,000 in the first year, making this one of the largest fund-raising events ever in that city. Each activity and image served multiple purposes and were used to do so consciously. In large part, the point of what was being done, and certainly how it was being done, was the building of community.

Health Educators and Community Building Practice

If a health educator operating from a community building practice orientation participated in a team producing an event such as the AIDSWALK, his or her focus might be on using the opportunity to educate, challenge, and enable everyone involved to be health educators around HIV and AIDS. He or she might provide opportunities for people to commit to the next step, whatever that would be for them, in educating and organizing around the epidemic.

The health educator in this situation would operate from an awareness that all of the people involved—whether as walkers collecting pledges or volunteers placing walk brochures at businesses—would be talking with many people about the walk. As a result, the health educator might explore a number of avenues to engage everyone as educators and organizers around the epidemic. On the individual level, this might include having part of the volunteer trainings address how to talk with people about HIV/AIDS, putting education information and a challenge in the walk brochure, and having an information packet for volunteers to give to businesses that provides information on HIV for employers and employees. On the organizational or institutional level, the AIDSWALK event might be used as a catalyst for engaging businesses and workplaces in a critical rethinking of their policies and practices that directly or indirectly affect employees and their families vis-à-vis HIV/AIDS. Opportunities for workplace-based HIV/AIDS education and outreach programs could be explored. Along with general HIV/AIDS information available at tables at the end-of-walk celebration, there might be sign-ups for groups or trainings for people wanting more information to educate themselves or an opportunity to be trained as HIV educators and organizers. On the broader state and societal levels, opportunities would be made available for engaging interested participants in working against ballot initiatives that discriminate against people with HIV/AIDS or for healthier public policy in regard to AIDS and people with AIDS.

All of these ideas and avenues are about making creative, multiple use of opportunities to engage and involve people in meaningful and useful ways. Health educators involved in community building practice find themselves working in any and all of the dimensions of practice and with people and organizations at many different levels. Whether planning a campaign, event, or program proposal; training peer educators and outreach workers; encouraging the participation of local community members in community advisory boards; conducting community assessments with people with HIV/AIDS; training professionals on how to incorporate health education and community organizing around the epidemic into their practices; using media advocacy to change the ways AIDS and people with AIDS are depicted in the mass media; or hosting celebrations for a job well done, we become community building practitioners through our perspective on community and the skills we employ more than through the role we play.

Dimensions of Community Building Practice

Community building practice encompasses practice within all of the dimensions of community. Whether we are actively engaged with all the dimensions or are simply holding an awareness of certain dimensions in any given moment, we have many avenues open to us as practitioners. And although the unique character of each dimension may invite different practice activities, community building practice suggests the possibility of engaging with and influencing multiple dimensions simultaneously.

To get a sense of what these avenues are, we can derive names and definitions of the dimensions of community building practice from the characteristics of each of the dimensions of community in the conceptualization I have proposed. Thus, community development derives from horizontal relationships; community planning, from vertical relationships; community action, from action; community consciousness, from consciousness; and the commons, from context. Each of these dimensions reflects unique features of the experience and expression of community practice, and they are useful in helping us conceptualize community practice. But within a community building practice orientation, they are each aspects of practice, not separate or exclusive forms of practice.

These seemingly diverse dimensions of practice are bound together by a focus on community building as a *way* of doing things, attending to all of the dimensions to involve everyone, to develop us as people, to build shared visions and goals, and to take action together. This can involve working with the consciousness and actions of people and organizations at many levels, from more remote bureaucratic organizations and the larger culture, to our own and other organizations engaged with the same issues and constituents, to the oppressed within the community, and to our own changing selves and practices. What unites this work is that it is grounded in constructing community through the building of trust, relationships, ways of working together, and understanding.

Community development manifests in the horizontal dimension. It is characterized by relationships involving mutual support, coordinated effort, development of new members, and what Marilyn French (1986) terms *power with*. Community development attends to community networks and the people in community. It is practiced through the eliciting of participation and contribution of unique talents, the building of skills and capacities, and the provision of respect and recognition, thus fostering growth of individuals, in groups, or between groups. Kibbutzes and cooperatives are examples of community development; so are those support groups that are concerned mainly with mutual aid for their members (see chapter 6).

Community planning manifests in the vertical dimension. It is characterized by relationships between people and organizations at different levels and involves command of resources, policy generation and implementation, organization, and "power over." Community planning attends to planning processes, allocation and utilization of resources, and development and implementation of projects and events. There are, of course, "implications of alternative planning structures for decision-making processes and outcomes" (Gilbert 1979, 644). Community planning also involves critical reflection and discussion of the implications for communities of policies, structures, and processes. Furthermore, it fosters the integration of efforts at different levels. Broad and diverse participation in planning from people and organizations at many levels is essential, playing a vital role in developing the participant's capabilities as builders of and resources for community. The HIV prevention planning councils described in chapter 19 are an example of community planning.

Community action manifests in the meeting of people, extending the boundaries of community through action. Community action is characterized by the power to, through activities and events involving people in community. Community action can be relational, constructive, and/or expressive. It may include engagement in a broad range of group activities and events, such as building a well, planting a garden, holding a meeting, marching or demonstrating, having a celebration, or participating in a ritual. The leadership of Dr. Martin Luther King in the civil rights movement embodied this dimension of community action; his strategic use of increasingly militant nonviolent action was a firm path toward mutual liberation from oppression within his vision of a "beloved community" of brothers and sisters (Nussbaum 1984, 155).

Community consciousness manifests in the depth of community. It is characterized by values, visions, communication, awareness, identity, affirmation, and the "power of." Community consciousness attends to the fostering of awareness of how relationships express values and of what values are being expressed. It is concerned with how identity and thus the experience of oneself and community are shaped by the words, images, and stories that predominate in the larger culture, and it addresses how we can influence the shaping of identity and perceptions in ourselves and the larger culture. Through awareness and communication, shared visions can be created that give meaning, purpose, and direction to relationships and actions. Community consciousness is also a crucial defense against the shortsightedness, condemned by Felix Rivera and John Erlich (1992), that derives from a focus on organizing the community, which leaves us susceptible to fixing problems at the community level and thus not acknowledging the influence of social forces in creating problems or encouraging discussion of these factors as a crucial process of developing critical consciousness.

This discussion of the dimensions of community building practice would not be complete without a look at the realm of the larger societal/cultural environment, the political and economic environments, and the physical environment, within which community exists and is formed and from which it draws many of its resources. This realm has been referred to by Roger Lohmann (1992) and Gary Snyder (1990) as "the commons."

The commons is a social institution, a way of perceiving, managing, and organizing the relationship of the community and its environment, and is "a level of organization of human society that includes the nonhuman" (Snyder 1990, 36).

Historically, the commons, which involved the immediate environment surrounding the community, served as a resource and was held in common; the access to and use of the commons were monitored and managed by the community with an eye toward sustainability. In contemporary society, "a commons can be thought of as an economic, political, and social space outside the market, households, and state in which associative communities create and reproduce social worlds" (Lohmann 1992, 59).

The commons as an approach to organizing human society requires a base of trust and partnership. Even though it is unlikely that this will become the predominant approach in the near future, efforts to combine this approach with market and state approaches, as in the case of public/private partnerships accenting true citizen participation, reflect the continued existence of the commons as a viable approach to organizing human society.

The dimensions of community building practice are fundamentally interrelated. Although to serve a particular purpose we might emphasize activity rooted in one of the dimensions, we will also invariably draw upon and influence the other dimensions as well. Those living in kibbutzes and cooperatives also plan, take action, and develop shared visions and values; both members of HIV planning prevention councils and evaluators focus not only on community planning or evaluation but also on developing people, uniting visions and goals, and taking joint action. In each of the dimensions and brief examples, we find people deeply involved with one another, a consciousness about what they are doing, and a willingness to challenge what is and to take action toward creating something new. This process sometimes involves conflict, and it definitely involves complete engagement. A quality that is shared regardless of strategy or method is a focus on fostering the elements of community, on building community.

Community building as an orientation to practice is not new. In fact, I suspect that the capacity to perceive and engage with all the different dimensions and elements of community may have been a major contributing factor in the success of our most esteemed community leaders, practitioners, and organizers throughout time. What is new is the attempt to articulate this framework for orienting ourselves in practice so that we have a tool for perceiving, working with, learning from, and talking with others about the complexity of the situations in which we practice and the vision of what we seek to create.

Skills and Principles for Community Building Practice

Since how we do what we do is essential to the building of community, it is critical that we develop translatable skills and principles for fostering community, participation, and creativity in the planning and conducting of activities and events. These skills and principles for building community must be relevant for use in a broad range of situations, with a broad range of people, and at many levels. They should also lend themselves to being taught to others through modeling and opportunity for practice. A preliminary list of skills for building community includes management of interconnectedness, communication, process awareness, process commentary, creative planning, and personhood.

Management of interconnectedness involves systems thinking, direction, coordination, facilitation, appreciation, and affirmation. *Communication* through the medium of speech, writing, music, art, film, or movement, coupled with the willingness and ability to listen, see, and understand, serves to make human experience accessible and thus human community possible. *Process awareness* involves awareness of the dynamic quality of community and the ability to attend to the here and now on multiple levels and in multiple dimensions simultaneously. *Process commentary* involves the ability to articulate process and to bring the discussion of process into the here and now. *Creative planning* involves the reconciliation and unification of multiple visions, where possible, toward the design of programs and the use of resources. *Personhood* involves clarity, strength, commitment, vision, integrity, flexibility, the willingness to take leadership, trust and respect, responsibility, follow-through, the ability to exchange positive energy, and the willingness to change. These are skills that can be developed and employed by us all in every aspect of community practice, whether as health educators, social workers, volunteers, consumers, or administrators; whether working with peers, clients, constituents, managers, coalitions, state or county workers, legislators, or students.

Along with skills for building community, there are "operating principles for building community" that can be used to guide our practice (Brown, Smith, and Isaacs 1996, 525–529). These principles include the following:

> Focus on real work.
> Keep it simple.
> Act.
> "Build from good, expect better, make great."
> Seek what unifies.
> Do it when people are ready.
> Design spaces where community can happen.
> Find and cultivate informal leaders.
> Learn how to host good gatherings.
> Acknowledge people's contributions.
> Involve the whole person.
> Celebrate.

Practicing these skills and principles is a lifelong process, both professional and personal. Ultimately, it is about the kind of community we want to be a part of. These are things we already do, whether consciously or not, whether well or not. Practicing them consciously while seeking to build community is community building practice.

References

Brown, J., B. Smith, and D. Isaacs. 1996. Operating principles for building community. In *The fifth discipline fieldbook: Strategies and tools for building a learning organization*, ed. P. M. Senge, A. Kleiner, C. Roberts, R. B. Ross, and B. J. Smith. New York: Currency Doubleday.

Freire, P. 1973. *Education for critical consciousness*. New York: Seabury Press.

French, M. 1986. *Beyond power: On women, men, and morals*. London: Abacus.

Gardner, J. W. 1991. *Building community*. Washington, D.C.: Independent Sector Leadership Studies Program.

Gilbert, N. 1979. The design of community planning structures. *Social Service Review* 53 (4):644–654.

Lohmann, R. A. 1992. *The commons: New perspectives on nonprofit organizations and voluntary action*. San Francisco: Jossey-Bass.

McKnight, J. L. 1987. Regenerating community. *Social Policy* (Winter):54–58.

Nussbaum, D. 1984. Social work and education in the beloved community. *Smith College Studies in Social Work* 54 (3):155–165.

Rivera, F. G., and J. L. Erlich. 1992. Introduction: Prospects and challenges. In *Community organizing in a diverse society*, ed. F. G. Rivera and J. L. Erlich. Boston: Allyn and Bacon.

Rothman, J. 1995. Three models of community organization practice, their mixing, and phasing. In *Strategies of community organization*, ed. J. Rothman, J. L. Erlich, and J. E. Tropman. 5th ed. Itasca, Ill.: Peacock.

Selznick, P. 1992. *The moral commonwealth: Social theory and the promise of community*. Berkeley and Los Angeles: University of California Press.

Senge, P. M. 1995. Creating quality communities. In *Community building: Renewing spirit and learning in business*, ed. K. Godzdz. San Francisco: New Leaders Press.

Snyder, G. 1990. *The practice of the wild*. San Francisco: North Point Press.

Tappen, R. N. 1995. *Nursing leadership and management: Concepts and practice*. Philadelphia: Davis.

Taylor, S. H., and R. W. Roberts. 1985. *Theory and practice of community social work*. New York: Columbia University Press.

Warren, R. L. 1963. *The community in America*. Chicago: Rand McNally.

Wheatley, M. H. 1994. *Leadership and the new science*. San Francisco: Berret-Koehler.

The Professional's Role in Organization and Empowerment
Part III for Health
Values, Assumptions, and Ethical Dilemmas

A PROFESSIONAL HAS BEEN DEFINED as "one who knows very, very well very, very little." Although professionals in fields such as community health education, health planning, and social work often pride themselves on being generalists rather than narrow technocrats, the humility implied in that definition is important, particularly in relation to our work with communities. For the more we appreciate the fact that we know "very well, very little" about communities, their needs, and their resources (at least in relation to how much communities tend to know), the more likely we are to engage in practice that is empowering in nature and respectful of the communities with which we are engaged.

In this part, we explore a number of roles and responsibilities of the professional as organizer, as well as some of the value dilemmas and tough ethical questions with which he or she may be confronted. Prior to examining these roles and issues, however, we take a further step back, with Ronald Labonte's careful look in chapter 6 at some of the assumptions underlying our notions of community and our related perceptions of community development work. Drawing on both his extensive work as a health promotion consultant internationally and his recent in-depth study of the Toronto Health Department, Labonte begins by asking professionals to shake loose from their often uncritical and romanticized notions of community. In a similar vein, he reminds us that community involvement and decentralized decisionmaking, although wonderful concepts in theory, may translate into tokenism and the sapping of a community's limited energy in the first instance and inadvertent support for government cutbacks in the second. These concepts, too, deserve our serious and critical reflection.

Labonte then applies this same attitude of critical rethinking to the whole domain of community development (which, he reminds us, has roughly the same meaning in Canada as community organizing does in the United States). Central to this discussion is the distinction Labonte draws between community-based efforts and true community development work. In the former, Labonte suggests, health professionals or their agencies define and "name" the problem, develop strategies for dealing with it, and involve community members to varying degrees in the problem-solving process. In contrast, community development or organizing supports community groups as they identify problems or issues and plan strategies for confronting them. Building on these and related distinctions, Labonte suggests that community development approaches are far more conducive to the building of authentic partnerships. The latter require, among other things, that "all partners have established their own power and legitimacy" and that community workers support community group partners, whether or not the latter "buy into" the concerns and mandates of the professional or his or her agency.

The appropriate roles and functions of professionals as organizers are examined in greater depth in chapter 7. Marc Pilisuk, JoAnn McAllister, and Jack Rothman describe the critical role health educators and other social change professionals can play by simply engaging in active listening and dialogue with community members. By drawing out community concerns and issues, uncovering themes, and, in some instances, determining how (or whether) a health department or outside professional's issue may have salience for the community in question, the organizer can play an important bridging role. This chapter also explores the delicate balancing act professionals as organizers need to play in enhancing community capacity without giving into the temptation to "do too much" merely to get the job done. Identity politics, conflicting agendas, and differing criteria for success in organizing efforts present challenges with which the outside professional as organizer must grapple.

The roles and functions described in this chapter would be difficult enough under the best of circumstances. But as Pilisuk and his colleagues suggest, they are made all the more difficult by the contemporary context in which grassroots organizing takes place. The chapter therefore begins and ends with a consideration of such contextual issues as the growing concentration of power in transnational corporations and other global entities, the consequent remoteness of information about power, and the disempowering effects of the mass media. Without minimizing the magnitude of these impediments to effective grassroots organizing, the authors point to strategies and approaches that are proving useful in confronting them. The growing use of media advocacy by community groups (see chapter 21), the effective linking of such groups with large public interest organizations, and the coming together of autonomous smaller community organizing efforts to form social movements are potent avenues for change.

In chapter 8, Meredith Minkler and Cheri Pies revisit many of the issues and challenges raised in chapters 6 and 7, focusing special attention on the ethical dimensions of these issues. Five areas are explored: the problem of conflicting loyalties; the difficulties involved in eliciting genuine, rather than tokenistic, community participation; the dilemmas posed by funding sources; the sometimes problematic, unanticipated consequences of our organizing efforts; and the whole matter of "common good" and whose common good is being addressed by the organizing effort.

Drawing on both the theoretical literature and relevant case studies, the authors highlight the ethical challenges raised in each of these areas and pose hard questions for the professional as organizer regarding his or her assumptions, appropriate roles, and potential courses of action. Although several "tools" are provided, such as the DARE criteria for measuring empowerment and the "publicity test of ethics" for helping communities decide whether to accept money from a controversial source, the purpose of the chapter is to raise questions rather than to answer them. A key message of the chapter—and indeed of this whole section of the book—is that careful questioning of our assumptions and values and careful exploration of the ethical dimensions of our work must be preliminary and ongoing aspects of our professional practice.

Chapter 6

Community, Community Development, and the Forming of Authentic Partnerships

RONALD LABONTE

Some Critical Reflections

It is hard to be critical of community when one spends most of the day working in the stuffy cubicles of a government building or in the isolated cubby-hole offices of universities. Community represents something more positive and affirming than the bureaucratic rigidities or academic competitiveness of one's daily working experience. It is difficult to question community's importance when the only positive comments about frontline workers' efforts come from small groups gathered in church basements or cluttered storefront agency meeting rooms. Yet questioning and critiquing the notion of community are precisely what I propose to do in this chapter. My concern is that an uncritical adoption of community rhetoric can, paradoxically, work against empowerment ideals that lie at the heart of many health practitioners' intent.

Let me clarify the meaning of a few key terms before proceeding. Several concepts bearing a community label are now common in the health sector, notably community organization, community mobilization, and community development. Different people use different terms to mean the same thing. In Canada, for example, community development is often used to describe what in the United States is called community organizing. For purposes of my argument, *community organizing* refers to efforts to create a new group or organization, often with the assistance of an outsider, such as a health promoter (Rothman and Tropman 1987). *Community mobilization* describes attempts to draw together a number of such groups or organizations into concerted actions around a specific

Portions of this chapter are based on "Community Empowerment: The Need for Political Analysis," *Canadian Journal of Public Health* 80 (2) (1989):87–88 and "Community Development and Partnerships," *Canadian Journal of Public Health* 84 (4) (1993):237–240. Adapted and reprinted by permission of the Canadian Public Health Association.

topic, issue, or event (Health and Welfare Canada 1992). *Community development* incorporates both but describes a particular health practice in which both practitioner and agency are committed to broad changes in the structure of power relations in society through the support they give community groups (Labonte 1996).

This chapter examines the continued conceptual confusion that surrounds the term *community* and offers five cautions about its uncritical invocation in health and social practice. Drawing in part on insights gained through my recent study of the Toronto Department of Public Health (Labonte 1996), I argue that, even though the concept of "community development" continues some of this confusion, the practice of community development has considerable potential for fostering self-reliance and the creation of authentic partnerships with communities. The chapter concludes by presenting nine characteristics of authentic partnerships that health educators and other social change professionals are encouraged to strive for in our practice.

The Contested Meaning of Community

Numerous historical developments have contributed to the conceptual prominence of community in health work. Although a detailed discussion is beyond the scope of this chapter, these factors include rising health care costs, the declining effectiveness and efficiency of medical treatment, and a growing appreciation of the role of individual and community factors in disease causation and prevention (Lalonde 1974; Hancock 1986).

As noted in earlier chapters, the centrality of community and the importance of community organizing for health were reflected in such influential documents as the Ottawa Charter for Health Promotion (World Health Organization 1986), which regarded "the empowerment of communities, their ownership and control of their own endeavours and destinies" as the heart of the "new" health promotion. Many commentators view community as the venue for, if not the very definition of, the new health promotion practice (Green and Raeburn 1988), a view commonly expressed by practitioners themselves (Feather and Labonte 1995). But there is little agreement on what community means. As Cheryl Walter suggests in chapter 5, a general weakness of professional/institutional discourses on community has been the largely atheoretical and uncritical way in which the term has entered common usage.

Initially in the health field, community was simply a reflexive adjective. In Canada, for example, hospitals became community health centers, nurses became community health workers, state health departments became community health departments, and health promotion and health education programs became community-based efforts. In the syntax of everyday language, community ceased being a subject, a group of people acting with their own intent, and became an object (community as a "target" for health programs) or an adjective to the real subjects, which remained health institutions, which had become, by linguistic sleight of hand, community modified. The problem was not that community-enamored practitioners and their agencies did not know their grammar well. The problem was the way in which community became objectified as fact and posited as a solution to all health problems rather than treated as a definitional conundrum whose development is inherently problematic.

When community is defined at all, it is usually in the static vocabulary of data, creating categories based on identity (the poor community, the women's community, a particular ethnocultural community), geography (the neighborhood, the small town, a particular housing project), or issue (the environmental community, the heart health community, the social justice community). Often, community is simply assumed to be those persons using the services of an institution and living within administratively drawn catchment boundaries (the hospital community, the school community, the university community).

Community has all of these elements—identity, geography, issue, even institutional relations—but it is also more. Community derives from the Latin *communitas*, meaning "common or shared," and the *ty* suffix, meaning "to have the quality of." Sharing is not some demographic datum; it is the dynamic act of people being together. Community is, in effect, organization. There is no "poor community" outside of poor persons coming together to share their experience and act upon transforming it. There is no "women's community" outside of two or more women sharing their reality, empowering themselves to act more effectively upon it. As the Toronto Department of Public Health (1994b) came to define community, it "is a group of individuals with a common interest, and an identity of themselves as a group. We all belong to multiple communities at any given time. The essence of being a community is that there is something that is 'shared.' We cannot really say that a community exists until a group with a shared identity exists."

Even recognition of the active, organizational nature of community, however, does not fully clarify the term. Community may be one of those "essentially contested concepts," so vast in territory (it routinely is used to describe any and every human group that falls between the individual and society) and so rich in evocation that it defies any rigid defining (Lyon 1989). But practitioners certainly need to be more critical in their use of the concept, and there are five considerations about its invocation that are helpful to ponder.

ROMANTICIZATION

Community, as implied in a WHO discussion paper (1984) and the Ottawa Charter (Epp 1986), can do no wrong. The building of stronger communities, for example, is often regarded as an elemental strategy for strengthening community health. Though it is important to accept community self-determination in principle, it is also vital to recognize that what communities do for their own health may be inimical to a broader public health. Nazi Germany was a classic example of a strong community. So, too, are many right-wing fringe groups, such as the Ku Klux Klan or other white supremacist militia organizations. One could even argue that lobbyists against stricter pollution controls are a community, as are people who work together to block supportive housing for persons with mental disabilities or disabled elders. Neighborhoods, towns, cities, and states are filled with myriad communities, as often in conflict with one another as seeking consensus and understanding. Under conditions of conflict, which community should be supported, and why? Without the question being linked to a political theory of social organization and change and an analysis of social power relations, it cannot be answered, and the notion of community becomes somewhat fatuous. Worse, it becomes romanticized in a way that can obscure very real and important power inequities between different communities that may subtly imperil the health and well-being of less powerful groups, for example, the community of urban land developers versus the community of the homeless.

BUREAUCRATIZATION

Whose interests are most served by increasing community involvement in health? What is it exactly that health workers are asking communities to become involved in? Apart from concerns over tokenism (participation without authority), community involvement in health programs may not always "strengthen" the community. Health professionals may bureaucratize thriving community initiatives if they are insensitive to the fact that a community organizing or community development approach to issues is intrinsically unmanageable by conventional planning standards, which rigidly specify goals, objectives, and outcomes before action can begin (Labonte 1993). Even when health agencies engender new initiatives, they may unintentionally sap the political vitality of community group leaders. One health educator was able to extract "permission" from her senior managers to involve local activists on a housing and health committee, but after a year little progress had been made (Labonte 1993). She had been involving community activists in her bureaucratic process of committee meetings, reports, and senior management approvals rather than assisting the activists in directly lobbying decisionmakers and collaborating with them in a partnership for social change. This effectively, if unintentionally, silenced the political voice of some of the strongest community leaders.

ANTIPROFESSIONALISM

Just as health authorities can risk elitism in their desire to demonstrate health promotion "leadership," community groups and some of their health worker supporters can undermine effective collaborations through a festering anti-professionalism. Professional is not the antithesis of community. Indeed, the Latin root of the word *professional* means to "profess" or "vow," a reference to the medieval practice of surrendering personal gain to the larger community of a religious order or workers' guild. It is true that health professionals, like others in the "poverty industry," can increase the victimization of people living in socially disadvantaged conditions through their attitudes and exercise of power over their "clients." But to imply, as some have, that most past public health practice has been wrong or that, as John McKnight (1987) has argued, "resources empower; services do not" denigrates the community of health workers. It reinforces a we/they polarity and ignores the formative role that respectfully delivered, useful, and usable services have often played in developing new community organizations and overcoming the isolation of society's most marginalized or oppressed (Hoffman 1989; Labonte 1993).

Many health professionals are also community activists, and all persons, employed or otherwise, are members of many different communities. If professionals respect the leadership prerogative of community groups, or if, as Walter suggests in chapter 5, they see themselves as part of the community, there is no reason for them to be self-deprecatory or to disparage the value of their own "professional" efforts. Indeed, community groups supported by health workers in Toronto specifically cite the professional status, legitimacy, and influence such workers bring to the relationship, which community groups use to enhance their own social change efforts (Labonte 1996). The process of policy change, for example, can be likened to a nutcracker (Labonte 1993). One arm is the data-rich reports, policy documents, charters, and frameworks produced by health professionals primarily for internal consumption and bureaucratic legitimacy. The other arm, exerting the greatest force, is community group pressure on politicians, "cracking" the issue against the more conservative arm of professional validation. Both arms are necessary, if different in their strategic placement and use in creating healthy social change.

DECENTRALIZATION

The decentralization of decisionmaking over public programs, another oft-cited tenet of community organization or community development, allows for programs unique to community groups and their perceived needs. But the concept must be tempered with the recognition that most economic and social policy is national and transnational in nature. Local decisionmaking can only be within narrow parameters at best and is unlikely to include substantial control over economic resources (see chapter 7). As a policy analyst with the Worldwatch Institute notes, small may be beautiful, but it may also be insignificant (Durning 1989). This is not to argue the intractable nature of the health-damaging aspects of our present social structure. Just as apathy can become a barrier to the organizing efforts of less powerful groups, cynicism (an apathy of the better-off with bigger vocabularies) can undermine the efforts of health workers to support such organizing efforts. Nonetheless, practitioners must append a strong advocacy component for macrolevel policy changes at senior government levels to their drive for decentralized decisionmaking. Otherwise, they may subtly "privatize" by rendering strictly local the choices available to people and mystifying the actual exercise of political power by national and transnational economic elites.

The rhetoric of decentralized local control may also inadvertently support growing social inequities by failing to defend social programs against fiscal restraint or regressive tax reform by more senior government levels (Labonte 1995). Indeed, part of the appeal of community, especially to neoliberals and neoconservatives, is that it can readily justify dramatic social service cutbacks in the name of increasing community control. It is instructive that, in Canada at least, decentralized community decisionmaking in health care is becoming a fact only as public funding for health care is shrinking, hospitals are closing, and thousands of health care workers are losing their jobs.

SELF-HELP

The promotion of self-help and mutual aid groups parallels the call for decentralized decisionmaking. Professional coordination of self-help networks is sometimes advanced as a means of "humanizing" the welfare system and of coping with program cutbacks driven by neoliberal economic policies. The first rationale is sound; the second accepts the reprivatization of social policy, better known as charity. That self-help groups can be empowering and health enhancing is undeniable. But there is typically no recognition in government policies on health promotion and community development that self-help primarily taps the volunteer energies of women, society's "traditional" care providers. Will government support and professional coordination of self-help simply increase voluntarism at the economic expense of women? Moreover, the type of self-help usually being promoted is what is sometimes called "defensive"—groups of people with a common problem or disease providing peer support.

There is also a history of "offensive" self-help, those groups concerned with meso- and macrolevel social change strategies. These groups are less likely to receive government or other outside support because they are regarded as being too political, self-interested, or advocacy oriented. Yet unless the right of groups to lobby for changes in government policy is recognized and supported in health promotion funding policy (though this again raises the dilemma of which groups advocating for which issues), the self-help ethos restricts to a personal level problems that have both personal and political dimensions.

Community Development: Assumptions, Cautions, and Potential

Many of the cautions just raised cut to the quick of community development as a specific health practice. (I remind American readers again that my use of this term includes much of what they may associate with community organization.) There is no theory of community development, anymore than there is a singular theory of or approach to health promotion. Rather, the term describes a range of practices within the many other sectors in which it has existed historically, such as international development, literacy, economic development, housing, and social work/social services.

Community development involves assumptions about the nature of society, social change, and the relationship among community developers, state agencies, and community groups. These assumptions are sometimes made explicit in community development and community organization literature and models (e.g., Rothman and Tropman 1987; Dixon and Sindall 1994). But they are rarely explicitly present in government or other health agency policy statements on community development and often remain unexplored among practitioners themselves (Labonte 1996). One succinct and representative statement of these assumptions is that of the Toronto Department of Public Health (1994b), which defines community development as "the process of supporting community groups in identifying their health issues, planning and acting upon their strategies for social action/social change, and gaining increased self-reliance and decision-making power as a result of their activities." There are five important components to this definition.

COMMUNITY DEVELOPMENT DESCRIBES A RELATIONSHIP BETWEEN OUTSIDE INSTITUTIONS AND COMMUNITY GROUPS

First, the "doer" of community development in the health field typically is a health department or nonprofit health agency or organization. This may strike some readers as patronizing. Do not communities develop themselves? Yes, but when they do, they engage in what Walter (chapter 5) terms *community building*; rarely (if ever) do they describe it as community development. The latter term historically refers to the actions of institutions in relation to citizens, whether conceived as interest groups or as persons living within some geographic space. When practitioners recognize themselves as the subjects of community development, they are forced to ask, "What do we intend by these relations?" Ideally, the answer should be to nurture relations with and among institutions and community groups that are more equitable in their power-sharing. As health workers with the Toronto Department of Public Health (1994a) note, "The goal of community development . . . is really trying to establish a more equitable power relationship between institutions and community groups." This requires that practitioners acknowledge the starting differences in power (status, authority, resources, legitimacy) that exist among themselves, their agency, and community groups. If practitioners presume without questioning that they are "equals" with community groups, they risk making invisible the types of power that they do hold "over" groups, thereby increasing the risk of abusing that power or of failing to recognize the potential for making it available to groups for their own use (see chapter 8).

COMMUNITY DEVELOPMENT IS ALWAYS A MATTER OF CHOOSING SOME GROUPS OVER OTHERS

Second, accepting a professional interest in community development compels practitioners to ask, "Which groups are we interested in, and why?" Allison Watt and Sue Rodmell (1988) argue that health promotion implies an "advocacy framework" that supports those whose living conditions provide them with less material forms of power, such as income, authority over resources, or political legitimacy. One of the difficulties encountered in practice is that the choices made by health workers and their agencies are rarely made explicit or include only those groups that might agree to mobilize around particular health issues, such as heart health or antitobacco advocacy. This renders choice a matter of personal preference or institutional convenience.

There is an ethical concern in the first instance: public agencies should be publicly accountable. Favoritism in choice should be informed by an explicit analysis of the social determinants of health and theories of social change and power relations, not simply by ideologies kept from organizational or public view and debate. There are both an ethical and a political concern in the second instance. One study of a Canadian health department found that social assistance recipients with the greatest health, organizational, and empowerment needs represented only 17 percent of practitioners' caseloads (Browne et al. 1995). Most health workers' time was spent with reasonably well-functioning and well-resourced middle-class individuals and groups, a finding common to many other local health departments (Labonte 1996). To the extent that community development is a public resource that can help to effect a redistribution in material resources, a high ratio of middle-class clients or groups represents an upward redistribution of resources that contradicts the social justice rhetoric of documents such as the Ottawa Charter.

COMMUNITY DEVELOPMENT INVOLVES "MAKING PRIVATE TROUBLES PUBLIC ISSUES"

Third, community development work is not support group work. We can distinguish a "support group" from a "community group" on the basis of whether its members primarily look inward to their immediate psychosocial needs or primarily look outward to the socioenvironmental context that creates those needs in the first place. To paraphrase C. Wright Mills (1956), community groups transform the private troubles of support groups into public issues for policy remediation. Support group work, or defensive self-help, is central to what many public health nurses, educators, social workers, and some community organizers do. It is fundamentally important work and necessary to community development, for without the support of a group, many historically marginalized people will lack the confidence to look outward to the harder-to-change sociopolitical conditions that created their marginality in the first place.

But whereas support group work concerns the creation of healthy (equitable) power relations within groups, community development concerns the creation of healthy (equitable) power relations among community groups and institutions, or offensive self-help. The reason for making this distinction is twofold. It prevents community development from becoming a term so large in practice that it no longer serves any useful conceptual purpose, a critique often, and aptly, made of health promotion. It also requires that health professionals and their agencies grapple with power relations at a higher level of social organization, and not restrict themselves to the necessary but insufficient work of support group development.

COMMUNITY DEVELOPMENT IS NOT SIMPLY BRINGING INSTITUTIONAL PROGRAMS INTO "COMMUNITY" SETTINGS

Fourth, we can distinguish between community-based and community development approaches to our work. The distinction lies in who sets the agenda and who names the issue or problem (see Table 6.1). In the community-based approach, the agency finds existing individuals or groups and links up its programs with them. It is an important approach to public health, but it is not community development, which attempts to support community groups in resolving concerns as group members define them. Of course, as already noted, not all groups or group concerns will or should be supported. Community development requires making choices that, in turn, require explicit analyses of social power relations and agency/staff commitments to shifting these relations toward greater equity. But much community organizing and community mobilizing work in health concerns itself primarily with specific diseases, lifestyle behaviors, and those public policies that influence their risks (Labonte 1993; Labonte and Robertson 1996). These issues may not always be of concern to poorer groups or localities. To the extent that institutional support and financial resources for community work are streamed through these "set agendas," the more political empowerment work of groups or localities can actually be undermined.

Community development, however, can emerge from a community-based program, just as community-based programs sometimes arise in the context of a larger community development effort (Labonte and Robertson 1996; Hoffman and

Table 6.1
Community-based and Community Development Programming

Community-based programming	Community development programming
The process of health professionals and/or health agencies defining the health problem, developing strategies to remedy the problem, involving local community members and groups to assist in solving the problem, working to transfer major responsibility for ongoing program to local community members and groups.	The process of organizing and/or supporting community groups in their identification of important concerns and issues and their ability to plan and implement strategies to mitigate their concerns and resolve their issues.
Example: Nobody's Perfect or Heart Health programs	*Example:* Healthy Communities projects
Characteristics • The problem name is given. • There are defined program time lines. • Changes in specific behaviors or knowledge levels are the desired outcome. • Decisionmaking power rests principally in the institution.	*Characteristics* • The problem name starts with that of the community group, then is negotiated strategically, i.e., to a problem naming that advances the shared interests of the group and the institution • Work is longer term, requiring many hours. • A general increase in the group's capacities is the desired outcome. • Power relations are constantly negotiated.

Dupont 1992). In the first instance, the practice issue becomes one of health workers and their agencies accepting as legitimate and finding ways to support action on more structurally defined health problems (e.g., unemployment, violence, racism) that participants in community-based programs (e.g., heart health) might raise as concerns. In the second instance, the practice issue becomes one of health workers and their agencies negotiating the content and timing of community-based programs with local citizens so that they fit within the context of other political mobilizations within localities.

COMMUNITY DEVELOPMENT PROMOTES SELF-RELIANCE, NOT SELF-SUFFICIENCY

Fifth, in defining community development as a process of creating more equitable relationships among groups and institutions, we can bury the myth of community self-sufficiency. According to that myth, the community group is able to mobilize and/or provide its own resources and the skills to enable it to function autonomously from others. This is often assumed to be the goal of community development or a measure of maximum community participation (Bjaras, Haglund, and Rifkin 1991). However, the health sector's rhetorical acceptance of such terms as *partnerships* and *intersectoralism* should lead practitioners and their agencies to foster equitable

and effective interdependencies rather than to promote the autonomy of localities. Self-reliance, as a contrasting concept, means that "the community group is
able to negotiate the terms of its interdependence with external professionals, organizations and institutions" (Toronto Department of Public Health 1994b). The
goal of community development is not self-sufficiency; it is the ability of the group
to negotiate its own terms of relationship with those institutions (agencies) that
support it.

Community Development and the Creation
of Effective and Authentic Partnerships

An equitably negotiated arrangement among different groups is often referred
to by the shorthand notion of "partnership." Whether practitioners and their
agencies rally behind the ideas of community organization, community mobilization, or community development, they are essentially entering a partnership
with a variety of different groups or organizations.

EFFECTIVE PARTNERSHIPS AND CONFLICT

Community development may strive for inclusivity in community building, for
agreement among as broad a collection of community groups as possible. The
reality, however, is that powerless groups usually seek to shift skewed social relations by limiting the power that other groups have over them. Powerless individuals
often create their identity as a community group only in opposition to or conflict
with groups that are more powerful than themselves. This dynamic has been at
the base of the confrontational approach to community organizing favored by Saul
Alinsky and his adherents (Alinsky 1971; Kling and Posner 1990) and has been
used successfully to create communities from the seemingly intractable conditions
of isolation and apathy (Ward 1987; Labonte 1993). More generally, research in
social identity theory finds that group identities often require conflictual forms of
"who's in/who's out" boundary setting (Abrams and Hogg 1990), and a large
body of sociological theory argues that intergroup conflict is the norm rather than
the exception and provides the necessary "fuel" for social change.

Even Barbara Gray (1989), whose work on collaboration theory is seminal
to an understanding of partnerships, acknowledges that collaboration usually
requires a period when less powerful groups establish their legitimacy through conflictual relations with more powerful groups. But conflict may also be necessary
during collaboration. One reason that environmental groups now participate in
collaborative policy bodies with industry and government is that they have
demonstrated they are able, through direct conflictual actions, to prevent unilateral
decisions by the other parties. Those environmental groups that participate in collaboration generally no longer engage in direct action. But if all environmental
groups ceased conflict relations with industry or government, what would prevent

a return to unilateral decisionmaking by either of the two more powerful stake-holders?

THE STRIVING FOR COLLABORATION

That intergroup conflict is healthy and perhaps essential to social change should not lead health workers to shun the necessity of uniting diverse, conflicting groups at some higher level of community. Community-as-ideal, the moral reso-nance of the word, is what gives it power and appeal (Lyon 1989), even if this ideal must be approached with an analytical caution about how it can be used for anti-community right-wing political agendas. Nonetheless, as Gardner (1991) remarks, pluralism without commitment to the common good is pluralism gone berserk. Pragmatically, the community born in conflict or struggle rarely survives the even-tual peace "unless those involved create the institutional arrangements and non-crisis bonding experiences that carry them through the year-in-year-out tests of community functioning" (14).

Gray (1989) provides a comprehensive partnership model for promoting those functions, which she describes as "collaboration." Successful intergroup col-laboration, which she defines as "a mutual search for information and solutions," has five features that characterize the process-as-outcome. First, recognition of stake-holder interdependence is enhanced. Second, differences are dealt with con-structively. Third, joint ownership of decisions is developed. Fourth, stakeholders assume collective responsibility for "managing the problem domain" through formal and informal agreements. Fifth, the process is accepted as continually emergent.

There are several steps in effective collaboration, the first and most important being problem setting. This requires a "common definition of the problem," a "com-mitment to collaborate," and "identification of the stakeholders." This stage sub-sumes a prenegotiation stage, the goal of which is to arrive at a common definition of problem and intent broad enough to get stakeholders to the table. This differ-entiates collaboration from the usual form of government or other health agency consultation, in which the issue and desired outcome are already defined.

Effective collaboration requires the efforts of persons Gray labels "midwives," the community developers of organizations-as-communities. These midwives (functionally distant from all of the stakeholders) work with the stakeholders before they come to the table, seeking to find the "superordinate goal" that Muzafir Sherif (1966) years ago argued was the basis for initiating any reduction in intergroup conflict. This goal must be "compelling for the groups involved, but . . . unattainable by [any] one group, singly; hence it is not identical with 'common goal.' . . . [It must also] supersede all other goals each group may have" (88).

Whatever the superordinate goal is that initiates intergroup collaboration and conflict resolution, the conditions for authentic collaboration allow a sharper delineation of the differences among consultation, involvement, and participation (collaboration). Briefly, *consultation* involves the seeking of information from citizens, but with no ongoing dialogue. *Involvement* does involve dialogue, but such dialogue is typically controlled by the government or outside agency. Citizen involvement tends to be advisory only, around a problem or issue that the government or outside agency has predetermined or named. There is no agreement on power-sharing. In contrast, true *participation* involves negotiated relationships with citizens, who are treated as constituencies and take part in "naming the problem" or selecting the issue. All affected groups participate, and resources are made available to enable the full participation of less powerful groups (Arnstein 1969; Doyle and Orr 1990; Labonte 1993).

What makes for the effective and authentic partnerships that community development creates? Building on the forgoing and drawing on Panet-Raymond's (1992) insights gleaned from attempts to forge relations between community health and social service centers and neighborhood volunteer centers in Quebec, we might say that partnerships exist only when

1. All partners have established their own power and legitimacy. This often requires a period of conflict and some enduring strain between powerful and powerless groups. The provision of resources to these groups is one facet of community development work, provided such resources remain in the autonomous control of the groups.
2. All partners have well-defined mission statements. They have a clear sense of their purpose and organizational goals.
3. All partners respect one another's organizational autonomy by finding a visionary goal that is larger than any one of their independent goals. This requires extensive midwifing work to set the shared agenda. The achievement of this shared agenda is another facet of community development work.
4. Community group partners are well rooted in the locality. They have a constituency to which they are accountable.
5. Institutional partners have a commitment to partnership approaches in work with community groups.
6. Clear objectives and expectations of the partners are developed. The partners create a commitment among themselves to jointly "manage the problem domain."
7. Written agreements are made that clarify objectives, responsibilities, means, and norms. Regular evaluation allows adjustments to these agreements.
8. Community workers have clear mandates to support community group partners without attempting to get them to "buy into" the institutional partner's mandate and goal. This distinguishes community development from community-based approaches to work.

9. All partners strive for and nurture the human qualities of open-mindedness, patience, respect, and sensitivity to the experiences of persons in all partnering organizations.

Conclusion

Community is a potent idea, but its reality is the more modest process of people organizing themselves, or being organized, into identity-forging, issue-solving groups. The multiplicity of people's group (community) experiences requires health practitioners and their agencies to specify clearly whom they mean when they invoke the term. Romantic notions of community are more likely to support neoliberal political agendas, the dismantling of social welfare programs, and the upward redistribution of wealth and power than to empower localities in any significant way. As health practitioners attempt to organize people, or support community groups, they must be wary of "colonizing" these groups with institutional, often disease-based ways of defining health issues. Moreover, they must locate their choice of issues and groups to support within some analytical framework of society and social change. This framework needs to take account of the many forms of power that partly constitute the relationship among institutions, health professionals, and community groups, for the essence of community development (community organizing) is the transformation of these power relations such that there is more equity within and between institutions and groups.

At base, community development opposes those inequalities between people that are created by people and their economic and political practices. For as French philosopher Raymond Aron once commented, "When inequalities become too great, the idea of community becomes impossible."

References

Abrams, D., and M. Hogg, eds. 1990. *Social identity theory: Constructive and critical advances*. New York: Springer-Verlag.

Alinsky, S. 1971. *Rules for radicals*. New York: Random House.

Arnstein, S. 1969. A ladder of citizen participation. *American Institute of Planners* 35 (4).

Bjaras, G., B.J.A. Haglund, and S. Rifkin. 1991. A new approach to community participation assessment. *Health Promotion International* 6 (3):199–206.

Browne, G., C. Roberts, J. Byrne, C. Byrne, J. Underwood, E. Jamiesen, M. Schuster, D. Cornish, S. Watt, and A. Gafni. 1995. Public health nursing clientele shared with social assistance: Proportions, characteristics, and policy implications. *Canadian Journal of Public Health* 86 (3):155–161.

Dixon, J., and C. Sindall. 1994. Applying the logics of change to the evaluation of community development in health promotion. *Health Promotion International* 9 (4):297–239.

Doyle, M., and J. Orr. 1990. *Opportunities for community empowerment and community-based planning*. Toronto: Social Planning Council.

Durning, A. 1989. Mobilizing at the grassroots. In *State of the World 1989*, ed. L. Brown et al. New York: Norton.

Epp, J. 1986. *Achieving health for all: A framework for health promotion.* Ottawa: Health and Welfare Canada.

Feather, J., and R. Labonte. 1995. *Sharing knowledge from health promotion practice: Final report.* Saskatoon: University of Saskatchewan, Prairie Region Health Promotion Research Centre.

Gardner, J. 1991. *Building communities.* Washington, D.C.: Independent Sector Leadership Studies Program.

Gray, B. 1989. *Collaborating: Finding common ground for multiparty problems.* San Francisco: Jossey-Bass.

Green, L., and J. Raeburn. 1988. Health promotion: What is it? What will it become? *Health Promotion* 3 (2):151–159.

Hancock, T. 1986. Lalonde and beyond: Looking back at "a new perspective on the health of Canadians." *Health Promotion* 1 (1):93–100.

Health and Welfare Canada. 1992. *Community mobilization.* Ottawa: Health and Welfare Canada.

Hoffman, K., and J.-M. Dupont. 1992. *Community health centres and community development.* Ottawa: Health Services and Promotion Branch.

Hoffman, L. 1989. *The politics of knowledge: Activist movements in medicine and planning.* New York: State University of New York Press.

Kling, J. M., and P. S. Posner. 1990. *Dilemmas of activism: Class, community, and the politics of local mobilization.* Philadelphia: Temple University Press.

Labonte, R. 1993. *Health promotion and empowerment: Practice frameworks.* Toronto: Centre for Health Promotion/Participation.

———. 1995. Population health and health promotion: What do they have to say to each other? *Canadian Journal of Public Health* 86 (3):165–168.

———. 1996. Community development in the public health sector: The possibilities of an empowering relationship between state and civil society. Ph.D. diss., York University.

Labonte, R., and A. Robertson. 1996. Health promotion research and practice: The case for the constructivist paradigm. *Health Education Quarterly* 23 (4):431–447.

Lalonde, M. 1974. *A new perspective on the health of Canadians.* Ottawa: Health and Welfare Canada.

Lyon, L. 1989. *The community in urban society.* Toronto: Lexington Books.

McKnight, J. 1987. Comments at Prevention Congress III, Waterloo, Ontario.

Mills, C. W. 1956. *The power elites.* New York: Oxford University Press.

Panet-Raymond, J. 1992. Partnership: Myth or reality? *Community Development Journal* 27 (2):156–165.

Rothman, J., and J. Tropman. 1987. Models of community organization and macro practice perspectives. In *Strategies of community organization,* ed. F. Cox, J. Erlich, J. Rothman, and J. Tropman. 4th ed. Itasca, Ill.: Peacock.

Sherif, M. 1966. *Group conflict and cooperation.* London: Routledge and Kegan Paul.

Toronto Department of Public Health. 1994a. Making choices. Toronto: Department of Public Health.

———. 1994b. *Making communities.* Toronto: Department of Public Health.

Ward, J. 1987 Community development with marginal people: The role of conflict. *Community Development Journal* 22 (1):18–21.

Watt, A., and S. Rodmell. 1988. Community involvement in health promotion: Progress or panacea? *Health Promotion* 2 (4):359–368.

World Health Organization. 1984. *Health promotion: A discussion document on the concepts and principles.* Copenhagen: WHO Europe.

———. 1986. *Ottawa charter for health promotion.* Copenhagen: WHO Europe.

Chapter 7

Social Change Professionals and Grassroots Organizing

Functions and Dilemmas

MARC PILISUK
JOANN MCALLISTER
JACK ROTHMAN

WHILE THE CONDITIONS of postindustrial society have increased the urgency of the need for grassroots organizing, they have also created new impediments to such activity. The current and increasingly global context in which grassroots organizing takes place raises anew questions about the appropriate role and functions of health edcuators, social workers, and other social change professionals who are involved in these processes at the community level.

This chapter presents a brief review of the conditions of the postindustrial era that have changed the context for grassroots community organizing. The paradoxical growth of such organizing in the face of often formidable obstacles is examined briefly, with most of the chapter then devoted to the functions and dilemmas of professionals engaged with communities in such organizing efforts.

The Contemporary Context for Grassroots Organizing

People excluded from the mainstream of organized power have come together throughout history to assert their needs. Frequently referred to as grassroots organizing, these diverse local efforts make up a special part of the human story, both psychologically and politically. They are essential for the human spirit and for the restoration of faith in democratic government, and they are taking place far more often than is publicized.

Grassroots community organizing is extremely varied. As discussed in chapter 3, *social action* approaches to such organizing are grassroots based, oriented more

Portions of this chapter are adapted from "Coming Together for Action: The Challenge of Contemporary Grassroots Advocacy," *Journal of Social Issues* 52 (1996): 15–37, by permission of the Society for the Psychological Study of Social Issues and the authors.

toward conflict than to consensus, focused upon direct action, and aimed at organizing a disadvantaged or aggrieved people to take action on its own behalf (Fisher and Kling 1991). Expected outcomes include changing the policies and programs of organizations and governments, achieving a role in community decisionmaking, and shifting power, status, or resources of individuals or communities. In contrast to social action, the emphasis in both *locality development* and the newer notion of *community building* is upon the slower process of creating a web of continuing relationships so that people may indeed come together, share their supportive attentions and resources, and experience a sense of belonging to their community. The building of a sense of belonging to a caring community, whether organized around a cooperative housing unit or a shared experience as survivors of breast cancer, requires skills and resources.

In each of these forms of community practice, there are roles for health educators, social workers, and other professionals in facilitating the development of local leadership, helping in the creation of an organizational framework for decisionmaking, and in other ways contributing to community building and empowerment. Certain conditions of the postindustrial era, however, have dramatically changed the setting for grassroots community organizing and present new challenges to professionals who are engaged with communities in these processes. Six of these changed conditions merit our attention here.

THE THREADBARE SOCIAL FABRIC

The fragmentation and decline in the supportive capabilities of communities represent a first major major contextual condition for contemporary grassroots organizing. Rapid change in industrial society has left the individual less securely embedded in a family, a workplace, a neighborhood, or a village (Putnam 1996). This condition both reflects and reinforces a disruption and decrease in the supportive capacity of communities. Nuclear families are smaller, less permanent, and more separated from extended kinship networks. Locally owned shops have been replaced by franchises of national or international chains, and the local doctor or lawyer has been replaced by corporate centers. People in need are more isolated from each other and further separated from the resources they require than ever before (Bellah et al. 1985; Pilisuk and Parks 1986). The community, once considered a secure place, all too often has become a source of fear (Pilisuk 1988).

Seventeen percent of Americans change residences each year (Putnam 1996), contributing to a decreased psychological sense of community (Lyon 1987). Associations among people have increasingly become consequences of opportunities pursued by choice and dependent upon transportation and communication resources, as well as a sense of efficacy. As the supportive web of indigenous ties has worn thin, the identity of individuals has been increasingly determined by their marketability within a global economy. People with little market value—children, frail elders, the poorly educated, the chronically ill, and the mentally disabled—have suffered the consequences, often falling between the cracks and/or being recategorized in the public dialogue as nonpersons. They may be sheltered or fed, imprisoned or deported, or herded out of public view. Such conditions make it difficult for people to get together, talk over their problems, and organize for action. Grassroots efforts to achieve specific ends will have to take into account the weakened fabric of social life.

LOCAL PROBLEMS, GLOBAL CAUSES

Although unmet needs are experienced at the most local and personal levels, the resources needed to address them are increasingly far removed (Pilisuk 1986–1987; Thurow 1996). Modern technology brings with it an intrusion of global forces upon domestic settings. As products of technology have dominated the ecology of each community, new needs have been created.

The global economy and modern technology have left a growing percentage of the world's population either unemployed or employed in alienating and underpaid forms of work. Resources that once sustained indigenous communities, such as forests and agricultural labor, are increasingly usurped for the production of commodities for export. Wars are fought in the Third World to determine whose interests are to be served by local resources. Likewise, in the United States and some other postindustrial societies, corporate pressures to relax occupational and environmental standards are working to ensure ever-greater profits at the expense of workers, their families and communities, and the ecosystem (Ross et al. 1984; Fischer 1993). These trends, too, form a critical part of the context of contemporary grassroots organizing.

THE CONCENTRATION OF UNACCOUNTABLE
TRANSNATIONAL POWER

Because grassroots organizing is about obtaining a share of resources, it is imperative to examine how wealth is now distributed. In the United States, 1 percent of the population owns 37 percent of the wealth. Ten percent own 86 percent of the wealth (Barlett and Steele 1992), leaving 90 percent of the population to compete for the less than 15 percent remaining. Once considered the pathway to increasing the pie, economic development has been transformed by the global economy into a means for increasing central control over local resources.

Governing bodies at all levels are indebted to those who supply the capital by which they can gain and hold office and with which they can provide services. Corporate managers of capital are closely tied, through interlocking personal and financial arrangements, to the major private financial institutions and to governments (Dooley 1969; Thurow 1996). Huge transnational corporations can seek tax favors, infrastructure promises, zoning concessions, and subsidy through government contracts and bond sales from the municipalities that pursue these corporations. Free to move their operations to a region with cheaper labor, fewer environmental restrictions, lower taxes, and a more favorable business climate, transnational corporations pose a formidable problem for any local community group that might challenge their decisions (Pilisuk, McAllister, and Rothman 1996; Ross et al. 1984).

THE REMOTENESS OF INFORMATION
ABOUT POWER AND CONTROL

The increasing distance between a community and the ownership of that community's resources, coupled with the increasing complexity of data, means that information on the causes of a local problem may be less and less available to local residents. Without such information, people easily blame scapegoats suggested to them by powerful interests in government, corporations, and the media.

The power of large corporations is protected by their ability to collect information and bring it to bear upon issues of concern. Such information is routinely applied to decisions of what resources to buy or sell; what people to employ, lay off, or buy out; where and when to relocate a branch; what legislation or candidates to support; and what information to release to the public. When a community hospital closes, or a toxic waste facility is approved, most people who would be seriously affected know little about how to identify the responsible parties. Unlike large corporate entities, community residents, particularly if they are in low-income areas, lack the research facilities that are needed to gather information that may be essential for their ability to take informed action (Villarejo 1980).

THE CENTRALIZED DOMINATION
OF SYMBOLS OF LEGITIMACY

The legitimacy of governmental authority justifies policies that assist the global corporate economy at the expense of local communities. The globalization of capital has reduced the power of government while forging an intimate interdependence between governmental powers and conglomerate interests (Thurow 1996). The power of nongovernmental bodies such as the Trilateral Commission— a group of prominent members of corporations, think tanks, and government— represents a recognition by the corporate and financial worlds that the national policies of developed countries are crucial to the orderly transformation to a global market economy.

Governments help to validate the belief that freedom for the individual and freedom for the corporation are identical and that "what's good for General Motors" is indeed "good for America." However, access to government and the media is severely limited for those without wealth (Bagdikian 1992). With the help of grassroots organizing, a group of Vietnam veterans may fast at the White House steps, or a busload of disabled elders may descend on a state legislator. But larger financial interests employ permanent lobbyists and, more important, have helped to select the residents of these capitals. Nevertheless, the state must legitimate itself as something more than an expression of capital interests (O'Connor 1976). In the United States, unemployment insurance, worker's compensation, Medicare, Social Security, voting rights, and consumer protection laws suggest an accountability to the interests of ordinary people. Such interests find form in grassroots actions long before they are represented by law. During times of severe fiscal retrenchment, however, groups that might otherwise be pushing for new protections and expanded programs instead find themselves lowering their sights to fight cutbacks in the already inadequate protections and safety net programs that are in danger of being stripped away.

THE DISEMPOWERING EFFECTS OF THE MASS MEDIA

Who has power depends in large part on who participates in the dialogue. Non-participation reflects both people's lack of control over dominant symbols of legitimacy and the habituation effects of media-induced passivity. Cornel West (1993) cites the need for a massive revival of public conversation, through which people can find expression and work toward their collective best interests. Although a number of factors have contributed to the decline in such civic engagement, the effects of television have been particularly striking. Americans now watch television for approximately four hours daily, not counting those periods when the television set is on in the background. A more conservative estimate of three hours daily would still mean that 40 percent of discretionary time is consumed with TV viewing (Putnam 1996). As Putnam (1996, 47) notes, "Television is . . . the only leisure activity that seems to inhibit participation outside the home. TV watching comes at the expense of nearly every social activity outside the home, especially social gatherings and informal conversations." The decreased availability of people for group association is a fact of contemporary life that contributes to the weakening of the social fabric.

In addition to a role in causing people to become less engaged in community life, television, together with the other mass media, can be problematic in light of the hegemony it maintains over what may be transmitted to the public (Bagdikian 1992). The major media are parts of transnational corporations. The increasing concentration of ownership of the mass media is reflected in the fact that fewer than thirty corporations control over 50 percent of all media output (Bagdikian 1992). As Lawrence Wallack et al. (1993, 59) argue: "This level of control, guided by commercial interests, results in a relatively narrow range of ideas, generally supported by the existing sociopolitical relationships in society. The potential for diversity in the large number of media outlets is deceptive, because the content tends to be uniform across the various forms and channels of mass media."

The messages brought to us through the mass media are transmitted through sensationalized "real-life" stories of crime or the salacious and luxurious private lives of celebrities. Even the news is presented as rapid-fire, attention-grabbing incidents that are sometimes difficult to distinguish from "entertainment" (Postman 1985). Television, even public television, includes messages from the sponsor, thereby transforming people into markets for created needs.

The media's monopoly over the means for projecting cultural symbols is also changing our concept of individual potency. With more bits of information readily available than ever before, people are becoming disempowered spectators to any but the most local of happenings. It is possible to see in a single telecast a famine in Africa, a toxic spill, a government official charged with accepting gifts in exchange for influence, and a local horror story of a violent killing, all sandwiched between weather, sports, the stock market, and commercials. Most of the information is presented without serious inquiry into why these problems recur. Who loses? Who gains? What difference does it make to the viewer, or what difference might the viewer make to the situation? These unaddressed questions are vital to democratic participation (Hermann and Chomsky 1988). The highly touted information highway is already cluttered with mindless pitches to the marketplace, and the interactive highways have almost no on-ramps in poor communities.

Perceiving themselves as unable to make a difference in a world characterized by injustice and inequality, people become easy prey to the depiction of the disadvantaged and the displaced as undeserving, as dangerous, and as responsible for the despair of those whose hard work has still not satisfied the marketed self-image of consumer (Katz 1995). Can grassroots groups overcome the disempowering manipulation of symbols? And can they gain access to the media to frame their own stories and effect changes in policy that can improve their health and quality of life?

The Paradox of Increased Activism

In the face of the preceding trends, a dramatic decline in participatory grassroots efforts might well be anticipated. To the contrary, however, the numbers of both domestic and international grassroots groups have been rising dramatically (Durning 1989; Lappe and DuBois 1994; Boyte and Riessman 1986). This growth has occurred among all classes of people, and some among the poor have shown a remarkable ability to persist actively for more than twenty years (Delgado 1986; see also chapter 4).

Grassroots groups are adjusting to the changed environment. Some have adopted sophisticated means to obtain, distribute, and use information. Some are building coalitions that cross the boundaries of geography and single issues and influence the policy process (Fisher and Kling 1991). Others are intentionally creating forms of mutual help once provided by intact communities (Pilisuk and Parks 1986). Finally, grassroots endeavors are helping to spread new symbols of value and legitimacy through such social movements as feminism, environmentalism, and cultural diversity (Hyde 1989; Hutcheson and Dominguez 1986). Nonentrepreneurial values of sustainability and socially engaged spirituality and a declining respect for governmental authority have encouraged new and creative forms of local action.

Since the 1960s, much local organizing in the United States and other developed countries has occurred among groups that were not economically impoverished. Many were middle-class people of color, women, people with disabilites, gays and lesbians, the elderly—all persons who had lived with injustices tolerated by the larger society. Others have joined in local action on issues of peace and the environment because governmental decisionmakers have shown little ability to face the threats posed by the very technologies they have fostered. Mutual aid groups of endless variety have formed, and many have moved beyond their original supportive purposes to the task of collective group action (Katz and Bender 1976; Leiberman and Borman 1979). What began as local breast cancer support groups, for example, have evolved into coalitions demanding effective care and opposing environmental contaminators (Soffa 1994).

Broader ideologies, such as independent living, environmentalism, and feminism, have inspired local efforts for battered women. A shelter for battered women now provides community education about domestic violence, promotes state legislation, and organizes the surrounding community to challenge the belief that men have a right to dominate women (Garske 1995). In this effort, the shelter joins a broad international feminist movement. In a like manner, a grassroots group formed after the accident at Three Mile Island tracked the bond holdings for nuclear plants in the portfolio of a state university's pension funds. Protesting public financing of nuclear power, the group made such investments less secure for financial lenders (Villarejo 1980). This work, together with pressure from other grassroots groups around the country, is a major reason that no new nuclear power plants have been built in this country since then.

Disability groups, too, demonstrate the power of grassroots efforts to reconstruct meanings that disempower them. The rights of people with disabilities to participate fully, live independently, and have equal access to education, housing, and other essential resources have emerged from local efforts and from powerful coalitions among persons with varied disabilities and from all regions. The Disabled People's International and the World Institute on Disability have provided a focus for groups around the globe concerned with issues of access, public education to confront stereotypes, and changes in public policy that support the rights of people with disabilities (Dreidger 1989). The Americans with Disabilities Act could not have come to pass without working coalitions of grassroots groups (McQuire 1994). So despite formidable impediments, grassroots organizing is alive and well at the dawn of the twenty-first century.

Roles, Functions, and Dilemmas of Social Change Professionals in Grassroots Organizing

Although most successful organizing efforts take place without the aid of social change professionals, the characteristics of postindustrial society, including the increase in information and skills needed to confront even local issues, have expanded the rationale for professional involvement. But what roles might health educators, social workers, and other social change professionals play as organizers, and what potentials and dilemmas do these roles present in relation to the goal of fostering community empowerment? A few of these roles and their corresponding dilemmas and challenges are illustrative.

BEGINNING CONVERSATIONS AND SHARING THE MESSAGE

People who have a common problem often have little awareness that the problem is shared by their neighbors or that getting together to discuss their distress is possible. The first task of the organizer is to begin such conversations, first with individuals, then with groups. Beginning such conversations involves first and foremost active listening. In Michael Miller's (1985, 1) words, "By asking questions, the organizer draws out of the people their hopes, aspirations, fears, problems, vision [and] dreams." In the process, the organizer may also learn of jealousies or rivalries within the group, members' past experiences with organizing, and their likes and dislikes. Such knowledge helps the organizer to bridge differences and affirm common aspirations. For Paulo Freire (1968, 1973), active listening also entails problem-posing, or asking questions that cause a small group of people to reflect critically on their reality, their shared problems, the linkages between those problems, and their root causes (see chapters 3 and 12 for a fuller discussion of this approach).

As discussed in chapter 3, even where the topic for organizing has been externally determined (as, for example, when a health educator wants to help mobilize a community around tobacco advertising or violence prevention), starting conversations and engaging in active listening are critical first steps. When gangs are the primary basis for self-esteem for youths in a poverty neighborhood, or when smoking is a popular means of coping in a work site characterized by boring, repetitive jobs and frequent layoffs, violence prevention and smoking cessation may take on a more complex reality. The organizer's role in such instances is to discover how an issue is perceived by the local community and then create a message that will "pique the interest" of members (Mondros and Wilson 1994). The message must be broad enough to attract sufficient numbers of people, and it must be delivered clearly and strongly in ways to which the community can relate (Mondros and Wilson 1994). For Nicholas Freudenberg (1984a, b), the message must not only present information that the organizer feels is critical (e.g., regarding the potential hazards of a toxic waste dump being proposed in a low-income community), but also reflect those community members' concerns that the health educator uncovered through the needs assessement process. Active listening, in short, is important for reaching more people with "the message" and for bringing their messages back to the health department, nonprofit agency, or other external group. Through active listening, the health educator may discover potential bridges between these issues that further enable him or her to tailor messages to specific subgroups in the community (Freudenberg 1984b).

The central dilemma faced by social change professionals with regard to beginning the conversation and sharing the message often involves relinquishing ownership of the problem and its definition. Yet as earlier chapters in this volume have suggested, the discrepancy between local perspectives and the ways that outside professional helpers understand the nature of local problems underscores the importance of having people define their own problems. Professional problem definition may result in a "problem" being identified that is important to the outsider but not a major concern to residents (Miller 1985). Alternatively, professionals may identify a problem of real salience to the community, yet define it in such a way that significant portions of the problem may be omitted. It was only after Act-Up, a grassroots organization of HIV-positive individuals and their friends, began organized direct action that health agencies began to view AIDS as a serious national epidemic. It was also local action by patients with AIDS, as with breast cancer, that called attention to the nonmedical, quality-of-life issues for persons facing these devastating diseases.

An assumption of voicelessness and an inability to articulate individual and community problems and concerns occur among well-meaning health and social service professionals more frequently than they would like to admit. The Interagency Council on the Homeless (1992) made important recommendations to a variety of federal departments and agencies toward integrating agency efforts, expanding housing options and alternative services, and improving outreach and access for existing rehabilitative programs. What the report lacked, however, was an analysis of why people are homeless and a strategy for prevention. The latter was provided through a self-help movement of formerly hospitalized patients, who viewed the problem as one of power and empowerment. In the services that have evolved from their grassroots organizing, clients are treated to the previously often neglected practice of informed consent for any form of assistance. They come to understand how their prior diagnoses and institutional handling have diminished what resources they have. They gain strength by exercising actual control over decisions in the facilities they use and many extend their grassroots efforts to political action on zoning restrictions, welfare reductions, or job training (Segal, Silverman, and Temkin 1991). The political nature of problems such as mental illness and homelessness leads to the inescapable conclusion that no solution can be found without participation of those most affected in problem definition and in subsequent organizing and social movements (Yeich 1994).

ENHANCING COMMUNITY CAPACITY

Although community members may identify a shared problem and express a desire to bring about change, they often do not know how or where to begin. As Miller (1985) notes, the fundamental task of organizers at this stage may be to help people "think through" what might be done, including, importantly, the gifts and resources they bring to the situation. Indeed, a major task of the organizer at this stage is to work with people in ways that enhance the capacities of the community to address its needs without continued reliance upon the organizer.

This can be difficult because people who have internalized repressive messages may believe their status is the inevitable consequence of the circumstances of their birth, class, gender, race, age, or disability or that it was ordained by fate. Some see change as wholly dependent upon powerful leaders. The organizer's special talent lies in a willingness to understand, and an unwillingness to collude with, such internalized oppression. This stance calls for realization on the part of the organizer that helpful outsiders have come before and left the community without bringing about desired change and without having increased community competence or problem-solving ability (Cottrell 1983). It means that the organizer will have to earn the trust of people and establish relationships with them in their surroundings. It means an ability to suspend the power, privilege, prestige, and protection offered by one's own background and be willing to be less safe.

The health educator, social worker, or other social change professional may have practical skills in setting up an effective meeting, enlisting community participation in assessing needs and resources, and in facilitating the process of developing goals and priorities. He or she may also be skilled at locating sources of information and other forms of power not known to the local community. And he or she may be effective in helping get people admitted to a hearing or appointed to a local city or regional committee (Chavis, Florin, and Felix 1993; Johnson 1994). But of ultimately greater importance than the utilization of these skills to faciliate a particular organizing effort is the transfer of such skills so that the community left behind is better able to organize itself in the future. There are many ways of doing this. The health educator or other social change professional may teach community members how to conduct "barefoot epidemiology," researching the etiology of health problems they have identified. He or she may help them understand the power structure as it relates to a particular issue, how to access information, and how to get invited onto task forces and other civic bodies. The outside organizer may do both formal and informal leadership training. Such simple things as role-playing a planned meeting with local health department officials to enable group members to practice how they might best put forward their objectives can make a real difference not only in the success of a given action but also in the building of community competence and the self-confidence of community members.

However, health educators, social workers, and other professionals must be careful in their approach to leadership training and related activities. As discussed in chapter 8, the teaching of leadership skills is not without risk, as when indigenous leaders become distanced from others or use the skills they have acquired to manipulate other community members. Resources are best used to reinforce actions that build a sense of community, develop an organizing plan, find information, locate sources of power not known to the community, and maintain accountability to the community.

STEPPING BACK VERSUS GETTING THE JOB DONE

Critical to organizer success in working with community groups is wisdom in knowing how and when to apply diverse skills and when to step back. A study of advocate planners found that those more highly educated were more likely to view their task as delivering some concrete gain for people. Others with a more populist bent were more content to work with people, defer to group judgement, and see mobilization of the group as an end in itself (Ross 1977). A frequent dilemma for the professional as organizer involves curbing the temptation to "do too much" in the name of task accomplishment; otherwise, in the process the organizer may lose sight of the equally important goal of advancing community competence. This dilemma is particularly likely to surface in relation to the fact that grassroots organizing exists in a world in which control of information is a form of power and concealment, a form of control. More than ever before, grassroots efforts that lack indigenous sophistication in obtaining information may require the technical assistance of outside professionals who can help the community uncover information about who controls social institutions, how decisions are made, and how dialogue is averted. The challenge for the organizer is to provide such information in ways that do not impose direction and thereby reduce the power of the community group for choice (Johnson 1994).

ADDRESSING COMMUNITY DIVISIONS AND IDENTITY POLITICS

As Ronald Labonte suggests in chapter 6, another dilemma for the organizer is that communities are not of one mind. Housing segregation, for example, leaves many African-American neighborhoods with a mix of economic levels. Some of the local

landlords may be the least able financially to provide good maintenance. Organized tenant struggles may drive them, rather than the large absentee landlords,
into bankruptcy. Indigenous leaders may or may not be representative of their constituencies (Cnaan 1991; Friedman et al. 1988). Race and gender issues often surface even among grassroots efforts intended to eliminate them. The organizer must
address the sometimes divisive "identity politics" of the dispossessed (Delgado 1994).
Men may try to speak for women or to withdraw from action led by women. Long-
term residents may resent immigrants, who are seen as competition for jobs and
services. Most American working people have never experienced a multiethnic
framework of political solidarity, and workers have traditionally belonged to
unions and political machines based upon ethnic solidarity and exclusion (Flacks
1990). The good organizer will require strong analytic skills to notice such differences
and will have to rely upon broader ethical and ideological frameworks for guidance in how to work with them.

COPING WITH CONFLICTING AGENDAS AND SUCCESS CRITERIA

Health educators and other organizers with expert knowledge in certain areas of
application, such as adolescent drug use, HIV/AIDS, or toxic contamination, face
other dilemmas as well. As discussed in greater detail in chapter 8, key among
these is the question of conflicting loyalties. Do social change professionals work
for the organization that has hired them because of their credentials or for the community constituency? Do they define success by improvements in the situation of
one particular "target group" in one community despite the fact that such success
may result in less local resources available to other groups with equally pressing
needs? Do they support conflictual tactics knowing that privilege rarely con-
cedes without pressure, or do they advocate for consensual tactics that work
against the exclusion of any parties? Again, leaders will have to rely upon broader
frameworks that are both ethical and political.

The dilemmas are real, but the underlying principle is clear. Grassroots community organizing is not about the creation of clients for services (see chapter 2).
The job is to help bring people together and to assist judiciously with tasks of empowerment and organization.

CONNECTING COMMUNITY GROUPS WITH PUBLIC INTEREST ORGANIZATIONS

When grassroots groups seek broader policy changes, they need organizations that
extend beyond the community confines. One important role for health educators
or other social change professionals, therefore, may be to connect community groups
with appropriate public interest organizations. Because local problems have distant
causes, public interest groups such as the Center for Science in the Public Interest

become important advocates enhancing grassroots activism at regional, national, and international levels. They often form broad-based coalitions and serve local community groups by making sophisticated information more widely assessible.

However, although many public interest groups espouse the goal of participation, they frequently abandon it in practice, with such groups often doing little to empower their members (Clark 1968). As Michael McCann (1986, 170) notes, "Actual forms of interest group organization have been built upon a structural logic at odds with the task of participatory grass roots movement building that reform rhetoric celebrates." Similarly, David Bunn (1983, 10–11) argues that

> difficulty fundraising and pressures for immediate results and
> mainstream public credibility tend to push public interest groups away
> from grassroots strategies and toward a more corporate structure and
> strategy. . . . It is far easier to write a foundation grant proposal or to ask
> . . . law firms for major contributions than it is to organize a canvass or
> a community fundraising event. It is . . . faster to build a direct mail
> membership list than it is to organize and train community activists.

Given these realities, the health educator or other social change professional may have an equally important role to play in working with public interest organizations to increase their responsiveness to community group members. With the latter, they can challenge the power of public interest groups to define the issues of dissent such that the linking of community groups with larger movements will result in real, rather than symbolic, participation.

USING THE MASS MEDIA FOR POWER AND EMPOWERMENT

As noted earlier, corporate hegemony over what is transmitted to the public by the mass media is a major contributor to the voicelessness and lack of participation and power experienced by people and communities in postindustrial society (Bagdikian 1992). Yet even as control of the media is being increasingly concentrated in a small number of corporations, new strategies are emerging that can help communities access the media to draw attention to their own issues, reframe the debate, and advance policies conducive to health. The most promising of these strategies is media advocacy, defined by Lawrence Wallack in chapter 21 as "the strategic use of mass media to advance a social or public policy initiative." A coalition of health, religious, and community organizations in Philadelphia that successfully prevented the test-marketing of a new brand of cigarettes targeted to African Americans succeeded in part because of its effective use of local media. Through careful bridge building, goal setting, message framing, and selection of appropriate media outlets, the group not only prevented the test-marketing of "Uptown" cigarettes in the city but also helped ensure that the new tobacco product was never even released (Wallack et al. 1993).

Health educators and other social change professionals have been among the key architects of media advocacy as a strategy for redressing power imbalances and promoting policies that improve the public's health. By becoming familiar with the concept and methods of media advocacy and sharing them with community groups, health education practitioners can play an important role in countering some of the disempowering effects of the mass media and helping communities access the latter to further their own health and social goals

Implications for Practice: A Final Note

There are two ways to interpret the implications of global trends for grassroots efforts. The first applies to the means that the organizer must use to assist community groups in acting in the face of a changed reality. These include building supportive ties into a project (where such ties may be lacking among constituents), obtaining information about power or ownership, or gaining access to media or governing bodies.

The second implication is to the *ends* that community organizing will have to address. At some appropriate point in each local action, the professional will need to help the community group articulate its analysis of the underlying reasons that resources to address their needs are scarce and how other groups like themselves are addressing this problem. The increasing control of local resources by national and global corporations is placing a serious cap on what any local group can accomplish. Affirmative action, fair wages and benefits, assured health care, aid for dependent people, and conversion of military development to civilian uses are examples of issues that cannot be resolved at the community level, despite the fact that they are not likely to be resolved without local efforts.

Communities, like individuals, need to know that they are not alone when their voices are raised. Some of the more effective coalitions have linked community efforts across the country and across continents to provide action on voter registration, the protection of women against violence, control over pollution, and the monitoring of nuclear weapons laboratories. These alliances help to keep alive a culture of caring and concern amid global trends toward competitive control. To stem the loss of community control over local resources, each separate project needs to be a source of education about where the control over resources really lies. Each local effort will have to offer a connection to other groups whose joint actions constitute a social movement to return a measure of global corporate accountability to the local community.

Conclusion

The postindustrial mileu for grassroots organizing is one of exacerbated need in the face of new and often formidable impediments. The resurgence and dramatic growth of local organizing in the face of these obstacles are heartening and speak to the continued role of grassroots organizing as an essential part of the human story. Although most organizing takes place without the aid of professionals, outside organizers clearly have important contributions to make. The challenge and the dilemma for health educators, social workers, and others engaged in social change are how to lend their special gifts and resources in ways that strengthen, rather than diminish, community capacity in the process.

Listening actively and empowering personal dialogues, nurturing community resources, helping to access hidden information, and transferring skills in locating information and other sources of power are among the contributions social change professionals can make to the grassroots organizing processes. Helping to connect local communities with public interest groups that have a presence in policy and media circles may also represent an important role. In each of these tasks, however, the challenge for the social change professional is to ensure that the steps taken serve to further, rather than undermine, the ultimate goal of community empowerment.

References

Bagdikian, B. H. 1992. *Media monopoly*. 4th ed. Boston: Beacon Press.

Barlett, D. L., and J. B. Steele. 1992. *America: What went wrong?* Kansas City, Mo.: Andrews and McMeel.

Bellah, R. N., R. Madsen, W. Sullivan, A. Swidler,and S. M. Tipton. 1985. *Habits of the heart: Individualism and commitment in American life*. Berkeley and Los Angeles: University of California Press.

Boyte, H., and F. Riessman 1986. *The new populism*. Philadelphia: Temple University Press.

Bunn, D. A. 1983. Structural development of a grassroots political organization in rural communities of California. Master's thesis, University of California, Davis.

Chavis, D. M., P. Florin, and M.J.R. Felix. 1993. Nurturing grassroots initiatives for community development: The role of enabling systems. In *Community organization and social administration: Advances, trends, and emerging principles*, ed. T. Mizrahi and J. Morrison. New York: Haworth Press.

Clark, T. 1968. *Community structure and decision-making: Comparative analyses*. San Francisco: Chandler.

Chaan, R. A. 1991. Neighborhood representing organizations: How democratic are they? *Social Service Review* 65 (4):614–634.

Cottrell, L. S. Jr. 1983. The competent community. In *New perspectives on the American community*, ed. R. Warren and L. Lyon. Homewood, Ill.: Dorsey Press.

Delgado, D. 1986. *Organizing the movement: The roots and growth of ACORN*. Philadelphia: Temple University Press.

Delgado, G. 1994. *Beyond the politics of place: New directions in community organizing*. Oakland, Calif.: Applied Research Center.

Dooley, P. 1969. The interlocking directorate. *American Economic Review* (June):314–323.

Dreidger, D. 1989. *The last civil rights movement: Disabled People's International*. New York: St. Martin's Press.

Durning, A. B. 1989. *Poverty and the environment: Reversing the downward spiral*. Washington, D.C.: Worldwatch Institute.

Fisher, R. 1993. Grassroots organizing worldwide. In *Mobilizing the community: Local politics in a global era*, ed. R. Fisher and J. Kling. Thousand Oaks, Calif.: Sage.

Fisher, R., and J. Kling. 1991. Popular mobilization in the 1990s: Prospects for the new social movements. *New Politics* 3:71–84.

Flacks, D. 1990. The revolution of citizenship. *Social Policy* (Fall):37–50.

Freire, P. 1968. *Pedagogy of the oppressed*. New York: Seabury Press.

———. 1973. *Education for critical consciousness*. New York: Seabury Press.

Freudenberg, N. 1984a. Citizen action for environmental health: Report on a survey of community organizations. *American Journal of Public Health* 74 (5):444–448.

———. 1984b. *Not in our backyards: Community action for health and the environment*. New York: Monthly Review Press.

Friedmann, R. R., P. Florin, A. Wandersman, and R. Meier. 1988. Local action on behalf of local collectives in the U.S. and Israel: How different are leaders from members in voluntary associations? *Journal of Voluntary Action Research* 17:36–54.

Garske, D. 1995. Transforming communities: Creating safety and justice for women and girls. In *Preventing violence in America,*. ed. R. L. Hampton, P. Jenkins, and T. P. Gollotto. Newbury Park, Calif.: Sage.

Hermann, E. S., and N. Chomsky. 1988. *Manufacturing consent*. New York: Pantheon Books.

Hutcheson, J. D., and L. H. Dominguez. 1986. Ethnic self-help organizations in non-barrio settings: Community identity and voluntary action. *Journal of Voluntary Action Research* 15:13–22.

Hyde, C. 1989. A feminist model for macro-practice: Promises and problems. In *Administrative leadership in the social services: The next challenge*, ed. Y. Hasenfeld. New York: Haworth Press.

Interagency Council on the Homeless. 1992. *Outcasts on main street: Report of the Federal Task Force on Homelessness and Severe Mental Illness*. Washington, D.C.: Interagency Council on the Homeless.

Johnson, A. K. 1994. Linking professionalism and community organization: A scholar/ advocate approach. *Journal of Community Practice* 1:65–87.

Katz, H. A., and E. L. Bender. 1976. *The strength in us: Self-help groups in the modern world*. New York: Franklin-Watts.

Katz, M. 1995. *Improving poor people*. Princeton: Princeton University Press.

Lappe, F. M., and P. M. DuBois. 1994. *The quickening of America: Rebuilding our nation, remaking our lives*. San Francisco: Jossey-Bass.

Leiberman, M., and L. Borman. 1979. *Self-help groups for coping with crises: Origins, members, processes and impact*. San Francisco: Jossey-Bass.

Lyon, L. 1987. *The community in urban society*. Philadelphia: Temple University Press.

McCann, M. W. 1986. *Taking reform seriously*. Ithaca: Cornell University Press.

McQuire, J. F. 1994. Organizing from diversity in the name of community: Lessons from the disability rights movement. *Policy Studies Journal* 22 (1):112–122.

Miller, M. 1985. Turning problems into actionable issues. San Francisco: Organize Training Center. Unpublished paper.

Mondros, J., and S. Wilson. 1994. *Organizing for power and empowerment*. New York: Columbia University Press.

O'Connor, J. 1976. What is political economy? In *Economics: Mainstream readings and radical critiques*, ed. D. Mermelstein. 3d ed. New York: Random House.

Pilisuk, M. 1986–1987. Family, community, and government: The value and the limits of local caregiving. *International Quarterly of Community Health Education* 7 (1):61–67.

———. 1988. Sacrificing the city. *Practice* 6 (1):29–49.

Pilisuk, M., J. McAllister, and J. Rothman. 1996. Coming together for action: The challenge of contemporary grassroots organizing. *Journal of Social Issues* 52:15–37.

Pilisuk, M., and S. H. Parks. 1986. *The healing web: Social networks and human survival*. Hanover, N.H.: University Press of New England.

Postman, N. 1985. *Amusing ourselves to death: Public discourse in the age of show business*. New York: Viking Press.

Putnam, R. 1996. The strange disappearance of civic America. *American Prospect* (Winter):34–48.

Ross, R. 1977. Professional advocates and the mobilization of constituencies. Paper presented at the annual meeting of the Society for Study of Social Problems, Chicago, Illinois, September.

Ross, R., K. Gibson, J. Graham, P. O'Keefe, D. M. Shakow, and P. Susman. 1984. Global capitalism and regional decline: Implications for the strategy of classes in older regions. In *Regional restructuring under advanced capitalism*, ed. P. O'Keefe. London: Croom Helm.

Segal, S., C. Silverman, and T. Temkin. 1991. *Enabling, empowering, and self-help agency practice*. Berkeley: Center for Self-help Research.

Soffa, V. M. 1994. *The journey beyond breast cancer: From the personal to the political*. Rochester, Vt.: Healing Arts Press.

Thurow, L. 1996. *The future of capitalism*. New York: William Morrow.

Villarejo, D. 1980. *Research for action*. Davis: California Institute for Rural Studies.

Wallack, L., L. Dorfman, D. Jernigan, and M. Themba. 1993. *Media advocacy and public health: Power for prevention*. Newbury Park, Calif.: Sage.

West, C. 1993. *Race matters*. Boston: Beacon Press.

Yeich, S. 1994. *The politics of ending homelessness*. Ladham, Md.: University Press of America.

Ethical Issues in Community Organization and Community Participation

Chapter 8

MEREDITH MINKLER
CHERI PIES

THE ACTIVE INVOLVEMENT of people, beginning with what they define as the needs and goals to be addressed, is the critical factor distinguishing true community organizing from other approaches, such as social planning (Rothman 1987) and public health consultation. For although some degree of community involvement often occurs in the latter processes, increasing community competence or problem-solving ability is usually not a primary objective.

From an ethical perspective, increasing community competence is important in part because it serves to make the community less vulnerable to outside manipulation in future encounters. A heavy emphasis on fostering community determination may at first suggest that the health or social change professional as organizer does not need to engage in extensive ethical reflection since many of the processes in which he or she is already involved make increased freedom of choice for the community a central goal. Yet despite these lofty goals and guiding principles, the practice of community organization is, in reality, one of the most ethically problematic arenas in which health educators, social workers, and other practitioners function.

All too often we find ourselves searching for answers to the ethical challenges we face in the hopes that by doing so, we can move ahead with plans and programs. But a resolution of these dilemmas may be less important than a continuing commitment to the process of articulating them, as well as the values and assumptions that inform our practice.

In the interest of real community participation and empowerment, how do we facilitate dialogue rather than direct it? How do we tease apart our own agenda from the community's? And what happens when there are multiple, and often conflicting, community agendas? These are just a few of the questions we face.

Whether and how we think about them will have critical implications for the future of community organizing and community building for health.

This chapter explores five areas in which health educators and other practitioners frequently experience tough ethical dilemmas in relation to the community organizing aspects of their roles. These areas are(1) the problem of conflicting loyalties; (2) the eliciting of real, rather than symbolic, participation; (3) the dilemmas posed by funding sources; (4) the unanticipated consequences of organizing; and (5) the matter of whose "common good" is being addressed through the organizing effort. Case examples in each of these areas are used to highlight some of the challenges faced, with particular attention drawn to the ethical questions raised for practitioners as organizers.

Conflicting Loyalties

Almost two decades ago, E. Richard Brown and Glenn Margo (1978, 8) argued that "in concrete attempts to develop consumer participation in health planning, health educators act as facilitators of co-optation more frequently than they increase the power and influence of consumers." This observation, although an overstatement, nevertheless points up a major and continuing dilemma faced by health educators and other health professionals who find themselves simultaneously responsible to a health agency employer, to the communities being served by that agency, and to the funding sources supporting the particular project or program. Particularly in instances in which the health education professional is charged with facilitating consumer participation in the agency and acting as an advocate for the community, conflicting goals and loyalties may be problematic. As Jerry Grossman (1971, 55) once noted, the health educator's role in helping people "set their own goals" often in reality means helping them set these goals "within the context of preexisting goals." When agency agendas fail to correspond to the needs and desires of the community, the health educator faces difficult ethical dilemmas involving the degree to which she or he will feel comfortable complying with agency expectations and directives.

Two ethical precepts that lie at the heart of community organizing and community building—self-determination and liberty—are helpful for thinking about and addressing such dilemmas. Both reflect an inherent faith in people's ability to accurately assess their strengths and needs and their right to act upon these insights in setting goals and determining strategies for achieving them.

In the language of health education, these ethical precepts are reflected in Dorothy Nyswander's (1956) early admonition to "start where the people are." Yet when an HIV/AIDS prevention program has as its goal the promotion of safer sex, in part through mobilization of a community around the epidemic, and when the community in question is more concerned about drug abuse or violence, should the health education practitioner put on the back burner, for the time being, the agency's formal agenda and truly start where the people are? Within the bounds of certain limiting conditions to be discussed later, our response to this question is affirmative since in choosing to start where the people are, the health professional asserts a commitment to the principles of self-determination and liberty and the rights of individuals and communities to affirm and act on their own values.

Yet there is a practical rationale for starting where the people are as well. When this ethical principle has been followed, when trust in the community has been demonstrated, and when the immediate concerns of people have received primary attention, the organizer's original health concerns frequently then are seen by the community's members as having relevance for their lives (Minkler 1978).

An early case study demonstrating this phenomenon had as its setting a family planning agency in New York City where eight low-income African-American and Puerto Rican women, all with large families, were hired to do community organizing around family planning in their communities. On meeting with the women, the agency's health educator quickly discovered that they had each taken the job out of sheer economic necessity and were in fact quite suspicious of family planning on both health and political grounds.

Consequently, the health educator began by scrapping the agency's formal agenda and instead engaging the women in a dialogue about their own perceptions of the paramount needs in their communities. Using the issues they identified, such as irregular garbage collection and drug dealers in the school yard, the health educator began a discussion of various effective organizing techniques the women might want to employ to get action from appropriate agencies on these and other issues. Within weeks the women, still on the payroll as family planning workers, were reporting the successes they were having in stirring community interest and, in some cases, getting actual changes in undesirable environmental conditions.

Convinced at this point that the agency really was concerned with their communities' overall welfare, and not merely with bringing down the birthrate, the women began to ask questions about birth control methods, their side effects, and the political ramifications of working in what was then a highly charged and sensitive area. Following these discussions, six of the eight women became convinced that family planning was in the best interests of their communities and began doing effective outreach and organizing in their neighborhoods (Minkler 1978).

Had the health educator failed to start with the concerns of the people she worked with, her chances of having effectively met the agency's health objectives would have been slim indeed. Yet in dropping the agency's formal agenda to assist the women in identifying and organizing around their own felt needs, she clearly took a risk. Objectives might have been set, or actions taken, that were incompatible with those of the funding agency.

A health educator working in a field such as HIV/AIDS prevention, and serving a community with very high seroprevalence rates among youths, may justifiably feel that continuing to work in this area is critical, even if the community does not share his or her perception of urgency. Such a situation may pose legitimate grounds for not starting where the people are. In instances like these, however, the health educator, even though borrowing methods and tools from community organizing, would not be doing "pure" community organizing since the community's felt needs were not determining the goals set or the actions pursued.

As discussed in chapter 6, a road around the choice between agency and community agendas may sometimes be found by health educators or other professionals charged with organizing around a problem that has been externally identified by the health department or another outside agency. Through careful listening and the asking of thoughtful, probing questions (Miller 1993), the organizer may learn how the issue she or he is concerned about is perceived by the local community, what the community's primary issues are, and whether bridges or links can be found between these seemingly disparate agendas. The Asian Pacific Environmental Network (APEN), for example, wanted to organize a local Laotian refugee community in Richmond, California, around the high levels of potential toxins to which it was being exposed. Toxic spills from the nearby oil refineries and other industries, contamination of the local fish on which many were dependent for their livelihood, and toxic waste in the plots of ground in which they grew vegetables were among the areas around which APEN, together with the university-based Labor and Occupational Health Program, hoped to organize (Center for Occupational and Environmental Health 1996). On meeting with the local refugees, asking questions, and really listening to the answers, however, APEN staff learned that the former had far more urgent questions, such as how to grow better vegetable crops. APEN's organizing agenda was consequently put aside while the organizers addressed the community's concerns. This show of genuine appreciation and acceptance of the community's agenda increased APEN's credibility among the refugees, some of whom subsequently began mapping toxic waste sites in their community and in other ways taking beginning steps in organizing around environmental hazards in their neighborhood (Center for Occupational and Environmental Health 1996; Leung 1996).

Although we have focused primarily on the problem of conflicting loyalties between "the community" and a health educator or other professional's agency, tensions around conflicting loyalties may also surface when there are multiple communities or community factions with different and often conflicting agendas. A community committed to AIDS prevention, for example, may be deeply torn over an effort to organize around getting a needle exchange program. A low-income Hispanic neighborhood near a toxic waste dump may likewise be divided between those residents wishing to organize against environmental racism and those who see the dump as a source of needed employment. The outside health professional's efforts to organize in situations like this may generate more conflict and confrontation than consensus among community members (Reynolds and Norman 1988). In such instances, the importance of questioning whether to intervene, and if so on what level and with what ethical precepts to guide us, takes on added importance (see chapter 11).

Dilemmas Posed by Funding Sources

The ethical dilemmas posed by conflicting community and/or community versus agency loyalties may be complicated still further by the realities of funding availability. The nature and source of funding for organizing projects can severely limit the extent to which the principle of starting where the people are can be put into practice. In the United States, nonprofit organizations with tax exempt 501(c)3 status, for example, "have to promise not to engage in partisan politics, and, with some exceptions, not to engage in any lobbying" (Paget 1990, 123). Although a different IRS category (501[c]4) permits somewhat greater degrees of freedom with respect to lobbying, even these organizations "must maintain, at least in rhetoric, a fuzzy line between non-partisan and partisan activities" (123). For the health educator or other social change professional working with either a 501(c)3 or a 501(c)4 agency, these constraints may greatly hinder efforts in organizing with communities around their political and social change agendas.

Where government funding has been received for a health promotion project that attempts to accent community participation, additional funding-related dilemmas also may arise. As noted in chapter 3, for example, the CDC's PATCH approach to community health promotion places a heavy accent on community involvement and participation, beginning with community needs assessment. As Marshall Kreuter (1992, 139) points out, this approach works well when the planning process "leads to a priority problem for which resources are available." However, "where the indicated problem is not a priority of the government, the community may have to choose between shifting focus to a health issue for which there are available resources or do without. This has been a long-standing problem with PATCH, and indeed all community based health promotion programs which require extensive technical assistance" (139).

Although PATCH is an example of a social planning approach rather than of true community organizing (see chapters 3 and 9), the dilemma it raises is nevertheless a familiar one to health educators and other social change professionals who engage in community organizing. Moreover, even when community members define their priority area for organizing and successfully seek government or foundation money to support their work, the community's priorities may shift over time, or members' interest may wane before project completion. Does the health educator or outside professional urge the community group to continue working on what is now a low priority in order to fulfill a funding mandate? Does she or he propose returning the remaining money to the funders? Or does she or he approach the funding source about accepting the community's change in direction and continuing to provide overall project support, despite the group's failure to complete the efforts originally emphasized?

Still another funding dilemma faced by health educators and other social change professionals as organizers involves the declining availability of both government and foundation funding and the resulting need to turn increasingly to other sources of support. In such a climate, community organizations and programs may find themselves considering or accepting financial support from sources they may not previously have countenanced—sources that sometimes have invisible strings attached. New York City's Coalition for the Homeless, for example, accepted a $100,000 grant from Phillip Morris, only to be pressured later to help defeat a bill mandating antismoking ads; Phillip Morris wanted the coalition to demand that the City Council address more important issues—such as homelessness (Quindlen 1992)!

Where a funding source may pose a direct real or perceived conflict of interest for an organization, such problems may intensify. For example, the early acceptance by Mothers Against Drunk Driving (MADD) of a sizable donation from Anheuser Busch, the nation's largest beer manufacturer, and MADD's increasingly close affiliation with the alcohol industry were widely viewed as having compromised MADD's ability to take a strong stand on the industry's role in the nation's alcohol problem (Marshall and Oleson 1994). In defense of MADD, William Dejong and Anna Russell (1995) stress the organization's leadership role in pushing for a national minimum drinking age and other policy changes opposed by the alcohol industry. Yet as these analysts also point out, MADD did not significantly strengthen its position on alcohol advertising until 1994—after it had cut its ties to an industry that, it belatedly concluded, "was truly not interested in solving problems due to the misuse of alcohol," despite its propaganda to the contrary (234).

Even when money comes without apparent strings, conflicts between an agency or group's values and those of a potential financial sponsor may raise difficult ethical questions. AIDS organizations around the country, for example, have been offered substantial financial support from alcohol and tobacco companies to help underwrite media campaigns and other projects and programs. For health professionals aware of the harmful effects of tobacco and heavy drinking, accepting such donations may be difficult indeed. Yet the community-based AIDS organizations or groups with which they work may either feel no conflict or agree with Saul Alinsky (1972) that in organizing, the end (in this case, getting support for a needed AIDS project) justifies the means.

To help avoid situations like these, some health educators have begun working with "alternative sponsorship projects," which link health and social programs and organizing efforts with alternative corporate or other sources of financial assistance, in the process dealing a public relations blow to alcohol and tobacco companies. Still other health educators have helped community coalitions and programs to decide whether to accept funding from a controversial source by applying what has been called the "the publicity test of ethics." This simple test involves having a group ask itself whether its reputation or integrity would be damaged if the source of funding for a particular project became known.

Such strategies are important, but in a time of major fiscal retrenchment in health and social services and declining support for a whole host of worthy organizing endeavors, they do not begin to solve the problem of severe funding constraints. When the need is great, where should the line be drawn? And when community participation and empowerment are a value, who draws the line? In meetings with community members about a financial offer of assistance from a source that may pose ethical implications, health educators not infrequently are confronted with the reaction "We need the money—go for it!" Are we truly promoting community participation and empowerment if we disregard the community's desire to accept needed resources from a source we may consider problematic?

Or will the community's long-run agenda be undermined if taking the money may at some point put constraints on decisionmaking, priority setting, or program direction? If what we are after is promotion of the common good, how do we accomplish this in a climate of declining public funding and the concurrent pull of likely support from potentially problematic sources? These are but a few of the kinds of questions health educators and other social change professionals need to ask themselves in relation to the funding of programs and organizing efforts with which they are associated.

Community Participation: Real or Symbolic?

Community participation historically has been recognized as a central value in community health education practice (Green 1990). In the 1970s, it gained increasing currency in the field of health planning as well, where calls for "maximum feasible participation" coincided with the birth of the neighborhood health center movement (Hatch and Eng 1984). More recently, as noted in chapter 3, community or public participation, together with the concept of empowerment, has emerged as the "defining feature" of the health promotion movement (Robertson and Minkler 1994).

Despite the increased rhetoric of participation in the health field, however, acting on the principle that calls for high-level community involvement has proved difficult indeed. As Gail Siler-Wells (1989, 142) points out, "Behind the euphemisms of participation and empowerment lay the realities of power, control and ownership." And even as we attempt to blur hierarchical distinctions by talking, for example, about health care "providers" and "consumers" (Neysmith 1990) and calling for partnerships between health professionals and communities, these power imbalances remain (Minkler 1994).

In an early attempt to bring clarity to these issues of control and ownership, health planner Sherry Arnstein (1969) developed a "ladder of participation." The bottom rungs of the ladder were two forms of "nonparticipation"—therapy and manipulation. In the middle were several "degrees of tokenism"—placation, consultation, and informing—through which community members were heard and might have a voice but did not necessarily have their input heeded. Finally, the top rungs of the ladder were three degrees of "citizen power"—partnership, delegated power, and true citizen power.

As Ann Robertson and Meredith Minkler (1994, 305) argue, much of current health promotion practice, although using the rhetoric of high-level community participation, in fact tends to operate at the lower rungs of Arnstein's ladder, as professionals "attempt to get people in the community to take ownership of a professionally defined health agenda." In Ronald Labonte's (1990, 7) words, such an approach "raises the specter of using community resources primarily as free or cheaper forms of service delivery in which community participation is tokenistic at best and co-opted at worst."

In other instances, the community's input may be sought and then discounted, further reinforcing unequal power relationships between health professionals and communities. The experience of some community advisory boards provides a good case in point. When taken seriously by professionals, community advisory boards or committees can make a real difference in the ways in which health educators and other practitioners approach their community-based programs. When allowed to serve as true partners in decisionmaking, such boards can provide valuable input on community needs and strengths, the likely effectiveness of alternative organizing strategies, and the cultural nuances and sensitivities that need to be respected and addressed.

As Lawrence Green and C. James Frankish (in press) point out, however, far too often community boards are established in response to a funding mandate or similar inducement rather than out of a sincere concern for eliciting and acting on community input. In such instances, community boards often perceive that they are expected to serve as rubber-stamp mechanisms for decisions that the health professionals have already made.

Finally, even programs committed to community participation through advisory boards and the like may occasionally find themselves ignoring input that conflicts with predetermined projects and plans—sometimes at considerable cost. An unfortunate example of this occurred in what is in many respects a national model for effective health promotion on multiple levels—the California Tobacco

Control Program (CTCP). We use this example to underscore that even the best programs can slip into paternalistic ways of doing things on occasion, with negative results.

The CTCP was created when a successful ballot initiative in 1992 put a twenty-five-cent tax on cigarettes and allocated a quarter of the money generated to anti-tobacco health education and advocacy. The program has been extremely successful and has been credited for the fact that the state's decline in cigarette smoking has recently been three times the national average (Skolnick 1994).

Part of the CTPC's activity has involved supporting groups such as the African-American Tobacco Control Education Network (AATCEN), which has addressed the heavy targeting of cigarette advertising to people of color and helped to mount a culturally sensitive counteradvertising campaign. When professionals at the CTCP first designed a proposed billboard aimed at the African-American community, they showed it to the AATCEN's Advisory Group for its feedback. The billboard depicted a young African-American man smoking a cigarette under the caption "Eric Jones just put a contract out on his family for $2.65. Secondhand smoke kills." Advisory Group members perceived the proposed ad as extremely racist, and they strongly urged that it not be used. Rather than heed the group's concerns, however, the CTCP did run the ad and received the same kind of negative reaction from community members (Ellis 1996).

The story behind that billboard is a sad and poignant reminder that it is not enough to "talk the talk" of community competence and community participation. We must indeed be willing to "walk the walk"—in this case, letting an advisory board composed of African-American community members teach the rest of us how to avoid further stigmatizing of their community in the name of health promotion.

It is easy to see how only paying lip-service to the concept of community participation can lead to a healthy suspicion on the part of communities and community groups regarding the agenda of the community organizer. Without a strong commitment to real community participation, we risk undermining our future efforts and dissipating the often fragile trust that communities invest in us. The credibility of the community organizer can be easily undermined when community group members sense that their participation is only symbolic, thus leading the community to question the commitment of the organizer and others to the community's real issues. Recognition of the importance of self-determination for communities, coupled with commitment to the concept of true partnership, must serve as guiding principles for ensuring meaningful community participation. (See appendix 11.)

A useful tool in applying these guiding principles is offered by community organizers Herbert Rubin and Irene Rubin (1992, 77) in the form of the DARE criteria of empowerment:

Who determines the goals of the project?

Who acts to achieve them?

Who receives the benefits of the actions?

Who evaluates the actions?

The more often we can answer these questions by responding, "the community," the more likely our partnerships and community organizing efforts are to be contributing to real community empowerment and high-level participation.

Unanticipated Consequences

The guiding principles of fostering self-determination and meaningful participation can go a long way in helping to avoid many of the problems that can plague the community organizing process. Yet even when these principles are followed, our organizing efforts may result in outcomes or by-products that were unanticipated and that may have negative consequences. Two examples are illustrative, one in the area of injury prevention campaigns and the second in the training of community health workers to enhance their skills in areas such as leadership and community organizing.

Many recent prevention and health promotion campaigns have done an excellent job of involving youth, people of color, and other traditionally neglected groups in the design and pretesting of programs and materials aimed at better reaching these populations (Ellis, Reed, and Scheider 1995; Wallerstein and Sanchez-Merki 1994). At the same time, however, health promotion and community organizing efforts often inadvertently reproduce and transmit problematic aspects of the dominant culture.

A poignant example of this is found in the work of Caroline Wang (1992), who identifies the stigmatization of people with disabilities that is often communicated through well-meaning injury prevention campaigns. A billboard sponsored by MADD, for example, featured a teenager in a wheelchair with the caption "If you think fourth period English is endless, try sitting in a wheelchair for the rest of your life!" Another, with the caption "One for the road," showed a man on crutches with his leg partially amputated. As Wang points out, the implicit message in such ads is "Don't let this happen to you!" Although well intended, these messages reinforce already powerful negative prejudices in our society against people with disabilities. At a time when the disabled are organizing to assert their rights and break down negative societal stereotypes, such campaigns can be particularly demoralizing. In the words of one person with a disability on viewing the injury prevention ads, "I feel like I should be preventing myself!" (Wang 1992).

In our attempts to avoid negative and unanticipated consequences like this one, the principle of high-level community involvement—and in this case, the reaching out to an overlooked community (people with disabilities)—can stand us in good stead. Such an approach is illustrated in the close coordination between two strong advocacy and organizing groups based in the San Francisco Bay Area— the World Institute on Disability (WID) and the Trauma Foundation. Although the latter's raison d'être is injury prevention, its president, Andrew McQuire, has served as chair of the board of WID, and he and other foundation staff are strong advocates for the recognition and treatment of disabled people as full participants in American society.

In some instances, of course, the very nature of the processes involved in community organizing can have negative unanticipated consequences. The training of "health promoters" or community health workers in both Third World and post-industrialized nations provides a good case in point. From a health education and a community organizing standpoint, such activities makes eminent sense, for they typically identify and build on the strengths of natural helpers in a community and address issues of homophily (e.g., that people often learn best and prefer to receive services from people who are "like themselves" in terms of race, social class, etc.). Many excellent models for community health worker training, moreover, put a heavy accent on empowerment, often employing methods such as Paulo Freire's (1968, 1973) "education for critical consciousness."

Yet as Freire (1968) himself has cautioned, leadership training can alienate the community members who are involved, making them strangers in their own communities. Once they have been trained and, in a sense, "indoctrinated" into the culture of the public health department or health clinic agency, community health workers may find it difficult to relate to or interact with their peers as they had previously. Is it the training they receive that gives them a new vocabulary and consequently a different way of addressing identified problems? Is it the fact that they feel some unstated pressure to "fit in" to the agency that hired them, where most people are professionally trained and where the culture of the office environment is different from the culture of the community or neighborhood? Or is it that once someone who is identified as a community leader tries to bring a particular health message to the community, she or he is distrusted as being "on the other side"? How should we proceed when we are committed to involving indigenous community workers in the process of education and organizing, yet are aware that such efforts may serve to alienate these individuals from their communities and serve to limit their credibility in the community?

Still another unanticipated consequence of training community members as health workers, group leaders, and organizers is that they may use the skills they have acquired to manipulate other members of the community. More than three decades ago, Herbert Kelman (1965, 35) warned that as a consequence of the training received, a community leader "may be able to manipulate the group into making the decision he desires, but also to create the feeling that this decision reflects the will of the group discovered through the workings of the democratic process."

There may always be some risk of community health workers or other recip-ients of training misusing the tools that we have helped them acquire. However, numerous examples from North America and around the world of effective com-munity health worker programs and leadership training activities on the local level suggest that this strategy is, on balance, a critical one for improving health and contributing to individual and community empowerment (Eng and Parker 1994; Ovrebo et al. 1994). The task for health educators and other social change pro-fessionals then remains one of determining how best to help participants acquire the tools they need for effective leadership and organizing, while at the same time communicating the responsibilities this new training imposes, as well as some of the difficulties and challenges they may need to anticipate.

Thoughts on Common Good

Acknowledging and confronting the dilemmas posed by conflicting loyalties; potential funding sources; the task of creating real, rather than symbolic, partici-pation in community organizing; and the possible unanticipated consequences of community organizing efforts may bring us close to greater community participation and ultimately greater empowerment of community groups. When we start where the people are, we make every attempt to be responsive to the needs, concerns, and agendas of a particular community, thereby affirming a commitment to self-determination and liberty, as well as promoting the rights of individuals to act on their own values. The question remains, however, Do we have an ultimate end in our efforts of promoting and preserving the common good of the communities with which we work? And if so, whose common good is being addressed, and who is determining what constitutes the common good? Finally, should we also be con-cerned with notions of common good that transcend local communities?

Alinsky (1972) long argued that a cardinal rule in effective community orga-nizing is to appeal to self-interest: people will not organize unless they see what is in it for them. However, particularly in a country such as the United States, which is characterized by a heavy accent on rugged individualism, stressing only self-interest may feed into an already impoverished notion of the common good. As Lester Thurow (1996, 159) points out, the dominant American ideologies—capitalism and democracy—"have no 'common good,' no common goals toward which everyone is collectively working. Both stress the individual and not the group. . . . Neither imposes an obligation to worry about the welfare of the other. . . . In both, individual freedom dominates community obligations."

In part because of the individual focus of these dominant ideologies, the very debate over public or common good in America has been badly constrained. In Larry Churchill's (1987, 21) words, our notions of justice are based on "a moral heritage in which answers to the question 'what is good?' and 'what is right?' are lodged definitively in a powerful image of the individual as the only meaningful level of moral analysis." Churchill goes on to argue that "a more realistic sense of community is one in which there are shared perceptions of the value of individual lives and a social commitment to protect them all equitably" (101).

The lack of a more realistic sense of community and of a well-developed notion of the common good may be particularly troubling for health educators and other social change professionals for whom a strong sense of social justice often lies at the base of their worldview and career choice (Mondros and Wilson 1994; see also chapter 1). Moreover, as suggested earlier, although an appeal to self-interest may be pragmatic in helping to mobilize a community for the achievement of its self-interested goals, there are dangers in this limited approach. Key among these is the fact that a local community group may fail to see or reflect on the connection between its goals and concerns and the broader need for social justice in a democratic society. Consequently, even though a focus on self-interest may be necessary from an organizing perspective, we would argue that it is too narrow to be sufficient.

We would, however, advocate against an overly simplistic utilitarian notion of the common good that focuses solely on achieving the greatest good for the greatest number. For the latter may not truly reflect the end that those engaged in community organizing are attempting to realize. Instead, we may want to look toward a definition of common or collective good that both speaks to local organizing efforts and includes a broader vision of society. The latter broader vision was frequently lacking in the Alinsky brand of organizing (Miller 1987) in which many community organizers have their roots.

Feminist leader Charlotte Bunch (1983) has offered one approach that may be usefully adapted and applied by community organizers attempting to create a bridge between local or small-scale organizing efforts and a broader social vision. She argues that any particular reform or change effort that is sought should be perceived and evaluated not as an end in itself but as a means toward a larger goal. For her, the latter is a revolutionary feminist agenda that leads to "a new social order based on equitable distribution of resources . . . , equal justice and rights for all, and upon maximizing freedom for each person to determine her own life" (204). If we replace "reform" with "community organizing effort" and "women" with "community members" in Bunch's statement, the criteria she sets forth for such evaluation include such questions as "(1) Does [the community organizing effort] materially improve the lives of community members and if so, which members and how many? (2) Does [participating in the organizing process] give community members a sense of power, strength and imagination as a group and help build structures for further change? and (3) Does the struggle . . . educate community members politically, enhancing their ability to criticize and challenge the system in the future?" (206–208). Overarching questions like these can help organizers engage the communities with which they work in the kind of broader reflection needed if we are indeed to build bridges between "acting locally" and "thinking globally."

The last decade of the twentieth century has been a time of renewed moral reflection in the United States (Elshtain 1995; Etzioni 1988, 1993; McKnight 1995). As part of this reflection, scholars and social analysts at different places along the political spectrum have begun reviving and refining a social vision of communitarianism in which, in Amitai Etzioni's (1993) words, the "restoration of the community [is] a core mission." For New Left commentator Michael Lerner (in Labonte 1996), the effort is no less that an attempt to "shift the dominant discourse of our society from an ethos of selfishness and cynicism to an ethos of caring and idealism." For the more centrist Etzioni, it calls for a return to the kind of community "in which people do not merely ask 'How are you?' . . but care about the answer."

Health educators, community organizers, and other social change professionals must engage in this discussion, reflection, and debate both to understand the issues and to bring their perspectives to a dialogue that will be critical to the future of communities, community organizing, and community participation. Through such discussions, we can help demonstrate how community organizing can serve as a bridge to thinking more deeply about the collective good not only of this or that community but also of the broader society.

Conclusion

Throughout this chapter, we have been asking hard questions that go to the core of our practice as community organizers. As health educators and other social change professionals, we often operate on the implicit assumption that our interventions are ethically justifiable since they are derived from community-identified needs. Yet the principles of starting where the people are and working closely with communities to translate their goals into reality, while critical to ethically sound practice, do not exempt us from the need to engage in frequent, thoughtful, ethical reflection. All too often, such reflection on the ethical issues in community organizing has been an afterthought, occurring as a result of unanticipated dilemmas and ethical issues. By making it instead an early and continuing part of our organizing efforts, we as professionals can enhance our ability to ensure that the actions we take in working with communities meet the criteria of ethically sound practice.

Although we have tried to address a number of specific ethical dilemmas in this chapter, many others cannot be anticipated, given the ever-changing context in which we work. We must commit ourselves to articulating the dilemmas we face in our practice as community organizers, with special attention to recognizing the contradictions with which we must cope and understanding where our responsibilities lie.

It is critical, moreover, for us to be able to identify and articulate not only the ethical dilemmas we face but also the underlying values that drive our work. How do we communicate the importance of the values of community participation and empowerment when we find ourselves in ethically challenging situations? When conflicting loyalties present us with the task of meeting different needs and different (and sometimes conflicting) agendas, how do we make explicit the values that can help ensure that we do "the right thing"? When our agencies or funders propose what is really only symbolic or lip-service community participation, how do we formulate effective value-based arguments to reinforce the importance of not only bringing community members to the table but also hearing their concerns and ensuring that their input is heavily reflected in the final product? Finally, what role can we play in helping community groups reflect on their own values as a means of grappling with difficult dilemmas over issue selection or whether to accept funding from a potentially ethically problematic source? And what role can we play in helping communities to explore the connections between their perceptions of their own common good and a broader vision of society?

Although we cannot anticipate the possible consequences of all our actions, we can anticipate that some consequences of our community organizing efforts will be different than expected. We must remind ourselves to expect the unexpected and to recognize that in the process we are likely to find ourselves in ethically challenging situations that require discussion, dialogue, and difficult choices.

References

Alinsky, S. D. 1972. *Rules for radicals*. New York: Random House.

Arnstein, S. 1969. A ladder of citizen participation. *Journal of American Institute of Planners* (July):216–224.

Brown E. R., and G. Margo. 1978. Health education: Can the reformers be reformed? *International Journal of Health Services* 8 (1):3–26.

Bunch, C. 1983. The reform tool kit. In *First harvest*, ed. J. Frideman. New York: Grove Press.

Center for Occupational and Environmental Health. 1996. LOHP to work with local Laotian community. *COEH Newsletter* (January):2.

Churchill, L. 1987. *Rationing health care in America: Perceptions and principles of justice*. South Bend, Ind.: University of Notre Dame Press.

Dejong, W., and A. Russell. 1995. MADD's position on alcohol advertising: A response to Marshal and Oleson. *Journal of Public Health Policy* 16 (2):231–238.

Ellis, G. 1996. Personal communication, March 26.

Ellis, G. A., D. F. Reed, and H. Scheider. 1995. Mobilizing a low-income African-American community around tobacco control: A force field analysis. *Health Education Quarterly* 22 (4):443–457.

Elshtain, J. 1995. *Democracy on trial*. New York: Basic Books.

Eng E., and E. Parker. 1994. Measuring community competence in the Mississippi Delta:

The interface between program evaluation and empowerment. *Health Education Quarterly* 21 (2):199–220.

Etzioni, A. 1988. *The moral dimension: Toward a new economics.* New York: Free Press.

———. 1993. *Public policy in a new key.* New Brunswick: Transaction Books.

Freire, P. 1968. *Pedagogy of the oppressed.* New York: Seabury Press.

———. 1973. *Education for critical consciousness.* New York: Seabury Press.

Green, L. W. 1990. The theory of participation: A qualitative analysis of its expression in national and international health policies. In *Community organization: Traditional principles and modern applications,* ed. R. Patton and W. Cissell. Johnson City, Tenn.: Latchpins Press.

Green, L. W., and C. J. Frankish. In press. Finding the right mix of personal, organizational, decentralized, and centralized planning for health promotion. In *Community health promotion,* ed. B. Beerly, E. Wagner, and A. Cheadle. Seattle: University of Washington Press.

Grossman, J. 1971. Health for what? Change, conflict and the search for purpose. *Pacific Health Education Reports* 2:51–66.

Hatch J. W., and Eng, E. 1984. Community participation and control. In *Reforming medicine: Lessons of the last quarter century,* ed. V. Sidel and R. Sidel. New York: Pantheon Books.

Kelman, H. C. 1965. Manipulation of Human behavior: An ethical dilemma for the social scientist. *Journal of Social Issues* 21:31–46.

Kreuter, M. 1992. PATCH: Its origins, basic concepts, and links to contemporary public health policy. *Journal of Health Education* 23 (3):135–139.

Labonte, R. 1990. Empowerment: Notes on professional and community dimensions. *Canadian Review of Social Policy* 26:1–12.

———. 1996. Community development in the public health sector: The possibilities of an empowering relationship between state and civil society. Ph.D. diss., York University.

Leung, Y. L. 1996. Personal communication, March 16.

Marshall, M., and A. Oleson. 1994. In the pink: MADD and public health policy in the 1990s. *Journal of Public Health Policy* 15 (1):54–68.

McKnight, J. 1995. *The careless society: Community and its counterfeits.* New York: Basic Books.

Miller, A. S. 1987. Saul Alinsky: America's radical reactionary. *Radical America* 21 (1):11–18.

Miller, M. 1993. The Tenderloin Senior Organizing Project. In *A journey to justice.* Louisville, Ky.: Presbyterian Committee on the Self-development of People.

Minkler, M. 1978. Ethical issues in community organization. *Health Education Monographs* 6:198–210.

———. 1994. Ten commitments for community health education. *Health Education Research* 9 (4):527–534.

Mondros, J. B., and S. M. Wilson. 1994. *Organizing for power and empowerment.* New York: Columbia University Press.

Neysmith, S. 1990. Closing the gap between health policy and the service needs of tomorrow's elderly. *Canadian Journal of Community Mental Health* 8:141–150.

Nyswander, D. 1956. Education for health: Some principles and their application. *California Health* 14 (November):65–70.

Ovrebo, B., M. Ryan, K. Jackson, and K. Hutchinson. 1994. The homeless prenatal program: A model for empowering homeless pregnant women. *Health Education Quarterly* 21 (2):187–198.

Paget, K. 1990. Citizen organizing: Many movements, no majority. *American Prospect* (Summer):114–128.

Quindlen, A. 1992. Good causes, bad money. *New York Times,* November 15.

Reynolds, C. H., and R. V. Norman, eds. 1988. *Community in America: The challenge of "Habits of the Heart."* Berkeley and Los Angeles: University of California Press.

Robertson, A., and M. Minkler. 1994. New health promotion movement: A critical exam-
    ination. *Health Education Quarterly* 21 (3):295–312.
Rothman, J. 1987. Three models of community organization practice, their mixing, and
    phasing. In *Strategies of community organization*, ed. F. M. Cox, J. L. Erlich, J. Rothman,
    and J. E. Tropman. 4th ed. Itasca, Ill.: Peacock.
Rubin, H., and I. Rubin. 1992. *Community organizing and development*. 2d ed. New York:
    Macmillian.
Siler-Wells, G. L. 1989. Challenges of the gordian knot: Community health in Canada.
    In *International symposium on community participation and empowerment strategies in
    health promotion*. Bielefeld, Germany: Center for Interdisciplinary Studies, University
    of Bielefeld.
Skolnick, A. 1994. Antitobacco advocates fight 'illegal' diversion of tobacco control
    money. *Journal of the American Medical Association* 271:1387–1389.
Thurow, L. 1966. *The future of capitalism*. New York: William Morrow.
Wallerstein, N., and V. Sanchez-Merki. 1994. Freirian praxis in health education: Research
    results from an adolescent prevention program. *Health Education Research* 9 (1):105–118.
Wang, C. 1992. Culture, meaning, and disability: Injury prevention campaigns in the pro-
    duction of stigma. *Social Science and Medicine* 3 (5):1093–1102.

Part IV

Community Assessement

FIELDS SUCH AS health education, health planning, and social work typically focus considerable attention on needs assessment, or the use of a variety of methods to determine the problems and needs being experienced by the groups with which the professionals work. Increasingly, however, the importance of shifting our gaze from a narrowly conceived needs assessment to a broader community assessment has been realized. Reflecting this change in emphasis, the two chapters in this part provide approaches to community assessment that go well beyond needs assessment as it is typically conceived and indeed reject the narrow needs assessment approach as rooted in a "deficit thinking" mentality that can harm, rather than enhance, our efforts at community organizing and community building for health.

Trevor Hancock and Meredith Minkler begin in chapter 9 by posing a series of questions that get to the heart of the whys and hows of community assessment for health. Drawing on the former's extensive experience as a key architect of the Healthy Cities Movement worldwide, they indeed suggest that the very focus of such efforts should move from *community health* assessment to *healthy community* assessment if we are to pay adequate attention to the numerous factors impacting on the health of communities. Arguing that community assessments are needed not only for the information they provide for and about change but also for empowerment, the authors make the case for assessment that is truly of, by, and for the community. Expanding on John McKnight's statement that "institutions learn from studies, communities learn from stories," they further point up the need for collecting both stories and more traditional "study" data as part of a comprehensive assessment process.

Hancock and Minkler use Sylvia Marti-Costa and Irma Serrano-Garcia's categorization of assessment techniques according to the degree of contact with community members that they entail as a framework within which to explore a number of assessment techniques and approaches. This chapter makes a strong case for the use of multiple methods, with an accent placed on those methods that empower individuals and communities, in part through their active involvement in and ownership of the assessment process.

A critical part of the shift from a needs assessment to a community assessment focus involves appreciating that communities are not simply collections of needs or problems but vital entities possessing many strengths and assets. Chapter 10 presents a classic contribution to the community assessment literature, namely, John McKnight and John Kretzmann's approach to "mapping community capacity." Pointing out that the needs-focused approach to low-income communities has led to deficiency-oriented policies and programs, they propose instead a capacity-oriented model. The community mapping technique they provide looks first to "primary building blocks"—those assets such as people and their talents and associations—located in the neighborhood and largely under its control. In a spirit consistent with Cheryl Walter's (chapter 5) expanded notion of community, however, they would also have us consider nonprofit organizations and the like that are located in the neighborhood and that, although largely controlled by outsiders, nevertheless may constitute important "secondary building blocks."

The sample neighborhood needs map and contrasting neighborhood assets map included in this chapter offer students and practitioners a graphic illustration of how changing our orientation from deficiencies to strengths can transform our perceptions of communities, as well as those communities' images of themselves. Although the chapter addresses itself to geographic communities, the approach it demonstrates clearly can be adapted for use in a workplace or common interest community as well.

Community Health Assessment or Healthy Community Assessment

Chapter 9

Whose Community? Whose Health? Whose Assessment?

TREVOR HANCOCK
MEREDITH MINKLER

A GREAT MANY QUESTIONS need to be asked concerning the performance of a community health assessment. In this chapter, we discuss a number of these questions and provide some examples of assessment processes that we believe illustrate promising approaches. As our title implies, we believe that assessment should be of the community, by the community, and for the community if it is to be truly empowering and health promoting.

Why Assess?

In a seminal article written in the early 1980s, Sylvia Marti-Costa and Irma Serrano-Garcia (1983) argued that, far from being neutral or objective, needs assessment is, in reality, an ideological process that can serve political purposes ranging from system maintenance and control to the promotion of social change and consciousness-raising. At one end of the ideological continuum are needs assessments designed to support and justify the status quo. Although they may include some efforts at "first-order change"—what Paul Watzlawick, John Weakland, and Richard Fisch (1974) describe as "fine-tuning" the way the system functions—they do not question or wish to change the ideological commitments on which that system is based (Marti-Costa and Serrano-Garcia 1983). The health educator trying to increase attendance at agency-sponsored community health fairs, for example, might well conduct an assessment to determine whether the event's hours and location were problematic for local residents. But if the agency had already committed to health fairs as its modus operandi for community health outreach, the health educator would not be expected—or wanted—to determine residents' perceptions of whether the fairs really addressed their primary health needs.

In contrast, an assessment open to broader "second-order change" would actively involve community residents in helping the agency or organization critically rethink its mission and activities. The purposes of such an assessment, as Marti-Costa and Serrano-Garcia (1983) have suggested, would be to

Measure, describe, and understand community lifestyles
Assess community resources to lessen external dependency
Return needs assessment data to facilitate residents' decisionmaking
Provide skill training, leadership, and organizational skills
Facilitate collective activities and group mobilization
Enable consciousness-raising

The purposes of a needs assessment and the values and assumptions underlying this process, in short, heavily influence the choice of assessment techniques, the interventions proposed, the utilization of data obtained, and the perceptions of who owns the data in the first place.

Although Marti-Costa and Serrano-Garcia's framework was designed to stimulate critical thinking regarding the goals and purposes of needs assessment as these relate to social services programs, their message is of equal relevance to community health assessment as an initial step in community organizing and community building. For example, a narrowly defined needs assessment designed and conducted by outside experts as a means of justifying and providing raw data for organizing around a predetermined community health need may be effective in achieving its objectives. But by failing to meaningfully involve community members in determining the goals of the assessment process, by focusing solely on needs rather than identifying and building on community strengths, and by failing to make empowerment of people a central goal of the assessment process, such an approach would fail to meet several critical criteria of community organizing and community building practice.

Rationale behind Community Health Assessment

For health professionals concerned with community organizing and community building for health, there are two reasons for the imperative placed on effective and comprehensive community health assessments: information is needed for change, and it is needed for empowerment.

INFORMATION FOR CHANGE

The first kind of information has three purposes: to stimulate change or action, to monitor change or action, and to assess the impact of change (Hancock 1989). Information that will *stimulate change* must carry what has been called "social and political punch." Such information would include hard data and stories that point up differences, particularly inequalities in health and its prerequisites among different groups and sectors in the community. In addition, indicators that carry social and political punch must, of necessity, be sensitive to short-term change given the short-term basis of much social and political action. Information that falls into this category would include stories and data about inequalities in health and the social and physical determinants of health in the community, preferably focusing on inequalities where there is a reasonable chance of seeing some change in a comparatively short period of time. Although it may be important in the long run to document differences in mortality rates for lung cancer or heart disease, for example, this needs to be balanced by information on people's perceived state of health, their social and physical living conditions, and their behaviors, all of which may be more likely to reflect changes in the short term following some policy or community action.

The change rationale for community assessment also involves the need for information about the *processes of change or of action.* In a discussion of healthy cities assessment, Leonard Duhl and Trevor Hancock (1988) note that because the focus is on the processes involved in a given city or community, assessment is heavily dependent on stories and observations rather than on hard data. Activities and related phenomena that appear to be precursors to change itself must be identified. These might include widespread community knowledge of the project, the establishment of participatory mechanisms such as intersectoral committees, evidence of the development of new skills among the population, and indicators of political commitment to the project at the local level. The linking rationale, which can be proved only in the long run, is that these activities will lead to other actions that will ultimately lead to better health.

Information that will *assess the impact of change* on health can function as a baseline of the individual and community dimensions of health. Here health is defined broadly to include physical, mental, and social well-being in both subjective and objective terms. Regular repetitions of the baseline measures via surveys and other instruments must be conducted to assess change.

INFORMATION FOR EMPOWERMENT

An entirely different reason for wanting information about health, and one of at least equal importance, is that knowledge is power and is therefore a component of empowerment. As noted in earlier chapters, the process of empowerment is central to, and indeed forms the core of, the World Health Organization's (1986) definition of health promotion. Individuals and communities can become truly empowered only if they have the knowledge required to assess their situation and to take action—backed by sufficient power—to make change happen (Hancock 1989).

The most obvious way of defining and obtaining information is to ask the community itself for its definition of a good or healthy community. In so doing, the health education or health promotion professional is helped to identify the most important components about which information must be collected. But by asking the community how to define health, assess progress, and measure change, the outside professional is also helping to further the process of empowerment.

If the community is to use information, it must be information that is easily collected by the community and easily understood and used by its members. Whether hard data or stories, the information must therefore be physically, socially, and culturally accessible to the community. Information should be presented via local media and be placed in local community settings such as libraries, community centers, faith organizations, and schools.

Reports need to be written simply, in plain English and/or in the dominant language of the community; even in postindustrial nations such as Canada and the United States between 21 and 25 percent of the population is either functionally illiterate or operating at the lowest level of literacy (Ontario Public Health Association/Frontier College 1989; U.S. Department of Education 1993). Thus, in addition to written information, it is important to disseminate information in audio and video formats through the media that the majority of the population routinely use.

Information from the healthy community assessment also can and should be used as the basis for study groups, work circles, and other adult and popular education strategies, including literacy training and English as a second language (ESL) courses. A good example of the latter can be seen in the work of Leadership to Improve Neighborhood Communication and Services, a neighborhood affiliate of the Healthy Boston project in the linguistically diverse Allston-Brighton area. A communitywide assessment meeting, conducted in half a dozen languages and attended by over three hundred people, uncovered concerns about inadequate housing, AIDS, and other topics. An effort then was made to incorporate some of these issues into the neighborhood's ESL programs. By combining ESL with leadership training, advocacy training, and field internships for over forty residents, the project further helped create a cadre of individuals who could serve as "cultural liaisons" between their cultural community and health and social service agencies, as well as the larger city and neighborhood (Lupo 1994; Dufour 1996).

Knowing how well one's community functions, how much it cares about the well-being and quality of life of its citizens, and how choices that affect health are made—and by whom—enables people to more fully and actively participate in the life of the community. This is a fundamental basis of health promotion and, even more broadly, of citizenship. And it underscores the importance of disseminating the information gleaned from a healthy community assessment through literacy training and a host of other channels.

Whose Community, Whose Health?

We have referred thus far to "the community." But as earlier chapters have suggested, the real question is, Which community are we referring to? Health educators and other health promotion professionals working with geographic communities often focus their attention on a particular neighborhood, and this is indeed the level with which people tend to identify. Yet since one of the intents of the healthy city/community process is to stimulate local government involvement in and commitment to improving the health of the community, the boundaries for assessment may also often be municipal boundaries. Within—and overlapping the boundaries of—any single municipality, of course, is a large number of smaller "communities." The first challenge, then, is to assess the healthy community process and situation both at the municipal level and at the level of the community or neighborhood.

The second challenge we face is to conceptualize health in a broad enough manner that we are able to look well beyond such traditional indicators as morbidity and mortality to embrace the World Health Organization's (1948) view of health as "a state of complete physical, mental and social well being, and not merely the absence of disease and infirmity." Community members know from their own experience that health is much more than the absence of illness or dysfunction, and they often have creative and meaningful ways of conceptualizing health for themselves. The challenge for the health professional is to pay more attention to how the members of the community define health and to incorporate their definitions for assessing the health of the community.

Needs or Capacities?

In chapter 2, John McKnight describes the importance of the "associational life," or the informal and formal community-based organizations and networks that form the underpinnings of the community. This is similar to what Robert Putnam (1993) calls "civicness" or social solidarity. As suggested in chapter 2, McKnight has been particularly concerned with having professionals change their focus from *individual and community deficits* that requires services to *assets and capacities* that enable community building. (See the next chapter for an approach to identifying and mapping these capacities.)

The implications of such a 180-degree shift in how we view people and communities are profound. For they suggest that we should reevaluate the entire way in which we conceive of the role of professionals in the community—as enablers and facilitators rather than providers of services—and the purpose of those services. From the perspective of assessment of the community's health, McKnight's approach has two important implications. First, it underscores the importance of assessing capacity and not merely "needs," and second, it reminds us that the process of that assessment should itself contribute to the capacity of people and communities and to community health.

Community Health Assessment or Healthy Community Assessment?

To understand the difference between a community health assessment and a healthy community assessment, it is necessary to begin with a clear understanding of what is meant by the term *healthy community*. The most commonly accepted definition was promulgated by Hancock and Duhl for WHO in 1986 (24): "A healthy [community] is one that is continually creating and improving those physical and social environments and expanding those community resources which enable people to mutually support each other in performing all the functions of life and in developing to their maximum potential."

There are several important points in this definition, key among them being that it is a definition of a process rather than of a status. Thus, even though high health status and low mortality and morbidity are important, a healthy community is not necessarily one that has the highest health status in a conventional sense, but one that is striving with every fiber of its being to be more healthy. Ideally, this would be reflected in a commitment at all levels from the political to the personal, across all sectors, and involving all stakeholders and indeed all members of the community around the common focus of improving the health, well-being, and quality of life of the community and its members. The closer a community is to this ideal, the closer it is to being a healthy community.

Reviewing a wide range of literature, Hancock and Duhl (1986) suggest the following eleven key elements of a healthy community:

1. A clean, safe, high-quality environment (including housing quality)
2. An ecosystem that is stable now and sustainable in the long term
3. A strong, mutually supportive, and nonexploitative community
4. A high degree of public participation in and control over the decisions affecting one's life, health, and well-being
5. The meeting of basic needs (food, water, shelter, income, safety, work) for all the city's people
6. Access to a wide variety of experiences and resources, with the possibility of multiple contacts, interaction, and communication
7. A diverse, vital, and innovative city economy
8. Encouragement of connectedness with the past, with the cultural and biological heritage, and with other groups and individuals
9. A city form that is compatible with and enhances the preceding parameters and behaviors

10. An optimum level of appropriate public health and sick care services accessible to all
11. High health status (both high positive health status and low disease status)

Only one of these eleven refers directly to health status, which is the usual focus of a community health assessment. As Hancock and Duhl contend, a community health assessment is just one component of a healthy community assessment. Furthermore, high positive health status and low mortality and morbidity are not the same. For example, a person can be healthy while dying, or a person who is a quadriplegic can be healthy in the sense that his or her mental and social well-being is high and physical health is as good as it can be.

A good place to begin a healthy community assessment is to consider the classical epidemiological elements of place, time, and person. Here, however, place refers to the geography and environment of the community, time refers to its history and development, and person refers to the demographic profile of the community. There is much that can be learned about the community's health by understanding these aspects of the community. The geography will reveal some of the factors likely to affect health, such as climate, natural resources (especially water and food sources), natural hazards, air and water quality, and wind direction, all of which usually define where low-income populations will live (downwind, downstream, and downhill—or uphill if the hills are dangerous!). The community's history provides important information on the major economic, political, and social forces that have shaped the community's evolution and that explain many of the present circumstances that influence the health of the community. Finally, the community's present demography—such factors as age and gender distribution, racial/ethnic and socioeconomic characteristics—provides further information that enables us to anticipate some of the health-related issues facing the community.

Specific issues can be examined regarding each of the eleven components of a healthy community and others that are considered important by the community.

> Do people in the community have access to such basic prerequisites for health as food, shelter, education, clean water, clean and safe environments, and sustainable resources?
> What is the degree of equity (or inequity) in the community?
> How strong is civic or associational life?
> How do urban design and architecture affect health in this community?
> What is being done to improve health?
> How rich is the cultural life of the community, its artistic, creative, and innovative elements?

What is the environmental quality of the community, what is its
   impact on regional and local ecosystems, and what is being done
   to minimize that impact?
Does everyone have access to basic primary care?

Several illustrations are useful in demonstrating what such an approach to
assessment might look like. The quality-of-life indicators in Pittsburgh, Pennsylvania, for example, include the amount of overcrowded housing, the high
school dropout rate, mass transit miles per capita, and the child abuse rate (University of Pittsburgh 1993). Similarly, the "sustainable Seattle" indicators
include wild salmon runs through local streams, gallons of water consumed per
capita, usage rates for libraries and community centers, and "provocative"
indicators (items for which the quality and validity of the data may be in
doubt but that make people think, such as the amount of beef eaten per capita
compared to the amount of vegetables eaten). Finally, a community in Hawaii
identified the presence of Manapua trucks—small fast-food trucks that visit local
communities—as an indicator of declining community health for four reasons:
they replace home cooking and family dining, the nutritional quality of the food
they provide is poor, they make it easier for children to buy cigarettes, and they
harm local businesses by undercutting them and taking money out of the community. As these examples suggest, communities can offer thoughtful indexes
of local health status.

A healthy community assessment would also need to look at the processes under
way in the community that are believed to be related to health and the extent to
which health is taken into account and/or is a focus for action. On the level of
the city or formally defined municipality, for example:

Does the municipal council take health into account in its policy
   deliberations?
Is there a mechanism for health impact assessment?
Do the local planning department and other government bodies
   understand the impacts of planning and design on health?
Is the economic sector (e.g., the chamber of commerce, business
   improvement associations) part of the process?
Do businesses understand the importance of health for their
   activities?
Do they understand the importance of equitable access to the basic
   determinants of health for the entire population?
Are neighborhood and resident groups involved? In what way?
Are the environmental groups and organizations involved? The
   school boards? Faith organizations? The police? Local politicians at
   all levels of government?

Finally, a healthy community assessment would take the time to determine not only formal leadership at the local level but also those informal leaders who can be identified through such methods as reputational and decisional analysis. The former technique involves having knowledgeable community members formally or informally "nominate" residents who play a powerful role in community affairs. The latter technique has informants describe recent community decisions and the roles played by various key participants in actually bringing about those decisions (Swanson and Swanson 1977). By studying the processes of community action and change on multiple levels and uncovering multiple players in these processes, the healthy community assessment greatly broadens its potential for subsequently involving these diverse stakeholders in building a healthier community.

We have argued so far that several categories of information for and about health are needed for assessment at the local level. These include the following:

People's perceptions of the strengths and resources of their communities, as well as their individual and collective health and well-being

Stories about the formal and informal processes of developing healthy cities and healthy communities

Data and stories about the community's physical and social environment

Data and stories about inequities in health and about the prerequisites necessary to address these inequities

Health status data, at the neighborhood or small-area level, incorporating mortality and morbidity data and both subjective and objective assessments of physical, mental, and social well-being   (Hancock 1989)

This is a much broader approach than is usually thought of when professionals develop a community health status report, which is for the most part concerned with only the last of these categories. A healthy community assessment is much more than a community health assessment.

How Do We Assess?

Knowing what to assess is only part of the approach to healthy community assessment; we also need to determine how the process can contribute to the health of the community. This question of the process of assessment is a vital one, requiring that we consider carefully both the type of information that is collected and the degree of contact with the community during the data collection process.

THE TYPE OF INFORMATION COLLECTED

As John McKnight is fond of pointing out, "Institutions learn from studies; communities learn from stories." Just as there is a critical difference between needs assessment and community assessment, important differences exist between the two main types of information for health on the community level—studies and stories. Studies are usually data rich and are carried out by academics and professionals. The data are analyzed to yield information, but the knowledge that is acquired is seldom transferred to the community, and as a result there is little increase in wisdom. Stories, in contrast, represent the accumulated and almost folkloric wisdom of a community. Stories contain knowledge that can be adapted and applied by other communities but seldom contain information in the form of hard data. Thus, for the most part stories hold little interest for academics and professionals. But if one accepts that knowledge is power and that stories are a means of transferring knowledge between and within communities, the empowering potential of stories as a source of information about health becomes apparent.

Both stories and studies have an important role to play in our efforts to assess health and well-being at the local level. People can learn much about the health of their communities by listening to and telling stories, whether around the kitchen table, at community meetings, through the media, or through events that celebrate successes or acknowledge loss. More structured means of exchanging stories can occur, taking the form of newsletters, videos, collections of stories (Ontario Healthy Communities Coalition 1994), or workshops at conferences or at regional, national, or international meetings.

Stories can form the basis of studies, with qualitative ethnographic research often providing a more formal means of listening to and learning from stories. The work of Penelope Canan (1993) and her colleagues in Molokai is illustrative. When these researchers asked villagers what they valued about their communities, one of the things they identified was "the slow pace of life." When then asked how to measure pace of life, community members suggested counting the number of alarm clocks in each village: if the number of alarm clocks went up, the villagers were clearly losing their slow pace of life. As this story illustrates, people know what is important to them, and they have the ability to identify innovative and meaningful measures that make sense in their own community. Ethnographic studies and other means of gathering and really listening to people's stories can provide critical information for an assessment of community health and well-being.

Of course, quantitative approaches and studies, have an important role to play in assessing communities and community health. Such approaches can provide documentation of health inequalities within and between communities, which are often starkly dramatized through studies of infant mortality rates and the like. Quantitative methods often have the advantages of perceived scientific rigor, large denominators, and forms of data analysis that make the findings readily accessible to policymakers and others who "need the numbers" to make a case for new legislation or other proposed actions. For quantitative studies to live up to their potential with regard to being an empowering community assessment, however, they must be empowering, transferring information and knowledge to members of the community and, ideally, involving community members in the research process as well. This approach, known as participatory research, has particular relevance to health promotion (Green 1995).

Two case examples are illustrative of how this empowerment may be achieved. The Oakland, California–based Grandparent Caregiver Study (Minkler and Roe 1993) was primarily concerned with exploring, through both quantitative and qualitative measures, the health and social status of African-American grandmothers who were raising young children as a consequence of the crack cocaine epidemic. Before any instruments were developed or data collected, however, local community-based organizations were sought out for their input, and a community advisory committee was established. Consisting primarily of older African-American women, the committee was heavily involved in decisionmaking about all aspects of the proposed study, including the topics and questions to be included. Once the initial data were collected, moreover, findings were presented first to the study participants themselves, both by word and in an easy to read, nontechnical report. At a luncheon in their honor, the seventy-one participants were consulted about where they wanted to see the information taken and which findings they felt most needed to be highlighted (and in one case, held back) in order to best benefit the community (Roe, Minkler, and Saunders 1995).

A similar accent on listening to the community, building its concerns into the research, and then "giving back" findings to facilitate empowerment can be found in the "State of the City Report" developed by the Healthy City Office in Toronto, Ontario (Toronto Healthy City Office 1994). The study began by determining what people said was important to the health of the city. The Healthy City Office then collected both data and stories that illustrated the extent to which the city was or was not healthy in the seven areas identified (housing, education, the economy, etc.). In addition to producing a thick report containing many pictures, charts, quotes, and stories, as well as hard data, the Healthy City Office generated a "citizen's guide," in plain language, containing highlights of the report, as well as pertinent questions. The intention was to have the Citizen's Guide become a basis for study circles that would enable residents to ask and discuss questions about the health of their own neighborhood or community, as well as the health of the city as a whole.

In short, a balance of studies and stories make up the information needed to assess communities and community health. How this information is collected, the purposes for which it is sought, and whether the findings are then returned to the community play a critical role in determining the empowering potential of the assessment process.

THE DEGREE OF CONTACT WITH THE COMMUNITY

Numerous techniques and approaches can be employed to obtain the types of information needed, and a comprehensive listing is beyond the scope of this chapter.
A helpful framework for thinking about these alternative methods, however, is
provided in Marti-Costa and Serrano-Garcia's (1983) suggestion that assessment techniques can be grouped into categories defined by the extent to which
they involve contact between the outside professional and members of the community. Since contact with and high-level involvement of community residents
in the assessment process are vital parts of community organizing and community building for health, special attention should be given to methods that foster community involvement and consciousness-raising as part of the assessment
process. At the same time, as noted earlier, the utility of studies that produce hard
data, including some that may involve no-contact or minimal contact methods,
should be appreciated.

NO-CONTACT METHODS. Demographic and social indicators, such as divorce and
unemployment rates and morbidity and mortality statistics are often the first
types of data looked at by health professionals charged with conducting a community needs assessment. Presented in the form of rates and percentages, small-
area analyses, or dynamic modeling, studies using such data often have the
advantages of a large numerical base and/or a representative sample and an aura
of "scientific objectivity." No-contact methods such as multivariate analysis can
document such factors as the impacts of race and class on mortality rates in
neighboring communities; as such, these methods can provide information that
may be vital in demonstrating health inequalities in a format that legislators and
advocacy groups can use in fighting for health resources.

However, utilization of such methods is based on the assumption that
"the community needs and problems that appear in official statistics are representative of community problems" (Marti-Costa and Serrano-Garcia 1983,
81). That assumption, of course, is not always warranted. As Linda Nettekoven
and Norman Sundberg (1985) point out, for example, treatment statistics may
indicate a dramatic change in the types of mental health problems in a given
community when what it fact has changed are the service categories for which
mental health agencies receive funding. Mental health professionals thus may
simply be using "creative labeling" in order to continue treating persons they
believe to be in need!

In addition to statistical studies, no-contact methods often include documents
review, with pertinent "documents" including community newspapers or newsletters,
written progress reports from health departments or other agencies, and community bulletin boards, whose contents may give a flavor for the kinds of issues and
resources represented in a given community. Like the collection by outside pro-

fessionals of health and other demographic and social indicator data, such methods, when used without community involvement, lack the potential to facilitate local empowerment or mobilization (Marti-Costa and Serrano-Garcia 1983).

Increasingly, however, the term *no-contact methods* is becoming something of a misnomer. With the advent of accessible computer technology, for example, opportunities are expanding for community members to be involved in the collection and use of data that were formerly within the exclusive purview of researchers and health professionals. Jeffrey Gould's (1994) small-area health analysis provides a good case in point. Through community workshops and similar educational forums, local community groups have been trained to access and use via personal computers previously unavailable data on perinatal outcomes and other health indicators specific to their zip codes or neighborhoods (Gould 1996). By training community members and actively involving them in such aspects of the assessment process, professionals can greatly expand the empowering potential of many so-called no-contact methods.

MINIMAL CONTACT OBSERVATIONAL METHODS. A variety of observational methods may be useful for the health professional wishing to gain some initial impressionistic sense of the community with which he or she will be working. Roland Warren (Warren and Warren 1977); Ronald Braithwaite, Cynthia Bianchi, and Sandra Taylor (1994); Eugenia Eng and Lynn Blanchard (1990–1991); and Linda Nettekoven and Norman Sundberg (1985) all propose the initial use of a neighborhood "windshield tour" or walk-through. The health educator or other social change professional is advised to walk or drive slowly through a neighborhood, ideally on different days of the week and at different times of the day, while being "on the lookout" for a whole variety of potentially useful indicators of community health and well-being. As described in appendix 1, observing the condition of houses and automobiles, the nature and degree of activity level, and social interaction between residents and the like can provide the health educator with valuable impressionistic information. Similarly, sitting in a neighborhood coffee shop, or observing at a community forum or PTA meeting, can provide useful initial insights.

As in the case of the no-contact methods, minimal contact methods can be modified in ways that enable community involvement and hold the potential for facilitating empowerment. Community organizer James Kent (1970), for example, has advocated that members of a community be trained to look at their community "through a stranger's eyes," checking their assumptions about how things should be in order to examine how things really are. Community members, and not merely outsiders, thus could undertake a windshield tour or in other ways gather "fresh" impressionistic data, which could then be shared and compared with that of other members of the assessment team. Once again, if our goal in community assessment is not solely to stimulate, monitor, and assess the impact of change but also to further empowerment, exploiting opportunities for increased community contact and involvement is critical.

INTERACTIVE CONTACT METHODS. This category of methods includes techniques such as key informant interviews, door-to-door surveys, and a variety of small-group methods for eliciting data and stories about a local community. Among the latter, three are particularly deserving of mention. The first of these, discussed in detail in chapter 12, is Paulo Freire's (1973) *education for critical consciousness*. Through the use of a problem-posing method, group members are asked questions that cause them to critically reflect on their lives and the life of their community. The "generative themes" that emerge from this process, and that capture the hopes and concerns of the people, frequently offer rich insights into their assessments of community and community health.

A second small-group method with particular utility in community assessment is Andre Delbecq, Andrew Van de Ven, and David Gustafson's (1975) *nominal group process*. A structured process designed to foster creativity, encourage conflicting opinions, and prevent domination by a few vocal individuals (Siegel, Attkisson, and Cohn 1977), the nominal group method is especially helpful in encouraging the participation of marginal group members.

Finally, *focus groups* hold perhaps the greatest current appeal among small-group methods used in community assessment. The focus group brings together, under the direction of a professional moderator, a small group of community members who, in a confidential and nonthreatening discussion, address a series of questions concerning their feelings about their community (Stewart and Shamdasani 1990). Employed by health agencies, philanthropic foundations, community-based organizations, and local policymakers, focus groups have considerable potential for providing the stories and perceptions that can greatly enrich the overall community assessment.

Although contact methods by definition involve community residents, their potential for truly facilitating empowerment depends on the how these methods are employed. Focus groups and key informant interviews, for example, can be disempowering if they only seek information about community needs and problems and ignore or discount the participants' knowledge of their community's resources and assets. In contrast, a contribution to community capacity building may be made when questions are asked that encourage residents to reflect on and contribute to a broader understanding of community strengths. Such questions might include "What are the things you like best about your community?" "What makes this a good or healthy community in which to live?" "Who do people go to, to get things done?" and "How have people here come together in the past to make a decision or solve a problem?"

By revealing an appreciation of the community by the outsider, and engaging informants in a process of thinking critically about the strengths and competencies of their community, such questions can make a real difference in the information obtained and in the community's willingness to be actively involved in the assessment process. Finally, training community members to conduct surveys and interviews themselves (and compensating them for their work) can contribute significantly not only to the assessment process but also to individual and community empowerment. The training of homeless persons to conduct an assessment with their peers for the University of California at Berkeley's "Suitcase Clinic" facilitated the attaining of far more sensitive information about the real needs and strengths of this population than the medical student volunteers had been able to attain by themselves. But it also enabled these homeless persons to gain self-confidence and skills that some could then draw upon in working to change their own lives (Ratner 1995). Similarly, the "Shooting Back" project in Washington, D.C., which provides homeless children with cameras and skills in photography (Hubbard 1991), is, as Caroline Wang and Mary Ann Burris (1994, 177) note, part of "the genre that allows the most vulnerable people within a society to convey their own vision of the world." Further developed by Wang and Burris (in press) as "photovoice," this approach offers new and "imaginative models for integrating community participation, health concerns and the visual image."

MULTIMETHOD ASSESSMENT   Clearly, no one method or approach to community assessment can capture the richness and complexity of communities and community health. A strong case should therefore be made for the use of multiple methods, or what researchers refer to as "triangulation." The U.S. Centers for Disease Control's PATCH model (Kreuter 1992) and the collaboratively developed Assessment Protocol for Excellence in Public Health (APEXPH) (1991) both include elaborate multimethod approaches to community assessment as a precursor to action plans for addressing priority health issues. Directed respectively to state and local health departments, both models emphasize the collection of hard data on a community's health status and needs, information on health department organizational capacity, and community participation in the identification of health issues and community resources and in the development of health promotion strategies.

Of course, the promise of methods such as PATCH and APEXPH has not always been fully realized. Ronald Labonte (1994) and George Bogan et al. (1992) cite a PATCH application in Chicago in which a community opinion survey's finding that violence and drugs were of major concern to residents was "put on the back burner" by health professionals so that they might attend to the problem of heart disease, for which funding was available. Similarly, Marshall Kreuter

(1995, 7) notes that in a few PATCH sites, what was being called community participation "was often a collection of health officials and formal interest groups talking to one another, with little or no attention being paid to the perceived needs of those they were supposed to be serving." Although such models as APEXPH and PATCH have a distance to go before the reality of their implementation matches the ideal, their expressed appreciation of the need for multimethod assessments that accent community participation and their increasing concern with facilitating this represent an important step forward.

On a much more modest scale, a good example of a multimethod approach to community assessment for health can be found in the assessment component of Braithwaite et al.'s (1994) Community Organization and Development approach to health promotion. Specifically designed to foster community empowerment in low-income communities of color, the COD model stresses "participatory ethnography," through which community members are involved with outside health educators in developing a systematic description of the health needs and resources of their neighborhoods. Personal interviews, surveys, videotaped documentation of the perceptions of local leaders, and focus groups designed to identify and prioritize health concerns are among the methods utilized. The development of a community resource inventory and the conducting of community forums similarly are among the participatory activities included in this component of the assessment.

But the COD approach also includes the obtaining of geographic and demographic information from local community planning and development agencies, including "block statistical maps" identifying census tracks and a variety of health indicator data (Braithwaite et al. 1989). The result is a rich portrait of a community and its health profile and priorities, which then serves as the basis for community action and change.

Regardless of the scale on which a community assessment is conducted, it is likely to be most effective if it combines multiple methods, respects both stories and studies, and places its heaviest emphasis on eliciting high-level community participation throughout the assessment process.

Summary

This chapter has attempted to build on the ideological framework provided by Marti-Costa and Serrano-Garcia (1983), as well as more recent insights developed through the Healthy Cities Movement, to propose an empowering approach to community assessment for health. Both stories and studies are vital if we are to stimulate, monitor, and assess the impact of change and at the same time facilitate the empowerment that comes with knowledge, specifically with the transfer of knowledge to communities. Likewise, no single assessment tool or technique is sufficient in and of itself to sensitively and accurately capture community or community health. That is better accomplished by multiple methods, especially those that serve to empower individuals and communities while making explicit the realities of the community, its resources, and its health.

References

Assessment protocol for excellence in public health. 1991. Washington D.C.: Centers for Disease Control/National Association of County Health Officials.

Bogan, G. III, A. Omar, S. Knobloch, L. Liburd, and T. O'Rourke 1992. Organizing an urban African-American community for health promotion: Lessons from Chicago. *Journal of Health Education* 23 (3):157–159.

Braithwaite, R. L., C. Bianchi, and S. E. Taylor. 1994. Ethnographic approach to community organization and health empowerment. *Health Education Quarterly* 21 (3):407–416.

Braithwaite, R. L., F. Murphy, N. Lythcott, and D. S. Blumenthal. 1989. Community organization and development for health promotion within an urban black community: A conceptual model. *Health Education* 2 (5):56–60.

Canan, P. 1993. Presentation at Emory University/CDC workshop on quality-of-life indicators, Atlanta, Georgia.

Delbecq, A., A. H. Van de Ven, and D. H. Gustafson. 1975. *Group techniques for program planning: A guide to nominal group and delphi processes.* Glenview, Ill.: Scott, Foresman.

Dufour, H. 1996. Personal communication, April 23.

Duhl, L., and T. Hancock. 1988. *A guide to assessing healthy cities.* Copenhagen: FADL.

Eng, E., and L. Blanchard. 1990–1991. Action-oriented community diagnosis: A health education tool. *International Journal of Community Health Education* 11 (2):93–110.

Freire, P. 1973. *Education for critical consciousness.* New York: Seabury Press.

Gould, J. 1996. Personal communication, April 16.

Gould, J. B. 1994. Pitfalls of summary statistics and workable solutions. In *Quantitative problem solving in maternal child health,* ed. J. B. Gould. Oakland, Calif.: Third Party.

Green, L. W. 1995. Study of participatory research in health promotion: Review and recommendations for the development of participatory research in health promotion in Canada. Vancouver: Institute of Health Promotion Research, University of British Columbia/B.C. Consortium for Health Promotion Research. Unpublished report.

Hancock, T. 1989. Information for health at the local level: Community stories and healthy city indicators. Unpublished paper.

Hancock, T., and L. Duhl. 1986. *Healthy cities: Promoting health in the urban context.* Copenhagen: WHO Europe.

Hubbard, J. 1991. *Shooting back: A photographic view of life by homeless children.* San Francisco: Chronicle Books.

Kent, J. A. 1970. Descriptive approach to a community clinic. Denver. Unpublished report prepared for the city of Denver.

Kreuter, M. 1992. PATCH: Its origins, basic concepts, and links to contemporary public health policy. *Journal of Health Education* 23 (3):135–139.

————. 1995. A brief, biased, and limited history of community-based strategies to prevent and control chronic disease. Paper presented to the National Chronic Disease Conference, Atlanta, Georgia, December 7.

Labonte, R. 1994. Health promotion and empowerment: Reflections on professional practice. *Health Education Quarterly* 21 (2):253–268.

Lupo, A. 1994. Tracing neighborhood needs. *Boston Globe,* July.

Marti-Costa, S., and I. Serrano-Garcia. 1983. Needs assessment and community development: An ideological perspective. *Prevention in Human Services* (Summer):75–88.

Minkler, M., and K. M. Roe. 1993. *Grandmothers as caregivers: Raising children of the crack cocaine epidemic.* Newbury Park, Calif.: Sage.

Nettekoven, L., and N. Sundberg. 1985. Community assessment methods in rural mental health promotion. *Journal of Rural Community Psychology* 6 (2):21–43.

Ontario Healthy Communities Coalition. 1994. *Stories to guide action.* Toronto: Ontario Healthy Communities Coalition.

Ontario Public Health Association/Frontier College. 1989. *The literacy and health project: Making the world healthier and safer for people who can't read.* Toronto: Ontario Public Health Association/Frontier College.

Putnam, R. 1993. *Making democracy work.* Princeton: Princeton University Press.

Ratner, R. 1995. Personal communication, October 16.

Roe, K. M., M. Minkler, and F. F. Saunders. 1995. Combining research, advocacy, and education: The methods of the grandparent caregiver study. *Health Education Quarterly* 22 (4):458–475.

Siegel, L. M., C. C. Attkisson, and I. H. Cohn. 1977. Mental health needs assessment: Strategies and techniques. In *Resource materials for community mental health program evaluation,* ed. W. A. Hargreaves and C. C. Attkisson. 2d ed. Washington, D.C.: GPO.

Stewart, D., and P. Shamdasani. 1990. *Focus groups: Theory and practice.* Newbury Park, Calif.: Sage.

Swanson, B. E., and E. Swanson. 1977. *Discovering the community.* New York: Irvington.

Toronto Healthy City Office. 1994. *The state of the city.* Toronto: Beacon Press.

University of Pittsburgh. 1993. *Pittsburgh benchmarks: Quality-of-life indices for the City of Pittsburgh and Allegheny County.* Pittsburgh: University Center for Social and Urban Research.

U.S. Department of Education. 1993. *National Association of Literacy survey.* Washington, D.C.: Office of Educational Research and Improvement, September.

Wang, C., and M. A. Burris. 1994. Empowerment through photo novella: Portraits of participation. *Health Education Quarterly* 21 (2):171–186.

———. In press. Photovoice: Concepts, methodology, and use for participatory needs assessment. *Health Education Quarterly.*

Warren, R. B., and D. I. Warren. 1977. *The neighborhood organizer's handbook.* South Bend, Ind.: University of Notre Dame Press.

Watzlawick, P., J. Weakland, and R. Fisch. 1974. *Change: Principles of problem formation and problem resolution.* New York: Norton.

World Health Organization. 1948. Constitution of the World Health Organization. Adopted by the International Health Conference in New York, 1946, and entered into force April 7, 1948.

———. 1986. *Ottawa charter for health promotion.* Copenhagen: WHO Europe.

Chapter 10	Mapping Community Capacity

JOHN L. McKNIGHT
JOHN P. KRETZMANN

No ONE CAN DOUBT that our older cities these days are deeply troubled places. At the root of the problem are the massive economic shifts that have marked the last two decades. Hundreds of thousands of industrial jobs have either disappeared or moved away from the central city and its neighborhoods. And while many down-town areas have experienced a "renaissance," the jobs created there are different from those that once sustained neighborhoods. Either these new jobs are highly professionalized, and require elaborate education and credentials for entry, or they are routine, low-paying service jobs without much of a future. If effect, these shifts in the economy, and particularly the removal of decent employment possibilities from low-income neighborhoods, have removed the bottom rung from the fabled American "ladder of opportunity." For many people in older city neighborhoods, new approaches to rebuilding their lives and communities, new openings toward opportunity, are a vital necessity.

Traditional Needs–oriented Solutions

Given the desperate situation, it is no surprise that most Americans think about lower-income urban neighborhoods as problems. They are noted for their defi-ciencies and needs. This view is accepted by most elected officials, who codify and program this perspective through deficiency-oriented policies and programs. Then, human service systems—often supported by foundations and universities— translate the programs into local activities that teach people the nature of their

Adapted from *Mapping Community Capacity* (Evanston, Ill.: Center for Urban Affairs and Policy Research, Northwestern University, 1988), by permission of the authors.

problems and the value of services as the answer to their problems. As a result, many low-income urban neighborhoods are now environments of service where behaviors are affected because residents come to believe that their well-being depends upon being a client. They see themselves as people with special needs to be met by outsiders. And gradually, they become mainly consumers of services with no incentive to be producers. Consumers of services focus vast amounts of creativity and intelligence on the survival-motivated challenge of outwitting the "system" or on finding ways—in the informal or even illegal economy—to bypass the system entirely.

There is nothing "natural" about this process. Indeed, it is the predictable course of events when deficiency- and needs-oriented programs come to dominate the lives of neighborhoods where low-income people reside.

The Capacity-focused Alternative

The alternative is to develop policies and activities based on the capacities, skills, and assets of low-income people and their neighborhoods.

There are two reasons for this capacity-oriented emphasis. First, all the historic evidence indicates that significant community development only takes place when local community people are committed to investing themselves and their resources in the effort. This is why you can't develop communities from the top down, or from the outside in. You can, however, provide valuable outside assistance to communities that are actively developing their own assets.

The second reason for emphasizing the development of the internal assets of local urban neighborhoods is that there is very little prospect that large-scale industrial or service corporations will be locating in these neighborhoods. Nor is it likely that significant new inputs of federal money will be forthcoming soon. Therefore, it is increasingly futile to wait for significant help to arrive from outside the community. The hard truth is that development must start from within the community and, in most of our urban neighborhoods, there is no other choice.

Unfortunately, the dominance of the deficiency-oriented social service model has led many people in low-income neighborhoods to think in terms of local needs rather than assets. These needs are often identified, quantified, and mapped by conducting "needs surveys." The result is a map of the neighborhood's illiteracy, teenage pregnancy, criminal activity, drug use, etc.

But in neighborhoods where there are effective community development efforts, there is also a map of the community's assets, capacities, and abilities. For it is clear that even the poorest city neighborhood is a place where individuals and organizations represent resources upon which to rebuild. The key to neighborhood regeneration is not only to build upon those resources which the community already controls, but to harness those that are not yet available for local development purposes.

The process of identifying capacities and assets, both individual and organizational, is the first step on the path toward community regeneration. Once this new "map" has replaced the one containing needs and deficiencies, the regenerating community can begin to assemble its assets and capacities into new combinations, new structures of opportunity, new sources of income and control, and new possibilities for production.

Mapping the Building Blocks for Regeneration

It is useful to begin by recognizing that not all community assets are equally available for community-building purposes. Some are more accessible than others. The most easily accessible assets, or building blocks, are those that are located in the neighborhood and controlled by those who live in the neighborhood.

The next most accessible are those assets that are located in the neighborhood but controlled elsewhere.

The least accessible are those potential building blocks located outside the neighborhood and controlled by those outside the neighborhood.

Therefore, we will "map" community assets based upon the accessibility of assets to local people. We turn now to a more detailed discussion of each of these clusters of building blocks.

PRIMARY BUILDING BLOCKS—ASSETS AND CAPACITIES
LOCATED INSIDE THE NEIGHBORHOOD,
LARGELY UNDER NEIGHBORHOOD CONTROL

This cluster of capacities includes those that are most readily available for neighborhood regeneration. They fall into two general categories: the assets and capacities of individuals and those of organizations or associations. The first step in capturing *any* of these resources is to assess them, which often involves making an *inventory*.

INDIVIDUAL CAPACITIES.   Our greatest assets are our people. But people in low-income neighborhoods are seldom regarded as "assets." Instead, they are usually seen as needy and deficient, suited best for life as clients and recipients of services. Therefore, they are often subjected to systematic and repeated inventories of their deficiencies with a device called a "needs survey."

The starting point for any serious development effort is the opposite of an accounting of deficiencies. Instead, there must be an opportunity for individuals to use their own abilities to produce. Identifying the variety and richness of skills, talents, knowledge, and experience of people in low-income neighborhoods provides a base upon which to build new approaches and enterprises.

To assist in identifying the skills and abilities of individuals, an inventory of capacities can be developed—a simple survey designed to identify the multitude of abilities within each individual. Neighborhood residents have used the "Capacity Inventory" to identify the talents available to start new enterprises. For example, people have begun a new association of home health care providers and a catering business. Public housing residents in a number of cities have formed local corporations to take over the management of their developments. They immediately needed to identify the skills and abilities of neighbors in order to be effective. The Capacity Inventory provided the necessary information allowing people to become producers rather than problems.

PERSONAL INCOME.   Another vital asset of individuals is their income. It is generally assumed that low-income neighborhoods are poor markets. However, some studies suggest that there is much more income per capita than is assumed. Nonetheless, it is often used in ways that do not support local economic development. Therefore, effective local development groups can inventory the income, savings, and expenditure patterns of their neighborhoods. This information is basic to understanding the neighborhood economy and developing new approaches to capturing local wealth for local development.

THE GIFTS OF LABELED PEOPLE.   There is rich potential waiting to be identified and contributed by even the most marginalized individuals. Human service systems have labeled these people "retarded, mentally ill, disabled, elderly, etc." They are likely to become dependents of service systems, excluded from community life, and considered burdens rather than assets to community life.

In the last five years, there have been a growing number of unique community efforts to incorporate "labeled" people into local organizations, enterprises, and community associations (O'Connell 1988a). Their gifts and abilities are identified and are introduced to groups who value these contributions. The results have been amazing demonstrations as the "underdeveloped" hospitality of neighborhood people has been rediscovered and gifts, contributions, and capacities of even the most disabled people are revealed.

INDIVIDUAL LOCAL BUSINESSES.   The shops, stores, and businesses that survive in low-income neighborhoods—especially those smaller enterprises owned and operated by individual local residents—are often more than economic ventures. They are usually centers for community life as well. Any comprehensive approach to community regeneration will inventory these enterprises and incorporate the energies and resources of these entrepreneurs into neighborhood development processes. The experience and insight of these individual entrepreneurs might also be shared with local not-for-profit groups and with students.

HOME-BASED ENTERPRISES. It is fairly simple to inventory the shops, stores, and businesses in low-income neighborhoods. However, as neighborhoods become lower income, there is often an increase in informal and home-based enterprise. Local development groups have begun to make an effort to understand the nature of these individual entrepreneurs and their enterprises. After gathering information about them, development groups can identify the factors that initiated such enterprises and the additional capital or technical assistance that could increase their profits and the number of people they support.

ASSOCIATIONAL AND ORGANIZATIONAL CAPACITIES

Beyond individual capacities are a wide range of local resident-controlled associations and organizations. Here is an initial inventory.

CITIZENS' ASSOCIATIONS. In addition to businesses and enterprises, low-income communities have a variety of clubs and associations that do vital work in assuring productive neighborhoods. These groups might include service clubs, fraternal organizations, women's organizations, artistic groups, and athletic clubs (see appendix 2). They are the infrastructure of working neighborhoods. Those involved in the community building process can inventory the variety of these groups in their neighborhoods, the unique community activities they support, and their potential to take on a broader set of responsibilities (O'Connell 1988b). Then these groups can become a part of the local asset development process. Or they may affiliate in other ways (e.g., by creating a congress of neighborhood associations).

ASSOCIATIONS OF BUSINESSES. In many older neighborhoods, local business people are not organized. Where they are organized, they are not informed about effective joint partnerships in neighborhood economic development. Connecting local businesses with each other and expanding their vision of their self-interest in community development are a major effort of effective community building activities.

FINANCIAL INSTITUTIONS. Relatively few older neighborhoods have a community-oriented financial institution, such as a bank, savings institution, or credit union. But where they do exist, they are invaluable assets.

One ambitious and successful example of a locally controlled financial

institution is the South Shore Bank in Chicago. The bank has been a continuing experiment in how to capture local savings and convert them to local residential
and commercial development. A related effort in Bangladesh, called the Gameen
Bank, is a successful experiment in very small capitalization for small community
enterprises. Similar experiments are taking place in the United States involving
credit unions. All of these inventions are new tools to capture local wealth for local
development. Their presence or potential is a central resource for the future of a
developing community.

CULTURAL ORGANIZATIONS. People in low-income neighborhoods are increasingly giving public expression to their rich cultural inheritance. Celebrating the
history of the neighborhood, and the peoples who have gathered there, is central
to forming a community identity and countering the negative images that originate outside the community. Neighborhood history fairs; celebrative block and
neighborhood parties featuring the foods, music, dancing, and games of diverse
peoples; cross-cultural discussions and classes; oral history projects; theatrical
productions based on oral histories—all these hold great potential for building strong
relationships among residents and for regaining definitional control of the community. In many neighborhoods, local artists are central to the creation of these
expressions.

COMMUNICATIONS ORGANIZATIONS. Strong neighborhoods rely heavily on
their capacity to exchange information and engage in discussions. Neighborhood newspapers, particularly those controlled by local residents, are invaluable
public forums. So, too, are less conprehensive media such as newsletters, fliers, even
bulletin boards. In addition, both local access cable TV and local radio hold promise
as vehicles relevant to community building.

RELIGIOUS ORGANIZATIONS. Finally, any list of organizational assets in communities
would be woefully incomplete without the local expressions of religious life.
Local parishes, congregations, and temples have involved themselves increasingly
in the community building agenda, sometimes through community organizations
or community development groups, sometimes simply building on the strengths
of their own members and networks. In fact, the ability of local religious institutions to call upon related external organizations for support and resources constitutes
a very important asset.

SUMMARY. In summary, then, the primary building blocks include those community
assets that are most readily available for rebuilding the neighborhood. These
involve both individual and organizational strengths. Our initial list includes:

Individual Assets	Organizational Assets
Skills, talents, and experience of residents	Associations of businesses
Individual businesses	Citizens' associations
Home-based enterprises	Cultural organizations
Personal income	Communications organizations
Gifts of labeled people	Religious organizations

SECONDARY BUILDING BLOCKS—ASSETS LOCATED WITHIN THE COMMUNITY BUT LARGELY CONTROLLED BY OUTSIDERS

Though a good many individuals and associational capacities are already within the control of the people who live in the neighborhood, others, though physically a part of the community, are directed and controlled from outside. To capture these assets for community building purposes, neighborhood actors will not only conduct inventories but will construct strategies designed to enhance the regenerative uses of these assets. The examples which follow fall into three categories: private and not-for-profit organizations; public institutions and services; and other physical resources.

PRIVATE AND NONPROFIT ORGANIZATIONS.

Institutions of higher education. Private and public junior colleges, colleges, and universities remain in, or adjacent to, many older urban neighborhoods. However, they are often quite detached from the local community. Community building groups are creating new experiments with partnerships in community development between local institutions of higher education and those who are mobilizing community capacities.

Hospitals. Next to public schools, hospitals are the most prevalent major institution remaining in many older neighborhoods. They are a tremendous reserve of assets and resources to support initiatives in community enterprise. In a few cases, hospitals have created innovative local partnerships. Creative development groups are exploring the nature of the development assets controlled by their local hospitals.

Social service agencies. Though often dedicated to the delivery of individual service to the clients—an activity that does not necessarily contribute to community building—local social service agencies do have the potential to introduce capacity-oriented strategies to their programs. Many, in fact, have begun to see economic development and job creation as appropriate activities, while others have entered into networks and partnerships with community organizations and neighborhood development groups for community building purposes.

PUBLIC INSTITUTIONS AND SERVICES. Of the range of public institutions and services that exist in low-income communities, a few deserve to be highlighted for their community building potential.

Public schools. Big-city schools have often become so separate from local community initiatives that they are a liability rather than an asset. The Carnegie Commission on Public Education has said that the primary educational failing of the local public school is its separation from the work and life of the community. Therefore, localities need to teach their schools how to improve their educational function by connecting themselves to community deveolopment efforts. As an integral part of community life, rather than an institution set apart, the local public school can begin to function as a set of economic and human resources aimed at regenerating the community (McKnight 1987).

Police. As with all other local institutions, the police need to participate in the neighborhood revitalization enterprise. Much of the hesitance about new investment of all kinds relates to issues of security. Therefore, local police officials should be asked to join the asset development team, acting as advisers and resources to development projects. In a number of instances, responsive police departments have joined with local community organizations and other groups to devise and carry out joint safety and anticrime strategies.

Fire departments. In both small towns and large cities, the local fire department boasts a tradition of consistent interaction with the community. Because of the sporadic nature of their important work, firefighters are often available for a variety of activities in the neighborhood. Retrieving and building upon that tradition are an important strategy for community building.

Libraries. Many older neighborhoods contain branches of the public library, often underfunded and underused. Considered not only as a repository for books and periodicals, but also as the center of a neighborhood's flow of information, the library becomes a potentially critical participant in community regeneration. For example, neighborhoods which choose to enter into a community planning process will need localized information on which to base their deliberations. The availability of library-based personal computers can enhance access to a variety of relevant databases. The library can also provide space for community meetings and initiate community history and cultural projects.

Parks. In many low-income communities, the local parks have fallen into disrepair and are often considered uninviting and even dangerous. But when local citizens organize themselves to reclaim these areas, they can be restored not only physically, but functionally. As symbols of community accomplishment, they can become sources of pride and centers for important informal relationship building. Often, groups of existing associations will take joint responsibility for renewing and maintaining a local park.

PHYSICAL RESOURCES. Besides the private and public institutions in the neighborhood, a variety of physical assets are available. In fact, many of the most visible "problems" of low-income neighborhoods, when looked at from an asset-centered perspective, become opportunities instead. A few examples follow.

Vacant land, vacant commercial and industrial structures, vacant housing. Most older urban neighborhoods are thought to be "blighted" with vacant lots, empty sites of old industry, and unused industrial and commercial buildings. However, in some U.S. cities, local groups have found creative and productive methods to regenerate the usefulness of both the land and the buildings. They identify potential new uses, create tools to inventory and plan for local reuses, and organize the redevelopment process. Similarly, abandoned housing structures are often structurally sound enough to be candidates for locally controlled rehabilitation efforts.

Energy and waste resources. The costs of energy and waste collection are relentless resource drains in older neighborhoods. As their costs escalate, they demand a disproportionate and growing share of the limited income of poorer people. As a result, maintenance of housing is often forgone, and deterioration speeds up. However, in some neighborhoods, this "problem" has become an opportunity. New local enterprises are developing to reduce energy use and costs and to recycle waste for profit. These initiatives need to be identified, nurtured, and replicated.

SUMMARY. These secondary building blocks are private, public, and physical assets, which can be brought under community control and used for community building purposes. Our initial list includes:

Private and Nonprofit Organizations	**Public Institutions and Services**
Higher education institutions	Public schools
Hospitals	Police
Social service agencies	Libraries
	Fire departments
	Parks

Physical Resources
Vacant land, commercial and industrial structures, housing
Energy and waste resources

POTENTIAL BUILDING BLOCKS—RESOURCES
ORIGINATING OUTSIDE THE NEIGHBORHOOD,
CONTROLLED BY OUTSIDERS

In this final cluster are resource streams which originate outside the neighborhood, but which nonetheless might be captured for community building purposes.

There is a sense in which all local public expenditures are potential *investments* in development. However, in low-income neighborhoods they are usually expenditures for the *maintenance* of an impoverished neighborhood and for individuals in the absence of work. We need tools and models for converting public expenditures into local development investments. In addition to the public institutions cited above, two other public expenditures are critical.

WELFARE EXPENDITURES. In Cook County, Illinois, over $6,000 is expended annually by government for low-income programs for every man, woman, and child whose income falls below the official poverty line. This substantial investment ($24,000 for a family of four) is distributed so that on a per capita basis, poor people receive only 37 percent in cash ($8,880 for a family of four) and 63 percent in services ($15,120) (Kallenback and Lyons 1989). This creates an impoverished family dependent on services. Creative community groups are developing new experiments where some of these welfare dollars are reinvested in enterprise development and independence.

PUBLIC CAPITAL IMPROVEMENT EXPENDITURES. Every neighborhood is the site of very substantial "infrastructure" investments. In downtown areas, these dollars leverage private investment. In neighborhoods, the same funds are usually applied only to maintenance functions. Effective community development groups are creating experiments to convert local capital improvement funds into development dollars.

PUBLIC INFORMATION. Wherever we have seen community innovation in local neighborhoods, the people there have had to gain access to information not normally available. What is the vacancy ratio in the worst buildings? How many teachers have skills that could help our development corporation? What time do the crimes that threaten our shopping center occur? How much property is off the tax roles? What does the city plan to invest in capital improvements? Unfortunately, most useful development planning data are collected for the use of "downtown" systems. But as neighborhoods become responsible for their future, information must be decoded and decentralized for local use.

Some neighborhoods have done pioneering work in developing methods to translate systems data into neighborhood information. This "neighborhood information" is an invaluable asset in the development process.

SUMMARY. These potential building blocks include major public assets, which ambitious neighborhoods might begin to divert to community building purposes. At the beginning, at least, these are:

Welfare expenditures
Public capital information expenditures
Public information

Two Community Maps

This chapter only begins to map the assets that exist in every neighborhood and town. It is a new map that can guide us toward community regeneration.

But there is another map, an old map of neighborhood deficiencies and problems. As we noted at the outset, it is a "needs-oriented" neighborhood map created by "needs surveys." This is a powerful map, teaching people in low-income neighborhoods how to think about themselves and the place where they live.

This map is initiated by groups with power and resources that ask neighborhood people to think of themselves in terms of deficiencies in order to access the resources controlled by these groups. Among the groups that ask neighborhood people to inventory their problems, needs, and deficiencies are government agencies, foundations, universities, United Ways, and the mass media. Indeed, the institutions that produce this map not only teach people in low-income neighborhoods that their needs, problems, and deficiencies are valuable. They also teach people outside these neighborhoods that the most important thing about low-income people and their neighborhoods is their deficiencies, problems, and needs. In this way, low-income people, helping institutions, and the general public come to follow a map that shows that the most important part of low-income neighborhoods is the empty, deficient, needy part. An example of this Neighborhood Needs Map is in Figure 10.1.

It is true that this map of needs is accurate. But it is also true that it is only half the truth. It is like a map of the United States that shows only that portion east of the Mississippi River. The United States is also the portion west of the Mississippi River, and a map omitting the west is obviously inadequate in the most fundamental ways.

Similarly, every neighborhood has a map of riches, assets, and capacities. It is important to recognize that this is a map of the *same* territory as the neighborhood needs map. It is different because it shows a different part of the neighborhood. But the most significant difference about this capacity map is that it is the map a neighborhood must rely on if it is to find the power to regenerate itself.

Communities have never been built upon their deficiencies. Building community has always depended upon mobilizing the capacities and assets of a people and a place. That is why a map of neighborhood assets is necessary if local people are to find the way toward empowerment and renewal. An example of a Neighborhood Assets Map is in Figure 10.2.

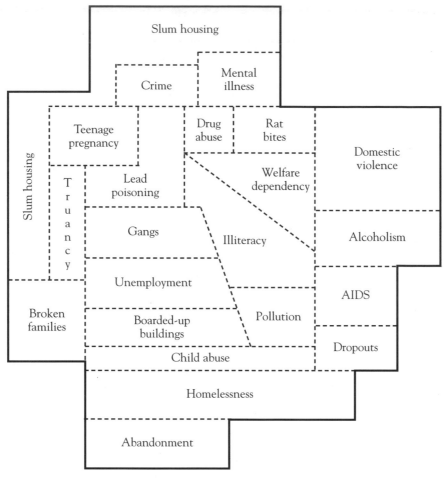

Figure 10.1. Neighborhood needs map.

Finally, it is important to remember that this assets map is very incomplete because it is new. It does not even begin to identify all of the assets of every community. Therefore, we know that as more and more neighborhood regeneration processes are created, residents will identify many more skills, capacities, riches, assets, potential, and gifts to place on the map.

Using the Capacities Map

Most of the assets listed above already exist in many low-income neighborhoods. They are waiting to be inventoried and turned toward the goal of rebuilding communities.

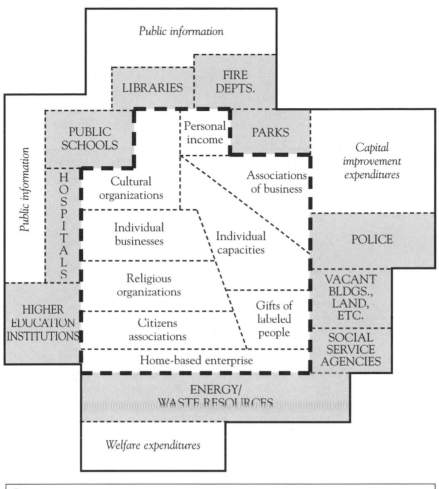

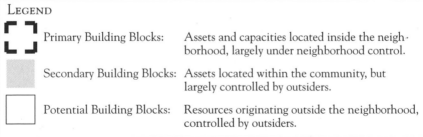

Figure 10.2. Neighborhood assets map.

Different communities will approach this challenge with different strategies. Leaders in every community, however, will need to consider at least three questions which are central to the rebuilding task.

1. Which organizations can act most effectively as "asset development organizations" in our neighborhood?
2. What kinds of communitywide research, planning, and decision-making processes can most democratically and effectively advance this rebuilding process in our neighborhood?
3. Having inventoried and enlisted the participation of major assets inside the community, how might we build useful bridges to resources located outside the community?

Asset Development Organizations

To begin with, who might lead the community building process? Where might the necessary asset development organizations be found?

Two kinds of existing community associations are particularly well suited to the task of knitting together a neighborhood's various assets and capacities. The first, already central to the lives of many older city neighborhoods, is the multi-issue community organization, built along the "organization of organizations" model of the late Saul Alinsky. Community organizers already understand the importance of associational life to the well-being of the neighborhood and to the empowerment of the local residents. A number of these community organizations are beginning to incorporate a capacity-oriented approach to community building in their ongoing activities.

The second potential asset development organization is, of course, the community development corporation. Groups that are dedicated to community economic development have often worked hard to asemble the business assets available to the neighborhood. Many have championed strategies emphasizing local purchasing and hiring and have encouraged homegrown enterprise development. All of these approaches can only be strengthened as the local development corporation broadens and deepens its knowledge of community capacity.

Together or separately, these two types of community-based organizations are well suited to the challenge of asset development. But in many communities, neither the multi-issue organizing group nor the development corporation may exist. In these settings, neighborhood leaders face the challenge of creating a new asset development organization. This new organization may be built on the strengths and interests of existing citizens associations and will challenge those associations to affiliate for these broader purposes.

The Community Planning Process

Having identified or created the asset development organization, community leaders face the challenge of instituting a broad-based process of community planning and decisionmaking. Capacity-oriented community planning will no doubt take many different forms. But all of them will share at least these characteristics in common:

1. The neighborhood planning process will aim to involve as many representatives of internally located and controlled assets as possible in the discussion and decisions. In fact, the map of neighborhood assets provides an initial list of potential participants in the planning effort.
2. The neighborhood planning process will incorporate some version of a community capacity inventory in its initial stages.
3. The neighborhood planning process will develop community building strategies which take full advantage of the interests and strengths of the participants and will aim toward building the power to define and control the future of the neighborhood.

Building Bridges to Outside Resources

Finally, once the asset development organization has been identified and has begun to mobilize neighborhood stakeholders in a broad-based process of planning, participants will need to assemble the many additional resources needed to advance the community building process. This will involve constructing bridges to persons and organizations outside the neighborhood.

It is clear that no low-income neighborhood can "go it alone." Indeed, every neighborhood is connected to the outside society and economy. It is a mark of many low-income neighborhoods that they are uniquely dependent on outside and human service systems. What they need, however, is to develop their assets *and* become *interdependent* with mainstream people, groups, and economic activity.

Organizations leading developing communities often create unique bridges to the outside society. These are not to government alone. Instead, they bridge to banks, corporations, churches, other neighborhood advocacy groups, etc. (McKnight 1987). These bridged relationships in the nongovernmental sector are vital assets in opening new opportunities for local residents and enterprises.

The task of the asset development organization, then, involves both drawing the map and using it. It involves leading the community interests into capacity-oriented planning and creating the organizational power to enable that process to become the map of the neighborhood's future. The challenge facing the asset development organization, and all of the participants in the neighborhood planning process, is both daunting and filled with promise. However, meeting this challenge to rebuild our neighborhoods from the inside out is crucial to the hopes and aspirations of city dwellers everywhere.

References

Kallenback, D., and Lyons, A. 1989. *Government spending for the poor in Cook County, Illinois: Can we do better?* Evanston, Ill.: Neighborhood Innovations Network, Center for Urban Affairs and Policy Research, Northwestern University.

McKnight, J. 1987. *The future of neighborhoods and the people who reside there: A capacity-oriented strategy for neighborhood development.* Evanston, Ill.: Neighborhood Innovations Network, Center for Urban Affairs and Policy Research, Northwestern University.

————. 1988. *A primer for a school's participation in the development of its local community.* Evanston, Ill.: Neighborhood Innovations Network, Center for Urban Affairs and Policy Research, Northwestern University.

O'Connell, M. 1988a. *Getting connected: How to find out about groups and organizations in your neighborhood.* Evanston, Ill.: Neighborhood Innovations Network, Center for Urban Affairs and Policy Research, Northwestern University.

————. 1988b. *The gift of hospitality: Opening the doors of community to people with disabilities.* Evanston, Ill.: Neighborhood Innovations Network, Center for Urban Affairs and Policy Research, Northwestern University.

Issue Selection and the Creating of Critical Part V Consciousness

INTERWOVEN throughout this book are such vital components of community organizing and community building as fostering participation and leadership and emphasizing the social, as well as the task-oriented, agendas of groups and communities. Although each of these issues ideally should be the subject of a chapter in and of itself, space limitations preclude this. Consequently, only a few key topics have been singled out for concentrated and in-depth attention. Two of these topics—issue selection and the creation of critical consciousness—are the focus of this part.

In chapter 11, Lee Staples, author of the classic organizing manual *Roots to Power* (1984), draws our attention to one of the most pivotal areas within community organizing, namely, selecting and "cutting" the issue around which community mobilization can take place. Echoing a theme that runs throughout much of the book, Staples argues that issues should come from the members and potential members of a community rather than from outsiders.

At the same time, he sees the outside professional as having a critical role to play in helping community groups become familiar with the criteria of good issues so that they can select foci for action that measure up against these important yardsticks for success. As he suggests, a good issue is one about which the community feels deeply. But it also is an issue that is winnable, serves to unite the community, provides opportunities for leadership development and broad-based member participation, and is consistent with the long-range goals and strategies of the organization.

Staples also explores in detail the process organizers refer to as cutting the issue, or deciding who gets what from whom and how and why they intend to get it. Using numerous examples from health and related organizing efforts in the United States, he describes and illustrates the issue-cutting process and how it fits within the conduct of a broader strategic analysis. Although largely based on a selection from *Roots to Power*, Staples's chapter has been significantly updated and revised, with a wealth of new case studies drawn upon to connect the principles provided with real-world community organizing for health.

In sharp contrast to issue selection, which has long been a critical part of community organizing practice, education for critical consciousness represents a far newer dimension. To date, in fact, few textbooks on community organizing give more than passing mention to adult educator Paulo Freire's (1973) development of this empowerment philosophy and method and its potential and actual applications in community building and community organizing.

The devotion of an entire chapter to Freire's pedagogy and its application in an innovative and nationally recognized alcohol and substance abuse prevention program reflects the editor's belief that this approach represents one of the most important contributions to community organizing and community building theory and practice in the last quarter century. Through an emphasis on equality and mutual respect between group members and facilitators and a use of problem-posing dialogue and action based on critical reflection, Freire's approach takes traditional community organizing in important new directions. It further complements and extends the approaches to community building described by McKnight, Walter, and others earlier in this text.

Although a number of promising applications of the Freire approach now can be found in health education and related fields, probably none has achieved the visibility or acclaim of Nina Wallerstein and her colleagues' Adolescent Social Action Program in New Mexico. Chapter 12 begins with a description of this unique university-community partnership, whose goals were to reduce morbidity and mortality among youths in high-risk areas, encourage their making of healthier choices in their own lives, and facilitate, through the use of Freirian praxis, their active engagement in their communities through political and social action.

The program's conceptual grounding in both Freirian philosophy and Ronald Rogers's (Rogers, Deckner, and Mewborn 1978) protection-motivation theory is then explored, with attention to how these two very different change approaches can in fact complement and enhance each other. Three steps in a Freirian approach—receptive listening, dialogue, and action—are explored in detail, along with their applications in this case example. Finally, the program's research processes and outcomes are examined, as are the implications for the use of this method in health education and community organizing for health.

References

Freire, P. 1973. *Education for critical consciousness*. New York: Seabury Press.

Rogers, R. W., C. W. Deckner, and C. R. Mewborn. 1978. An expectancy-value theory approach to the long-term modification of smoking behavior. *Journal of Clinical Psychology* 34:562–566.

Staples, L. 1985. *Roots to power: A manual for grassroots organizing*. New York: Praeger.

Chapter 11

Selecting and "Cutting" the Issue

LEE STAPLES

In community organizing, issue campaigns are both ends and means. Organizations are formed as vehicles to address issues, and the issues that they are created to resolve help the organizations grow and flourish. The capacity of an organization to deal successfully with an issue is a function of its level of organizational development. Like the people within them, organizations grow through experience and practice; issue campaigns are the very lifeblood of the process. Through them, new people are attracted, existing members remain active, and leadership abilities flower. The interrelationship between organizational development and issue campaigns cannot be overemphasized. The group builds in order to win and by winning builds an even stronger power base.

Good issue campaigns should have the twin goals of winning a victory and producing organizational mileage while doing so. Therefore, when choosing an issue, the organization must be concerned with not only whether it can be won but also how the campaign can be used to develop the group. The choices frequently will be difficult, and decisions should be made carefully.

The issues should come from the members and potential members rather than from outsiders. As discussed in chapter 3, issues are found by talking with people and testing out various themes. This kind of testing can be done in a variety of settings where significant numbers of people are found, such as organizational meetings, actions, and events. Two of the best ways of surfacing and testing new issues are through door knocking and house meetings. For health educators, social workers, and other professional change agents, focus groups or community forums

Adapted from "Analyze and Strategize: Issues and Strategies," in *Roots to Power: A Manual of Grassroots Organizing*, by Lee Staples, 53–92 (New York: Praeger, 1984), by permission of the Greenwood Publishing Group, Inc., Westport, Conn. Copyright © 1984 by Praeger Publishers.

have also achieved popularity as methods for finding and testing issues and community perceived needs. (See chapter 9 for a fuller discussion of some of these methods.) Regardless of the method chosen, the role of the organizer is one of listening actively (Miller 1993), asking questions, agitating, and in other ways engaging in the issue-cutting process.

There are no shortcuts for testing new issues. Sometimes it may be tempting simply to discuss a potential issue among the top leadership, but this common mistake overlooks one key factor. The highest leaders may be so committed to the organization that their notion of self-interest has broadened to the point where they are no longer typical of members. Thus, they may be very poor judges of what issue campaigns will appeal most widely and deeply to the rest of the membership. Within the organization, issues should be tested and selected with as much bottom-up participation as possible. To do otherwise is to risk a campaign without a large base of committed people.

Of course, at times the organization will have little choice but to respond to a particular issue. For instance, the threatened closure of a large public hospital in a low-income community without other reliable sources of medical care almost "chooses itself" as a salient issue for community mobilization. The positive aspect of such a situation is that many people will be angry and ready to take action. The danger is that the group may be forced to bite off more than it can chew. Regardless, in instances such as these the organization really cannot afford to walk away if it hopes to retain its credibility.

Many organizations will also choose to be involved in more than one issue campaign at a time. This usually is desirable providing the organization has a multi-issue focus that helps create a broad base of participation and a wide range of influence. However, the group must be aware of the danger of spreading itself too thin in the process. There is no simple answer to the question of how many issues an organization should take on. Resources are a key factor, as are the level of organizational development and the demands of the other issue campaigns. Another significant factor is timing. It is certainly possible to run several campaigns simultaneously if some are relatively quick hits, while others are more protracted. In the final analysis, each situation must be assessed individually within the context of the two primary goals of winning basic issues of immediate concern to the members and further developing the organization.

The normal rules for decisionmaking will vary according to the particular organization's structure, but fundamentally, the process should be democratic and involve as many members as possible. In addition to being a worthy organizational end in itself, a democratic process will help ensure that a broad base of members begins to feel ownership of the issue campaign and the developing strategy. Large numbers of people will usually be necessary both to achieve a victory on the issue and to develop increased organizational mileage.

In addition, the decisions should be made on a strategic basis. A strategy is simply a well-thought-out plan to achieve a specific goal or set of goals. Strategic thinking is systematic, logical, and analytical; it is highly rational and focuses on a methodical line of action necessary to achieve the desired result. Formulating a successful strategy requires the ability to anticipate likely outcomes. Each possible option for organizational action will produce a reaction; strategic analysis allows predictions of the most probable results of each alternative. Based on those predictions, wiser choices and decisions can be made.

As organizations mature, their leaders and members will be able to take on increasingly more complex issue campaigns with strategies that unfold in a series of steps, each predicated on the outcome of the last. Like a chess master, the best strategists will be able to think through the implications of most variables and will be able to lay out the stages of the campaign well into the future to an ending point.

Since organizational resources are limited and every issue cannot be addressed, it is not sufficient to simply choose an issue and then develop a strategy. That approach locks the organization into a campaign before all factors can be evaluated. Rather, issues should be chosen on the basis of a strategic analysis that determines in advance whether they are winnable and capable of building the organization. When community groups and organizers are assessing the potential of a possible issue campaign for developing the organization, the following questions will help focus attention on the most vital considerations. Of course, the complete answers to many of them will not be known until after the organization actually engages in the campaign. Indeed, the questions should be reexamined in even greater detail as part of a systematic postcampaign evaluation process. Nevertheless, much can be determined and predicted ahead of time. The following list is illustrative of the kind of thinking called for in order to do a strategic analysis:

- Is the issue consistent with the long-range goals of the organization?
- Will the issue be unifying or divisive?
- Will the campaign help the organization grow?
- Will the campaign provide a good educational experience for leaders and members, developing their consciousness, independence, and skills?
- Will the organization receive credit for a victory on the issue, improve its credibility, and increase its overall visibility?
- How will the campaign affect organizational resources?
- Will the campaign develop new allies and/or enemies?
- Will the campaign emphasize direct action and produce new tactics or issues?
- Will the campaign produce a significant victory?

Consistency

Is the issue consistent with the long-range goals of the organization? How will this issue campaign fit in with the overall organizational agenda? Will it help move the organization along that path, or will it involve a detour or even a basic change in direction? For instance, a health access organization in a low-income neighborhood might be considering involvement in a campaign to fight cutbacks in bus service—an issue of concern to many members. Although not dealing specifically with health in the narrow sense, the transportation issue is one that might have a direct impact on many of the organization's low-income constituents. One of the many factors the group should consider before making a decision on this issue will be the campaign's impact on future organizational directions. Will other health access issues be neglected while this transportation campaign is undertaken, or will this fight complement other organizational actions? Does this signal the start of a new multi-issue approach? Will this campaign build the power of the organization to represent the interests of low-income residents better than other issues? Beyond these questions, what are the long-range goals, and how have they been determined?

Unity or Division

Will the issue be unifying or divisive? Serious internal splits will weaken an organization, so it is important to consider how a potentially divisive issue relates to the organization's ultimate goals. Sometimes people on each side of an issue may argue that it is intimately intertwined with the organization's long-term goals. One faction may contend that by taking a position, the organization will virtually destroy itself, while others argue that if a stand is not taken, the organization will not be worth saving. These situations often have no easy solution, and feelings will run high, but a clear understanding of one fundamental principle is essential: any issue campaign that weakens the organizational base jeopardizes the attainment of all other goals.

An organization that bites the bullet on too many divisive issues may find itself with a pure ideological record but only a handful of self-righteous true believers. An organization needs to stand up for its principles and goals, but to be effective, it also needs lots of people standing up with it. One important safeguard is a democratic decisionmaking process. Both organizers and leaders need to avoid imposing their own ideological goals and visions on the rest of the organization. When controversial, divisive issues arise, organizers and leaders need to come to grips with their own feelings and try to separate them from their roles within the group. When this is not possible, it should be acknowledged honestly, and those whose positions run counter to the group's consensus should withdraw as much as possible from the issue or in some cases even leave the group.

Any good campaign on a significant issue will attract new people who agree with the organization's position and action. But it will also, to a lesser degree, flush out some members who did not really understand or accept the basic aims of the organization to begin with. Such minor losses of membership are healthy and should be expected.

Oftentimes, a possibly divisive issue can turn out to be unifying if it is cut in a positive way. An inner-city community hard hit by epidemics of drug use and HIV/AIDS may be heavily divided over whether to mobilize in favor of a needle exchange program when the issue is cut in terms of condoning or not condoning the use of illicit drugs. But when the health educator or other social change professional can provide evidence that needle exchange programs reduce the spread of HIV without encouraging drug use, the issue can be cut instead in positive terms of disease prevention.

Problems of divisiveness are often more complex for multi-issue organizations than for single-issue groups, since the former usually have a more diverse multi-constituency base. Again, the interests of different constituent groups need to be weighed against the group's long-term goals.

Organizations also need to be aware of possibly counterproductive external divisions. Sometimes, for example, opponents will be able to divide an organization from its potential allies. Tobacco companies thus frequently provide funding for "Cinco de Mayo" parades and other cultural events in heavily Latino areas. In so doing, these companies may drive a wedge between community groups and health educators working together to fight the increased targeting of people of color in cigarette advertising and others in the community who want the tobacco companies' financial backing for these prized cultural events (see chapter 8). Obviously, questions of unity and divisiveness must be considered carefully before any issue is selected. A mistake in this area can have profound and lasting impact on the organization.

Growth

Will the campaign help the organization grow? An organization's ultimate source of power is its membership. The best campaigns will appeal to a broad range of people and attract new members. Such campaigns will also provide ample opportunity for direct participation by large numbers of people through direct actions and other organizational activities. The recruitment and involvement of large numbers of people will provide much of the leverage necessary to win the issue campaign while simultaneously expanding and building the membership base.

In addition to increasing membership, a good campaign should also involve and develop new leaders—a principle that is not emphasized adequately in many organizations. Organizational leadership should be spread among many people rather than be lodged in the hands of a few. This collective form of leadership depends on the infusion of new people who bring added skills and energy to the group. A good issue campaign should be able to attract new leaders and involve them in important roles. In some cases, they will be people who have never before been active with the organization, whereas in other instances former "second-line" leaders will move into positions of increased responsibility and prominence. Most organizations will periodically suffer the loss of some leaders, and the infusion of new leadership blood through issue campaigns can compensate for such losses.

Some issues are particularly effective in expanding organizational membership and leadership because they appeal to more than one natural constituency. Environmental issues increasingly fall into this category. Although continuing to appeal primarily to young, white, middle-class constituencies, some environmental groups have begun in earnest to tackle the "environmental racism" reflected in the disproportionate location of toxic waste dumps in low-income communities of color. And across the United States, low-income communities of color have themselves organized locally against their status as "the unchallenged dumping ground for toxic waste" (Pilisuk, McAllister, and Rothman 1996; Avila 1992). By forging linkages with these local efforts and moving concerns with environmental justice to the top of the agenda, larger environmental organizations can expand their constituencies while tackling one of the most critical environmental problems facing low-income communities.

Finally, organizations that hope to expand their geographic territory or turf can do so most easily through systematic recruitment on a hot issue. Much of the suspicion and resistance common to such an expansion effort will melt away in the face of a hot issue and an appealing action plan to deal with it.

Education

Will the campaign provide a good educational experience for leaders and members, developing their consciousness, independence, and skills? In organizing, the principles of adult education leader John Dewey (1946) should be borne in mind: people learn best through action and experience. An issue campaign can provide an educational experience that dozens of consciousness-raising sessions, workshops, or seminars could never accomplish. In a campaign, learning takes place within the context of actual life experience; there is a unique opportunity for the development of political awareness and analytic, strategic planning abilities. Skills can be learned in a wide range of areas, including, but not limited to, recruitment, the holding of effective meetings, direct-action tactics, negotiation, work with the media, and supportive grassroots fund-raising. The development of these abilities and skills will lessen the organization's dependence on organizers and other "professionals."

Learning should take place in a three-step process that involves as many people as possible: analyzing situations and making plans accordingly, carrying those plans into action, and evaluating the results. There is often a tendency among organizations to concentrate on developing top leadership while overlooking the rest of the membership, but that is a serious mistake. It is important to use campaign opportunities to educate the membership at large, especially second-line leaders who will be moving into top positions in the future.

Obviously, it is not always functional to have the entire membership involved in intricate strategic planning, but people can be polled by the leadership on various options, and briefings before all actions can explain the strategic line of thinking to everyone. The more people feel part of the process of making organizational decisions and plans, the greater will be their sense of ownership and investment in the campaign, creating a more committed and loyal membership.

The evaluation of issue campaigns provides an excellent opportunity to develop increased political awareness and more sophisticated analysis of how social systems work. For instance, a campaign against an increase in electric rates can lead to increased knowledge of how a private utility corporation functions, how electric rates are structured, and how the regulatory process works. The immediate campaign provides a specific context and experience within which these larger issues can be raised. This process, it is hoped, will lead to new campaigns on the larger issues themselves. The battles of Association of Community Organizations for Reform Now (ACORN) against utility rate hikes, for example, have developed into statewide initiative campaigns to change the rate structure and to replace appointed regulatory bodies with elected representatives. As people develop a better understanding of their organization's potential to bring about small but important changes in their lives, they will become more committed to building an organization that can win larger victories and achieve more significant systemic changes.

Credit

Will the organization receive credit for a victory on the issue, improve its credibility, and increase its overall visibility? Although we may resent the person who always wants the acclaim when good things happen, an organization should be aggressive about taking credit where it is due. For one thing, an organization's ability to raise funds and secure additional resources may be linked to the credit it gets for its victories. For another, new members may be attracted by the organization's publicity and winning image. And the group may be able to establish greater respect and credibility as a result of receiving credit.

Organizations may receive both internal credit within the community and external credit outside it. External credit most typically is secured through the press and electronic media. Most groups are very conscious of the type of press and media coverage they receive and go to some pains to secure it. Unfortunately, it is not always forthcoming. When this happens, the group still may receive proper credit "on the street" within its own community.

Sometimes the organization must help the process along at the local level. For example, a community group may have successfully pressured city officials to improve trash collection in the neighborhood. The mayor, who ordered the sanitation commissioner to correct the problems only after being confronted by angry organization members (an event that the press failed to cover), may have gotten credit in a news story for "taking bold, aggressive action to improve neighborhood conditions." Leaders and members could attempt to tell the real story through phone calls, the group's newsletter, and word of mouth. There might also be an effort to enlighten the media by framing the story in a new way and in other ways using media advocacy to get the community group's message highlighted (Wallack et al. 1993). (See chapter 21 for a full discussion of this strategy.) Regardless of the method or methods chosen, however, the organization would be able to get some measure of credit within its own community.

A distinction should be made between credit and credibility; the two go together frequently but not necessarily. A group that has credibility will be taken seriously. In the preceding example, there was a lack of external credit, but the organization undoubtedly increased its credibility with the mayor. On rare occasions, things may work the other way. A group may get credit for a victory when in fact it played a minor role. For instance, a piece of health legislation for which an organization lobbied may have passed a legislative body simply as a bargaining chip in a power struggle played out between two politicians. The organization may claim and receive credit for the bill's passage, but if the group plays this game too often, as many are tempted to do, it may actually lose credibility among legislators who know the real story. There also is the added danger of leaders and members believing their own press clippings even when they are untrue. This can lead to overconfidence, confusion over the group's true source of power, and a drift away from direct-action tactics.

Many leaders and members may be inclined to say, "Who cares who gets the credit as long as we get a victory on our issue?" But to build organizational mileage, credit and visibility will be important. Although this is difficult to predict, the best campaigns should have the potential for giving the organization increased visibility, credit, and credibility.

Resources

How will the campaign affect organizational resources? The availability of organizational resources will, of course, greatly affect the outcome of an issue campaign. But the reverse is true; campaigns, both successful and unsuccessful, will often have a lasting impact on an organization's resources. Clearly, internal and external visibility, credit, and credibility will have a direct bearing on fund-raising efforts. The organization that can attach an impressive list of victories along with an array of good press clippings to a funding proposal certainly will stand a better chance of receiving external funding. Private foundations or large individual contributors often have "favorite issues," such as health care or education. An organization should never prostitute itself by choosing issues simply to get funded, but a working knowledge of the fund-raising potential of a campaign is certainly a legitimate factor for leaders and members to consider when making a decision.

Of course, the effect of issue campaigns on external funding can cut both ways. For example, an organization that funds part of its staff through local government moneys had better be aware of the implications of taking on the mayor in a nasty fight. This type of example is the major reason that organizations should think long and hard before accepting any government funds. Or a group funded by a conservative foundation should not be surprised when a militant campaign for health care for the homeless leads to a cutoff of funding. Organizations may choose to engage in those campaigns anyway, in spite of the risk. But the funding implications of campaigns should be considered and weighed carefully before any decisions are made. There may be sound organizational reasons for taking on a campaign that jeopardizes funding, but there is no excuse for not anticipating and preparing for the contingencies of such decisions beforehand.

Door-to-door canvassing for large numbers of small contributions falls somewhere between external and internal fund-raising. Although many factors affect a canvasser's ability to raise money, organizational name recognition and issues that appeal to the donor's own self-interest are usually key ingredients for success.

Finally, internal fund-raising, both through membership dues and various grassroots events, will be affected by issue campaigns. Obviously, the greater are the visibility, credit, and credibility of the organization in its own community, the greater will be its ability to raise funds. Certain issue campaigns will generate more new members than others, and people will be more willing to buy a raffle ticket, attend a fund-raising event, or make a donation if they care about the issues the organization is tackling. Internally divisive issues will naturally split the organization's grassroots funding base.

Beyond direct funding, other organizational resources will be affected by any issue campaign. These range from supplies, use of equipment, and technical expertise, to, most important, the time of leaders, members, staff, and volunteers. Successful campaigns will frequently attract future donations of supplies and equipment along with an increase in the number of volunteers. As organizer and advocate Herbert Chao Gunther (see appendix 10) explains, "More than anything else, Americans want be on the winning side."

Just as leaders and members develop political and organizational skills through actual campaigns, so, too, do staff members learn through direct experience. A good issue campaign should provide an opportunity to increase the knowledge and skills of new staff and challenge the abilities of the veterans. Generally, success breeds success in organizing, with the best staffs developing in the most effective organizations. Like any other organizational resource, staff must be cultivated and nurtured carefully and used wisely.

Once there is an answer to the question "Do we have the resources necessary to win?" another question remains: "Is this the best use of our resources, and what will be the effect of this campaign on the rest of the organization?" Even though the resources to win on an issue may exist, the organizational payoff may not be worth the sacrifices. Choosing to work on a particular issue may mean not taking on several others or becoming involved in an all-consuming effort that forces other issues and activities to be neglected. Thus, when community groups and organizers are examining potential issues, it is not enough to analyze whether they are winnable; the overall impact on funding and other organizational resources should be considered as well.

Allies and Enemies

Will the campaign develop new allies and/or enemies? An old labor union saying goes, "Make no permanent friends or enemies." These still are wise words for both unions and other social action organizations, particularly when dealing with politicians. Allies and opponents can, and frequently will, shift from issue to issue. Nevertheless, relationships may be established that have lasting effects, especially between organizations. Texas Industrial Areas Foundation leader Ernesto Cortes Jr. (1993) has described how in 1975 San Antonio's Communities Organized for Public Service (COPS) staged major and highly publicized actions against several prominent downtown business leaders who had refused to work with COPS on a budget for improving conditions in the city's neglected West Side. The actions were successful, and dialogue was begun between the business leaders and the COPS organization. Two decades later, one of the major business leaders involved in the earlier confrontation and its follow-up was serving as chair of the board of a job training program designed and implemented in part by COPS. He also played a key role in 1990 in bringing the other business leaders to the table with COPS and the local IAF organization to plan a community assessment in the areas of income and job training. In Cortes Jr.'s words, "Establishing and maintaining relationships with both adversaries and allies is a critical component of the capacity to survive the contradictions of politics. . . . If you cannot have a real conversation with your opponent, he or she will never become your ally" (5).

Organizations that work together formally in coalitions or more loosely as allies on an issue campaign have an opportunity to cooperate on specific actions, activities, and tasks. A relatively new and unknown organization might derive both concrete assistance and a measure of needed legitimacy from working with another large, established organization. Both positive and negative experiences are bound to have some carryover effect, and where the former is true, the stage is set for future joint efforts. The development of such relationships can be a source of increased organizational mileage.

But sometimes an organization also helps define itself and what it stands for through the opposition it tackles (Wallack et al. 1993). United Indian Nations, the Circle of Strength/Healthy Nations Project, several local Native American health centers, and other local and national organizations concerned with the health of multicultural communities thus underscored their commitments in this area when they organized a campaign against Hornell Brewing Company. The company had expropriated the name and image of a revered Native American spiritual leader, Crazy Horse, to sell forty-ounce malt liquor to young people, targeting inner-city communities. Denouncing the use of the Crazy Horse name as "insulting and degrading" to Native Americans, and unable to convince the brewing company to cease using this label, the groups formed the Campaign Against Cultural Exploitation. The latter organized a widely publicized boycott of both Crazy Horse malt liquor and the manufacturer's popular Arizona Ice Tea.

As this example illustrates, organizations establish much of their identity through the kinds of issues and targets they pick and the types of campaigns they wage. When community groups are making these decisions, it is important to look at the long-term organizational significance of the friends and enemies who are chosen.

Tactics

Will the campaign emphasize direct action and produce new tactics or issues? The best victories will be those achieved through direct action on the part of large numbers of people. Campaigns featuring a high level of direct action enable the leaders and members to experience their own collective power. The organizational lesson is, "We won because lots of us stuck together and fought like hell."

Direct-action organizations are always searching for imaginative new tactics. The elements of surprise and unpredictability are important for most good actions, and innovative tactics can make the difference between success and failure. The Gray Panthers in Denver, Colorado, amply demonstrated this principle after encountering resistance from city officials to its request for a slower-timed stoplight at a major intersection. Many elderly senior center participants, and especially those with disabilities, had been unable to get from their bus stop to the senior center across the intersection before the light changed. The Panthers organized a demonstration in which some three hundred seniors, many of them with canes and wheelchairs, all attempted to cross with the light at the same time. The ensuing traffic tie-up effectively made its point, and the officials reversed themselves by giving into the Panthers' original demand. Although the tactics do not necessarily have to be brand new, they should be unexpected by the opposition (Alinsky 1972). Potential issue campaigns may hold possibilities for standard tactics that an organization has not used before—sit-ins or vigils, for example—and opportunities to engage in these tactics will broaden the experience and repertoire of the group's leaders and members.

In other instances, it may be necessary to develop a new variation of an old tactic or something entirely new. ACORN's campaigns against abandoned housing illustrate that a wide range of innovative tactics is often available. When city officials in Little Rock, Arkansas, refused to board up vacant buildings, ACORN members did it themselves and presented the city with a bill for materials. The press covered the action; the city paid up and improved its performance. Faced with a similar situation in New Orleans, Louisiana, ACORN members provoked city officials to act by tearing down an unsalvageable eyesore. In more than a dozen cities, ACORN members have squatted in vacant houses, moving in, beginning repairs, and demanding title to the properties.

In addition to producing new tactics, a good campaign may also create opportunities for new but related campaigns. Sometimes a logical progression can be seen ahead of time. For instance, the primary value of a campaign to establish a landlord-tenant commission is that it sets up future campaigns and establishes a new arena in which to resolve grievances. In other cases, a campaign may set the stage for escalation. For example, neighborhood efforts to obtain street repairs can progress to campaigns for fairer allocation of Community Development Block Grant money. Victory on one issue lays the groundwork for future battles. The potential for either spinning off or escalating campaigns can be an important factor in an organization's evaluation of how much mileage any one issue might produce.

Victory

Will the campaign produce a significant victory? There may be times when a group is forced to take on an issue and fight the good fight even though prospects for success are dim. But to grow and flourish, organizations need victories. In the vast majority of cases, issues should not be chosen unless there is a real possibility for victory, especially when the organization is newly formed.

What constitutes a "significant" victory? Despite the importance of external credit and credibility, the organization's members are the final judge of whether a victory will make a substantial difference in their lives. At one level, the test is whether an issue is important and whether it can be won. At another level, the test is whether the organization can be strengthened in the process, thereby increasing its power and the members' capacity to gain a greater measure of control over their lives in the future.

Of course, there will be times when almost certain victory evaporates into defeat. In other instances, a campaign will lose momentum, getting bogged down by forces beyond the organization's control. Occasions such as these often precipitate an organizational crisis as the energy and anger that are usually focused on the opponent turn inward. Infighting, scapegoating, low morale, and other internal problems can result. At just such a juncture, a "fight in the bank" can provide the needed remedy. The idea is to delay taking action on an easily won issue until a propitious moment. Then when the organization finds itself caught in an impasse or defeated on an issue campaign, it draws on the fight in the bank in order to gain a quick, easy victory with all its attendant benefits (Alinsky 1972).

When community groups and organizers are considering questions of organizational mileage, it is important to make one further distinction between types of issues. "Recruitment issues" lend themselves to systematic outreach efforts that can attract large numbers of new participants and members. Examples include any issue that great numbers of people care about deeply—for instance, the closing of a neighborhood health center or the discovery of a plan for a new hazardous waste dump near a low-income residential area. These issues can help build the organization, providing a steady influx of new leaders and activists.

"Maintenance issues," in contrast, do little to build the organization numerically but may provide mileage in other ways. These are issues that do not have a strong self-interest draw for lots of people but nevertheless are of concern to the organization's leadership and core group of activists. Often maintenance issues present opportunities to develop better social policy. Frequently, such issues involve taking positions on a specific piece of legislation. Maintenance issues can provide mileage by producing victories, establishing new allies, increasing visibility and credibility, generating new resources, and developing increased political skills.

Organizational mileage is enhanced when maintenance campaigns are politicized and unite different neighborhoods. For example, vacant lots are a traditional neighborhood concern, and campaigns to clean them up are a common focus for sustaining local group activity. But the efforts will produce more organizational mileage if a number of neighborhood groups combine to advocate a city ordinance that charges landlords the cost of cleanups and places liens on their property for unpaid bills. Winning the ordinance creates new campaign opportunities, targeting individual landowners and demanding city enforcement. However, serious problems can arise when organizations stop recruiting and concentrate too heavily on maintenance issues that involve only a small core of activists.

Winning victories, empowering people, and bringing about change are what organizing is all about. Without good strategic thinking, however, none of this is possible. Before organizers and community groups make an action plan, a preliminary phase of strategy development is critical. One of the central components of this strategic development is cutting the issue.

Cutting the Issue

To develop the basic outlines of an issue, four questions should be explored by community groups and the organizers working with them: Who makes up the constituency that will participate? What are their goals? Who are the targets of their action? How will the community group members gain the necessary leverage or handle to move into action effectively? Thus, the process of cutting the issue lays out the basic dynamics of the conflict—who wants what from whom and how and why they intend to get it (Katz 1980).

CONSTITUENCY

People will participate in an issue campaign if they feel it is in their own self-interest to do so. That self-interest can be tested through the application of Saul Alinsky's (1972) criteria of whether the issue is immediate, specific, and winnable.

Obviously, issues will appeal differently to various constituencies. For instance, antitobacco organizing has been an issue of deep concern to many middle-class activists. Yet in a low-income neighborhood where issues of basic survival confront people daily, tobacco may have little immediacy compared to illicit drugs, AIDS, inadequate housing, unemployment, and violent crime. If the issue is cut properly, however, it may well attract both constituencies. In some low-income communities, for example, people of color have recognized self-interest in opposing the heavy targeting of their communities by tobacco advertisers and have mobilized effectively around this issue (Ellis, Reed, and Scheider 1995).

Even in a low-income neighborhood with severe housing problems, an organizer might have little success recruiting people to a "housing" meeting. The general problem is too broad to organize around. Specific issues must be cut to appeal to particular constituencies: rent control to tenants, low-interest home improvement loans to homeowners, a lead paint program to renters with young children.

Of course, the better the chances for success are, the greater is the likelihood that people will make a commitment to get involved. Thus, a campaign to raise welfare benefits by 25 percent in the face of drastic cuts in state expenditures certainly would be met with skepticism, if not laughter. But an effort to stop an ill-conceived, highly criticized "workfare" program from being implemented might be attractive to many people. Before getting involved, people need to have some clear sense that a victory is possible. The rough outlines of the campaign will have to be laid out before general recruitment is done.

To predict a campaign's potential constituency, it is important that the organizer analyze both the breadth and depth of the issue's self-interest draw. Some issues may be mildly attractive to a broad range of people, whereas others may appeal very strongly to a more narrow segment. For instance, there might be more people who would express an interest in establishing new recreation programs than would seek action on an abandoned building. However, the smaller number affected by the abandoned building might feel much more deeply about that issue than those "interested" in recreation.

The depth of an issue's appeal is partly a function of the emotional response it triggers. Frequently, defensive fights (e.g., "stop the cutbacks") seem to arouse more passion than do efforts to win a positive reform or program. Often, positive efforts are actually phrased in the negative. Thus, a campaign to bring in more city services adopts the slogan "Save the neighborhood," whereas an effort to win a traffic light is conducted under the banner of "Stop endangering our kids." The famous ACORN chant "We're fed up, won't take it no more!" captures the essence of the defensive fight; it is an active response to an intolerable situation. Like the proverbial "straw that breaks the camel's back," such issues may be able to move people into action who have never moved before. Not surprisingly, most spontaneous organizing efforts have grown out of defensive situations.

Campaigns to bring about a positive change do, of course, often generate plenty of emotion and anger. Issues such as HIV/AIDS, drugs, abortion, and day care have moved large numbers of people on both the Right and the Left into action over the past few years. Furthermore, any organization that seeks to empower people must move beyond the realm of defensive responses to the proactive campaigns that change power relationships. But it is critical to generate sufficient passion to move lots of people in these positive efforts. Only if an organization involves many people who care deeply about an immediate, compelling issue can it be won.

GOALS

The goals of a constituency are whatever people want done to solve the problem they have identified—removal of lead paint or asbestos from a local school, prevention of threatened cutbacks in medical care access for the poor, establishment of smoke-free workplaces. The goals of an issue campaign have to be clear, concrete, and compelling. It does little good to have realizable goals that no one really supports.

Possible solutions to the problem at hand should be tested with a number of people as part of the issue-cutting process. It is important to start by finding out which options people really want. There should be a true bottom-up process, not merely a ratification of the goals of leaders, organizers, planners, politicians, or various interested parties. This process of testing different alternatives helps people develop the ownership of both the issue and the strategy that will be essential if the campaign is to be truly broad based and participatory (see chapter 9).

Once there is a general sense of the preferable solution(s), a determination must be made of what is realistic. This is an area where research plays a key role. Good research is essential for predicting what potentially can be won from an opponent and what levels of organization and effort will be necessary to achieve success. As information is learned, it should be shared. Similarly, where drastic cuts in federal funding or local tax revenues make a proposed solution totally unrealistic, there should be a discussion of the obstacles rather than an avoidance of the subject. The formulation of goals is a dynamic process that evolves as more information is gathered and viable options are presented.

The specific objectives will continue to be shaped and refined as more and more factors are weighed and analyzed. At this point in time, as the issue is first cut, it is sufficient to draw the broad outline of what is wanted. Again, the demands will be a function of who the constituency is, who the target will be, and how the organization can find points of leverage to bring pressure to bear.

TARGETS

The language of social services is replete with references to "target" groups, areas, and populations. Invariably, the people who are defined as having the problem are targeted for some sort of program, service, or other form of assistance. Organizing looks outside the affected constituency and targets those who cause the problem or those who have the power, directly or indirectly, to bring about a change. Thus, in organizing, the people with an interest in a particular issue take collective action on their own behalf against external targets that have the ability to meet their demands. Those targets arise from an analysis of potential (or actual) opposition, what is needed to overcome it, and who has the power to make the decisions necessary to produce an organizational victory. It is important to distinguish between opposition and targets because they are not always the same. James Katz (1980, 4) phrases the distinction nicely:

> The opposition is anyone who is opposed to you and capable of acting against you; the targets are the persons and institutions you act against. Not everyone in the opposition is a worthwhile target; some may be too inaccessible, too powerless, or too peripheral to the resolution of the issue. However, there might be other players who are not necessarily opposed to your campaign—they might even be neutral or favorable—but who may influence the outcome in your favor. These are known as "indirect targets."

Targets typically are straightforward and direct. Aside from vulnerability, a good target should have the power to make concrete, specific decisions on the organization's demands. Saul Alinsky's (1972, 130) famous dictum says it all: "Pick the target, freeze it, personalize it, and polarize it." Thus, when community organizations are targeting an institution, it is important to understand the decisionmaking process thoroughly and then accurately fix responsibility with the key individuals who have the relevant power. Organizers and the community groups they work with must distinguish between formal and informal decisionmaking processes, remembering that those who wield the most power may not always occupy the most visible positions. The organization may have to move first on those who are officially responsible, thereby smoking out the real powers that be. In other instances, the best strategy will be to move directly on the hidden powers.

Here again, good research is a must. It is impossible to fight a whole bureaucracy; individuals who can make the necessary decisions should be singled out as targets and not allowed off the hook. It is critical that the right target be chosen in the first place. Clearly fixing responsibility on the proper person helps focus the organization's energy and brings the issue to life for people. There is nothing like a villain to energize a campaign. Thus, during a winter when Boston cut off service for unprecedented numbers of hard-pressed customers, Massachusetts Fair Share's campaign for rate reform gathered new momentum as the company's president was singled out as "Shutoff King of the Year." From small landlords to presidents of multinational corporations, from city councillors to U.S. senators, the best targets will generate anger and emotion in organization members.

Accessibility, vulnerability, and ability to meet the organization's demands will help determine the best targets. At times, indirect targets will have to be chosen, whereas in other instances multiple targets will work best. As more is learned about the opposition, many options will become clearer, and wise decisions will be easier to make.

HANDLES

A door cannot be opened without some form of handle; neither can an organizing issue. Handles can be laws, regulatory processes, or bureaucratic rules and procedures that may be open to interpretation in ways than could benefit the local organization or community. Proposals by the Republican Congress in the mid-1990s to rescind the hard-won Nursing Home Reform Act, which had dramatically reduced the use of physical and chemical restraints in nursing homes (Kane et al. 1993), provided important ammunition for local, state, and national organizing in the area of long-term care. Not only was the act allowed to stand, but also renewed media and public attention to the issue of long-term care helped spur subsequent organizing efforts in this area.

Handles can also be precedents, broken promises, or conflicts of interest, each of which provides a natural opportunity for a community group to apply pressure backed by some historical and/or moral justification. When the prestigious Hastings Law School in San Francisco reneged on promised internal security patrols for low-income residents of four apartment buildings it owned, residents tried without success to convey their concerns to management. The law school's broken promise was then used by the Tenderloin Senior Organizing Project as the basis for helping concerned residents organize a tenants' association. The latter won an out-of-court settlement from the law school and was able to establish a system whereby the property manager met regularly with the tenants' group to explore and address their concerns (Minkler in press; see also chapter 15).

Finally, incidents, events, and situations (e.g., an upcoming election) can provide critical handles or "hooks" and have the added virtue of often lending themselves to media coverage. When a Hawaii chapter of Mothers Against Drunk Driving learned of a planned substantial weakening of the state's drunk driving law, the organization kicked off a campaign on Memorial Day, in front of the state's eternal flame war monument, and urged people to remember their highway dead along with their war fatalities. A large sign in front of the podium bore the phone numbers of the governor and the senate president, who received record numbers of calls and letters in response to this well-publicized event (Wallack et al. 1993). The choice of a good and media-worthy handle—the symbolic linking of a MADD campaign with Memorial Day—set the stage for subsequent and effective organizing to defeat the proposed policy change.

Whatever form handles may take, they help explain how the organization can win and why its position is justifiable. Thus, the concept entails both a tool that the organization can use to maximize its power on the issue and a rationale that underscores the legitimacy of the campaign. Once again, however, the goal in organizing is to involve as many people as possible, not simply to win on an issue and solve the problem. The best handles will maximize participation and emphasize the organization's direct-action focus.

These four factors—constituency, goals, targets, and handles—are the essentials that must be considered in a cutting of the issue. As pointed out earlier, all four are interrelated and should not be considered separately and sequentially. Indeed, the cutting of an issue can start with any of these factors and then move forward to integrate the others.

Issue Selection and Strategic Analysis: A Final Note

This chapter has focused on the criteria that groups and communities should consider in the issue selection process. It then examined the factors that make up the process of cutting the issue, a vital part of strategic development. Although a discussion of all the parameters of a strategic analysis is beyond the scope of this chapter (see Staples 1984), a few key points are worthy of mention.

First, a strategic analysis is a straightforward, useful way of examining the helping and hindering forces that will affect any change effort. Kurt Lewin's (1946) method of "force field analysis" (described and illustrated in detail in chapter 14) provides an excellent tool for conducting a strategic analysis. Briefly, this approach enables organizers and the communities they work with to lay out the forces working for and against a change and to consider a variety of change strategies that take these forces into account.

Second, Roland Warren's (1975) three major types of change strategies should be considered, with attention to the conditions under which each is most appropriate. *Collaborative strategies* are effective when there is broad agreement among all parties on the goals of the change effort. *Campaign strategies* are used when there are differences among the parties that could be resolved by consensus. Finally, *contest strategies* are used when there are significant differences among the parties and little hope of achieving consensus.

Third, although the mechanics of a strategic analysis are quite simple, the *depth* of the analysis is what really counts. Assumptions should not be made quickly or superficially, and nothing should be taken for granted. Most important, the various factors should be viewed dynamically rather than statically. Action and change are the goal, not just analysis of the status quo for the sake of analysis. Too often, when done by academicians, such studies lead to explanations and rationalizations for why no change is possible. Organizers and leaders must avoid such analysis paralysis and concentrate on how action can alter the various forces to achieve victory.

Finally, several key factors should be part of any strategic analysis. These are *opposition, objective conditions, organizational capacity*, and *support*. Analysis of these four factors answers several basic questions: Who is against you? What is beyond your control? What is your group capable of doing? What is the possibility for help via coalitions and other mechanisms? Whether done formally through a strategic analysis or more informally, analysis of these factors, in conjunction with the process of cutting the issue, should give a reasonably accurate picture of the level of organizational action and clout necessary to achieve success.

In sum, an organization must weigh a tremendous number of factors and consider many variables when choosing and cutting issues and developing strategies. But the group should be careful not to analyze and strategize to the point where no campaign can materialize. It is impossible to figure out every single possibility. There is a time to act!

References

Alinsky, S. D. 1972. *Rules for radicals*. New York: Random House.

Avila, M. 1992. Environmental racism and issues of social justice. Keynote address to the University of Michigan Law School, Ann Arbor, Michigan, January 23.

Cortes, E. Jr. 1993. No permanent friends, no permanent enemies. *Shelterforce* (January-February):3.

Dewey, J. 1946. *The public and its problems: An essay in political inquiry*. Chicago: Gateway Books.

Ellis, G., D. F. Reed, and H. Scheider. 1995. Mobilizing a low-income African-American community around tobacco control: A force field analysis. *Health Education Quarterly* 22 (4):443–457.

Kane, R. L., C. C. Williams, T. F. Williams, and R. A. Kane. 1993. Restraining restraints: Changes in a standard of care. *Annual Review of Public Health* 14:545–584.

Katz, J. 1980. *Action research*. Washington, D.C.: Institute for Social Justice.

Lewin, K. 1946. *Field theory in social sciences*. New York: Harper Touchstone.

Miller, M. 1993. Community Organizing. In *A journey to justice*. Louisville, Ky.: Presbyterian Committee on the Self-development of People.

Minkler, M. In press. Empowerment of the elderly in San Francisco's Tenderloin District. In *Health and society: Case studies*, ed. B. Amick and R. Rudd. Cambridge, Mass.: Harvard University Press.

Pilisuk, M., J. McAllister, and J. Rothman. 1996. Coming together for action: The challenge of contemporary grassroots organizing. *Journal of Social Issues* 52:15–37.

Staples, L. 1984. *Roots to power*. New York: Praeger.

Wallack, L., L. Dorfman, D. Jernigan, and M. Themba. 1993. *Media advocacy and public health: Power for prevention*. Newbury Park, Calif.: Sage.

Warren, R. 1975. Types of purposive social change at the community level. In *Readings in community organization practice*, ed. R. M. Kramer and H. S. Specht. 2d ed. Englewood Cliffs, N.J.: Prentice-Hall.

Chapter 12

Freirian Praxis in Health Education and Community Organizing

A Case Study of an Adolescent Prevention Program

NINA WALLERSTEIN
VICTORIA SANCHEZ-MERKI
LILY DOW

TODAY'S ADOLESCENTS are confronted with many risks, including fears about the future, lack of employment opportunities, media targeting by the alcohol and tobacco industry, family and community violence, and social norms of peer pressure to engage in risky behaviors. In addition to these risks, young people are bombarded with the "don't" messages of health professionals and preventionists, such as "Don't drink and drive," "Don't have sex," or "Don't use drugs." Implicitly, adolescents are asked to assume full individual responsibility for their behavior in the face of social conditions that foster powerlessness and alienation. For adolescents in low-income communities of color, real and perceived powerlessness is often particularly profound.

This chapter illustrates how a university and community partnership works with youths to address the interconnectedness of personal choices and social conditions through a mix of empowerment education and community organizing strategies. In New Mexico, a group of interdisciplinary university faculty, staff, and graduate students in collaboration with school administrators, teachers, and middle and high school students have sought to understand and address the interplay between individual and social change in one health education intervention, the Adolescent Social Action Program. The intervention incorporates Paulo Freire's (1970) empowerment education theory of dialogue and praxis with community organizing strategies and Ronald Rogers's (1984) protection-motivation behavior change theory.

After offering an overview of the ASAP program and its theoretical framework and processes, we give a brief summary of results from a qualitative study on the interaction of individual and community change processes. We conclude by discussing the implications for health educators and community organizers of using a Freirian approach with youths.

The Adolescent Social Action Program

ASAP is a youth-centered, intergenerational, and experiential prevention program that was initiated in 1982 among schools, both on and off reservations, that serve predominantly Native American, Hispanic, and low-income Anglo communities. The program is a collaborative effort among the University of New Mexico, University Hospital, the county detention center, and over thirty multiethnic schools and communities throughout New Mexico. Formerly known as the Alcohol and Substance Abuse Prevention Program, ASAP's goals are to reduce morbidity and mortality among adolescents who live in high-risk environments, to encourage them to make healthier choices in their own lives, and to facilitate, via empowerment education, their active engagement in political and social action in their communities.

ASAP consists of a seven-week experience for small groups of youths brought into the hospital and detention center to interview and interact with patients and jail residents who have problems related to drug, tobacco, and alcohol abuse; interpersonal violence; HIV infection; and other risky behaviors (Wallerstein and Bernstein 1988). The ASAP facilitators (trained university graduate students from the health professions and social sciences) follow an extensive curriculum that includes structured dialogue about the patient and jail resident stories and exercises in decisionmaking, conflict mediation, communication, problem-posing, and resistance to peer pressure. In each session, they help the youth develop questions for the interviews, construct role plays, and address specific anxieties or fears that arise in the hospital and jail setting.

At the heart of the program is Freire's educational empowerment approach (Wallerstein and Sanchez-Merki 1994). With the guidance of the ASAP facilitators, the adolescents apply and practice the Freirian model, that is, a listening-dialogue-action reflection cycle with the patients and jail residents. The youths listen to the patients' and residents' life stories. After the interviews, the youths engage in dialogue about the issues they have heard, exchange personal experiences about their lives, and analyze the social, medical, and legal consequences of risky behaviors. The debriefing component of the program takes the participants beyond a "scared straight" model, which has been proved to be ineffective (Rogers and Mewborn 1976; Job 1988), and allows for the practice of critical thinking skills.

At this juncture, the adolescents begin to explore action strategies to make healthier choices for themselves and their communities. ASAP incorporates protection-motivation theory directed at increasing students' threat appraisal and coping self-efficacy for behavior change (Rogers 1984; Stainback and Rogers 1983). The integration of behavior and social change is especially important for youths of color who face poverty, racism, and unemployment and who are therefore overrepresented in injury and mortality statistics.

As the seven-week curriculum ends, ASAP typically offers the adolescents two options: to participate in a peer education component or to work on a social action project. The peer education program allows the adolescents to continue the Freirian model with elementary school students. They can practice the craft of conducting empowerment education and act as role models for younger children. The social action model, however, is the one that extends into community organizing. Adolescent participants are encouraged to devise their own social or health projects for their schools and neighborhoods. This approach encourages the youths to explore existing social/legal policies and community resources, to evaluate prevention strategies for risky behaviors, and to participate in actions to transform alcohol and tobacco norms in their communities.

Philosophical and Theoretical Bases of ASAP

The underlying theory and philosophical framework for ASAP come from Brazilian educator Paulo Freire (1973, 1970). He originally developed his ideas through highly successful literacy programs in the 1950s for slum dwellers and peasants in Brazil. Choosing emotionally and socially charged words and pictures of students' problems, he generated discussion on how to improve their lives. In the last three decades, Freire's educational ideas have been a catalyst for world-wide programs in literacy (Fiore and Elsasser 1982), English as a second language (Wallerstein 1983; Auerbach and Wallerstein 1987), health education (Minkler 1985; Werner and Bower 1982; Wallerstein and Bernstein 1994), worker health and safety education (Wallerstein and Weinger 1992), youth programs (Alschuler 1980; Reed 1981), college courses (Shor 1980, 1987; Shor and Freire 1987), and community development (Hope, Timmel, and Hodzi 1984; Barndt 1989; Vella 1994, 1995; Arnold et al. 1991).

To Freire, the purpose of education is human liberation, which means people are subjects of their own learning, not empty vessels filled by teachers' knowledge. To promote the learner as subject, Freire proposes a structured dialogue approach in which everyone participates as colearners to create a jointly understood reality. Through dialogue, individuals engage in critical reflection, or conscientization, to analyze the societal context for personal problems and their own role in working on the problems. The goal of dialogue is praxis, or the ongoing interaction between reflection and the actions that people take to promote individual and community change. In health education and community organizing, there has been a growing interest in the role of Freirian theory in health enhancement through people collectively moving beyond feelings of powerlessness and assuming control in their lives (Wallerstein 1992).

ASAP also incorporates protection-motivation theory, an attitudinal change theory that assumes that intention to act is an indicator or a predictor of behavior change. Protection-motivation theory proposes that decisions to act are initiated through a variety of informational sources and mediated through a nonlinear cognitive perceptual process (Rogers 1984; Rogers, Deckner, and Mewborn 1978), resulting in either an adaptive or a maladaptive response. Variables in Rogers's model include personal vulnerability, severity, response and self-efficacy, and a set of beliefs around rewards and costs. Rogers's model purports that a positive, adaptive response occurs when exposure to a stimulus increases one's threat appraisal and one's coping appraisal and when rewards decrease for engaging in a maladaptive behavior (Rippetoe and Rogers 1987).

The coping appraisal variables of self-efficacy (the belief that one has the ability to successfully complete a task) and response efficacy (the belief that one's actions will make the desired difference) improve the likelihood of self-protective behavior. Socially responsible behaviors can increase through enhanced self-efficacy to help others, strengthened collective efficacy (the belief that the group can make a difference), and political efficacy (the belief that one can make a difference in the political arena).

The Integration of Freire and Protection-Motivation

Through the Freirian model, ASAP links educational processes to individual changes and community organizing. During the hospital/detention center sessions, the predominant model is the cultivation of decisionmaking, critical consciousness, leadership skills, and community building. Starting from the youths' emotional responses as they listen to the patients' and jail residents' stories (their threat appraisal), Freirian dialogue creates a cognitive awareness of precursors and consequences of alcohol problems that leads participants to increased coping appraisal to protect themselves. Through empathy with each other and critical analysis of societal forces in a safe group context, a bridge is created between one-dimensional behavioral change and group efforts for social change. The youths are encouraged to engage in dialogue about their own lives and their relationships to their communities and to develop an awareness of school and neighborhood resources in order to develop socially responsible behaviors. Active participation is a key tenet of ASAP in the issues that adolescents bring to the dialogue and in their choice of follow-up activities.

To implement the Freirian structured dialogue model, which integrates threat and coping appraisals, ASAP uses a listening-dialogue-action methodology. This three-part process encompasses a participatory orientation to learning rather than a passive mode of receiving information. ASAP participants enter the program at the listening stage and, upon completion of the curriculum, leave in an action mode. Yet listening, dialogue, and action are not linear processes; rather, they are overlapping, cyclical components of learning and change. For example, listening continues throughout the program as students interview patients, discuss issues with facilitators, select an action project, evaluate and relisten to their own analysis of the impact of their actions, and choose other actions. This cyclical process is the embodiment of the Freirian concept of praxis and also reflects a cognitive-perceptual process that encourages attitudinal and behavior change. Figure 12.1 provides an illustration of the interaction between protection-motivation variables and the Freirian listening-dialogue-action model.

LISTENING

ASAP begins in the receptive, listening stage as students interview individuals who have experienced medical, social, or legal consequences related to their alcohol use, other drug problems, or interpersonal violence. The small-group context of seven students and two facilitators creates a supportive environment, essential for promoting the active participation of youths. Key to this environment is the ability of the facilitators, as colearners, to model and promote empathy, reinforce active listening skills, and encourage participatory discussion.

Students are prepared to immediately adopt an action stance as they engage in the role of questioner versus passive recipient of information. For students from high-risk environments in particular, this process provides an opportunity to adopt a new role in the dominant-culture hospital environment. Not only do they interview the patients, but they also are given the opportunity to interview the hospital personnel who care for the patients: the helicopter flight crews, paramedics, technicians, nurses, and physicians.

The motivation to explore the meaning of the interviewees' stories comes from the development of empathy—often spurred by curiosity and wonder about people in the hospital or in jail but kept alive by facilitators through guided discussion. Motivation to continue also comes from personal identification (the initial step toward increased susceptibility) with the patients or inmates. Students wonder, "Could I be here? Or could my father, mother, or friend?"

DIALOGUE

Once the key issues are elicited in the listening stage, the Freirian process proposes the use of discussion catalysts or "triggers" to pull together the issues into a concrete example so that people can interpret and project meaning onto the reality they see. A good trigger is a creation from the listening process that captures the emotional meaning of key problematic issues and the social context of these issues in participants' lives, yet does not present solutions.

In ASAP, the patient and jail resident stories are the major triggers for discussion. These stories portray the consequences of risky behaviors and the rich complexities of problems and solutions. Other triggers in the curriculum are role-plays, student stories about their own lives, videotapes, collages, and photographs.

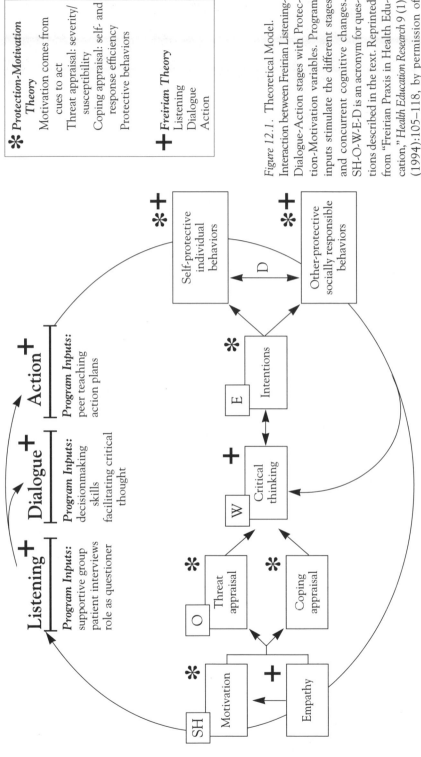

Protection-Motivation Theory
Motivation comes from cues to act
Threat appraisal: severity/susceptibility
Coping appraisal: self- and response efficiency
Protective behaviors

Freirian Theory
Listening
Dialogue
Action

Figure 12.1. Theoretical Model. Interaction between Freirian Listening-Dialogue-Action stages with Protection-Motivation variables. Program inputs stimulate the different stages and concurrent cognitive changes. SH-O-W-E-D is an acronym for questions described in the text. Reprinted from "Freirian Praxis in Health Education," *Health Education Research* 9 (1) (1994):105–118, by permission of Oxford University Press.

Although triggers present open-ended situations, critical thinking does not occur spontaneously. To promote different levels of critical thinking, the facilitators use an inductive questioning guide, S-H-O-W-E-D (Shaffer 1983). Sample questions for the acronym might include the following:

What do we *s*ee, or how do we name this problem?

What's really *h*appening to this individual in his or her life?

How does this story relate to *o*ur lives, and how do we feel about it?

*W*hy has this person experienced these problems at an individual and family or community level?

How might we become *e*mpowered now that we better understand the problem?

What can we *d*o about these problems?

The questions ask the youths to describe the problem, consider how it affects their personal lives, develop a critical analysis of the context of the problem, and strategize social actions.

As an immediate emotional reaction to the patient and jail resident stories, the youths begin to personalize the stories and life experiences of the patients and inmates. Protection-motivation's variables of personal susceptibility and severity are increased for the youths: "This could happen to me," and "This is serious." Almost without facilitator prompting, youths are asking themselves, "What do we see, what is really happening here, and how does this relate to our lives? Our families? Our communities?"

To move the youths toward an adaptive coping response, at this juncture facilitators must acknowledge the feelings elicited by the interviews, yet help participants move past their emotions to a cognitive understanding of what happened in these peoples' lives to create their medical, legal, or social problems. Especially for youths, facilitators must push them to think beyond their peers and their families to a societal analysis. To do so, facilitators ask questions such as "Why does the homeless person in the emergency room feel helpless? Why does he drink? Does he have the support or resources to go into treatment?"

It is this component of critical thinking leading to action (or conscientization, in Freire's terms) that separates ASAP from other health education programs, which appeal solely to individual behavior change. Through the dialogue, students can acquire beliefs in their ability to help themselves and others. A belief in personal power and skill may be important for low-income or minority youths who have heightened vulnerabilities and powerlessness.

As students discuss their own lives through the dialogic model, they bring in their personal experiences, cultural backgrounds, and norms. ASAP students are encouraged to draw on their strengths (such as pride in their family and culture) to help them address the problems they face in their lives.

ACTION

Although the action stage is last, it is not the final step, merely a component of the reflection-action-reflection cycle, or praxis. Group actions that emerge during the dialogue process are reflected upon and in turn promote further actions that address problems in the participants' communities.

Youths are asked to take an action stance from the beginning of the program (e.g., by assuming the role of interviewer for patients and medical personnel), but by the fourth week, the action stage becomes prominent. Students have completed their work with patients and inmates, have worked through many of the emotions elicited by the interactions, and are now engaging in a community action project.

In the past, ASAP students often defined their actions solely in the arena of presentations and peer teaching. For the past few years, however, the social action approach has facilitated greater organizing opportunities within their schools and larger communities. These have included neighborhood organizing and community-based research in the production of their own curriculum, community murals, and ethnic-cultural institutes that reflect their community, culture, and the voice of local youths. ASAP adolescents have conceptualized, written, and produced several fotonovellas and ASAP videos, which have then been used as aids to other educational and organizing efforts in local schools and community centers.

Increased interest in youth issues statewide has led to ASAP youths participating in larger endeavors. At the New Mexico State Fair in 1994, for example, they helped plan and participate in "A Day Without Alcohol Is Fair." In Albuquerque's Civic Plaza, adolescents took part in "A Day Without Colors" by directing activities and running the ASAP booth. They have linked with Street Reach, a gang prevention project, in which ASAP adolescents share the health information and coping strategies they have learned. ASAP adolescents have been involved in a local youth-produced series of television programs on teenage life in New Mexico. Service has often been a part of ASAP social actions, with youths from Laguna-Acoma Pueblos, for example, helping senior citizens with house cleaning and repair and engaging in environmental cleanup campaigns.

In the policy arena, a group of ASAP youths played an active role in the New Mexico Peer Leadership Conference, which produced policy recommendations on tobacco use for the legislature and governor's office. They have joined Youth Link, a statewide endeavor that seeks to engage young people in statewide policy development.

Thus, Freirian action emphasizes youths becoming advocates for healthier schools and communities. By taking the emphasis off the individual as lone actor, Freirian action places individuals within their social and political context. This is particularly important for health educators who work in nondominant cultures (e.g., with the Native American and Hispanic youths in ASAP), where communal decisionmaking and traditional community responsibility are highly valued (Spector 1979).

Summary of Research Process and Outcomes

Although there are many Freirian-inspired programs throughout the world, few efforts have been made to research the processes created by these programs or to evaluate their health and social outcomes. Research into Freirian programs poses special difficulties because, like most community organizing efforts, change targets evolve over time as people become engaged in their community. Community-level change requires long-term commitment, with both intended and unintended results. In essence, there are two major research questions that require careful investigation: What are the major processes or outcomes of this type of intervention? What are the interactive relationships between individual- and community-level change? In other words, how does leadership development promote increased community participation and community capacity?

A qualitative exploratory study undertaken by Nina Wallerstein in 1986–1988 sought to answer these questions (see Wallerstein and Sanchez-Merki 1994, for a complete review of the research methodology and findings). Two ASAP sites were selected: a large Albuquerque high school, with 1,700 students, 39 percent from low-income families, almost 70 percent Hispanic; and a reservation middle-high school (sixth through twelfth grade), an hour outside of Albuquerque, with 450 students. Over 90 percent of the students in the latter school were Native Americans from the Laguna and Acoma reservations, and unemployment on the reservation at the time ranged from 50 to 75 percent.

The study population consisted of two groups of high school students from each site who were observed and interviewed throughout their participation in ASAP. Questions focused on several areas: perceptions of and satisfaction with the program, teenager concerns, beliefs in control and feelings about the future, individual substance use behaviors, relationships with friends and family, participation in groups, perception of community strengths and problems, and actions related to community change.

To deepen the study of the program's context and the cultural differences at each site, a limited multisite case study approach was also taken (Yin 1984). Two subunits were chosen within each site: the individual participating students to assess individual change possibilities and the school and community context and implementation of the intervention to assess community change possibilities.

Although the initial research questions had focused to a great extent on how a Freirian program could promote community change, the continuing data analysis pointed toward a refocus on individual actors and how they engage in a larger change process. In the final data analysis, five major themes emerged: (1) the changes in the youths' abilities to engage in dialogue, (2) the youths' emotional changes related to connectedness with others and self-disclosure, (3) the youths' critical thinking ability to perceive the social nature of the problems and their personal link to society, (4) the youths' level of actions to promote changes, and, most important, and (5) the youths' own perception of how they could be involved in change.

A three-stage model of change that combined the five processes into one central pattern of change surfaced. That pattern concerned the youths' perception of their changing self-identity, the fifth process just mentioned (see Figure 12.2).

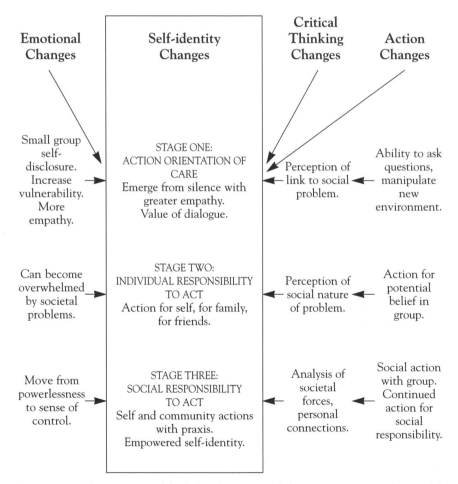

Figure 12.2. Three-stage model of change. Reprinted from "Freirian Praxis in Health Education," *Health Education Research* 9 (1) (1994):105–118 by permission of Oxford University Press.

Participatory dialogue from the program appeared to start a three-stage process of self-identity change: action orientation of caring, individual responsibility to act, and social responsibility to act within each stage. The youths experienced changes on emotional, critical thinking, and action levels.

In the first stage, the youths developed an action orientation of caring about the problem, about each other, and about their ability to act in the world. The key processes involved in this stage were the recognition (emotionally and cognitively) of one's personal connection and susceptibility to the problem and the nonjudgmental small-group environment, which enabled dialogue and self-disclosure, the development of empathy for others, and the new active role of question-asker. In the words of one Laguna student, "It's scary at times to talk about feelings . . . but once feelings got out, it wasn't so hard. Everyone could share. . . . If you want to cry, cry" (Wallerstein 1989).

In the second stage, the youths began to act for individual changes, expressing an ability to help others who were close to them. This second stage, that of individual responsibility, evolved naturally as individuals attempted to fulfill their new ethic of care. The motivation for action was significant in that it arose directly out of the participatory and caring dialogue in the hospital/jail experience. The students' increased self-efficacy to talk and help others and their own self-articulated behavior changes reinforced their self-confidence and their own recognition of their personal changes in self-perception and in perception of others. As one student commented, "Talking to these people at the hospital, they really got me to think, wow, just think, some of these people around my neighborhood might want to just talk. Maybe if we just talk to them and tell them I did care about you, maybe that would make an impression in their life" (Wallerstein 1989).

In the third stage, the youths reached a level of understanding of the need for social responsibility and the possibility for larger social actions. This third stage, that of social responsibility, requires critical thinking and ongoing support to maintain the commitment to work on problems over the long term, despite having an appreciation for the difficulties of both personal and social change.

Many students from both schools suggested that group actions could be more effective than individual actions. In the words of one, "Probably anyone can do something, if you get enough people against it. [You] need more people to change the community, working together that are informed. . . . Alone, [you] can't make the ideal community happen" (Wallerstein 1989).

Interesting cultural differences also emerged from the data. For example, although both the Native American and the Hispanic students expressed a belief that groups could make a difference, the Hispanic students saw an important role for individuals: "Groups can have a bigger influence, [but] maybe individuals can help set up groups." "[It's] people working together, one person has to stand up and say something. A group is easier; you have support" (Wallerstein 1989).

In contrast, the Native American students expressed the opposite point of view: "Individuals can do nothing, maybe talk to officials, but I don't think they'll do anything. . . . I went to the tribal council and said bars just make people go bad. The first lieutenant agreed, but the governor didn't want to close the bars because the tribe gets half the profit" (Wallerstein 1989).

However, the latter comments of hopelessness were not congruent with the students' actions: all but two of the ten Laguna/Acoma students were involved in peer education and tribal council presentations, for example. Whether their comments reflected a cultural belief that figures of authority are the ones to make the changes, an accurate appraisal of the situation, or some combination of these and other factors is not known. Such findings point up the need for far greater attention to the interaction of social and cultural factors in community organizing and interventions research.

In addition to identifying three stages of change, research results from this study underscored the role of many of the individual change processes as intermediate variables to community empowerment outcomes or as psychological empowerment outcomes (Zimmerman 1995). Variables identified within this qualitative study included the protection-motivation variables for self- and other protection, empathy, critical thinking, belief in group action, and group behaviors, such as extent of participation in social actions. ASAP has incorporated these variables into student questionnaires for research using an experimental design with intervention and control schools. Early analysis of this research shows intervention youths developing a statistically significant increase of certain other-protective socially responsible efficacies over the control youths.

Although individual outcomes are possible to measure in a construct of psychological empowerment that may interact with community empowerment, community outcomes are more problematic. Direct impact on the school and community is hard to gauge, even when ASAP has concentrated on community action. One example of a community change was that ASAP students from Laguna-Acoma were asked to make presentations at the tribal council and at several village meetings. Although girls normally are not permitted to attend village meetings, the ASAP girl students were given their first opportunity to participate in the political system of their tribal villages.

Community empowerment research within community psychology and public health has supported further interest in the measurement of psychological, organizational, and community changes and in the use of research processes to strengthen community organizing (Zimmerman and Rappaport 1988; Zimmerman and Perkins 1995; Israel et al. 1994; Wallerstein and Bernstein 1994; Fetterman, Kaftarian, and Wandersman 1996). But research still needs to be undertaken to link individual changes in self-efficacy, participation, and action orientation with indicators of competent or empowered communities, that is, communities with the capacity for solving problems, developing support structures, and increasing access to resources (Cottrell 1976; Wallerstein 1992; Parker 1995). In the last decade, evaluations of lay health adviser interventions in particular have contributed to the development of community competence indicators (Eng 1989; Eng and Parker 1994).

In ASAP, community competence goals for the school become possible when several groups from one school go through the program at a time. ASAP participants then spread their influence through peer education presentations and social actions. On an annual basis, several hundred youths participate in ASAP, though the maximum number at each school is four groups per year.

Even with instruments that measure change with the community as the unit of analysis, assessment of the impact of Freirian interventions, like all open-ended community organizing efforts, must largely be a discovery process. Community researchers have argued that empowerment is a dynamic construct that may vary across time, across domains (i.e., school or family), and across contexts; as such, empowerment cannot be measured through a universal or global measurement tool (Zimmerman 1995). Qualitative research should therefore accompany any measurement instruments in order to take into account the preconditions for change, that is, the existence of other viable community groups, the barriers imposed from inside and outside the community, and the particular culture, power dynamics, and history of the community undergoing the change. Part of the evaluation will always be a case study that provides a detailed account from which others can learn.

Implications for Community Organizing within Health Education Practice

Some core issues exist about the limits and benefits of community organizing within a program such as ASAP. The first issue is the ability of youths to assume full responsibility for organizing. The acquisition by the adolescents of skills from colearning with adults is a primary step for community organizing. They learn to work across age and ethnic cultural borders, yet in the end, due to the many financial, ethical, legal, and mechanistic issues, youths still depend on adults. Their organizing strategies may go only as far as the alliance formed with supportive adults. For example, resources such as transportation, materials, supplies, money, and personal contacts exist within adult supporters. Even if youths have access to these resources, they also depend on family support. They need parental/legal guardian consent to remain involved or to conduct the organizing events. The hope is, however, that after participating in ASAP, youths will develop decisionmaking skills, a belief in group action, awareness of social responsibility, and a belief and confidence in themselves as leaders who can make a difference.

The second issue is that because the school is the starting place for the program, this raises questions of community as an organizing base. Unfortunately, many youths identify with their school, their neighborhood, their ethnic culture, or their gang and will not work across these boundaries. Broader organizing would have to take these polarized subcommunities into account in order to help bridge the differences and build a community of youths who could have citywide policy impact.

The third organizing issue is that the majority of funding for ASAP is categorical—for alcohol and other drug prevention. Since alcohol and drugs have been a prominent concern for teenagers, and adolescents have been able to choose projects within the broad range of adolescent risky behaviors, categorical funding so far has not proved a major obstacle in this project. As discussed in chapter 8, however, in a situation where a community or group's perceived needs or concerns do not correspond to those of the funding source, the ethical and practical utilization of a model like this one would be hampered.

The fourth organizing issue is the challenge of integrating Freirian listening-dialogue-action educational methods into health education programs and community organizing strategies. This challenge is important for established health education programs, such as ASAP, or for other organizing efforts that depend on group processes. The Freirian education skills of listening, structured dialogue, and responsiveness to emotions that emerge in the dialogue require practice and a commitment to communities over time, which is especially important in building trust with youths. Actions that yield results need to be built in from the beginning of any effort in order to sustain youth commitment. Continual reflection on actions, or praxis, is critical for movement from stage two, or individual responsibility to act, to stage three, or social responsibility to act. Without critical awareness, participants who may be motivated to become actors for change can redevelop feelings of hopelessness and powerlessness.

The final organizing issue is the challenge for Freirian facilitators to be colearners and to honor youths as full decisionmaking partners in a health education or organizing effort. In reality, power dynamics permeate most relationships between adults and youths, whether because adults bring expectations or because adult facilitators often come from a different class or ethnic group than that of their target population (Labonte 1994). Although a focus on disfranchised communities may inadvertently perpetuate power dynamics and racism (Pinderhughes 1990), a Freirian approach enables both sides (adult facilitators and youths) to analyze social problems and learn how to challenge the hierarchies together. Organizers would themselves would find it useful to engage in self-reflection and self-renewal as they seek to understand their role in community change and how actions they take with the group may either challenge the status quo or promote further dependency.

Conclusion

ASAP presents a comprehensive model that combines Freirian empowerment education, critical consciousness, and praxis with such community organizing principles as leadership development, community building, high-level participation, and advocacy. Though direct community organizing is not the starting place, the ASAP model illustrates how young people are introduced to the skills required to participate in community organizing and to explore the processes of working with the barriers and resources presented to them. The process engages them in learning to combine many of the principles with an overarching social change agenda.

As demonstrated throughout this chapter, a Freirian approach can be integrated with individual cognitive change theories to create programs directed at both individual and community change. The three-stage model of change suggests that people engaged in Freirian programs can evolve beyond powerlessness to create a sense of empowerment—that they can make a difference in their worlds.

Because a Freirian approach presupposes an interactive model of behavior and social change, it acknowledges that individuals can best develop a sense of self-direction and empowerment in the context of transforming community powerlessness. With praxis, health educators and organizers can model and promote their own growth as they promote the growth of the youths with whom they work.

References

Alschuler, A. S. 1980. *School discipline: A socially literate solution*. New York: McGraw-Hill.

Arnold, R., B. Burke, C. James, D. Martin, and B. Thomas. 1991. *Educating for a change*. Toronto: Doris Marshall Institute.

Auerbach, E., and N. Wallerstein. 1987. *ESL for action: Problem-posing at work*. Reading, Mass.: Addison-Wesley.

Barndt, D. 1989. *Naming the moment: Political analysis for action*. Toronto: Jesuit Centre for Social Faith and Justice.

Cottrell, L. S. Jr. 1976. The competent community. In *Further explorations in social psychiatry*, ed. B. H. Kaplan, R. N. Wilson, and A. A. Leighton. New York: Basic Books.

Eng, E. 1989. *Pinah evaluation progress report*. Chapel Hill: Department of Health Behavior and Health Education, School of Public Health, University of North Carolina.

Eng, E., and E. Parker. 1994. Measuring community competence in the Mississippi Delta: The interface between program evaluation and empowerment. *Health Education Quarterly* 21 (2):199–220.

Fetterman, D., S. Kaftarian, and A. Wandersman. 1996. *Empowerment evaluation: Knowledge and tools for self-assessment and accountability*. Thousand Oaks, Calif.: Sage.

Fiore, K., and N. Elsasser. 1982. Strangers no more: A liberatory literacy curriculum. *College English* 44 (2):115–128.

Freire, P. 1970. *Pedagogy of the oppressed*. New York: Seabury Press.

———. 1973. *Education for critical consciousness*. New York: Seabury Press.

Hope, A., S. Timmel, and C. Hodzi. 1984. *Training for transformation: A handbook for community workers*. Vols. 1–3. Gweru, Zimbabwe: Mambo Press.

Israel, B., B. Checkoway, A. Schulz, and M. Zimmerman. 1994. Health education and community empowerment: conceptualizing and measuring perceptions of individual,

organizational, and community control. *Health Education Quarterly* 21 (2):149–170.
Job, R. F. 1988. Effective and ineffective use of fear in health promotion campaigns. *American Journal of Public Health* 78 (2):163–167.
Labonte, R. 1994. Health promotion and empowerment: Reflections on professional practice. *Health Education Quarterly* 21 (2):253–268.
Minkler, M. 1985. Building supportive ties and sense of community among the inner-city elderly: The Tenderloin Senior Outreach Project. *Health Education Quarterly* 12 (4):303–314.
Parker, E. 1995. Conceptualizing community problem-solving capacity in seven African-American southern communities: The results of a grounded theory study. Ph.D. diss., School of Public Health, University of North Carolina.
Pinderhughes, D. 1990. *Understanding race, ethnicity, and power: The key to efficacy in clinical practice*. New York: Free Press.
Reed, D. 1981. *Education for building a people's movement*. Boston: South End Press.
Rippetoe, P., and R. W. Rogers. 1987. Effects of components of protection-motivation theory on adaptive and maladaptive coping with a health threat. *Journal of Personality and Social Psychology* 52 (3):596–604.
Rogers, R. W. 1984. Changing health-related attitudes and behavior: The role of preventive health psychology. In *Interfaces in psychology*, ed. R. McGlyn, J. Maddox, C. Stoltenberg, and R. J. Harvey. Lubbock: Texas Tech University Press.
Rogers, R. W., C. W. Deckner, and C. R. Mewborn. 1978. An expectancy-value theory approach to the long-term modification of smoking behavior. *Journal of Clinical Psychology* 34 (2):562–566.
Rogers, R. W., and C. R. Mewborn. 1976. Fear appeals and attitude change: Effects of a threat's noxiousness, probability of occurrence, and the efficacy of coping responses. *Journal of Personality and Social Psychology* 34 (1):54–61.
Shaffer, R. 1983. *Beyond the dispensary*. Nairobi: Amref.
Shor, I. 1980. *Critical teaching and everyday life*. Boston: South End Press.
———, ed. 1987. *Freire for the classroom: A sourcebook for liberatory teaching*. New Haven: Boynton/Cook.
Shor, I., and P. Freire. 1987. *A pedagogy for liberation*. South Hadley, Mass.: Bergin and Garvey.
Spector, R. E. 1979. *Cultural diversity in health and illness*. New York: Appleton-Century-Crofts.
Stainback, R., and R. Rogers. 1983. Identifying effective components of alcohol abuse prevention programs: Effects of fear appeals, message style, and source expertise. *International Journal of Addictions* 18 (3):393–405.
Vella, J. 1994. *Learning to listen, learning to teach: The power of dialogue in educating adults*. San Francisco: Jossey-Bass.
———. 1995. *Training through dialogue: Promoting effective learning and change with adults*. San Francisco: Jossey-Bass.
Wallerstein, N. 1983. *Language and culture in conflict: Problem posing in the ESL classroom*. Reading, Mass.: Addison-Wesley.
———. 1989. Empowerment education: Freire's theories applied to health: A case study of alcohol prevention for Indian and Hispanic youth. Ann Arbor, Mich.: UMI Dissertation Information Service.
———. 1992. Powerlessness, empowerment, and health: Implications for health promotion programs. *American Journal of Health Promotion* 6 (3):197–205.
Wallerstein, N., and E. Bernstein. 1988. Empowerment education: Freire's ideas adapted to health education. *Health Education Quarterly* 15 (4):379–394.
———, eds. 1994. *Health Education Quarterly* 21 (2–3).
Wallerstein, N., and V. Sanchez-Merki. 1994. Freirian praxis in health education: Research results from an adolescent prevention program. *Health Education Research* 9 (1):105–118.

Wallerstein, N., and M. Weinger, eds. 1992. Empowerment approaches to worker health and safety education. *American Journal of Industrial Medicine* 22 (5):619–784.

Werner, D., and B. Bower. 1982. *Helping health workers learn*. Palo Alto: Hesperian Foundation.

Yin, R. 1984. *Case study research: Design and methods*. Applied Social Research Methods Series, vol. 5. Beverly Hills, Calif.: Sage.

Zimmerman, M. 1995. Psychological empowerment: Issues and illustrations. *American Journal of Community Psychology* 23 (5):581–600.

Zimmerman, M., and D. Perkins, eds. 1995. *American Journal of Community Psychology* 23 (5).

Zimmerman, M., and J. Rappaport. 1988. Citizen participation, perceived control, and psychological empowerment. *American Journal of Community Psychology* 16:725–750.

Community Organizing and Community Building Within and Across Diverse Groups

Part VI

THE PAST FEW YEARS have witnessed a growing appreciation of the community organizing and community building efforts that are taking place among and with women, people of color, people with disabilities, gays and lesbians, and other diverse groups. For the most part, however, this wealth of experience has not been well represented in the literature. Furthermore, what literature does exist has suggested that traditional models of community organizing are often ill-suited to work with disfranchised groups, whose reality tends to differ markedly from that of the architects of many of these models.

This part begins with Lorraine Gutierrez and Edith Lewis's thoughtful approach, in chapter 13, to organizing with women of color, which stresses the utility of feminist perspectives for developing a culture- and gender-relevant model of practice. Utilizing as a framework interrelated principles of education, participation, and capacity building, the authors draw on the literature, and on a wealth of personal experience in social work, to develop an approach that acknowledges and confronts the combined effects of racism, classism, and sexism. Building in part on the work of Felix Rivera and John Erlich (1995), Gutierrez and Lewis's model sees varying roles for organizers, depending, in part, on their degree of oneness and identification with the community in question. Regardless of the role played, however, Gutierrez and Lewis argue that a number of precepts are critical to effective organizing with women of color, among them learning actively, recognizing and embracing the conflict inherent in cross-cultural work, involving women of color early on in leadership roles, and in other ways contributing to community capacity.

Whereas the history of activism among women of color in the United States is traced by Gutierrez and Lewis to the early part of the nation's history, organizing among gays and lesbians tends to be a more recent phenomenon. In chapter 14, Dan Wohlfeiler provides an in-depth case study of an important piece of this history—the community building, education, and organizing among gay and bisexual men around HIV/AIDS prevention that has taken place through San Francisco's STOP AIDS Project. Like the Adolescent Social Action Program discussed in chapter 12, STOP AIDS is a good example of a health education effort that attempts to achieve both individual behavior change and increased community building and organizing, in this case around the AIDS epidemic. As such, the chapter draws on a variety of conceptual perspectives, including the AIDS Risk Reduction Model, diffusion theory, and theories stressing social support and community building. STOP AIDS provides a stark contrast to both "radical" social action organizing efforts such as Act-Up and the growing number of programs that stress primarily or exclusively treatment and services provision for people with AIDS. Yet as Wohlfeiler points out, the project's steadfast focus on prevention, although sometimes unpopular, has been critical to its effectiveness in helping to curb infection and seroconversion in this very-high-risk population.

In addition to providing a fascinating account of a difficult and important experiment in community building and individual- and community-level change, this chapter demonstrates the utility of Kurt Lewin's (1947) force field analysis in the retrospective analysis of our community organizing and community building efforts. By laying out the forces working for and against the changes that STOP AIDS wanted to promote, and then discussing the various actions taken to address these forces, the chapter amply illustrates the continued usefulness of Lewin's model for diagnosing and overcoming resistance to change.

Chapter 15 has as its setting another community in San Francisco. Unlike the city's gay and bisexual communities, which have an excellent track record of mobilizing effectively around gay and lesbian rights prior to the AIDS epidemic, the low-income elderly in the city's Tenderloin hotels has long been viewed as an "unorganizable" population. In chapter 15, Meredith Minkler chronicles the birth and evolution of the Tenderloin Senior Organizing Project, an outreach and organizing effort that was largely successful in proving this dictum false. Grounded ,in the philosophy and methods of Saul Alinsky (1972), Paulo Freire (1973), and John McKnight (1987), the project differs from more traditional health and social programs serving the elderly in emphasizing individual and community empowerment and resident determination of needs and goals.

The transformation of the Tenderloin Senior Organizing Project over time from an outreach to a true organizing project is discussed, as are its efforts in areas such as leadership building, coalition formation around issues, and creation of social support networks and tenants' organizations as vehicles for grassroots organizing. Factors contributing to the demise of the project after sixteen years are explored, as are efforts and challenges in the area of evaluating or measuring project outcomes. Although this chapter illustrates the often impressive changes that disfranchised and oppressed communities can achieve by identifying and building on their strengths, it also vividly points up the impossibility of large-scale change without a deep societal-level commitment to the reduction of social inequalities.

References

Alinsky, S. D. 1972. *Rules for radicals*. New York: Random House.

Freire, P. 1973. *Education for critical consciousness*. New York: Seabury Press.

Lewin, K. 1947. Quasi-stationary social equilibria and the problem of social change. In *Readings in social psychology*, ed. T. M. Newcomb and E. L. Hartley. New York: Holt, Rinehart and Winston.

McKnight, J. 1987. Regenerating community. *Social Policy* (Winter):54–58.

Rivera, F., and J. Erlich, eds. 1995. *Community organizing in a diverse society*. 2d ed. Boston: Allyn and Bacon.

Education, Participation, and Capacity Building in Community Organizing with Women of Color

Chapter 13

LORRAINE M. GUTIERREZ
EDITH A. LEWIS

THE FIELD OF COMMUNITY ORGANIZING has only recently begun to address the need for an approach to practice that respects and builds on the special challenges posed by our increasingly diverse society. Although much community organizing has taken place among women and communities of color, for example, surprisingly little attention has been paid to the ways in which race, gender, ethnicity, or social class will affect the organizing effort. This oversight has often prevented organizers from working effectively with women or communities of color (Bradshaw, Soifer, and Gutierrez 1994; Burghardt 1982; Rivera and Erlich 1995). By failing to recognize and take into account the many ways in which issues of oppression affect organizing work, organizers can perpetuate the objectification and exploitation of these groups (Burghardt 1982). Organizers whose own racial or ethnic stereotypes distort their view of communities of color, for example, will be ineffective in building leadership or working in partnership (Bradshaw et al. 1994; Rivera and Erlich 1995). In this way, community organizing efforts can perpetuate the very problems they were designed to solve.

This chapter begins by examining several recent contributions to our thinking about organizing with women of color, with special attention to the contributions of feminist perspectives on organizing. An empowerment framework stressing education, participation, and capacity building is then developed and used to explore different dimensions of effective community organizing with women of color. Examples of organizing both within and across racial/ethical groups are provided to illustrate many of the points made and offer lessons for social change professionals in their roles as organizers.

Multicultural Perspectives on Community Organizing

Much of the literature that does exist on multicultural organizing emphasizes the ways in which organizers can develop cultural competence for working in partnership with communities. In particular, this literature has stressed the ways in which organizers can use their own self-awareness to build bridges for work within communities. Organizers are encouraged to take the role of the learner in approaching a community and discovering its problems and strengths (Burghardt 1982; Bradshaw et al. 1994; Rivera and Erlich 1995).

A critical contribution to organizing with communities of color may be found in Felix Rivera and John Erlich's (1995) approach to identifying the appropriate roles for the organizer in light of his or her relationship to the community. If the organizer is a member of the community, these analysts argue, then primary contact is appropriate. Primary contact would involve immediate and personal grassroots work with the community. In contrast, an organizer who is of a similar ethnic or racial background but not of the community should instead be involved on the secondary level. This level would involve participation as a liaison between the community and the larger society. The tertiary level of contact would be most appropriate for those who are not members of the group. They can provide valuable contributions to the community through consultation and the sharing of technical knowledge. For example, outside professionals interested in participating in community work with a local African-American neighborhood could first establish relationships with key individuals in the community. The professional as organizer's responsibilities would be those defined by the community, no matter how insignificant these might seem on the surface. Efforts to learn the strengths of the community as they are exemplified in daily learning activities within the community would be a primary activity for the organizer. In this way, the organizer's willingness to use the culturally competent perspective of "noninterference" would be recognized in time by residents, and more opportunities for work with that community might be revealed (Lewis 1993; Lewis in press).

In work on organizing with communities of color, Catherine Bradshaw, Steven Soifer, and Lorraine Gutierrez (1994) propose a "hybrid model" of organizing that integrates aspects of the Saul Alinsky (1972) approach to social action organizing with relevant perspectives from feminist organizing. Flexibility, leadership identification and training, the appropriate use of both collaborative and confrontational tactics, and the role of the organizer as a learner and facilitator are among the characteristics of this hybrid model. Of particular importance in this model are skills for developing cultural competence that enable the outside organizer to better understand, respect, and learn from the community. These skills involve (1) cultivating awareness of one's own understanding of the community,

(2) finding ways to learn more about the local community through key informants, (3) working as partners to develop local leadership, and (4) focusing on ways to build cohesiveness within and between ethnic communities. As is by now clear, the most critical role of the organizer indeed is that of a learner who approaches the community to understand and facilitate change.

Contributions from Feminism

Much of the conceptual and practice-based literature on organizing with women has been written from a feminist perspective (Gutierrez and Lewis 1995; Hyde 1986; Weil 1986). Feminist approaches can contribute to organizing with women of color through their emphasis on integrating personal and political issues through dialogue. Feminist organizing assumes that sexism is a significant force in the experiences of all women and one that lies at the root of many of the problems they face. Therefore, a major focus for organizing with women of color is to identify ways in which sexism, racism, and other forms of oppression are affecting their lives (Bricker-Jenkins and Hooyman 1986; Gould 1987; Hyde 1986; Kopasci and Faulkner 1988; Morell 1987; Zavella 1986). Common methods for feminist organizing include the development of consciousness-raising groups, creation of alternative services, and social action that incorporates street theater and other holistic methods (Hyde 1986).

An important focus of feminist approaches is reflected in their concern with developing ways to work across differences. All women are thought to be a part of a "community" of women, as well as members of their own specific communities. Therefore, organizers need to work to bridge differences between women based on such factors as race, class, physical ability, and sexual orientation on the principle that diversity is strength. According to this perspective, "Feminist practitioners will not only strive to eliminate racism, classism, heterosexism, anti-semitism, ableism, and other systems of oppression and exploitation, but will affirm the need for diversity by actively reaching out to achieve it" (Bricker-Jenkins and Hooyman 1986). This goal for feminist organizing has been most effective when carried out from a multicultural perspective (Gutierrez and Lewis 1994).

Organizing with Women of Color

Very little literature has looked specifically at methods for organizing women of color. Yet as we have discussed elsewhere (Gutierrez and Lewis 1994, 1995), organizing by women within ethnic communities in the United States has a rich and diverse history. For example, the organization of Black Women's Clubs in the United States a century ago by leaders such as Ida B. Wells Barnett was instrumental in developing nursing homes, day care centers, and orphanages within

African-American communities. These clubs also organized for social change, particularly on antilynching and antirape campaigns and in the foundation of organizations such as the National Urban League (Collins 1991; Gutierrez and Lewis 1995; Macht and Quam 1986; Smith 1986).

Women of color have always worked to improve conditions within their communities and in society in general and have been more likely than European-American middle-class women to see community activism as a natural outgrowth of their gender role (Ackelsberg and Diamond 1987; Gilkes 1981). During the mid- to late twentieth century, for example, women played important roles in the movement for equality and civil rights within ethnic minority communities (Evans 1980; Muñoz 1989; West 1990; Withorn 1984). Neighborhood violence, economic issues, and environmental concerns are but a few of the areas on which women of color in urban communities have organized ("Fighting Back" 1988; Hirsch 1991; "Mothers' Group" 1989).

Effective community organizing efforts will build upon these traditions. By looking at these historical and contemporary efforts, we can identify ways to draw upon their strengths and learn from and adapt the strategies that already exist. As noted earlier, the role of the organizer can and should vary according to her relationship to the community or the issue being addressed (Rivera and Erlich 1995). To determine the appropriate role, we must involve the community in defining the issues it wishes to address and the strategies it feels will be most effective and culturally appropriate in attempting to achieve collectively set goals. For example, a Native American woman may be able to use her role as a member of the community and a designated leader to work on the primary level with her community to bring about change. A very different role in relation to the community would be taken by a Latina or Japanese-American organizer, who could provide important technical assistance or research skills but would not work on this primary level. Although we emphasize the necessity of participation by community members in primary roles, the important roles that can be played by nonmembers of the community on the secondary and tertiary levels should not be overlooked.

Education, Participation, and Capacity Building

What does this analysis suggest about community organizing with women of color? Utilizing an empowerment framework that stresses the core concepts of education, participation, and capacity building, we can develop sensitive and effective methods for community practice. Many of the methods described here are equally relevant to organizers and community members, and the processes of education, participation, and capacity building should take place within the organizer as well as with community members. These reciprocal process methods can be summarized as follows:

Education
1. Learn about, understand, and participate in the women's ethnic community.
2. Recognize and build upon ways in which women of color have worked effectively within their own communities; build upon existing structures.
3. Serve as a facilitator, and view the situation through the lens or vision of women of color.

Participation
4. Use the process of praxis to understand the historical, political, and social context of the organizing effort.
5. Begin with the formation of small groups.
6. Recognize and embrace the conflict that characterizes cross-cultural work.

Capacity Building
7. Involve women of color in leadership roles.
8. Understand and support the need that women of color may have for their own separate programs and organizations.

EDUCATION

Educational efforts toward community organizing and change need to be grounded in the ways in which women of color share similarities and differences with European-American women and men of color. Community organizers have often recognized the impact of powerlessness on women of color from the perspective of institutional racism. Frequently overlooked in this process, however, is the role of gender inequity in influencing the life chances of women of color. The history of community participation by women of color has often been ignored by the field. When women of color are viewed solely as members of their racial or ethnic group and gender is not taken into account, community organizers may alienate women of color and reinforce ways in which sexism, both in the larger society and within ethnic minority communities, is a form of oppression (Aragon de Valdez 1980; Collins 1991; Weil 1986; Zavella 1986).

As suggested in earlier chapters, an important first step in effective community organizing involves defining community. The fact that women of color can be members of multiple communities and hold multiple identities based on race, gender, geography, and other factors presents both a challenge and an opportunity for organizers. From an organizing perspective, however, the central issue for organizing will often define the community. For example, if the issue is toxic waste dumping in a community, then the neighborhood or city may be an appropriate level for work. If the issue is sterilization abuse and reproductive rights, then gender may be the focus. Awareness of these memberships in multiple communities can be helpful when an organizer is building coalitions or alliances between different groups.

An organizer who is from a different racial, ethnic, or class background than the women she works with must recognize how her life experience has colored her perceptions and how her status has affected her power relative to the political structure. Her beliefs and perceptions should not dominate the organizing effort. She must work toward serving as a facilitator and view the situation through the "lens" or "vision" of women of color. In part, this requires allowing this vision to alter the way the organizer views her own work and sharing that new information with others hoping to organize and work within communities of color.

When organizing with low-income women in a housing project, one of the authors initially attempted to separate individual from community concerns. She believed at first that group members would work on individual problem resolution for eight weeks and then, having established a pattern of interaction within the group, would be able to work cooperatively on analysis and resolution of community concerns. It became clear within the first two meetings that the group could not separate and sequentially work with individual and community concerns. As one participant put it, "My individual problems are the community's problems." The flexibility to alter the design based on the realities of the community allowed the group to continue working toward resolution of its identified goals, not those of the facilitator/researcher. This example illustrates the importance of understanding the community's lens on reality and the process of praxis, or action based on critical reflection, to unravel and address the salient historical, social, and political forces at work. In the preceding example, had the outside organizer insisted on separating the individual from the community problem, she would have alienated and probably lost committed community activists for whom this separation was an artificial and inappropriate one. By respecting the community's vision of the intimate interdependence of these levels, however, she was able to facilitate a process through which participants proceeded to make change on both the individual and community levels (Lewis and Ford 1990).

Organizers should also use the process of praxis to understand and address the historical, political, and social contexts of the organizing effort. This means that the organizing process as well as the outcome will inform both the organized community and "community" of the organizer. As organizers and community groups analyze the process and outcome of organizing efforts, the outcome of a tactic often emerges as less important than what the community and organizer learn about the nature of the problem being addressed. In this way, community issues are often redefined (Freire 1970; Lewis 1993).

The involvement of women of color in the battered women's movement nicely illustrates this principle. When many feminist shelters observed that they were unsuccessful in reaching women of color, they defined the problem as that of inadequate outreach. When this outreach was unsuccessful, women of color in some localities provided feedback to many shelter programs that their approach was alienating and foreign to communities of color. They often identified the lack of women of color in administrative or permanent staff positions as one way in which the program indicated a lack of commitment to their community. Programs that have been most successful with women of color have been those that addressed their own racism, classism, and ethnocentrism in the development of alternative programs (Schechter 1982).

PARTICIPATION

Participating in the women's ethnic community is an important step for educating the organizer and building bridges for future work. This participation can result in an analysis of societal institutions, including the one represented by the organizer, and how they might ultimately benefit or hurt the community. Churches, community centers, schools, and social clubs can be avenues for reaching women of color and effecting change within the community. Knowledge can also be gained about specific communities of color through reading and participation in community events (Kopasci and Faulkner 1988). Particularly for an organizer who is not an ongoing member of the community of women with whom she will be working, developing an understanding of the community's cultural context is vital.

In an effort to become involved in the community, one organizer participated in activities sponsored by the local community center. She worked for several months in enrichment programming for the children of the community before proceeding to work with the women. During this time, she became aware of community members' patterns of interaction, their relationships with agencies in the city, and other potential issues in the community. Community members and group participants had the opportunity to meet and talk with the community worker and to watch her interact with their children. Many of the initial participants in subsequent organizing efforts later mentioned that their decision to participate in the work was directly related to their approval of the facilitator's work with their children and the nature of her presence in the community (Lewis and Ford 1990).

Effective organizing often begins with the formation of small groups. The small group provides the ideal environment for exploring the social and political aspects of "personal" problems and for developing strategies for work toward social change (Gutierrez 1990; Hyde 1986, Pernell 1985; Schechter, Szymanski, and Cahill 1985). It can also be a forum for identifying common goals among diverse groups of women.

The latter strategy involves organizing small groups of individuals to work on specific problems and later coordinating these small groups so that they can work in coalition with others on joint issues. On the community level, the small group, or house meeting strategy, has been the primary way in which women of color have been organizing movements to improve conditions in ghettos and barrios (Hirsch 1991; "Mothers' Group" 1989; "Fighting Back" 1988). For example, Clementine Barfield's work with Save Our Sons and Daughters in Detroit began with discussions among a small group of mothers who had experienced the loss of a child through a violent death in the inner city.

The building of these alliances to develop community efforts can be particularly challenging when they involve more than one ethnic or other group. This is particularly true because the United States remains a highly segregated society in which many people experience little meaningful interaction with those outside their own race, class, ethnic group, or sexual orientation. Effective organizing across diverse groups requires breaking down societal boundaries to build alliances. Furthermore, it necessitates recognizing and embracing the conflict that characterizes cross-cultural work. Conflicts will inevitably arise both within those organizations that have been successful in reaching a diverse group and between the organization and a larger community that may be threatened by the absence of expected boundaries. In some respects, the emergence of conflict is an indication that meaningful cross-cultural work is taking place. However, the sources and resolution of conflict will affect the outcomes of the organizing effort. The extent to which the organizer anticipates conflict related to group interaction, the effects of internalized oppression, wider political strategies to hinder or destroy the community change effort, and similar factors will often determine whether organizing efforts are successful (Ristock 1990; West 1990).

Conflict includes the discomfort many organizers feel when they find themselves the sole person from a different ethnic or class background in a group of women of color or when they attempt to participate for the first time in a community event that has previously been attended solely by persons from the community. It is important for organizers to recognize that they will be "tested" by community members to determine whether they, as others who came before, are present only to "take." Giving on the community's terms, as illustrated in the earlier example of the author's work with children, is one example of the testing process experienced by someone attempting to enter the community.

It is our experience that European-American organizers are often less comfortable than women of color with the conflict engendered by the development of a multicultural organization. Conflicts are a part of our everyday lives. They reflect choices about fact, value, and strategy alternatives that we face intra- or interpersonally (Lewis 1988). Too often, women have been socialized into conflict-avoidance behaviors. These behaviors only temporarily delay conflicts, which will resurface when issues are not addressed directly. Addressing a conflict has often been misconstrued as synonymous with confrontation, another conflict resolution strategy. They are, however, quite different. Confrontation often means the minimization of or attack on a party with which there is conflict. This minimization, either at the personal or political levels, can easily be perceived as a threat, which inevitably leads to an escalation of the conflict rather than a dialogue about its nature.

Addressing conflict directly means employing interpersonal skills such as engagement, active listening, and consensus building. It means viewing the situation through various lenses in the presence of all who are involved in the conflict and then managing to reach some consensus about how to proceed. The process of reaching this consensus often involves being open about our differing conflict styles and managing to hear the content, rather than just the affect, of the messages being presented. To do so also requires taking a strengths approach—in this case, acknowledging the capacity or strengths in the conflict style of the group—on the part of those who have only been privy to one way of handling conflicts. In this way, conflict-avoidance techniques may be valued for their ability to offset the attack, whereas confrontation approaches may be valued for their ability to focus immediate attention on the conflict.

Conflict resolution that results in genuine dialogue and analysis of the basis of difference will have a direct effect on the outcome of an organizing effort. For example, only after European Americans involved women of color in their organizations did many European-American women encounter a different view of gender roles and how they translate into different strategies and goals. Once women of color were included in such organizations, work around sexual assault had to recognize and deal with the fears of many European-American women concerning men of color. In one organization, it was only after the group began a campaign confronting "the myth of the black rapist" that women of color within the organization and in the larger community came to believe that the organization represented their needs.

Dealing with such conflict is difficult but valuable. If we are to work toward a more equitable society, this vision must be integral to the work of our organizations. We must know ourselves and be open to knowing others. Dealing with community backlash and conflict also requires taking risks to speak out in support of our vision. The inability to resolve these conflicts has resulted in the death of some organizations and has minimized our ability to work in coalition.

CAPACITY BUILDING

Contemporary organizing by women of color has often taken a grassroots approach based upon existing networks of family, friends, or informal and formal ethnic community institutions. In this way, individual, family, and community interests are viewed as compatible and integrated with one another. Many African-American women, Latinas, and other women of color describe themselves as motivated to engage in activism because of their commitment to their communities and ethnic group (Collins 1991; Barrera 1987; Gilkes 1981, 1983; Lacayo 1989). Women also have often been active in the mutual aid societies within ethnic communities, such as the Hui among the Chinese, the Ko among the Japanese, and the tribal councils among Native Americans (Gutierrez and Lewis 1995). Each of these organizations has served as a vehicle for assisting individual ethnic group members, families, and entire communities through the establishment of business loans, funerals, and community programs.

Organizers must recognize and build upon these networks and the myriad ways in which women of color have worked effectively within their own communities. Outside organizers, regardless of their own race or ethnicity, need to work with community leaders and learn from them the most effective ways of working in particular communities. Working with existing leaders may involve organizers in different types of activities than those in which they may usually engage. For example, to provide survival services, existing community leaders may be active in church-related activities or with municipal agencies (Bookman and Morgan 1986). Organizers can learn from these women ways that they have found to survive and leverage political power.

Organizers also need to recognize how women of color have been involved in advocating for women's rights since the beginning of the feminist movement. For example, many of the first shelters for battered women were founded by women of color responding to the needs in their communities (Schechter 1982). Recognition of the contributions of women of color to feminist causes can help to break down some of the barriers and difficulties that exist in this work.

As suggested earlier, however, community organizing with women of color may involve a broader perspective than the one initially envisioned by the organizer. This broader perspective would recognize the many ways in which race, gender, class, and ethnicity are intertwined. Consequently, it would underscore the impossibility of separating the needs of women from those of their families and communities (Gutierrez and Lewis 1994). The role of women in the civil rights movements of the 1950s and 1960s certainly illustrates the importance of gender to mobilization efforts. The successful Montgomery Alabama bus boycott, for example, is usually credited to African-American male ministers who were in public leadership positions. However, the impetus for the boycott was a group of African-American women who impressed on the ministers that the cause was just and that they would launch the boycott themselves if the ministers did not take a public stance. The women raised the consciousness of the ministers and in this way contributed significantly to social action. However, they were willing to work behind the scenes, rather than spearheading the boycott themselves, because they thought it was imperative that African-American men's leadership be supported. This delicate interaction of race, ethnicity, class, and gender must be in the forefront of the organizer's praxis perspective.

All too often, organizing with women of color has taken the unidirectional "outreach approach," in which communities of color are targets of change rather than active participants and collaborators. When this former approach is used, women of color often resist organizing efforts and, in some cases, undermine them (Schechter 1982; Kopasci and Faulkner 1988). It is crucial, therefore, to involve women of color in leadership roles from the onset. Predominantly European-American organizations wishing to collaborate with women of color will need to incorporate women of color as leaders and active participants *before* taking on this kind of work. Such collaboration may require redefining the kind of work the organization does, as well as looking critically at its members' attitudes toward institutions such as the church and family. The history of attempts at collaboration suggests that cross-cultural work requires identifying how racism may exclude women of color from leadership roles (Burghardt 1982; Schechter 1982). Successful collaboration will require that European-American organizers change their interactions with women of color and be capable of sharing power and control of their programs. This type of organizational work embraces the tenet of feminist organizing that "diversity is strength."

Issues of perceived or actual social class differences must be taken into account, even when the organizer is from the same ethnic or gender background as the community in which she is working. As noted earlier, the definition of community may be psychological as well as geographic. Those entering, or reentering, communities need to be cognizant that their economic or educational backgrounds may be perceived as making them somehow different from other community members. They must anticipate suspicion or backlash as a possible consequence. As in other conflict situations, a process of dialogue and action can be used to work through this problem, such that the organizer can then participate in the community on the latter's own terms. Perhaps one of the highest compliments paid to one of the authors was in a community meeting in which she was introduced to others as "not an educated fool."

One method for building effective coalitions is the incorporation of informal "debriefing" groups for community workers. These groups would include all members of the community and would provide opportunities for input and clarification of the organizing process. Those in key leadership positions would model their ongoing praxis experiences by being open about the choices made in the organizing effort and the assumptions upon which these choices rested. Debriefing sessions would allow for community members who are not an integral part of the organizing effort to share additional strategies and to evaluate the impact of the design on the community to date. Some groups have used the house meeting strategy to provide debriefing opportunities, whereas others have relied upon formal written materials such as community newsletters to keep community members informed. Consistent ongoing debriefing efforts need to be built into the organizing design and expanded as needed.

Within the realm of organizing, there is room for multiethnic organizations and cross-ethnic coalitions, but also for organizations developed by and for women of color. In the latter regard, organizers need to understand and support the need that women of color may have for their own separate programs and organizations. For women of color, a separate group or organization in which we can explore who we are in relation to the communities in which we live can often provide the basis for creating a vision for future work. A separate organization is one means for building on strengths and nurturing capacity within a community. In work with women of color in an educational setting, the formation of a women of color caucus had positive impact on the ability of a women's studies program to hire more faculty of color and to develop courses that were more racially and ethnically inclusive. Although the formation was initially viewed by some as divisive, all participants in the program ultimately recognized that the caucus was a critical element in the empowerment of women of color and their capacity to work for positive change for all.

Summary

This chapter has used a framework of education, participation, and capacity building to explore empowering strategies and approaches for community organizing with women of color. Borrowing in part from Rivera and Erlich (1995), we have argued that different roles are appropriate for an organizer depending upon her relationship to the community (e.g., whether she is a member, a nonmember with a similar racial or ethnic background, or a person of a different racial or ethnic group).

Regardless of the role played, however, several principles are critical in effective organizing with women of color. These include being an active learner and facilitator who can view a given situation through the "lenses" of women of color, recognizing and embracing the conflict that characterizes cross-cultural work, involving women of color in leadership roles, and in other ways contributing to the building of community capacity. Both feminist perspectives and cultural perspectives on organizing in communities of color offer valuable lessons for organizers who cross race, ethnic, gender, class, and other lines in their organizing efforts.

References

Ackelsberg, M., and I. Diamond. 1987. Gender and political life: New directions in political science. In *Analyzing gender: A handbook of social science*, ed. B. Hess and M. Feree. Newbury Park, Calif.: Sage.

Alinsky, S. D. 1972. *Rules for radicals*. New York: Random House.

Aragon de Valdez, T. 1980. Organizing as a political tool for the Chicana. *Frontiers* 5:7–13.

Barrera, M. 1987. Chicano class structure. In *From different shores: Perspectives on race and ethnicity in America*, ed. R. Takaki. New York: Oxford University Press.

Bookman, A., and S. Morgan. 1986. *Women and the politics of empowerment*. Philadelphia: Temple University Press.

Bradshaw, C., S. Soifer, and L. Gutierrez. 1994. Toward a hybrid model for effective organizing with women of color. *Journal of Community Practice* 1 (1):25–41.

Bricker-Jenkins, M., and N. Hooyman. 1986. *Not for women only: Social work practice for a feminist future*. Silver Spring, Md.: National Association of Social Workers.

Burghardt, S. 1982. *The other side of organizing*. Cambridge, Mass.: Schenkman.

Collins, P. 1991. *Black feminist thought: Knowledge, consciousness, and the politics of empowerment*. New York: Routledge.

Evans, S. 1980. *Personal politics*. New York: Vintage Books.

Fighting back: Frances Sandoval and her mother's crusade take aim at gangs. 1988. *Sunday Chicago Tribune Magazine*, October 16, 10–24.

Freire, P. 1970. Cultural action for freedom. *Harvard Educational Review* 40:205–225, 452–477.

Gilkes, C.. 1981. Holding back the ocean with a broom: Black women and community work. In *The black woman*, ed. L. F. Rodgers-Rose. Beverly Hills, Calif.: Sage.

———. 1983. Going up for the oppressed: The career mobility of black women community workers. *Journal of Social Issues* 39:115–139.

Gould, K. 1987. Feminist principles and minority concerns: Contributions, problems, and solutions. *Affila* 3:6–19.

Gutierrez, L. 1990. Working with women of color: An empowerment perspective. *Social Work* 35:149–154.

Gutierrez, L., and E. Lewis. 1994. Community organizing with women of color: A feminist approach. *Journal of Community Practice* 1 (2):23–43.

———. 1995. A feminist perspective on organizing with women of color. In *Community organizing in a diverse society*, ed. F. Rivera and J. Erlich. 2d ed. Boston: Allyn and Bacon.

Hirsch, K. 1991. Clementine Barfield takes on the mean streets of Detroit. *Ms.* 1 (4):54–58.

Hyde, C. 1986. Experiences of women activists: Implications for community organizing theory and practice. *Journal of Sociology and Social Welfare* 13:545–562.

Kopasci, R., and A. Faulkner. 1988. The powers that might be: The unity of white and black feminists. *Affila* 3:33–50.

Lacayo, R. 1989. On the front lines. *Time*, September 11, 14–19.

Lewis, E. 1988. The single door: Social work with the families of disabled children. *Social Casework* 69 (1):61–63.

———. 1993. Continuing the legacy: On the importance of praxis in the education of social work students and teachers. In *Multicultural teaching in the university*, ed. D. Schoem, L. Frankel, X. Zuniga, and E. Lewis. New York: Praeger.

———. In press. Ethnicity, race, and gender: Training and supervision issues in the treatment of women. In *Women, gender, and group psychotherapy*, ed. B. De Chant, J. Cunningham, J. Lazerson, and R. Perls. New York: American Group Psychotherapy Association Monograph.

Lewis, E., and B. Ford. 1990. The network utilization project: Incorporating traditional strengths of African Americans into group work practice. *Social Work with Groups* 13 (3):7–22.

Macht, M., and J. Quam. 1986. *Social work: An introduction*. Columbus, Ohio: Merrill.

Morell, C. 1987. Cause is function: Toward a feminist model of integration for social work. *Social Science Review* 61:144–155.

Mothers' group fights back in Los Angeles. 1989. *New York Times*, December 5.

Muñoz, C. 1989. *Youth, identity, and power: The Chicano movement*. London: Verso.

Pernell, R. 1985. Empowerment and social group work. In *Innovations in social group work: Feedback from practice to theory*, ed. M. Parenes. New York: Hawthorn Press.

Ristock, J. 1990. Canadian feminist social service collectives: Caring and contradictions.

In *Bridges of power: Women's multicultural alliances*, ed. L. Albrecht and R. Brewer. Philadelphia: New Society.

Rivera, F., and J. Erlich. 1995. *Community organizing in a diverse society*. 2d ed. Boston: Allyn and Bacon.

Schechter, S. 1982. *Women and male violence: The visions and struggles of the battered women's movement*. Boston: South End Press.

Schechter, S., S. Szymanski, and M. Cahill. 1985. *Violence against women: A curriculum for empowerment*. New York: Women's Education Institute.

Smith, A. 1986. Positive marginality: The experience of black women leaders. In *Redefining Social Problems*, ed. E. Seidman and J. Rappaport. New York: Plenum Press.

Weil, M. 1986. Women, community, and organizing. In *Feminist visions for social work*, ed. N. Van DenBergh and L. Cooper. Silver Spring, Md.: National Association of Social Workers.

West, G. 1990. Cooperation and conflict among women in the welfare rights movement. In *Bridges of power: Women's multicultural alliances*, ed. L. Albrecht and R. Brewer. Philadelphia: New Society.

Withorn, A. 1984. *Serving the people: Social services and social change*. New York: Columbia University Press.

Zavella, P. 1986. The politics of race and gender: Organizing Chicana cannery workers in northern California. In *Women and the politics of empowerment*, ed. A. Bookman and S. Morgan. Philadelphia: Temple University Press.

<table>
</table>

Chapter 14 | Community Organizing and Community Building among Gay and Bisexual Men

DAN WOHLFEILER | *The STOP AIDS Project*

G AY AND BISEXUAL MEN are commonly held up as having made public health history (Choi and Coates 1994; Coates et al. 1995; McCusick et al. 1990). In San Francisco, when faced with a new, terrifying, fatal HIV epidemic, they changed their behavior rapidly and brought new infections down from a high of approximately 8,000 annually in the earliest years of the epidemic to approximately 650 by the mid-1980s (San Francisco Department of Public Health 1994; Stryker et al. 1995). By that time, almost one out of two of the estimated 58,000 gay and bisexual men in San Francisco had become infected, making ongoing prevention efforts that much more difficult and important (Stryker et al. 1995; San Francisco Department of Public Health 1992).

The gay community rapidly incorporated AIDS into its agenda and used its political and organizational power to develop the "San Francisco model" of AIDS prevention and treatment. So large was this mobilization that many members of the community voiced concern that it had "hijacked" the other important agendas of gay rights and gay community building (Fitzgerald 1986). This chapter describes the formation of a key community HIV prevention program, the STOP AIDS Project, its closure, and its subsequent reopening and how it began to turn itself inside out in order to help remobilize the community to reduce new infections.

The STOP AIDS Project's emphasis on volunteerism and well-honed educational and community organizing strategies has led to it being widely cited as an example of a successful HIV/AIDS prevention intervention (Smith 1996; DeCarlo 1995). Diverse communities have attempted to replicate its programs (Miller et al. 1990). At a time when many individuals still relied heavily on distributing information to promote behavioral change, the project recognized, as early as 1984, that its target community was highly informed about HIV transmission, but that information was insufficient by itself to create and maintain behavioral change (Puckett and Bye 1987).

This chapter first describes the project's conceptual grounding in social support theory and in the community building practice orientation set forth by Cheryl Walter in chapter 5. Kurt Lewin's (1947) force field analysis is then discussed as a useful conceptual tool for examining and better understanding the forces working for and against the changes that STOP AIDS wished to introduce in its community. After a description of the early days of the project, its closure in 1987, and its reopening three years later, the chapter uses force field analysis to explore both the driving forces and the barriers confronted by STOP AIDS staff and volunteers in the project's later years. Three new programs are used to illustrate how the project addressed some of these forces, and reflected key tenets of social support theories and community building, in carrying out its mission. Finally, implications for other organizers are presented.

Theoretical Framework

Like most community-based organizations, STOP AIDS did not begin as a consciously theory-based project. The organization was among the many that emerged out of the well-organized gay communities around the country in response to the epidemic. Almost immediately, however, the project founders, themselves gay San Franciscans, looked to theory to help shape the project. In relation to the individual behavior change aspects of its work, for example, the project quickly adapted the AIDS Risk Reduction Model (Catania, Kegeles, and Coates 1990), which highlights the importance of perceived threat, response efficacy, personal efficacy, and peer support. The project also relied heavily on diffusion theory, which suggests that only those early adopters, who make up a relatively small segment of the population, need to initiate a new behavior for it to spread throughout the population (Rogers 1983). Diffusion theory has been demonstrated to be effective in AIDS prevention programs for gay and bisexual men in diverse settings (Kelly et al. 1991).

Of great relevance to both personal behavior change and the organizing aspects of STOP AIDS has been its grounding in theories linking social support and health (Cohen and Syme 1985). Social support theory maintains, in part, that supportive social relationships reduce the risk of disease and disability. Conversely, this body of theory suggests that individuals, such as gay and bisexual men, who are at high risk for multiple losses in their social networks may be particularly vulnerable to illness. Finally, a tenet of social support theory with special relevance to this project suggests that identifying, strengthening, and working through preexisting networks will enhance the effectiveness of health-related interventions (Israel 1985). Peer support for safe behavior was correlated with safe behavior among gay and bisexual men in San Francisco as early as 1985 (Ekstrand and Coates 1990).

In addition to a conceptual grounding in social support theory, STOP AIDS fits comfortably within the framework of community building. As described in chapter 5, the latter stresses being one with the community and emphasizes community strengths rather than deficits. That STOP AIDS staff and volunteers viewed themselves from the beginning as "of" the community (San Francisco's gay and bisexual population) rather than as "outside organizers" or educators and that the project relied heavily on volunteers and increasingly on indigenous networks reflected its strong community building orientation.

A final conceptual area helpful in understanding the STOP AIDS project and its metamorphosis over time is Kurt Lewin's (1947) force field analysis. Lewin argues that any given social change situation is in a state of "quasi-stationary equilibrium" caused by driving and resisting forces working in opposition to each other. When the forces are weighted heavily on the driving side of the equation, change is likely to take place. When the resisting or restraining forces are the more powerful, no change is likely to occur. According to Lewin, strengthening or adding driving forces or weakening or removing resisting forces could help change take place, with the latter (removal or weakening of resisting forces) the most likely to be successful in achieving sustained change.

The Early Days

The early history of the AIDS epidemic in San Francisco has been well documented (Fitzgerald 1986; Garrett 1994; Shilts 1987). Community organizations took responsibility early for distributing information as it became available. Community activists began storefront telephone hotlines. Materials with early warnings about "gay-related cancer" appeared in the early 1980s.

In 1984, educators and market researchers gathered to conduct focus group research of gay and bisexual men to determine the elements of a marketing campaign to promote safe sex. What the researchers observed was that the men in the room were benefiting as much, if not more, from the discussion as the researchers were. Many men had been experiencing no small degree of anxiety and fear as a result of the sudden explosion of a fatal disease in their community.

Many of the participants realized that they were not alone in their anxieties and that, contrary to their unspoken assumptions, others wanted and expected behaviors that would not place them or their partners at risk. Many quickly perceived the benefits of breaking down some of the silent assumptions of different community members through explicit conversation about, and in support of, safe behavior.

The focus group organizers realized that such small group activities could have a substantial motivational and educational benefit and quickly mobilized their friends and acquaintances to hold these same groups in private living rooms around the city. This marked the birth of the STOP AIDS Project, which the founders described as a "community experiment in communication." Using aggressive outreach techniques, including stopping men on the streets and in bars and other gathering spots to describe the project, volunteers recruited men to participate in "the STOP AIDS Meeting." Between 1985 and 1987, the project reached approximately thirty thousand men through outreach.

The STOP AIDS meeting followed the basic outlines of the original focus groups. Trained volunteer facilitators asked participants a series of questions: "How has AIDS affected you?" "What do you think about the safe sex guidelines?" "What makes them difficult to follow?" In keeping with the project's community building orientation, the facilitators also asked, "What do you want from the community?" "What are you willing to do for the community?" Increasing community consciousness around values and the promotion of visions of the future was a key component of the STOP AIDS community building process and one vital to making community norms explicit, thereby increasing the community's ability to fight the epidemic. The element that made STOP AIDS meetings community organizing, rather than solely behavior change workshops, came at the end of the meeting, when the facilitator would ask each member of the group to make a commitment regarding his own behavior and community activism. Such an agreement might be "I commit to staying safe and to volunteering for an AIDS organization." Many of these participants would begin the next week to do outreach, schedule participants into workshops, mobilize people for participation in a rally, or get trained to facilitate future meetings themselves, becoming peer AIDS educators in the process.

The organization's own estimates put the number of men who went through these meetings at seven thousand (Puckett and Bye 1987). Such a number demonstrates the magnitude of the community's interest in openly discussing HIV prevention and in taking action into its own hands. The project had struck a chord at the right time and in a way that allowed community members to learn facts, gain and give support to act on those facts, and decide for themselves their most appropriate action.

To complement outreach and small-group meetings, the project developed a media campaign, through which it promoted meeting attendance and volunteerism. In addition, for those men who never stopped to speak to an outreach worker or who never attended a meeting, the media promoted open dialogue about these issues in the community.

In 1987, however, two major factors led to the project taking the unprecedented step of closing its doors. First, the number of men who were interested in attending meetings after their initial contact with an outreach volunteer declined considerably. Second, epidemiological studies showed that the level of new infections had decreased from 18 to 1 percent, perhaps as low a figure as was realistically attainable. While acknowledging that some men would continue to have unsafe sex, the project declared that it had reached the critical mass of early and even later adopters necessary to bring about continued behavior change. The project declared victory and closed its local operations, consciously freeing up resources for other communities that were just beginning to perceive the impact of the AIDS epidemic and conducting STOP AIDS training programs in other cities around the country.

Reopening

Unfortunately, the project's closing proved to be premature. A variety of factors, including the transient nature of the population, caused STOP AIDS to reopen its doors in 1990. For the next two years, the project maintained the same model as before. With volunteers from the first project as well as participants-turned-volunteers, the project reached an average of six thousand men through outreach and eleven hundred men in its four-hour meetings each year from 1990 through 1996. Although these were still significant numbers, the project clearly was not attracting as many men as it had originally.

To better understand the challenges facing STOP AIDS during this difficult later period in the epidemic, it is helpful to conduct a force field analysis. Some of the forces working to impede change were identical to those that had operated from the beginning. Others, however, reflected new developments and realities with which the project needed to cope. And a number of new and continuing driving forces could be identified that aided the project staff and volunteers by suggesting potential programmatic directions.

From the beginning, but increasingly recognized as important, the strongest resistant force was the massive strength of the epidemic itself. The HIV/AIDS epidemic is so extensive, with almost one out of two gay or bisexual men in San Francisco being infected, that any one unsafe incident carries a much higher risk than it would in other settings where HIV is less prevalent, such as among gay and bisexual men in Seattle, Washington (14 to 21 percent; Seattle–King County Department of Public Health 1995) or among lesbians in San Francisco (1.2 percent; Lemp et al. 1995). This means that even those men who are highly committed to safe sex but have a rare incident of unsafe sex with an unknown partner carry a high risk of exposure and infection (Ekstrand et al. 1990; Morris and Dean 1994).

A second key resisting force lies in the fact the Project's message was and has remained unattractive to many: the reduction of unprotected sex, which for many is inherently more pleasurable than safe, protected sex. It is not a choice that most men would make willingly if there were no risk attached. Nor is prevention an agenda that most communities would easily adopt.

A third resisting force was that the epidemic had already captured and overwhelmed the community's resources and time for emotional and practical support for those already infected with HIV. As of June 30, 1996, 16,072 persons in San Francisco had already died of HIV, and 23,176 cases had been diagnosed, of which 91 percent were among gay and bisexual men (San Francisco Department of Public Health 1996). The resulting needs for practical and emotional support and medical care and organizing to demand more resources for care and treatment were massive. In the community, in many organizations, and in the San Francisco Department of Health's own AIDS Office, which had been set up to provide both prevention and care services, care took precedence. In 1996, for example, Project Open Hand, a meals delivery service (Redis 1996) and the Shanti Project (Grossi 1996), which provides practical and emotional support to those infected, together could count on 650 volunteers. In contrast, 125 were actively volunteering for STOP AIDS.

These three resisting forces—the sheer size of the epidemic, its overtaxing of community resources, and the continued negative perceptions of safe sex by many —were the initial reasons for the project's existence and are the primary reasons for its continued relatively narrow focus on AIDS prevention for gay and bisexual men. Most community-based AIDS prevention programs exist within organizations that house prevention, care, and social service programs (Freudenberg and Zimmerman 1995). Additionally, many organizations target multiple communities. By maintaining an exclusive focus, however, the Stop AIDS Project has been able to develop expertise and concentrate its efforts on mobilizing the community to stay focused on prevention, while resisting the almost inevitable pull of the immediate needs posed by care and services for those infected by HIV.

Two additional resisting forces became more apparent as the project reopened. First, the highly transient nature of San Francisco creates an ongoing challenge for AIDS prevention efforts. Like other major metropolitan areas, San Francisco attracts many gay men who desire to live openly. One-third of the city's gay men are estimated to have lived in San Francisco for less than six years, and the proportion of men who had lived in San Francisco less than two years doubled between 1984 and 1989 (Communication Technologies 1990). In most cases, these men were coming from areas with less intensive education efforts. In addition, these men were not part of the initial community mobilizations that took place in the early 1980s and were likely to perceive less ownership of those organizations that had been founded prior to their arrival in the community. Q Action, the Young Men's Program of STOP AIDS, was created to address this issue while utilizing the driving force of a new generation of young gay and bisexual men with interest in and energy for organizing.

A second resisting force that became more apparent in later years involved the fact that some members of the community externalized responsibility for their risk behavior and resulting infections while not recognizing the individual's share of that responsibility. Blame for new infections was at times attributed to schools (Gay and Lesbian Alliance Against Defamation 1994), AIDS education (Odets 1995), and even STOP AIDS itself (Moon 1994). In one extreme case, a newspaper publisher blamed the project for not having stopped HIV transmissions (Chalker 1995). To consciously and explicitly return ownership of AIDS prevention to the community, and to provide an environmental context that would support small-group workshops and outreach efforts, the Stop AIDS Project created its Neighborhood Mobilization Program. This program took advantage of the driving force of a well-organized community, including many businesses that were willing to incorporate AIDS prevention into their activities. To further weave AIDS prevention back into the community and reduce the impression that AIDS prevention was the work of nonprofit agencies, the project took advantage of the multiple networks existing in the community by offering workshops to pre-existing social groups.

Q Action

The willingness of many young gay and bisexual men to serve as social activists provided a first significant driving force for addressing the resisting force of the highly transient nature of the community. The challenge for the project was to promote that activism while simultaneously encouraging explicit peer support for healthy behavior. The combination of high rates of new infection among young men and lack of ownership by young men of prevention efforts led STOP AIDS to create Q Action, a program by and for young men.

The project hoped that by young men creating a separate identity, members of this population would be more attracted to taking part in AIDS prevention activities. The creation of Q Action also built on health education and community organizing principles that people who feel a sense of program ownership are more likely to engage in high level participation and to take seriously the program agenda (Bracht and Tsouros 1990; Green 1986). Project media efforts promoted Q Action as a place where young men could take the epidemic into their own hands and on their own terms. Q Action set about to promote the dual agenda of political action and internal behavior change. Its messages were aimed at highlighting homophobia, racism, and other external social obstacles to safe behavior and the need for the individual to take responsibility for safe behavior.

To address those segments of the population for which AIDS prevention was likely to be less of a priority than many other issues, and to combat the perception that STOP AIDS was only an agency for white gay men, Q Action developed a special series of activities. To attract young African-American and Latino men, who were experiencing the highest rates of unsafe sex and seroconversion, the project began to sponsor film screenings about subjects that staff and volunteers of these communities felt were likely to be of interest to those populations, including racism, masculinity, and community. At these screenings, facilitators helped draw the connection between those issues and the project's priority, HIV prevention. For example, facilitators led participants in a discussion about why African-American and Latino men reported more unsafe sexual behavior than did Caucasians or Asians and how racial stereotypes influenced expectations by sexual partners.

In addition, the project created Boy+Boy, a direct-action group with substantial autonomy from the rest of the project. This was intended to further mobilize young gay and bisexual men to take actions that would help move HIV prevention up their peers' list of priorities. Actions included street theater, political demonstrations, and materials development. These actions were often targeted both at young men's peers and at political officials to pressure the latter into supporting explicit primary prevention efforts.

Group members decided to spend one out of four meetings discussing issues in their own lives related to HIV prevention, thereby once again providing explicit social support for safe behavior. The balance of this internal and external focus demonstrated the young men's successful adoption of the project's agenda, as well as a sophisticated understanding of the importance of taking both individual and collective action.

Neighborhood Mobilizations

Although not directly working under the project's umbrella, many community members were willing to participate in efforts to promote risk reduction. Collectively, these individuals had the potential to serve as a second, vital driving force for promoting behavior change. They could provide ongoing social support, on a larger and more diffuse scale, for the behavior that the workshops promoted on a more intimate level. Community members played a pivotal role in neighborhoods where HIV was a relatively lower priority than other issues.

Project organizers created the Neighborhood Mobilization Program in 1994 in an attempt to bolster the workshops' effect and to aggressively mobilize key opinion leaders to explicitly encourage their neighbors to have safe sex. By doing so, this program aimed at helping to reduce dependence on the project and other agencies as being the sole sources of social support.

The project began recruiting bar owners, restaurant owners, shopkeepers, and large and small businesses of all kinds to assist in the promotion of safe sex. As a means toward building long-term support, the project invited businesses and other organizations to participate in mobilization weekends, with massive distributions of materials and promotional activities. The project developed a scale of involvement of each key opinion leader, adapted from a scale developed by investigators involved in the CDC-funded Prevention of HIV in Women and Infants Projects (Person and Cotton 1996). The scale enabled project staff to document and measure the level of voluntary involvement in HIV prevention among key members of the community. The minimal level of participation, endorsement, involved key opinion leaders agreeing to place materials and condoms in their places of business. The next level, support, involved giving better placement to these materials. At the third level, opinion leaders would actively promote and distribute the materials to their customers. On the fourth level, they would create a safe-sex window display. The fifth and final level of participation involved becoming organizers by assisting in recruiting other opinion leaders.

The project community organizers originally targeted several neighborhoods around San Francisco. These included the Castro, heavily gay and the site of numerous gay-owned businesses and organizations; Haight-Ashbury, home to many young adults and recent arrivals to San Francisco, with a large street person population; the Mission, center of the city's Latino community, including several gay bars catering mostly to Latino men; the Polk, which had a large street youth and hustler population; and South of Market, where a very heterogeneous and mostly working-class residential population was joined at night by men patronizing gay bars and dance clubs.

The project had varying degrees of success in working with these neighborhoods. The variations in success reflected the organizers' familiarity with and understanding of the neighborhoods and the extent to which the neighborhood in question prioritized AIDS among a list of other competing issues. As anticipated, for example, the Castro was where the most opinion leaders signed on quickly and where it was the easiest for organizers to gain access to the local merchants' association. Many of these merchants dedicated substantial time and resources to assisting in the efforts.

In contrast, the Mission and Polk neighborhoods were much more challenging to organizers. The Mission, while home to a sizable number of self-identified gay men, is also home to sizable native-born and immigrant Latino populations. Among these population groups, there were many more readily identifiable high-priority issues, including violence, drugs, and immigration. Gay life typically is less open and is concentrated in a relatively small area of the neighborhood. The Polk, once the center of San Francisco gay life, is now characterized by high levels of drug use and male and female prostitution. Both neighborhoods have far fewer economic resources to dedicate to AIDS prevention than does the relatively affluent Castro. Organizers had to spend relatively greater amounts of time with local groups in these neighborhoods and accept much slower progress as they sought to promote HIV prevention.

By far the easiest goal to reach was that of distributing materials. The project provided condoms, brochures featuring well-known volunteers in each neighborhood, and posters advertising a "mobilization weekend." Encouraging the opinion leaders to take more active roles took much more effort. Nevertheless, many proactively offered the materials to their customers, and several took the initiative in verbally expressing their support for safe sex to patrons.

In addition, each neighborhood was the site of a safe-sex window display contest. Merchants were asked to put together a window display that would encourage clientele and passersby to stay safe. The windows were an easy barometer of the resources of each neighborhood, as well as the priority placed on HIV prevention. In some neighborhoods, only a handful of merchants would put together a collage of newspaper articles. In the Castro, however, over two dozen merchants participated, many spending considerable staff time and resources of their own to develop lavish displays. One local and highly popular gift store took individual pictures of fifteen employees, asked each of them to write short paragraphs about the importance of HIV prevention in their lives, and carefully arranged them in the window. This demonstrated the potential for the mobilizations to tap into an often unexpressed but present source of neighborhood-based support for safe sexual behavior.

Access to and Work through Social Organizations

The third driving force that the project attempted to harness was the extent to which gay and bisexual men had organized themselves into a complex social network. Since the inception of STOP AIDS, it had been largely an organization distinct from and outside of other community efforts. The project's effort in its later years to reach preexisting groups was an explicit attempt to reintegrate AIDS prevention efforts into the fabric of the community and to promote explicit expression of ongoing social support for healthy behavior.

In many ways, San Francisco's gay community was hyperorganized. A mere glance through the pages of one of the three or four gay newspapers published weekly reveals a vast array of social organizations: there are gay political, musical, recreational, religious, and athletic groups. Project organizers sought out methods to take advantage of the social support inherent in these groups to maximize the effect of the workshops. The project also hypothesized, based on social support theory, that preexisting groups would have a greater impact on unsafe sex than meetings where the participants had been recruited at random through outreach. If the conversation started in a STOP AIDS meeting, it would likely continue in informal ways between some members as time went on. This was consistent with research that indicated that gay men who found their sexual behavior problematic turned to friends for help.

The project hired a community organizer to recruit and facilitate the groups. Despite initial feedback gathered during interviews, many groups were very reluctant to commit their time to conducting a STOP AIDS meeting. Groups often rejected the idea of holding a workshop because they knew all about AIDS. This meant that the organizer had to redouble his efforts to explain the difference between giving information and offering the kind of explicit support that had to accompany this information to bring about sustained behavior change. In addition, many groups were suffering the frequent loss of their members. Many were reluctant to dedicate any more time to AIDS in the social outlets that they often perceived as a momentary escape from the harsh daily reminders of the ongoing epidemic.

The organizer went to extraordinary lengths to earn groups' trust. In keeping with the community action dimension of community building (see chapter 5), for example, he engaged with other community members in a broad range of activities. These included attending more than five masses of Dignity, a gay Catholic group; chanting along with the members of another spiritual group; attending multiple rehearsals of a gay marching band; and going to meetings of the Sisters of Perpetual Indulgence, a gay activist group, which had, in fact, helped launch the city's first AIDS prevention efforts.

The organizer also recruited project volunteers who were members of these organizations to assist in the recruitment. This proved to be helpful since the volunteers could serve as effective bridge builders to their own organizations. In addition, the project attempted to recruit several volunteers and staff to recruit their friends who were members of diverse informal social networks.

Qualitative feedback included reports from many participants who indicated that the meetings challenged their assumptions about their need for support beyond information. The meetings also catalyzed discussion and debate about the role of friends in encouraging each other to have safe sex and about, in the words of one participant, "whose business it is" if someone has unsafe sex.

Additionally, the project showed some promising signs of helping other groups place a higher priority on explicit support for prevention. The gay men's marching band, for example, without any prompting from the project, decided to hold a second workshop on its own. Other groups continued to discuss HIV prevention issues in their newsletters and in both formal and informal settings.

Together, Q Action, the Neighborhood Mobilization Program, and work to gain access to preexisting groups all demonstrated the project's desire to strengthen its community building and community organizing orientation rather than become a service organization. By actively turning itself inside out, the project sought to reduce potential dependence on itself as the holder of "the solution" to the problem of ongoing HIV infections among gay and bisexual men. Rather than be seen as the sole organizational provider of support, the agency aggressively sought to mobilize others to express that support and to come to regard HIV prevention as a greater priority in their individual lives and that of their community.

Suggestions for Practitioners

Several lessons emerge from the project's experience that are relevant to others involved in health promotion, community building, and community organizing. First, no matter what other agendas exist in a community, it is imperative that those working in prevention remain focused on their own agenda. This is not to say that other agendas should not be understood or that coalitions should not be built. But the unique nature of prevention—a topic that by definition is almost guaranteed to fall to the bottom of any community's list of priorities—means that organizers cannot rely exclusively on what communities say they want. Few people will ever say they want prevention. It is incumbent on organizers to base their efforts on epidemiology, using organizing techniques to build a long-term, effective response. By doing so, organizers can benefit from greater epidemiological impact, as well as an increased community ability to pursue other agendas.

Second, AIDS education has tended to become dangerously confused with treatment and social services. All AIDS activism is not AIDS prevention. If community-based organizations are to be truly effective, they must maintain a stance—however unpopular—that they cannot be held responsible for individuals' sexual actions. Organizations can and should help a community target external obstacles to safe sex, including bigotry against gay and bisexual men in the government and private sector. But organizers must be careful not to allow victimization to predominate because victimization is inherently contradictory to the kind of individual responsibility required to prevent transmission in the most intimate and irrational of human behaviors. AIDS organizations should be clear about highlighting the shared responsibility of communities to stop AIDS.

Third, it is imperative to build a strong cadre of critical thinkers and highly skilled organizers. As Ronald Labonte suggests in chapter 6, it is entirely consistent to be a health promotion professional and to be an organizer. Just as there are many fine physicians who serve in community settings, but of whom we rightfully expect good medical training, we need to support and demand that our educators and organizers are as well trained as possible. Community assessment, issue selection, planning, evaluation, and effective management are highly complex areas that benefit from training that includes a heavy emphasis on critical thinking and the application of relevant theory.

Fourth, AIDS educators need to build sound organizations while assuming the worst: that funding will dry up. They should not build dependence on themselves for AIDS prevention; they should instead attempt to build as strong a foundation in the community as possible. Organizers must do what they do best: rather than "serve their communities" from the outside, they must stress community building and organizing from within.

Acknowledgments

I wish to express my gratitude to the volunteers and staff of STOP AIDS for their exemplary dedication to HIV prevention for gay and bisexual men and to the UCSF Center for AIDS Prevention Studies.

STOP AIDS educational materials, including training manuals, may be obtained through the project's web page (http://www.stopaids.org) or through the project at 201 Sanchez Street, San Francisco, CA 94114.

References

Bracht, N., and A. Tsouros. 1990. Principles and strategies of effective community participation. *Health Promotion International* 5 (3):199–208.

Catania, J. A., S. M. Kegeles, and T. J. Coates. 1990. Towards an understanding of risk behavior: An AIDS risk reduction model (ARRM). *Health Education Quarterly* 17 (1):53–72.

Chalker, R. 1995. Publisher's note. *San Francisco Sentinel*, March 29.

Choi, K. H., and T. J. Coates. 1994. Prevention of HIV infection. *AIDS* 8:1371–1389.

Coates, T. J., M. Faigle, J. Koijane et al. 1995. *Does HIV prevention work for men who have sex with men?* Report prepared for the Office of Technology Assessment, Congress of the United States, August 31.

Cohen, S., and S. L. Syme. 1985. *Social support and health*. New York: Academic Books.

Communication Technologies. 1990. *Report on HIV-related knowledge, attitudes, and behaviors among San Francisco gay and bisexual men: Results from the fifth population-based survey*. San Francisco: Department of Public Health, January 31.

DeCarlo, P. 1995 Can HIV prevention make a difference for men who have sex with men? Center for AIDS Prevention Studies Fact Sheet. San Francisco: University of California, April.

Ekstrand, M. L., and T. J. Coates. 1990. Maintenance of safer sexual behaviors and predictors of risky sex: The San Francisco men's health study. *American Journal of Public Health* 80:973.

Ekstrand, M. L., R. Stall, C. Frutchey, and P. Christen. 1990. Averting disaster: Addressing relapse and ongoing AIDS prevention programs for self-identified gay and bisexual men of all colors. San Francisco: San Francisco AIDS Foundation/Center for AIDS Prevention Studies, University of California. White paper.

Fitzgerald, F. 1986. *Cities on a hill*. New York: Simon and Schuster.

Freudenberg N., and M. A. Zimmerman, eds. 1995. The role of community organizations in public health practice: The lessons from AIDS prevention. In *AIDS prevention in the community: Lessons from the first decade*. Washington, D.C.: American Public Health Association.

Garrett, L. 1994. *The coming plague*. New York: Farrar, Straus and Giroux.

Gay and Lesbian Alliance Against Defamation. 1994. KRON-TV considers follow-up to HIV series. *Update* (January):1.

Green, L. 1986. The theory of participation: A qualitative analysis of its expression in national and international health policies. *Advances in Health Education and Promotion* 1 (A):211–236.

Grossi, S. 1996. Personal communication, May 14.

Israel, B. 1985. Social networks and social support: Implications for natural helper and community-level interventions. *Health Education Quarterly* 12 (1):65–80.

Kelly, J. A., J. S. St. Lawrence, Y. E. Diaz, L. Y. Stevenson, A. C. Hauth, T. L. Brasfield, S. C. Kalichman, J. E. Smith, and M. E. Andrew. 1991. HIV Risk behavior reduction following intervention with key opinion leaders of population: An experimental analysis. *American Journal of Public Health* 81:168–171.

Lemp, G. F., M. Jones, T. A. Kellogg, G. N. Nieri, L. Anderson, D. Withum, and M. Katz. 1995. Seroprevalence among lesbians and bisexual women in San Francisco and Berkeley, California. *American Journal of Public Health* 85:1549–1552.

Lewin, K. 1947. Quasi-stationary social equilibria and the problem of social change. In *Readings in social psychology*, ed. T. M. Newcomb and E. L. Hartley. New York: Holt, Rinehart and Winston.

McCusick, L., T. J. Coates, S. Morin, L. Pollack, and C. Hoff. 1990. Longitudinal predictors of reductions in unprotected anal intercourse among gay men in San Francisco: The AIDS behavioral research project. *American Journal of Public Health* 80:978–983.

Miller, T. E., C. Booaraem, J. V. Flowers, and A. E. Iverson. 1990. Changes in knowledge, attitude, and behavior as a result of a community-based AIDS prevention program. *AIDS Education and Prevention* 2 (1):12–23.

Moon, T. 1994. Prevention taboo. *San Francisco Sentinel*, August 17.

Morris, M., and L. Dean. 1994. Effect of sexual behavior change on long-term human immunodeficiency virus prevalence among homosexual men. *American Journal of Epidemiology* 140:217–232.

Odets, W. 1995. Why we stopped doing primary prevention for gay men in 1985. *AIDS and Public Policy Journal* (10) 1 (Winter).

Person, B., D. Cotton, and the Prevention of HIV in Women and Infants Demonstration Projects. 1996. A model of community mobilization for the prevention of HIV in women and infants. *Public Health Reports* 111 (supplement 1):89–98.

Puckett, S., and L. Bye. 1987. The STOP AIDS Project: An interpersonal AIDS prevention program. San Francisco: STOP AIDS Project. Unpublished paper.

Redis, C. 1996. Personal communication, May 14.

Rogers, E. M. 1983. *Diffusion of innovations*. New York: Free Press.

San Francisco Department of Public Health. 1992. HIV Incidence and prevalence in San Francisco in 1992: Summary report from an HIV consensus meeting. San Francisco: Department of Public Health, February 12

———. 1994. Projections of the AIDS epidemic in San Francisco, 1994–97. San Francisco: Department of Public Health, February 15.

———. 1996. AIDS surveillance report. San Francisco: Department of Public Health AIDS Office, April 30.

Seattle-King County Department of Public Health, HIV/AIDS Epidemiology Program. 1995. *HIV/AIDS epidemiology profile for community planning*. Seattle: Department of Public Health.

Shilts, R. 1987. *And the band played on*. New York: St. Martin's Press.

Smith, W. 1996. The power of prevention science. Poster presentation at HIV Prevention Community Planning Cochairs' Meeting/1996 Prevention Summit, Atlanta, Georgia, March 7–8.

Stryker J., T. J. Coates, P. DeCarlo, K. Haynes-Sanstad, M. Shriver, and H. J. Makadon. 1995. Prevention of HIV infection: Looking back, Looking ahead. *Journal of the American Medical Association* 273:1143–1148.

Chapter 15

Community Organizing among the Elderly Poor in San Francisco's Tenderloin District

MEREDITH MINKLER

I N INNER-CITY single-room occupancy hotel (SRO) neighborhoods such as San Francisco's Tenderloin District, large numbers of low-income elders live on "the bottom rung on the housing ladder" (Ovrebo, Minkler, and Liljestrand 1991, 179). Often just a step removed from homelessness, many of these residents confront daily the interrelated problems of poor health, social isolation, and powerlessness as a result of poverty and social marginalization (Minkler in press).

Yet the elderly residents of the nation's impoverished and high-crime "Tenderloin districts" also possess many strengths and competencies. This chapter presents a case study of the Tenderloin Senior Organizing Project (TSOP) to demonstrate the role of community organizing as a vehicle for individual and community empowerment in a population previously labeled "unorganizable." After a brief description of the setting in which this project took place, the chapter examines TSOP's theoretical underpinnings and historical development. Particular attention is devoted to TSOP's evolution from a program that tried to "empower the elderly" to one in which elders and their neighbors could empower themselves. Project outcomes are described, as are a number of the problems and challenges faced in the course of TSOP's sixteen-year history.

Background

A culturally diverse "mixed-use" residential area, the forty-five-block area North of Market Street district, the Tenderloin, is home to large numbers of elders on small fixed incomes, younger people with physical and mental disabilities, immi-

Portions of this chapter are based on "Community Organizing among the Elderly Poor in the United States: A Case Study," *International Journal of Health Services* 22 (2) (1992):303–316. Copyright © 1992 by the Baywood Publishing Company, Inc., Amityville, N.Y. All rights reserved.

grants, and homeless people. Three hundred times more densely populated than the city as a whole, this neighborhood for years has had the highest crime rate in San Francisco. The city's failure to enforce housing codes or building ordinances, the absence of any major grocery store chain, and the highest density of alcohol outlets in the city (North of Market Planning Coalition 1992) contribute to such prevalent problems as inadequate and unsafe housing, undernutrition, and alcoholism (Minkler in press).

Although the Tenderloin suffers from a plethora of unmet needs, it also has many strengths on which to build, including its multiculturalism. The Tenderloin has for years had its own multilanguage newspaper. Several large and widely respected churches, a comprehensive and progressive local health center, and an active neighborhood planning coalition and housing clinic were among the "building blocks" identified by early TSOP organizers as potential supporters, allies, and advocates in the effort to create an environment in which residents could become empowered.

The overall goal of TSOP was to facilitate such empowerment by assisting elderly residents and their neighbors as they worked to organize and improve their community. The project's objectives were to draw out the competence, self-confidence, and leadership skills of residents (Ferrante 1991) and to reduce social isolation by enhancing social support networks within Tenderloin SRO hotels and other low-income residences.

Theoretical Base

Three major conceptual domains guided the project from its inception. The first, social support, is based on the large body of evidence demonstrating the critical role of social support and social interaction in influencing health status (Bloomberg, Meyers, and Braverman 1994; Cohen and Syme 1985; House, Landis, and Umberson 1988). Whether through "buffering stress" or contributing to an increased sense of "control over destiny" (Syme 1993), interventions that build supportive networks may be particularly important in neighborhoods like the Tenderloin, where social marginality and isolation are endemic.

A shortcoming of many social support theories lies in their tendency to focus on the individual and his or her supportive network as the sole unit of analysis. Empirical studies thus often overlook the more macrolevel changes that may take place as individuals and communities, empowered by increased social support, work collectively to attack those shared problems that have contributed to their oppression. In applying theories of social support to the Tenderloin, TSOP staff and volunteers attempted to look beyond individual-level outcomes of increased social support to focus as well on institutional- or community-level changes (Minkler 1992).

This perspective is in keeping with TSOP's second theoretical underpinning—the approach to empowerment theory elucidated by Brazilian educator Paulo Freire (1968, 1973) as "education for critical consciousness." As discussed in chapter 12, Freire's educational methodology centers on a relationship of equality and mutual respect between group participants and "teacher-learners," with the latter using a process called problem-posing to ask questions that challenge members of the group to look for root causes and other consequences of the problem under discussion and eventually develop a plan of action. Although TSOP originally was conceived of, in part, as a "Freire project" through which student facilitators would attempt to use this educational approach in leading hotel-based support and discussion groups, the regular applications of this methodology proved difficult. Ongoing discussions of the root causes of problems, for example, often proved impractical when residents were motivated to organize quickly around problems demanding immediate action. Consequently, although Freire's education for critical consciousness continued to provide an important philosophical and ideological base for the project, the method per se was not employed in a regular and rigorous fashion (Minkler 1992).

Of greater day-to-day usefulness in TSOP's work has been a third, eclectic approach to community organization best typified by the philosophy and methods of the late Saul Alinsky (1969, 1972) and supplemented by the work of John McKnight (1987, 1993; see also chapter 2) and Michael Miller (1985, 1993). As discussed in chapter 4, Alinsky viewed the low-income community as powerless and disfranchised in relation to the "haves" and to society as a whole. The goal of his approach was to facilitate a process whereby people coming together around a shared interest or concern could collectively identify a specific issue or target, garner resources, mobilize an action campaign, and through their collective action help realign power within the community.

In recent years, TSOP has increasingly drawn on the work of several post-Alinsky theorists and organizers who go considerably farther than Alinsky did in identifying and stressing the strengths of the local community and in developing creative methods for capacity building. The emphasis of McKnight and his colleagues (chapter 10) on helping communities identify their preexisting resources or assets has been a central conceptual underpinning of the TSOP approach. Similarly, TSOP has borrowed from community organizer and theorist Michael Miller (1993) the notion that "action rooted in deeply held values is more likely to be sustained than that which relies solely on addressing a specific injustice." The relationship between community organizing and democratic citizenship is stressed by Miller, who argues that discussions of values should form part of the community organizing process. Through such discussions, community members ideally begin to challenge such values as rugged individualism, consumerism, and a status system that exploits the poor and causes them to internalize their oppression. By helping residents see their work in relation to deeper values and ideologies, TSOP attempted to apply Miller's approach and make it a fourth conceptual project base.

Project Origins and Evolution

Originally known as the Tenderloin Senior Outreach Project, TSOP was established in 1979 with the dual goals of (1) improving physical and mental health by reducing social isolation and providing relevant health education and (2) facilitating, through dialogue and participation, a process whereby residents would work together in identifying common problems and seeking solutions to those shared problems and concerns (Wechsler and Minkler 1986). Specific methods included helping residents form discussion and support groups, and later tenants' associations and interhotel organizations and coalitions, that could serve as vehicles for increasing community competence or problem-solving ability, and bringing about concrete changes (e.g., reductions in the neighborhood crime rate) that in turn could promote individual and community well-being (Minkler in press).

Architects of what was to become TSOP began by conducting a community assessment, which revealed that forty-three different "helping agencies" and organizations existed in this forty-five-block area. Of these, one in particular— St. Boniface Church—appeared universally respected by residents. Following Alinsky's (1972) admonition to organizers to establish their legitimacy by linking with a preexisting organization, the first project volunteers—students in a graduate community organizing class at the University of California at Berkeley—became St. Boniface volunteers and as such approached hotel managers about the possibility of serving refreshments in the hotel lobby one morning a week as a means of encouraging resident interaction. With the help of these inducements, an informal "coffee hour" and discussion group was formed in an initial hotel; the group met weekly and included a core of eight to twelve residents and two outside facilitators. As levels of trust and rapport increased, members began to share personal concerns around issues such as fear of crime, loneliness, rent increases, and their own sense of powerlessness.

Student facilitators used a combination of organizing and educational approaches to help foster group solidarity and, eventually, community organizing. A Freirian problem-posing process was used as appropriate, for example, to help residents engage in dialogue about shared problems and their causes and to generate potential action plans. Similarly, Alinsky's (1972) admonition to create dissatisfaction with the status quo, channel frustration into concrete action, and help people identify specific, winnable issues was among the community organizing precepts followed. Finally, drawing on social support theories stressing the importance of social interaction opportunities per se, the student facilitators attempted to create a group atmosphere conductive to meeting the social, as well as the more political and task-oriented, concerns of group members. (See appendix 6.)

As the first hotel discussion group became an established entity, more student volunteers were recruited, and seven additional groups were organized in other Tenderloin hotels. To provide coordination and continuity for the project, staff secured a small foundation grant to fund a part-time director, and TSOP became incorporated as a nonprofit organization with a twelve-member board of directors. In recognition of the importance of building on community assets (see chapter 10), TSOP invited representatives of a popular neighborhood church, the powerful local planning coalition, and the neighborhood health clinic to join the board, along with community residents and allies from the business and professional communities.

Among the early issues identified and confronted by several of the hotel groups was the problem of undernutrition, particularly lack of access to fresh fruits and vegetables. After much discussion of alternative approaches, the residents of three hotels contracted with a local food advisory service and began operating their own hotel-based "minimarkets" one morning per week. In a fourth hotel, residents organized and ran a modest cooperative weekly breakfast program, thereby qualifying their hotel for participation in a food bank where large quantities of food could be purchased in bulk at reduced prices. Still other residents worked with TSOP staff to produce a "no-cook cookbook" of inexpensive and nutritious recipes. Later published by the San Francisco Department of Public Health, the cookbook was distributed free of charge to hundreds of residents of the Tenderloin, and more than one thousand copies were sold outside the community to generate additional money for the project. Early activities like these were important in making tangible changes (e.g., improved food access) but, more significantly, in contributing to resident feelings of control, competence, and collective ability to bring about change. Moreover, these early accomplishments gave residents the self-confidence needed to confront more difficult challenges in the future.

Although each hotel group developed and retained over time its own unique character, several common trends among the groups were evident. In all but one hotel group, for example, decreased reliance on outside facilitators was observed over time, with broader resident participation in discussion and decisionmaking. Greater concern for residents throughout one's hotel was increasingly witnessed among TSOP members and was particularly well demonstrated during stressful times, as when several hotels were temporarily evacuated in the aftermath of San Francisco's October 1989 earthquake.

Another trend observed in the groups, and one critical to TSOP's evolution, was the realization among residents of the need to look beyond hotel boundaries and work with residents of other hotels and community groups on shared problems. TSOP residents of several hotels thus identified crime and safely as their key area of concern and formed an interhotel coalition to begin work on this problem. The coalition in turn started the Safehouse Project, recruiting forty-eight neighborhood businesses and agencies to serve as places of refuge, demarcated by colorful posters, where residents could go for help in times of emergency. Coalition members also convinced the mayor to increase the number of police patrol officers in the neighborhood and, through this and other measures, helped effect a dramatic reduction in crime, including an 18 percent reduction in the first twelve months after the coalition's inception ("Safehouses" 1982).

Two other outcomes of TSOP's organizing around the crime issue are worthy of note. First, having experienced success in increasing personal safety and well-being, the TSOP elderly began turning their attention to the safety needs of other vulnerable groups. Elderly TSOP members, for example, had their Safehouse materials translated into Cambodian and Vietnamese, and they arranged for articles about the project to appear in the Asian-language pages of the community newspaper. They were also able to recruit several Asian merchants in the neighborhood to open safehouses, bringing the total to more than one hundred at the height of this project.

Second, even though the Safehouse Project received considerable local and national publicity, several of the project's resident founders began to critically question the narrowness of the crime prevention approach they had developed. Their discussions of the root causes of the high crime rates in poverty neighborhoods and their involvement, albeit sporadically, in areas such as advocacy for the homeless, job training for the unemployed, and voter registration reflected increasing appreciation of the need for working toward broader social change. As E. Richard Brown (1991) notes in critically analyzing the TSOP experience: "Successful actions that resulted in desired changes in the health related environment may reduce the needs to which community members originally responded, but they may also increase community members' organizational skills, experience, leadership, and feelings of empowerment. They thus may encourage further action for more far reaching goals of social change."

Increasing Community Competence: Progress and Problems

TSOP's commitment to "starting where the people are" (Nyswander 1956) by helping residents organize around issues, such as crime and nutrition, that they themselves had identified was in keeping with the organization's commitment to empowerment. Yet even with resident-initiated goals and activities, there was often a danger of slipping into the inadvertent creation of dependency. By the mid-1980s, for example, the cooperative breakfast program and hotel-based minimarkets, as well as a health promotion resource center that TSOP residents planned and originally ran themselves, had begun to look more and more like direct service activities. Although residents remained interested in reaping the benefits of these programs, they lost interest in running them themselves, and project volunteers and staff were alternating their organizing roles with direct service type functions.

TSOP staff discussed with residents the increasing tensions and contradictions between the organization's desired role in stimulating community organization and leadership development and its de facto service role. In the words of former project director Diana Miller: "We needed to clarify that what we do is build public power. [TSOP's role] was getting distorted because the organizers were spending a lot of time and energy on mutual aid programs" (Vanover 1991, 45).

After these discussions, and with the support of the board of directors, TSOP began gradually to terminate its direct service programs. The Health Promotion Resource Center, for example, was spun off to another community-based organization, while the minimarkets and cooperative breakfast program were gradually phased out. At the same time, and in a further effort to clarify the project's mission, TSOP formally changed the O in its name from Outreach to Organizing and adopted a new a mission statement that stressed the organization's values and its commitments to drawing out and building on the skills of residents and creating community competence through organizing.

TSOP's new operational model, which remained in place until the project's closure in 1995, involved entering new hotels and residences only at the request of residents. Through personal conversations, the TSOP organizer clarified the organization's role as being not one of advocacy *on behalf of residents* but one of helping residents advocate *on their own behalf*. He or she would begin dialogues about some of the advantages of organizing over help seeking and challenge residents to take the next step, speaking to a few of their neighbors and helping to form a small committee made up of individuals identified as potential leaders. Working with committee members on "thinking organizationally" (Miller 1993), or strategically and tactically, the organizer would help residents form a tenants' association, which in turn would identify issues, assess resources, and mobilize to achieve collectively set goals (Ferrante 1991). A total of fourteen tenants' associations were established with the help of TSOP and achieved a number of impressive victories.

Critical to TSOP's goal of fostering community empowerment and problem-solving ability was its emphasis on leadership training. Through one-on-one and small-group activities, residents were helped to improve interpersonal skills, learn to facilitate meetings, and discover ways of working through (or against) bureaucracies to bring about change.

Early approaches to leadership training included a day-long leadership training conference attended by eighty residents and three "media workshops" in which TSOP members met with journalists and reporters, who helped them practice articulating their concerns to the press. Of greatest importance, however, was the ongoing nurturing of individual and small-group leadership, including the extensive use of role-plays prior to confrontations with landlords, meetings with city officials, and so on. Through these "trial runs," TSOP members could practice creating and responding to alternative hypothetical scenarios and could learn to function effectively as leadership teams. Such exercises, and the selection and preparation of back-up leaders on any given issue in the event that a designated leader was ill on the day of a planned action, were among the strategies that enabled TSOP to develop a strong leadership cadre from among its membership. (See appendix 8.)

More advanced leadership training was undertaken during the later years of the project, with twenty TSOP members attending intensive national leadership training programs sponsored by the San Francisco–based Organize Training Center. Led by a prominent Alinsky-style organizer, the four-day training covered such topics as issue selection, values and critical reflection, and negotiation processes. Reporting back on the experience of one such training, one elderly participant said: "The workshop gave me an overall theoretical construct in which to place the things our tenants' association had learned from our TSOP organizer . . . so I could better grasp how one thing (such as values) ties into the next (such as action). I saw how our individual work can lead to building part of a community. Who would have thought an atheist in an apartment in a major city would be sharing concerns with a Lutheran pastor who ministers to farmers in rural Nebraska?" (Miller 1993).

Although TSOP has been concerned with individual and community empowerment since its inception, the TSOP model's change over time reflected the organization's more sophisticated understanding of what empowerment entails and the preconditions necessary for its achievement. By helping residents create their own tenants' organizations and cross-group organizations rather than playing a direct role in their creation, and by offering resources (e.g., leadership training) as requested, the newer TSOP model was more effective in fostering true community organizing and empowerment.

TSOP continued to experience its share of problems, including residents tiring or "burning out" on some issues they had earlier decided to tackle, occasional power plays within groups, and leadership turnover as a consequence of illness, transiency, and other problems. Ethical issues also arose, as when the proposed closing down of the cooperative breakfast program was strongly opposed by one very elderly and disabled resident for whom the breakfast had become a high point of the week. As TSOP shifted to a "pure" community organizing project, it also discovered that its goals (e.g., community empowerment and leadership development) were less attractive to most traditional foundation and corporate sponsors than were such tangible "deliverables" as hotel-based minimarkets and health promotion resource centers. Moreover, even progressive foundations that understood and applauded TSOP's new directions tended to avoid refunding the same project, such that new sources of income continually had to be located. With an over-worked board and no staff or volunteers specifically devoted to raising money, TSOP's two full-time organizers found themselves unable to respond to many requests to help organize in new buildings because they were too busy engaging in extensive fund-raising.

Project Accomplishments and the Problem of Evaluation

As with many efforts aimed primarily at community organization and empower-ment, separating TSOP's methods from the outcomes of those processes is diffi-cult. Of at least equal difficulty, moreover, is determining project impacts on such health and social outcomes as malnutrition, depression, and social isolation in a neighborhood where concurrent adverse developments (e.g., cutbacks in supple-mental security income [SSI] checks and escalating violence deriving, in part, from the drug epidemic) have often conspired to exacerbate these problems (Minkler in press). Finally, the strong objection of many residents to "being studied" led to a reluctance of project staff to engage in or allow formal evaluation efforts until very late in the organization's history. In spite of these limitations, however, a num-ber of project outcomes can be examined.

TSOP's greatest achievement was its formation of eight hotel-based support groups and fourteen tenants' associations. The support groups met weekly over peri-ods ranging from six months to, more typically, several years and averaged eight to twelve regular members. All but one of these groups moved from staff or stu-dent volunteer facilitation to resident facilitation or cofacilitation, and from dis-cussion of issues to the taking of concrete actions to bring about change.

A number of tangible victories were achieved by these groups. Members of one support group organized a protest against a sudden (and illegal) 30 percent increase in rent, which as a consequence of resident organizing was reduced to 10 percent. In another hotel, residents demanded and got a change in the landlord's harsh eviction policy, and in a third they pressured successfully for architectural changes to make their shared bathrooms wheelchair accessible. Support group orga-nizing also focused on accommodating the purely social or spiritual needs of resi-dents and included the planning of elaborate holiday parties and memorial services for some group members who had passed away.

Finally, resident organizing sometimes led to cross-group activities (for example, with the formation of a Tenderloin chapter of the Nuclear Freeze and of the interhotel coalition Tenderloin Tenants for Safer Streets) and to increased involvement with and on behalf of younger groups. On a 1982 visit to TSOP, Gray Panthers' founder Maggie Kuhn called the project "the best example I've ever seen of the Gray Panthers' motto—'age and youth in action.'" She made this comment in reference to the fact that elderly TSOP support group members had increasingly broadened their focus to work with younger disabled people, persons who were homeless or unemployed, and advocates for children in this very heterogeneous neighborhood.

In several instances, TSOP support groups formed the basis of subsequent tenants' associations that were able to build upon the formers' effective leadership base and prior collective organizing efforts. The early victories of one such organization included getting a hated furniture rental policy abolished, substantial rent rebates, and pet deposits reduced from $300 to $100 (Goldoflas 1988).

Other tenants' associations were formed in buildings where no previous organizing had taken place. Victories achieved by the fourteen tenants' associations that TSOP helped to create included:

- Appealing to the Rent Board and winning $10,000 in compensation for a hotel elevator that had been out of service for five months
- Getting management to install in a hotel lobby a vending machine with low-cost, nutritious foods
- Successfully protesting a provision in a new lease agreement that would have limited residents' rights to freedom of speech and expression
- Winning improved pest control and upgrading of substandard plumbing and wiring
- Getting an agreement for lead-based paint removal
- Winning an out-of-court settlement against a prestigious local law school that owned four neighborhood buildings and had reneged on promised internal security
- Getting hot water turned on in a building that had gone without it for ten years   (Ferrante 1991; Miller 1993; Minkler in press)

Like the earlier TSOP support groups, the tenants' associations went beyond their buildings' borders to work with other groups, organizations, and agencies on problems affecting the larger community. Through collaboration with several local businesses and the San Francisco Department of Public Health, for example, residents were able to secure the cleanup of a vacant lot that had become such a noxious and rat-infested dumping ground that its odors had prevented neighbors from opening their windows (Miller 1993). Similarly, tenants' association members successfully negotiated with the San Francisco Department of Parking and Traffic Safety for a senior crossing sign and an increase in pedestrian crossing time after the death of a resident at a local intersection.

Unfortunately, measurement of actual changes in health and quality of life that may be attributed, at least in part, to TSOP organizing efforts is difficult. In a few instances, TSOP was able to collect "hard data" on project accomplishments. An evaluation of the minimarkets, for example, included twenty-four-hour diet recalls that demonstrated a significant increase in the consumption of fresh fruits and vegetables among participants (Wechlser and Minkler 1986). Similarly, the marked decline in the neighborhood crime rate during the first two years of TSOP organizing in this area was attributed by the chief of police in large part to tenant organizing and to the increased community solidarity that it inspired (Minkler in press).

Qualitative data, albeit often anecdotal, has suggested potential impacts on health and well-being. Many residents, for example, reported that, as a consequence of group participation through TSOP, they no longer felt depressed and lonely. A formerly depressed woman in her early sixties commented: "I can't tell you what a difference the group had made in my life. When I moved to the Tenderloin three years ago, my husband had just left me. All I kept thinking was, 'Who's going to want me now?' I think I would still be alone in my room if it weren't for [TSOP]" (Minkler in press).

Changes in health habits, including smoking cessation, decreased alcohol consumption, and improved adherence to medical regimens, were attributed by a number of residents to their involvement with TSOP. A mentally disabled resident who had frequently failed to take her prescribed medication reported that she had become religious about taking it now that she was heavily involved in several TSOP activities that relied upon her leadership skills. And a younger TSOP member remarked, "TSOP is the only group I belong to not because I'm poor or disabled or HIV positive but because of my strengths" (Minkler in press). Although such stories are difficult to translate into hard outcome data, they provide important anecdotal evidence of the effectiveness that TSOP groups and activities may have had in improving health and particularly in reducing depression among participants.

TSOP's focus on developing leaders and on increasing the problem-solving capacity of individuals and groups resulted in some important outcomes in terms of community empowerment. Several tenants' associations, for example, became recognized by management as the organized voice of building residents. In some of these residences, landlords now meet regularly with the associations to discuss the latter's concerns, whereas in other buildings tenants' associations have a regular hand in decisionmaking on any issues that might affect them (Miller 1993; Minkler in press).

Effective tenants' association outreach to and collaboration with other community groups, local businesses and agencies, and such government bodies as the Department of Public Health, the Department of Housing and Urban Development, and the Department of Public Safety were indicative, in part, of the former's growing sophistication in problemsolving. The formation of interhotel groups and coalitions such as Tenderloin Tenants for Safer Streets and the TSOP Leaders' Council suggests a growing identity with the community beyond one's individual building, and this, too, appears to have contributed to neighborhood empowerment.

Joint mobilization to bring down the crime rate, arrange for vacant lot cleanup, and in other ways improve quality of life for members of the neighborhood are outcomes that may be illustrative of the increased problem-solving ability, on the community level, that TSOP helped to foster.

An extensive formal evaluation based on structured interviews with residents, unstructured interviews with key informants, and documents review was conducted during TSOP's final year of operation (Shaw 1995). The survey research component of the study compared 150 residents of TSOP-organized and nonorganized buildings. Significant differences between the two groups were found along fourteen dimensions, including social isolation, morale, feelings of safety, perceived ability to improve building living conditions, and overall quality of life. Unfortunately, however, the study failed to document statistically significant changes in health or sense of empowerment and also pointed to major organizational limitations, including lack of adequate strategic planning.

Although the evaluation produced important data on numerous aspects of TSOP's accomplishments and problems, the largely quantitative nature of the study may have limited its ability to capture some of the essence of the project. An alternative approach grounded in the philosophy and methods of empowerment evaluation (see chapter 18) might have overcome these difficulties. As Stephen Fawcett et al. (1996, 183) note, empowerment evaluation works toward the competing ends of "maximizing community control" and "understanding . . . the processes outcomes of a community initiative" or organizing effort. Empowerment evaluation ideally involves community members in all phases of the evaluation process and values qualitative, as well as quantitative, data so that the stories of community members and others become a critical part of the database. In both these respects, empowerment evaluation would, in retrospect, have been more in keeping with TSOP's philosophy and methods than was a more tradition survey research approach.

Project Closure and Replication Efforts

TSOP's closure after sixteen years came as a result of the increasing difficulty of raising the project's annual budget (approximately $100,000), most of it from private foundations. As suggested in the project evaluation, improved long-term strategic planning and earlier, more concerted efforts to develop a diversified funding base might have helped prevent the project's demise. At the same time, the general absence of government support for efforts such as TSOP and the increased competition among community groups for individual, foundation, and corporate dollars as a consequence of severe government cutbacks make the closure of projects like this one an all too frequent reality.

Several years prior to closure, however, and in response to growing numbers of requests for technical assistance from other community groups, TSOP developed a detailed project replication manual (Ferrante 1991). Outlining steps and barriers to starting and maintaining a grassroots organizing project, the guide includes discussions of such topics as the role of the organizer, choice of strategies and tactics, and the role of values in organizing, with case study examples and quotes from TSOP residents used to illustrate the points made. The manual was distributed upon request to organizers in the United States and Canada, and several replications have been attempted. A disabled veteran in New York City, for example, used the early TSOP model to help organize chronically schizophrenic veterans who had recently entered a residential treatment center (Pounder 1988). And in Vancouver, British Columbia, a government-funded project operates in nine SRO hotels and has achieved high credibility with the Ministry of Health (Jones and Sommers 1994). Replication efforts like these and the inclusion of the TSOP model in an innovative "health education models project" currently being developed by the Centers for Disease Control represent an important potential means of helping to ensure that the TSOP approach can continue to be refined and built upon in the years ahead.

Conclusion

The TSOP experience offers a number of lessons for those concerned with community organizing for health. Prominent among these are (1) the importance of community, rather than outside organizer, definition of need; (2) the need for a preliminary community assessment, as well as ongoing efforts to uncover and build upon community strengths; (3) the need to implement theories and methodologies flexibly, adapting them as necessary in order to ensure their greatest possible relevance in real-world contexts; (4) the importance of building in comprehensive, participatory, and empowering strategies for community organizing project evaluation; and (5) the need for attending early on to broad strategic planning, including the development of a diversified funding base (Minkler in press).

But as the TSOP experience also demonstrates, even the most committed community organizing effort will have limited success in improving health and quality of life in neighborhoods like the Tenderloin without a broad societal commitment to the reduction of social inequalities. A project like TSOP can make significant inroads in helping reduce feelings of social isolation and powerlessness endemic in low-income inner-city communities, especially as these feelings are often intimately tied to poor health. By helping to identify and nurture indigenous leaders, and by helping to build tenants' associations and other structures that can act as a unified voice for residents, TSOP was able to help the latter increase their power in fighting for and getting small but important changes in their health and living conditions. Furthermore, changes such as a drop (albeit temporarily) in the neighborhood crime rate, increased social support, and improvements in access to inexpensive, nutritious foods can have a direct bearing on malnutrition, depression, and other health and social problems prevalent in low-income communities (Minkler in press).

Yet conditions in the Tenderloin District, like those in many inner-city neighborhoods in the United States, have actually deteriorated over the last two decades as a result of broader economic and social conditions over which even the best-organized communities have little or no control. The economic problems of the early 1980s, combined with the politics of retrenchment that have continued to the present, have taken a particular toll on the poor. Severe cutbacks in SSI, subsidized housing, Medicaid, and a plethora of health and social service programs, combined with the growing epidemics of drugs, violence, and AIDS, wreak havoc on communities like the Tenderloin (Minkler in press).

Against this backdrop, the victories of organizations like TSOP take on added significance. Yet they also are dwarfed by the magnitude of the problems confronted, which can be adequately addressed only through a more fundamental societal-level commitment to reducing the social inequities that lie at the base of such problems. When poverty remains perhaps the single greatest risk factor for disease and premature death, and when the links among poverty, alienation, and a plethora of health and social problems are documented in study after study (Adler et al. 1994; Haan, Kaplan, and Syme 1989), our failure to deal with these more fundamental problems becomes increasingly troubling. Projects like TSOP do not operate in a vacuum, and without a broader social commitment to reducing social inequalities, the problems plaguing inner city communities like the Tenderloin will continue largely unabated into the twenty-first century (Minkler in press).

At the same time, however, and while health educators and other concerned professionals increase our commitment to working for broader social change at the societal level, we must not lose sight of the very real impacts a project like TSOP can have in the lives of the both individuals and communities. In the words of one elderly TSOP leader who credited the project with keeping her from succumbing to severe clinical depression: "I thought when you're way down like this, way down below the poverty level, you're powerless. But I realized you can make the big shots stand up and listen. It was amazing to me to learn that if you work together you can do something" (Ferrante 1991, 8).

References

Adler, N. E., T. Boyce, M. A. Chesney, S. Cohen, S. Folkman, R. L. Kahn, and S. L. Syme. 1994. Socioeconomic status and health: The challenge of the gradient. *American Psychologist* 49:15–24.

Alinsky, S. D. 1969. *Reveille for radicals*. Chicago: University of Chicago Press.

———. 1972. *Rules for radicals*. New York: Random House.

Bloomberg, L., J. Meyers, and M. T. Braverman. 1994. The importance of social interaction: A new perspective on social epidemiology, social risk factors, and health. *Health Education Quarterly* 21 (4):447–463.

Brown, E. R. 1991. Community action for health promotion: A strategy to empower individuals and communities. *Journal of Health Services* 21 (3):441–456.

Cohen, S., and S. L. Syme. 1985. *Social support and health.* New York: Academic Books.

Fawcett, S. B., A. Paine-Andrews, V. Francisco, J. Schultz et al. 1996. Empowering community health initiatives through evaluations. In *Empowerment evaluation: Knowledge and tools for self-assessment and accountability,* ed. D. Fetterman, S. Kaftarian, and A. Wandersman. Thousand Oaks, Calif.: Sage.

Ferrante, L. 1991. *The Tenderloin Senior Organizing Project's replication manual.* San Francisco: Tenderloin Senior Organizing Project.

Freire, P. 1968. *Pedogogy of the oppressed.* New York: Seabury Press.

———. 1973. *Education for critical consciousness.* New York: Seabury Press.

Goldoflas, B. 1988. Organizing in a gray ghetto: The Tenderloin Senior Organizing Project. *Dollars and Sense* (January-February):1–19.

Haan, M. N., G. A. Kaplan, and S. L. Syme. 1989. Socioeconomic position and health: Old observations and new thought. In *Pathways to health: The role of social factors,* ed. J. P. Bunker, D. S. Gromby, and B. H. Kehrer. Palo Alto: Stanford University Press.

House, J. S., K. R. Landis, and D. Umberson. 1988. Social relationships and health. *Science* 241:540–545.

Jones, J., and J. Sommers. 1994. Grant proposal. Vancouver, Canada: Vancouver Second Mile High Society. Unpublished.

McKnight, J. 1987. Regenerating community. *Social Policy* (Winter):54–58.

———. 1993. Local social community development and economic development issues. Paper presented at the annual meeting of the American Public Health Association, San Francisco, California, October 27.

Miller, M. 1985. *Turning problems into actionable issues.* San Francisco: Organize Training Center.

———. 1993. *The Tenderloin Senior Organizing Project.* Louisville, Ky.: Presbyterian Committee on the Self-Development of People.

Minkler, M. 1992. Community organizing among the elderly poor in the U.S.: A case study. *International Journal of Health Services* 22 (2):303–316.

———. In press. Empowerment of the elderly in San Francisco's Tenderloin District. In *Society and health: Case studies,* ed. B. Amick and R. Rudd. Cambridge, Mass.: Harvard University Press.

North of Market Planning Coalition. 1992. *Final report: Tenderloin 2000 survey and plan.* San Francisco: North of Market Planning Coalition.

Nyswander, D. 1956. Education for health: Some principles and their applications. *Health Education Monographs* 14:65–70.

Ovrebo, B., M. Minkler, and P. Liljestrand. 1991. No room in the inn: The disappearance of SRO housing in the United States. *Journal of Housing for the Elderly* 8 (1):77–92.

Pounder, R. F. 1988. Social learning for schizophrenic adults: The Lanchester model. Ph.d. diss. prospectus, Teachers College.

Safehouses now easing the fears of elderly residents. 1982. *Los Angeles Times,* November 21.

Shaw, F. 1995. Tenderloin Senior Organizing Project evaluation. Woodland, Calif.: Wellness Foundation. Unpublished report.

Syme, S. L. 1993. Control of destiny: A key to good health. Paper presented at the fiftieth anniversary symposium Shaping the Future of Public Health: Perspectives from Berkeley, University of California School of Public Health, Berkeley, California, April 17.

Vanover, J. 1991. Some seniors in San Francisco: An interview with Diana Miller. *Organizing* (Spring-Summer):44–47.

Wechsler, R., and M. Minkler. 1986. A community-oriented approach to health promotion: The Tenderloin Senior Outreach Program. In *Wellness and health promotion for the elderly,* ed. K. Dychtwald. Rockville, Md.: Aspen Systems.

Building and Maintaining Effective Coalitions

Part VII

As community organizer Tom Wolff (1995, 13) notes, "The language and practice of health and human services in the 1990's are dominated by two catch phrases: coalition building and empowerment." Loosely used, seldom defined, and frequently mandated by funding sources, this "mismatched pair of phrases," he points out, often breaks apart in our community coalition building efforts.

Although Wolff's concerns are accurate, well stated, and widely shared, he and other social change professionals also note the power of coalitions for bringing about change. Particularly in times of diminished fiscal resources and support, coalitions that can create a more powerful unifying structure for organizations sharing a goal or concern have an important role to play.

In chapter 16, Abraham Wandersman, Robert Goodman, and Frances Butterfoss discuss the growing popularity, as well as the unique role and capabilities, of coalitions for addressing complex public health issues. Borrowing as a conceptual framework the open systems perspective on how organizations develop and thrive, the three authors examine coalitions in terms of four key components: resource acquisition, maintenance, production, and the attainment of external goals. A coalition's membership is its primary resource, although external resources such as concerned public officials and funders and a variety of external groups and organizations may be important as well. Organizational structure—that aspect of the coalition whose functions include accessing resources and organizing members—should give special attention to issues of leadership, decisionmaking, and conflict resolution processes. Both *target activities*, including setting and fulfilling a coalition mission, and *maintenance activities* (e.g., recruiting and training new members, facilitating leadership development, and fund-raising) are, according to Wandersman and his colleagues, vital to the production functions of a coalition. Finally, coalition accomplishments, or the attainment of external goals, are described as constituting for many the "bottom line" in terms of coalition effectiveness and worth. As Wandersman and his colleagues note, both short-term successes and longer-term impacts should be considered and evaluated, as both are necessary to long-range coalition viability and impact. The benefits and the costs of coalitions are discussed in this chapter, and questions are posed for health educators and other social change professionals about these powerful, yet often difficult vehicles for social change.

Many of the principles and challenges laid out in chapter 16 are illustrated within a real-world context in the chapter that follows. In chapter 17, Daniel Kass and Nicholas Freudenberg present a case study of New York City's Coalition to End Lead Poisoning and describe how this umbrella organization has sought to educate diverse constituencies and influence public policy in this important public health problem area. After a brief overview of the problem and the elements of a meaningful lead poisoning prevention effort, the authors describe the genesis and evolution of the coalition. Its activities, which included bringing a lawsuit against the city, are explored, and their consequences are analyzed. Although the lawsuit has yet to be definitively settled, its early benefits, such as getting city officials to meet regularly with coalition members and encouraging progressive City Council members to introduce new legislation in this area, have been impressive.

A particularly useful contribution of this chapter lies in its critical analysis of the structure and functioning of the coalition against some of the dimensions laid out in the preceding chapter. The coalition's relative informality, reflected in its fluid, non-dues-paying membership, for example, is seen to have a number of positive benefits. Members are unlikely to use the threat of dropping out to get their positions adopted, and coalition resources are conserved for production rather than expended on maintenance functions. Yet this same informality has drawbacks as well, including a slow pace of production and a heavy reliance on a few founding members, whose departure could jeopardize the coalition's very existence.

This chapter closes with a thoughtful look at lessons that can be drawn from the case study for coalition building around other public health concerns. Defining issues broadly and helping diverse groups feel a personal connection to the issue are described as essential for a coalition concerned with influencing public policy. Similarly, the necessity of responding to policy shifts by changing strategies and, in some cases, projecting a different image of the coalition to the public is among the lessons offered. At a time when coalitions are formed—and dissolved —with increasing frequency, the experiences of the New York City Coalition to End Lead Poisoning are a useful reminder of the considerable impact that such vehicles can sometimes have.

References

Wolff, T. 1995. Coalition building: Is this really empowerment? In _From the ground up: A workbook on community building and community development_, ed. G. Kaye and T. Wolff. Amherst, Mass.: Area Health Education Center/Community Partners.

Chapter 16

Understanding Coalitions and How They Operate

ABRAHAM WANDERSMAN
ROBERT M. GOODMAN
FRANCES D. BUTTERFOSS

An "Open Systems" Organizational Framework

COALITIONS, PARTNERSHIPS, AND CONSORTIA are "hot strategies" for dealing with complex health and social problems. But bringing diverse partners together and running a successful coalition are very hard work. We believe that it is helpful to view a consortium or coalition as a type of organization. Like any organization, it needs resources, structure, activities, and accomplishments in order to survive. These are the essential elements of an open systems framework, so named because it is open to and interacts with the environment (Katz and Kahn 1978). This chapter begins with a brief look at the growing popularity of coalitions in public health practice and at the unique capabilities of these vehicles for action. The chapter then links the available research on coalitions to the open systems framework in an effort to better understand coalitions and how they operate.

The Rise of Coalitions as a Vehicle for Addressing Complex Public Health Issues

Substance abuse, smoking, violence, AIDS, and unplanned pregnancy are among the many complex health problems whose multiple causes are deeply imbedded in our social fabric. As earlier chapters have suggested, dealing effectively with such problems will require greatly increased efforts on the state and national levels and a societal-level commitment to broader social change. Yet as a number of the case

Portions of this chapter are based on "Understanding Coalitions" by Abraham Wandersman (April 1993), a report commissioned by the Community-based Public Health Evaluation Team, University of Minnesota, and funded by the W. K. Kellogg Foundation. Adapted by permission of the author and Connie C. Schmitz, P.I., University of Minnesota.

studies in this book suggest, local community action has an important role to play.

Effective community efforts to address substance abuse, violence, and other complex health and social problems are increasingly understood to require partnerships among numerous sectors. These may include the schools, business, the mass media, the health sector, academia, the criminal justice system, government, and grassroots community groups.

In recent years, both government and private sector funding agencies have begun to require coalition formation as an essential ingredient of the programs they support (Green and Frankish in press). The W. K. Kellogg Foundation's Community-Based Public Health Initiative, for example, was specifically designed to "strengthen the practice and teaching of public health by creating partnerships with an informed and involved public" (W. K. Kellogg Foundation 1994, 1). Consortia consisting of community, academic, and public health agency partners were funded in seven states beginning in 1992 toward the end of creating sustainable models of "a 'new' public health paradigm"—one that was to be "community driven and not merely "community placed" (W. K. Kellogg Foundation 1994).

The health promotion grant initiatives of the Henry J. Kaiser Family Foundation (Tarlov et al. 1987) and the "Fighting Back" substance abuse prevention programs funded by the Robert Wood Johnson Foundation are among the other major private sector grant initiatives that have mandated coalition building as a key dimension of the efforts they support. On the government level in the United States, the Centers for Disease Control's PATCH health promotion program, the Native American tribal health promotion programs sponsored by the U.S. Office of Minority Health, and the hundreds of "community partnerships" funded by the Center for Substance Abuse Prevention are among numerous recent initiatives that require coalition building as a condition of funding. These and other public health efforts assume that programs designed, implemented, and owned by community coalitions will be far more effective than those developed either by government alone or by a single group. Yet research with voluntary organizations suggests that coalitions are variable in their effectiveness and vulnerable to decline (Green and Frankish in press). Empirical evidence is needed to document how they operate, how they maintain their viability, and whether, indeed, they improve the impact of public health initiatives.

Unique Capabilities of Coalitions

Two definitions capture our understanding of coalitions. The first of these views a coalition as "an organization of *individuals* representing diverse organizations, factions, or constituencies who agree to work together in order to achieve a common goal" (Feighery and Rogers 1989, 1; emphasis added). The second sees a coalition as "an organization of diverse *interest groups* that combine their human and material resources to effect a specific change the members are unable to bring about independently" (Brown 1984, 4; emphasis added).

As both of these definitions suggest, coalitions are interorganizational, cooperative, and synergistic working alliances. The word *coalition* is derived from two Latin roots: *coalescere* (to grow together) and *coalitio* (a union). Coalitions unite individuals and groups in a shared purpose. But unity and purpose are common ingredients in many types of groups and cannot serve alone as distinguishing characteristics of coalitions. Recent definitions emphasize coalitions as multipurpose alliances that accommodate more than one mission or set of goals (Black 1983; Perlman 1979; Stevenson, Pearce, and Porter 1985), exchange mutually beneficial resources (Allensworth and Patton 1990; Hord 1986), and direct their interventions at multiple levels, including policy change, resource development, and ecological change (McLeroy et al. 1988).

As the growing body of literature on coalitions suggests, these vehicles serve several important purposes. Coalitions can

1. Enable organizations to become involved in new and broader issues without having the sole responsibility for managing or developing those issues (Black 1983).
2. Demonstrate and develop widespread public support for issues, actions, or unmet needs. This can help create the political will to make hard choices (Klitzner 1991).
3. Maximize the power of individuals and groups through joint action. They can increase the "critical mass" behind a community effort by helping individuals achieve objectives beyond the scope of any one individual or organization (Brown 1984).
4. Minimize duplication of effort and services. This economy of scale can be a positive side effect of improved trust and communication among groups that would normally compete with one another (Brown 1984; Feighery and Rogers 1989).
5. Help mobilize more talent, resources, and approaches to influence an issue than any single organization could achieve alone. Such "strategic devices" "enhance the leverage" that groups can amass (Roberts-DeGennaro 1986a).
6. Provide an avenue for recruiting participants from diverse constituencies, such as political, business, human service, social, and religious groups, as well as less organized grassroots groups and individuals (Black 1983; Feighery and Rogers 1989).
7. Exploit new resources in changing situations (Boissevain 1974).

The Open Systems Framework as a Model of Coalition Viability

How can the core elements of these synergistic working alliances be conceptualized? As noted earlier, we employ as a theoretical framework Daniel Katz and Robert Kahn's (1978) open systems perspective on how organizations function and maintain momentum as they interact with the surrounding environment. The framework proposes that organizations can be seen as *mechanisms for processing resources obtained from the environment into products that affect that environment.*

Using Katz and Kahn's work as a departure point, John Prestby and Abraham Wandersman (1985) developed a framework of organizational viability that suggests that there are four components of organizational functioning: (1) resource acquisition, (2) maintenance subsystem (organizational structure), (3) production subsystem (actions or activities), and (4) external goal attainment (accomplishments). This model indicates that any organization that fails to obtain adequate and appropriate resources, develop an organizational structure for obtaining resources and conducting work, mobilize resources efficiently and effectively, turn out appropriate "products" (e.g., action, benefits to members), and/or accomplish something will eventually cease to operate. The elements of the open systems framework are diagrammed in Figure 16.1.

Resource Acquisition

For a coalition to maintain itself, it must acquire the resources to keep going. For coalitions, resources consist primarily of those brought to the organization by its members and those recruited from external sources.

MEMBER RESOURCES

A coalition's membership is its primary asset. Several variables related to the members have been associated with organizational maintenance (Prestby and Wandersman 1985), including the size of the membership, depth of members' attachment to the mission, and members' personal and political efficacy.

Each member brings a different set of resources and skills to the coalition. For instance, one member may provide transportation to or space for meetings, another may contribute staff support, a third may assist in fund-raising, and a fourth may provide access to and influence with relevant policymakers (Knoke and Wright-Isak 1982). The pooling of member assets is especially significant when participation is voluntary and the coalition has few material resources of its own (Knoke and Wood 1981; Prestby and Wandersman 1985). Diversity among members enables the coalition to reach and represent a larger constituency.

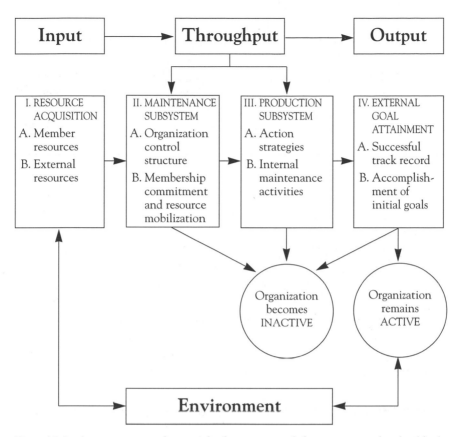

Figure 16.1. An open systems framework of organizational characteristics related to block organization maintenance.

However, this diversity may lead to diversity in assumptions and needs, which may lead to conflict.

The effective implementation and maintenance of a coalition require not only motivated and involved members but also members with the skills or capacity to participate in a partnership and to gain legitimacy (Gray 1985). For instance, a coalition that worked with problem youths demonstrated that the competence and performance of members were positively related to coordination among participating organizations and negatively related to conflict (Hall et al. 1977). Similarly, a skills training program conducted with members and chairpersons of an advocacy coalition resulted in increased reporting of issues by members, improvements in the chairpersons' ability to conduct action-oriented meetings, and overall improved effectiveness of the consumer organization (Balcazar et al. 1990).

EXTERNAL RESOURCES

Coalitions also benefit by linking with external resources, especially those concerned with policy, planning, and services (Butterfoss, Goodman, and Wandersman 1993). Examples of external resources include elected officials and government agencies, religious and civic groups, neighborhood and community development associations, foundations, and national sources of technical assistance. These resources can provide expertise, facilities for meetings, mailing lists, referrals, additional personnel for special projects, grant funding, loans or donations, equipment and supplies, and cosponsorship of events (Chavis et al. 1987; Prestby and Wandersman 1985). Such external support may be reduced when granting sources undergo funding cutbacks or when the coalition has small, overworked, inefficient staff; inadequate communication channels; or inflexible organizational policies (Whetten 1981).

A coalition's relationships with external resources may be classified along four dimensions: *formalization* (the degree of official recognition of the relationship), *standardization* (the degree to which procedures for linking are specified), *intensity* (the frequency of interactions and flow of resources), and *reciprocity* (the degree of mutual exchange of resources). High levels of these dimensions are related to greater satisfaction with the collaborative relationship but may also produce more conflict (Marrett 1971). Collaboration with external resources may also be conceptualized along a continuum from mild to intense linkage in which the stronger the linkage is, the greater are the trust and investment of time and resources by member agencies (Andrews 1990).

Access to local communities is an important link for many coalitions (Roberts-DeGennaro 1986b), particularly those concerned with health promotion. Such coalitions often benefit by linking with individuals and organizations active in community affairs. For instance, Prestby and Wandersman's (1985) study of block associations demonstrated that those that endured tended to have strong linkages with local community organizers and with other neighborhood associations. Exchange of needed resources with other community organizations occurred more often in active associations (Chavis et al. 1987). Finally, improved linkages with several other community organizations was reported by Paul Florin, Roger Mitchell, and John Stevenson (1989) as an important intermediate outcome of a substance abuse task force. Members of this group reported higher levels of participation, satisfaction, positive expectations, and greater intentions of future participation among their members.

Maintenance Subsystem

Organizational structure is the aspect of the coalition that obtains the resources and organizes the members. If coalitions are to be viable, they must be able to set goals, administer rewards, and mediate between members' individual needs and the task requirements of the organization. Leadership; formalized rules, roles, and procedures; and decisionmaking and problem resolution processes are important mechanisms for accomplishing these tasks.

LEADERSHIP

Strong central leadership is an important ingredient in the implementation and maintenance of coalition activities (Butterfoss et al. 1993). Regardless of size, coalitions tend to have a few core leaders who dominate coalition activities (Roberts-DeGennaro 1986b). When these leaders are attentive to and supportive of individual member concerns and are competent in negotiation, garnering of resources, problem-solving, and conflict resolution, the coalition tends to be more cohesive in reaching peripheral members and in maintaining coalition operations (Brown 1984). Other important qualities of leadership include

Personal resources (such as self-efficacy), membership in other
   community organizations, and level of education
A high degree of political knowledge, commitment, and competence
Proved administrative skills in setting agendas, running efficient
   meetings, garnering resources, and delegating responsibilities
Skill in communication and interpersonal relations
The ability to promote equal status and encourage overall
   collaboration in the member organizations
Flexibility
Easy access to the media and decisionmaking centers of the
   community   (Butterfoss et al. 1993)

FORMALIZED RULES, ROLES, AND PROCEDURES

Many authors assert that formalization is necessary for the successful implementation and maintenance of collaborative activities. Formalization is the degree to which rules, roles, and procedures are defined precisely. The higher the degree of formalization is, the greater are the investment of resources and exchanges among agencies, the satisfaction with the effort itself, and the willingness of member agencies to take responsibility and be committed. Examples of formalization include written memoranda of understanding, bylaws, and policy and procedures manuals; clearly defined roles; mission statements, goals, and objectives; and regular reorientation to the purposes, goals, roles, and procedures of collaboration (Butterfoss et al. 1993; Goodman and Steckler 1989). Formalization often results in the routinization or persistent implementation of the coalition's operations. The more routinized operations become, the more likely it is that they will be sustained (Goodman and Steckler 1989).

DECISIONMAKING AND PROBLEM RESOLUTION PROCESSES

The influence that participants have in making decisions is vital to a coalition. Wandersman (1981) describes a continuum of decisionmaking power in groups from advice to control. Advisory power means that the coalition develops recommendations but that professionals and government officials have the final responsibility for decisionmaking. Control means that the coalition itself has the final decisionmaking power.

Cheri Brown (1984) suggests that small, single-issue coalitions may adopt a decision-by-consensus method, whereas larger, multi-issue coalitions may aim for a working consensus (two-thirds majority) when time is limited. She advises coalitions to encourage open discussions and urge members to share in decisionmaking. If this is not done, group members may not understand or be committed to the issues under discussion. They may "sabotage" a decision by withholding objections initially and then failing to support the decision later. She also urges coalitions to avoid overrepresentation in decisionmaking by limiting the maximum number of votes to each member organization.

Strong, effective coalitions depend on shared leadership and shared decisionmaking. The latter can be affected by a "status differential" in the group, where one professional or organization has more authority or greater resources than others (Andrews 1990, 157). Howard Zuckerman and Arnold Kaluzny (1990) suggest that key stakeholders and leaders of an alliance be extensively involved in a joint decisionmaking process. Consensus and agreement require relationships among participants that are "collegial and egalitarian" and a manager who seeks to "balance constituencies rather than to control subordinates."

Prestby and Wandersman (1985) found that active block associations in the Neighborhood Participation Project were more likely to use a democratic decisionmaking process, whereas inactive associations used an autocratic or mixed democratic/autocratic process. The Block Booster project (Chavis et al. 1987) reported that active block association members felt that they had a greater influence in deciding on the policies and actions of the group than did inactive block association members. Active block associations used consensus and formalized decisionmaking procedures more often and were more decentralized than inactive block associations. Decisionmaking frequently involves conflict, negotiation, and compromise. Arlene Andrews (1990) warns that the problem-solving approach of the group must be clearly defined so that solutions will not conflict with the individual responsibilities of participants. In addition, conflict (usually interpersonal in nature) is reduced when a consensus is reached by using group techniques, such as nominal group process. Brown (1984, 26, 27) provides extensive guidelines for managing conflict and maintains that "almost every decision by an existing coalition, or one in the process of forming, necessitates negotiation." She suggests that conflicts should not be suppressed because they can be "energizing"—forcing both sides to develop new options and new ways of working together.

Richard Hall and others (1977) report that both conflict and coordination appeared to be a consequence of frequent interorganizational interactions. Personnel competence, performance, quality of communications, and compatibility of philosophy were all positively related to coordination and negatively related to conflict among youth-oriented organizations.

Terry Mizrahi and Beth Rosenthal (1992) argue that conflict is an inherent characteristic of coalitions. It may arise between the coalition and its targets for social change or among coalition partners concerning issues such as leadership, goals, benefits, contributions, and representation. Mizrahi and Rosenthal identify four "dynamic tensions" that account for conflict in coalitions: (1) the mixed loyalties of members to their own organizations and to the coalition, (2) the autonomy a coalition requires and the accountability it has to its member organizations, (3) the lack of clarity about the coalition's purpose as either a means for specific change or a model for sustained interorganizational cooperation, and (4) the diversity of interests of its members. (See appendix 3.)

Michael Edelstein (1992) suggests several aspects of coalitions that may be useful in understanding the context in which conflicts emerge:

1. *Voluntary versus required formation:* some coalitions are entered into voluntarily, whereas others are formed because they are required (e.g., to obtain funding).
2. *Reactive versus proactive formation:* some coalitions form in reaction to a crisis, whereas others form to develop a new program or fill a gap.
3. *Confrontation versus cooperation:* some coalitions take an adversarial approach to the power structure, whereas others attempt to work with the power structure.
4. *Previous history of coalition partners:* some coalition functioning will be influenced by the extent and type of previous history that the coalition partners have.
5. *Consensus versus dissensus:* some coalitions work with similar members (e.g., representatives of local community-based organizations working on domestic violence), whereas some attempt to coalesce potentially opposing partners (e.g., public health educators working in a substance abuse coalition with representatives from the beer and wine industry).

How the coalition manages these dynamics affects its cohesiveness and effectiveness. Systematic study of these factors is required to better understand how coalitions deal with conflict.

VOLUNTEER-STAFF RELATIONSHIPS

Although not all coalitions have the resources to employ staff, they can reduce the burdens placed on a coalition's membership. When a coalition employs staff, it is likely to be more harmonious if staff and members are clear about their respective roles and if staff are given latitude to carry out daily tasks (Brown 1984). Ellen Feighery and Todd Rogers (1989) suggest that staff roles should be clarified as soon as a coalition is formed. They believe that in the early stages of the coalition, staff must help educate some volunteer members to the issues that influence the coalition's mission and strategies and that staff must guide members in assuming new roles and responsibilities.

The effectiveness of the staff may be judged by how well they balance their provision of technical assistance to members with the members' ability to make informed decisions. Staff seem more likely to improve the atmosphere of a coalition when they possess an appreciation for the voluntary nature of coalitions and have organizational and interpersonal skills to facilitate the complex collaborative process (Croan and Lees 1979).

The literature on different types of roles for volunteers in coalitions is sparse. A volunteer in a coalition can be an instrumental founding board member, a committee chair or dependable member, or an occasional participant working on a single activity. We believe that each role has its own challenges, benefits, and costs and has a different relationship with staff. Additional research is needed to fill this gap in the literature.

COMMUNICATION PATTERNS

Smooth internal communication among the membership and staff may be the most essential ingredient for enhancing the climate of a coalition. Open communication helps the group focus on a common purpose, increases trust and sharing of resources, provides information about one another's programs, and allows members to express and resolve misgivings about planned activities (Andrews 1990; Feighery and Rogers 1989). Viable coalitions often have frequent meetings, which members are actively encouraged to attend (Benard 1989; Hord 1986), and a well-developed system of internal communication to keep staff and members informed (Andrews 1990; Cohen, Baer, and Satterwhite 1991; Croan and Lees 1979).

MEMBERSHIP COMMITMENT AND MOBILIZATION

Membership commitment and resource mobilization are key aspects of the operation of organizations, especially when they depend upon voluntary effort. As Marilyn Gittell (1980, 263) concludes, "We need to know more about why people join organizations and what encourages them to devote time and energy to those organization's aims." Political economy theory suggests that in organizations a social exchange takes place in which participants will invest their energy in the organization only if they expect to receive some benefits. Some of the potential benefits and costs of participation are as follows:

Benefits
- Increased networking, information sharing, and access to resources (Hord 1986; Kaplan 1986)
- Involvement in an important cause and attainment of the desired outcomes from the coalition's efforts (Rich 1980; Zapka et al., 1992)
- Enjoyment of the coalition's work (Benard 1989)
- Receipt of personal recognition (Rich 1980; Roberts-DeGennaro 1986b; Wandersman and Alderman 1993)

Costs
- Time given to coalition lost to other obligations (Bailey 1986; Rich 1980)
- Lost autonomy in decisionmaking, expenditure of scarce resources, overcoming of any unfavorable image held by other partners (Schermerhorn 1975)
- Lack of direction from coalition leadership or staff, perception of lack of recognition or appreciation, burnout, lack of necessary skills, pressure for additional commitment (Wandersman and Alderman 1993)

Several studies have systematically studied the benefits and costs of participation in voluntary organizations for individuals. Prestby et al. (1990) found two main sources of motivation: "personal gain" benefits (such as learning new skills and gaining personal recognition) and "social/communal benefits" (such as improving the neighborhood and helping others). In a related study, Wandersman et al. (1987) found that members and nonmembers agreed that the greatest benefits were in making a contribution and helping others rather than in satisfying self-interest or a need for personal gains. More active participants further reported receiving significantly more social/communal benefits and personal benefits than less active participants (Prestby et al. 1990).

There are, however, costs involved in participation: "personal costs" (e.g., time, effort, and the things people give up in other parts of their lives in order to participate) and "social/organizational costs" (e.g., interpersonal conflict and lack of organizational progress) (Wandersman et al. 1987). Furthermore, the least active members have reported more social/organizational costs than more active members (c.f. Prestby et al. 1990). Such costs may act as a barrier to more active participation.

Several studies have also looked at the *ratio* of benefits to costs. Prestby et al. (1990) found that the more actively a person participated, the higher the benefit/cost ratio was. In addition to an understanding of the costs and benefits of participation to an individual, it would be useful to examine the benefits and costs of participation for an organization to participate in a coalition. In other words, what does an organization get out of participating in a coalition?

Production Subsystem

A coalition must engage in two types of activities: (1) target activities, or those that work directly toward the consortium's intended goals and products, and (2) maintenance activities, or those that clarify processes and sustain and renew the infrastructure.

TARGET ACTIVITIES

If a coalition is to survive, it must produce more than a sense of safety in numbers or camaraderie among members; it must engage in the tasks and produce the products for which it was created. Examples of tasks in the early stages of a coalition are creating a mission statement, setting up committees, performing a needs assessment, and developing a comprehensive plan. In the implementation phase of the coalition, the actual activities (e.g., training, advocacy, education programs) are carried out. For example, a community partnership to prevent alcohol and other drug problems might develop after-school activities, parent training, media or red ribbon campaigns, and coping skills programs, or the partnership might advocate for policy change.

MAINTENANCE ACTIVITIES

To sustain momentum and rebuild, a coalition has to recruit and orient new members, train leaders, prepare leaders-in-waiting to take over when there is turnover, address and resolve conflict, engage in public relations, celebrate its accomplishments, and raise funds (Prestby and Wandersman 1985). Many voluntary organizations, including coalitions, appear to be vulnerable in this area because maintenance activities do not always have the "glitz," visibility, or priority that target activities do.

Tension can and frequently does arise between target and maintenance activities. For example, how much time should be spent on each type of activity when people's energy is limited? Although we cannot say that there is a known "best ratio," we believe that each type is necessary for viability but insufficient for a coalition to be effective. Perhaps understanding the importance of both types can lead to a more productive balance of time and energy. For example, staff might spend more time on maintenance activities, and volunteers might focus on target activities. (See appendix 3.)

External Goal Attainment

What has the coalition accomplished? For many, including coalition members and funders, this is the bottom line. Has the coalition taken any actions that have achieved its initial goals and objectives? For example, has it reduced the incidence of substance abuse? Has it improved the training of public health professionals?

SHORT- AND LONG-TERM CHANGES

Program evaluators often discuss two types of program effects, which may be thought of as short-term and long-term effects. *Outcome evaluation* attempts to determine the short-term or direct effects of the program. In contrast, *impact evaluation* is concerned with the long-term, ultimate effects desired by a community organizing effort or program. In alcohol and other drug prevention programs such as the New Mexico–based Adolescent Social Action Program described in chapter 12, impacts can include reduction in overall drug use and a decrease in drunk driving–related fatalities.

Several analysts emphasize the need for coalitions to accomplish "quick wins" and short-term successes to increase member motivation and pride and to enhance the credibility of the coalition (Brown 1984; Croan and Lees 1979; Hord 1986). Once a coalition attains a quick win, it may direct its efforts at more complex tasks (Cohen et al. 1991). Short-term successes should not, however, be mistaken for ultimate solutions to complex health problems and social concerns (Sink and Stowers 1989).

In addition to evaluating the outcomes produced by the programs of the coalition, some coalitions are concerned with system change, such as alterations in service delivery and system reform (Kagan 1991). Measurement of system change, such as new community linkages and cross-referrals among agencies, is difficult. There are few widely accepted measures and few studies that have attempted to measure systems change.

CHALLENGE TO EVALUATORS

Ultimately, if coalitions are to contribute to the improved health status of the community, they have to evaluate the impact they have on improving the social and health systems and outcomes of the community. Thorough evaluation is one mechanism that is frequently cited for improving outcome effectiveness (Bailey 1986; Feighery and Rogers 1989; Andrews 1990; Cohen 1989; Wandersman and Goodman 1991; Cohen et al. 1991). Clearly, there is a great need for additional conceptualization and new methodological tools in the assessment of coalition functioning and outcomes (see chapters 18 and 19 for a discussion of recent developments in empowerment evaluation that offer promise in this regard).

CHALLENGE TO COALITION LEADERS

The complex issues that many coalitions address take concerted and long-range efforts. Therefore, successful activities and programs probably need to be repeated. This requires the institutionalization of the program or community organizing effort. The latter can be institutionalized either in the coalition or in one of its member agencies. In addition to the institutionalization of programs or organizing projects, institutionalization of the coalition itself (or its functions) should be a long-range consideration for most coalitions and a marker for coalition success. Robert Goodman and Allen Steckler (1989) have used an open systems framework to assess program institutionalization.

Conclusion

Community coalitions and partnerships represent exciting experiments in social change and powerful weapons in the battle to solve complex challenges in the public's health. They can be viewed as a panacea, as the only solution to getting things done, or as the way to break the gridlock of opposing forces or insufficient power. But as Lawrence Green and C. James Frankish (in press) point out, coalitions can also be time consuming and difficult, particularly in times of limited resources.

Coalitions form at the local level when grassroots groups seek safety or power in numbers. They may form when opportunities for new funding arise or cutbacks necessitate consolidation or cooperation. The basic idea is that "working together can move us forward." However, knowing how to really make a coalition work is paramount. The challenges to an effective coalition are enormous. Collaboration has been called an "unnatural act between unconsenting adults." While this remark is made in humor, it appears to reflect a truism that collaboration is challenging because of turf issues, personalities, group dynamics, power, and status. Therefore, a coalition that attempts to achieve stability should be even more challenged.

Although the research literature on coalitions as organizations is relatively thin, we believe that there is enough research and experience to suggest that if a coalition is to be successful, there has to be an *organization* of roles and people. The *resources* of a coalition (its greatest potential) must be organized in a *structure* that clarifies roles and relationships and produces *activities* that work toward the goals of the coalition and sustain and renew the organization. A successful coalition yields perceivable *accomplishments* and *impacts*.

Within this perspective, health educators and other social change professionals engaged in coalition building and maintenance may benefit from reviewing how their consortia operate as organizations. What resources do members bring? What additional external resources are necessary? Are both target and maintenance activities occurring simultaneously? Do members feel that the benefits of participation outweigh the costs for themselves as individuals and for their organizations? The posing of such questions, as well as others described in appendix 3, can help us be realistic about the costs and the many benefits of coalitions and can help in our efforts to have these social change vehicles realize their full potential.

References

Allensworth, D., and W. Patton, W. 1990. Promoting school health through coalition building. *Eta Sigma Gamma Monograph Series* 7.

Andrews, A. 1990. Interdisciplinary and interorganizational collaboration. In *Encyclopedia of social work*, ed. A. Minahan et al. 18th ed. Silver Springs, Md.: National Association of Social Workers.

Bailey, A. 1986. More than good intentions: Building a network of collaboratives. *Education and Urban Society* 19:7–23.

Balcazar, R., T. Seekins, S. Fawcett, and B. Hopkins. 1990. Empowering people with physical disabilities through advocacy skills training. *American Journal of Community Psychology* 18 (2):281–296.

Benard, B. 1989. Working together: Principles of effective collaboration. *Prevention Forum* (October):4–9.

Black, T. 1983. Coalition building—some suggestions. *Child Welfare* 62:263–268.

Boissevain, J. 1974. *Friends of friends*. Oxford: Basil Blackwell.

Brown, C. 1984. *The art of coalition building: A guide for community leaders*. New York: American Jewish Committee.

Butterfoss, F., R. Goodman, and A. Wandersman. 1993. Community coalitions for prevention and health promotion. *Health Education Research* 8 (3):315–330.

Chavis, D., P. Florin, R. Rich, and A. Wandersman. 1987. *The role of block associations in crime control and community development: The block booster project*. Final report to the Ford Foundation, New York.

Cohen, D. 1989. Collaboration: What works? *Education Week* (March):13.

Cohen, L., N. Baer, and P. Satterwhite, P. 1991. Developing effective coalitions: A how-to guide for injury prevention professionals. Paper presented at a meeting of the U.S. Department of Health, Maternal Child and Adolescent Health, January.

Croan, G., and J. Lees. 1979. *Building effective coalitions: Some planning considerations*. Arlington, Va.: Westinghouse National Issues Center.

Edelstein, M. 1992. Building coalitions for sustainability: An examination of emergent partnerships addressing environmental and community issues. Paper presented at the annual meeting of the Environmental Design Research Association, Boulder, Colorado, April.

Feighery, E., and T. Rogers. 1989. *Building and maintaining effective coalitions*. How-to Guides on Community Health Promotion no. 12. Palo Alto: Stanford Health Promotion Resource Center.

Florin, P., R. Mitchell, and J. Stevenson. 1989. Rhode Island Substance Abuse Prevention Act questionnaire. Providence: Department of Psychology, University of Rhode Island.

Gittell, M. 1980. *Limits of citizen participation: The decline of community organizations*. Beverly Hills, Calif.: Sage.

Goodman, R. M., and A. Steckler. 1989. A framework for assessing program institutionalization. *Knowledge in Society: The International Journal of Knowledge Transfer* 2 (1):57–71.

Gray, B. 1985. Conditions facilitating interorganizational collaboration. *Human Relations* 38:911–936.

Green, L. W., and C. J. Frankish. In press. Finding the right mix of organizational, decentralized, and centralized control in planning for health promotion. In *Community health promotion*, ed. B. Beery, E. Wagner, and A. Cheadle. Seattle: University of Washington Press.

Hall, R., J. Clark, P. Giordano, P. Johnson, and M. Van Roekel. 1977. Patterns of interorganizational relationships. *Administrative Science Quarterly* 22:457–473.

Hord, S. 1986. A synthesis of research on organizational collaboration. *Educational Leadership* (February):22–26.

Kagan, S. L. 1991. *United we stand: Collaboration for child care and early education services.* New York: Teachers College Press.

Kaplan, M. 1986. Cooperation and coalition development among neighborhood organizations: A case study. *Journal of Voluntary Action Research* 15 (4).

Katz, D., and R. L. Kahn. 1978. *The social psychology of organizations.* 2d ed. New York: Wiley.

Klitzner, M. 1991. *National evaluation plan for fighting back.* Bethesda, Md.: Robert Wood Johnson Foundation.

Knoke, D., and J. R. Wood. 1981. *Organized for action: Commitment in voluntary associations.* New Brunswick: Rutgers University Press.

Knoke, D., and C. Wright-Isak. 1982. Individual motives and organizational incentive systems. *Research in the Sociology of Organizations* 1:209–254.

Marrett, C. 1971. On the specification of interorganizational dimensions. Sociology and Social Research 56:83–99.

McLeroy, K. R., D. Bibeau, A. Steckler, and K. Glanz. 1988. An ecological perspective on health promotion programs. *Health Education Quarterly* 15 (4):351–377.

Mizrahi, T., and B. Rosenthal. 1992. Managing dynamic tension in social change coalitions. In *Community organization and social administration: Advances, trends, and emerging principles,* ed. T. Mizrahi and J. D. Morrison. New York: Haworth Press.

Perlman, J. 1979. Grassroots empowerment and government response. *Social Policy* 10:16–21.

Prestby, J. E., and A. Wandersman. 1985. An empirical exploration of a framework of organizational viability: Maintaining block organizations. *Journal of Applied Behavioral Science* 21 (3):287–305.

Prestby, J., A. Wandersman, P. Florin, R. Rich, and D. Chavis. 1990. Benefits, costs, incentive management, and participation in voluntary organizations: A means to understanding and promoting empowerment. *American Journal of Community Psychology* 18(1):117–149.

Rich, R. 1980. The dynamics of leadership in neighborhood organizations. *Social Science Quarterly* 60 (4):570–587.

Roberts-DeGennaro, M. 1986a. Building coalitions for political advocacy. *Social Work* (July-August):308–311.

―――. 1986b. Factors contributing to coalition maintenance. *Journal of Sociology and Social Welfare* 248–264.

Schermerhorn, J. Jr. 1975. Determinants of interorganizational cooperation. *Academy of Management Journal* 18 (4):846–856.

Sink, D., and G. Stowers. 1989. Coalitions and their effect on the urban policy agenda. *Administration in Social Work* 13:83–98.

Stevenson, W., J. Pearce, and L. Porter. 1985. The concept of coalition in organization theory and research. *Academy of Management Review* 10:256–268.

Tarlov, A., B. Kehrer, D. Hall, S. Samuels, G. Brown, M. Felix, and J. Ross. 1987. Foundation work: The health promotion program of the Henry Kaiser Family Foundation. *American Journal of Health Promotion* 2 (2) (Fall):74–78.

Wandersman, A. 1981. A framework of participation in community organizations. *Journal of Applied Behavioral Science* 17:27–58.

Wandersman, A., and J. Alderman. 1993. Incentives, costs, and barriers for volunteers: A staff perspective for volunteers in one state. *Review of Public Personnel Administration* 13 (1):67–76.

Wandersman, A., P. Florin, R. Friedmann, and R. Meier. 1987. Who participates, who does not, and why? An analysis of voluntary neighborhood associations in the United States and Israel. *Sociological Forum* 2 (3):534–555.

Wandersman, A., and R. Goodman. 1991. Community partnerships for alcohol and other drug abuse prevention. *Family Resource Coalition Report* 10 (3):8–9.

W. K. Kellogg Foundation. 1994. *Working together toward healthy communities*. Community-based Public Health Initiative program brochure. Battle Creek, Mich.: W. K. Kellogg Foundation.

Whetten, D. 1981. Interorganizational relations: A review of the field. *Journal of Higher Education* (52):1–27.

Zuckerman, H., and A. Kaluzny. 1990. Managing beyond vertical and horizontal integration: Strategic alliances as an emerging organizational form. University of Michigan. Unpublished manuscript.

Chapter 17

Coalition Building to Prevent Childhood Lead Poisoning

DANIEL KASS
NICHOLAS FREUDENBERG

A Case Study from New York City

How can public health professionals influence public policy in order to promote health and prevent disease? What methods are effective when the targets for behavior change are institutions and policymakers, as well as patients, clients, and consumers? How can educators for health define for themselves a role that bridges the gap between health professional and advocate? In the late 1980s, public health professionals and other advocates from around New York City asked themselves these same questions to arrive at a concerted and comprehensive understanding of, and response to, the problem of childhood lead poisoning. This chapter describes the thinking and efforts that drove a coalition's formation as well as the coalition's intended and actual, direct and indirect achievements.

The Public Health Scope of Childhood Lead Poisoning

According to the Centers for Disease Control and Prevention, childhood lead poisoning is the most serious environmental health threat facing young children (U.S. Department of Health and Human Services 1991). Very high blood lead levels (greater than 80 µg/dl) can cause convulsions, coma, even death. Mortality from lead poisoning in the United States has been all but eliminated through the reduction of lead in gasoline and the banning of lead-containing solder from food storage cans, the two sources that contributed most to blood lead levels in the general population. Whereas 152 deaths from lead poisoning in New York City occurred between 1954 and 1974, for example, none has occurred since (Office of the Controller 1986). Although the health consequences to children are less grave than they once were, they are just as pernicious. And the single greatest source for childhood lead poisoning is ingestion of deteriorating lead-based paint.

278

Though toxic to all humans, the effects of lead are particularly dangerous to children younger than six. Their still-developing nervous systems are damaged by very small amounts of lead exposure. Children also absorb lead from the digestive system six times more efficiently than do adults and because of their small size receive far greater effective doses. Several studies have demonstrated that children with blood lead levels below 40 µg/dl suffer from a variety of development delays and learning disorders, including delayed speech development and verbal processing, poor attention span, and decreased IQ scores (Needleman et al. 1979; Goyer 1993). Behavioral disorders, including juvenile delinquency, have similarly been linked to childhood exposures to lead (Needleman et al. 1996). At low levels of exposure of short duration, the effects of lead poisoning are largely reversible. Sustained or high doses can lead to permanent damage, affecting neurological functions and behavior through adulthood. Exposures in children can lead to delayed symptoms in adults when calcium is liberated from bones, where lead is stored. This biological phenomenon can lead to prenatal exposure from mothers with a childhood lead burden.

According to the National Health and Nutrition Examination Survey completed in 1991, more than 8.9 percent, or 1.7 million, children in the United States have blood levels at or above 10 µg/dl, the "level of concern" set by the CDC. Lead poisoning is not evenly distributed across demographic groups. Low-income children are four times more likely than middle- and high-income families to have elevated blood lead levels. African-American children are four times more likely to be lead poisoned than white children are. Nationally, 37 percent of urban African-American children have blood levels at or above 10 µg/dl (National Center for Health Statistics 1991). In 1993, 8 percent of all reported U.S. lead poisoning cases occurred in New York City alone. The city estimated that 65,000 children had blood lead levels greater than 10 µg/dl in 1994 and that more than 2,000 had blood lead levels considered poisoning cases ($\geq$ 20 µg/dl) (New York City Department of Health 1994). Of these, 82 percent of lead-poisoned children were African American or Hispanic.

The societal cost of childhood lead poisoning includes medical costs for affected children and exposed mothers, costs of special education, lost lifetime occupational productivity, personal injury claims by victims, and a host of related expenses (Schwartz 1994). These total costs have been estimated at $400 million to $1 billion (Provenzano 1980). Preventing cases of poisoning could save $43 million per year in medical costs and $96 million per year in special education costs and could increase lifetime earnings by $600,000 per year (Lead-Based Paint Hazard Reduction and Financing Task Force 1995).

Ingestion of lead-contaminated dust is the most common exposure pathway that leads to childhood lead poisoning. Lead dust that contaminates easily reachable surfaces is ingested by children through normal hand-to-mouth activity.

This dust comes from deteriorating painted surfaces, from the result of friction between two paint surfaces such as doors and windows, and from damage or repair to building structures. According to 1990 estimates by the Department of Housing and Urban Development, 57 million housing units contain lead-based paint. Of these, 20 million are contaminated by chipping and peeling lead-based paint or by elevated levels of lead dust, and 3.8 million units housed children under seven years of age (U.S. Department of Housing and Urban Development 1990). Though residences are the most common source of exposure, children may also be exposed in day care centers, schools, and playgrounds. Even park soil that has accumulated lead from automobile and industrial emissions may have dangerously high levels capable of significantly elevating blood levels of lead.

Elements of a Meaningful Lead Poisoning Prevention Program

Reducing the incidence of new cases of childhood lead poisoning requires a multi-faceted approach that combines public health, medical, and housing interventions. Identifying cases depends upon screening children for blood lead levels as early as possible and at regular intervals. Successful screening programs depend upon knowledgeable medical care providers and informed parents. When cases are identified, further exposure to lead dust must be minimized through careful evaluation of dwellings and other places frequented by affected children. Where the potential for lead paint exposure is found, corrective action is required to ensure that peeling or chipping paint is removed and lead containing dust is entirely abated. Where lead paint remains, leaking roofs and pipes, unstable plaster, and damaged ceilings, all of which cause paint to deteriorate, must be repaired. Permanent correction of these hazards depends upon the safe removal of all lead paint.

Although a general consensus exists on what needs to be done, little agreement has emerged on how to go about doing it, who should bear the cost, and how to appropriately make interim progress on the problem while waiting for permanent solutions. It is clear, however, that prevention efforts must involve the coordination of public health agencies, medical practitioners, landlords, housing inspectors, and health educators and that these efforts must be driven by uniform local policies that set minimum standards for preventive and corrective efforts. It was around the call for improved local policy to prevent childhood lead poisoning that a coalition in New York City was born.

The Formation of a Citywide Coalition

The New York City Coalition to End Lead Poisoning (NYCCELP) was created at a time when there was widespread prevalence of lead poisoning, growing medical evidence that exposure to very low levels of lead causes serious health problems, and lack of confidence in the city government's willingness to confront the problem. Some fourteen years before the coalition's creation, scientists, housing activists, and parents of lead-poisoned children formed Citizens to End Lead Poisoning. This group successfully mounted pressure to force the City of New York to develop an agency infrastructure to screen and medically treat poisoned children and to educate health care providers on lead poisoning. Although the group did not last, the problem of lead poisoning did, and the response of the city to the problem waned (Freudenberg and Golub 1987).

In the early 1980s, several organizations emerged to address neighborhood environmental quality concerns. The Washington Heights Health Action Project organized a local coalition against lead poisoning that met for two years and helped to improve screening and educational services in northern Manhattan. The Lead Poisoning Prevention Project was begun in 1981 at Montefiore Medical Center in the Bronx with the aims of educating the community about lead, inspecting apartments, offering blood lead screening, and providing follow-up medical care.

These two organizations' successes in mobilizing people on this issue, as well as their failures in making substantive changes in city policies on lead poisoning, created the impetus for a citywide coalition against lead poisoning. In 1983, leaders of these two community-based efforts called together a group of housing activists, health professionals, and staff of advocacy groups to form a new organization dedicated to making lead poisoning once again a citywide political issue. The group called itself the New York City Coalition to End Lead Poisoning. Its members initially included social workers, community organizers, health educators, physicians, and housing activists. It would later expand its membership to include legal advocates, construction trade unions, private consulting firms, and progressive municipal agency personnel.

The Coalition's Activity

The coalition's first task was to review the New York City government's entire lead poisoning control program. After nine months of meetings with officials of the Departments of Health and Housing Preservation and Development, reviewing data on program performance, and consulting with medical experts on lead poisoning, NYCCELP wrote a report entitled *The Problem That Hasn't Gone Away: Childhood Lead Poisoning in New York City*. One week before its scheduled release, a newly formed interagency task force on lead poisoning, convened by the Mayor's Office, urgently requested that the coalition not release its report. The task force also outlined several new initiatives on lead poisoning, including more community education, more screening, and better interagency coordination. After much discussion, NYCCELP decided that it would release the report, hoping the latter would generate additional political support for stronger city action. The report recommended actions that addressed each of the essential elements of a preventive program just outlined.

In the months following the release of the report, NYCCELP members worked with another consortium of public health and advocacy groups to craft a budget proposal that would offer initial funding for implementing its recommendations. Though the City Council ultimately increased the budget by $300,000 for lead poisoning control, the funds were allocated to study control measures that would, in the opinion of the coalition, only serve to delay needed apartment repair. Little money was allocated to crucial screening, education, and lead paint abatement (Freudenberg and Golub 1987).

In early 1985, the coalition decided that it would initiate a lawsuit against the city. This decision was based on the coalition's perception that the city government had failed to act decisively to prevent lead poisoning and on the city's refusal to meet with coalition members after the release of the report. With representation by Bronx Legal Services, a class action lawsuit was filed on behalf of five lead-poisoned children and their parents against the mayor and the commissioners of health and housing preservation and development. Though monetary awards were requested, the broader hope was that the lawsuit would force the development of improved policy and enforcement of city regulations. Filed in a mayoral election year, the lawsuit, so the coalition hoped, would politicize the issue of lead poisoning and force candidates to define their position on this and other related public health and housing issues.

Ten years have passed since the lawsuit was filed. Five times, the courts have ruled for the coalition and the plaintiffs. Three times, the city has been held in contempt of court for failing to comply with the court's order to enforce city housing and health codes in ways the courts have interpreted were necessary to comply with the city's mandate to protect the health of children. Although it is frustrating that even court orders have not yet forced compliance or improved programming, the lawsuit has had several anticipated and unanticipated benefits in the ongoing struggle to prevent child lead poisoning:

- City officials now meet regularly with coalition members to discuss issues. In fact, coalition members lobby each year to increase (though more recently preserve) the budgets of agencies named as defendants in the lawsuit. There is now a more sophisticated recognition within agency staff of the Health Department of the role that the coalition can play in helping realize agency objectives.

     The politicization of the lawsuit has encouraged progressive City Council members to introduce legislation designed to improve the city's prevention efforts.

- In 1992, the mayor convened a task force, which included coalition members, to review city policy on lead poisoning. Though many suspected that the effort was intended to appease the city's critics, coalition members participated and helped to prevent a consensus from emerging that ultimately would have resulted in ineffective approaches to the problem. The coalition also gained membership from the ranks of this task force who had become frustrated at the disproportionate power of the real estate industry and profit-oriented environmental consultants.

- Though the lawsuit has dragged on, it has helped to sustain the coalition. The success in the courts has helped to legitimate the coalition in the media and among politicians and candidates. Status reports are discussed at meetings. Settlement offers have helped to solidify the positions of coalition members. Media coverage and legal affiliations have served to link coalition members to organizations and efforts outside of New York City and have strengthened the coalition's role in national alliances to address lead poisoning.

Though the lawsuit has been the most sustained and visible of NYCCELP's work, the coalition's activity has included other outward-reaching and inward-strengthening efforts. NYCCELP has, for example, developed community education curricula, conducted trainings, and cosponsored conferences. On the political front, NYCCELP members engage in state and local advocacy for improved enforcement and expanded budgets. They have also drafted legislation to mandate lead abatement worker training and certification (since improper abatement can lead to serious lead exposure among already poisoned children) and set minimum standards for abatement procedures. NYCCELP has for years served as a referral service for families, helping them to navigate the byzantine structures of city government and referring them to legal representation to redress hazardous conditions.

A Critical Analysis of the Structure of the Coalition

Throughout the existence of NYCCELP, it has depended principally on the use of member resources. Because many of the organizations that its participants represent have stable staff and financial resources (e.g., hospital- and university-based programs and legal offices), NYCCELP has not sought its own funding and has never had paid staff. NYCCELP has eschewed a great degree of formalization and standardization in its structure. Membership is fluid. Members are not charged dues. Leaders are democratically selected, but there is little concentration of power in their positions. An individual's failure to attend each monthly meeting is not met with approbation, and there is no mechanism for expulsion. The voluntary and flexible nature of the coalition's structure has contributed positively to its work and sustenance in two important ways: (1) the threat of dropping out that members of many coalitions use to have their position adopted has not occurred here, adding to the coalition's stability; and (2) scarce human resources are not expended on the operation of the coalition but are directed instead toward the primary objective of influencing citywide lead poisoning prevention policy. (See appendix 4.)

The coalition's informality also has its drawbacks. Flexible membership increases a coalition's risk of collapse or cooptation. NYCCELP has survived these threats because several original founding members have maintained strong, central roles throughout its existence. The withdrawal of their support, therefore, whether because of ideological reasons or because of sheer burnout, would imperil the coalition. The voluntary nature of NYCCELP also contributes to a slow pace of production, or what Abraham Wandersman, Robert Goodman, and Frances Butterfoss refer to in the previous chapter as "low intensity." Without staff, the coalition often depends on squeezing time and product from already overburdened members.

NYCCELP depends almost entirely on the financial and material resources of its organizational members. Resource inputs of staff time for mobilization, advocacy, legal representation, report writing, education, and other work products, as well as postage and transportation expenses, are contributed by individual and organizational members. This has ultimately helped to sustain the coalition in several ways:

- Members have had to work within their own base organizations to convince their boards or supervisors of the importance of the issues and the relevance of the proposed activities. The net effect has been that member organizations have expanded their own missions to better incorporate child lead poisoning prevention.

- The coalition generally has not opted to engage in activities its members are not capable of sustaining, thereby leading to more successes, fewer failures, and less frustration.

- Each member organization pledges its support fully aware of its own resource limitations and is less likely not to deliver on its promises. This has helped to solidify the partnerships and minimize internal divisiveness.

- Resource inputs have been balanced among organizational members; whereas some member organizations are able to offer financial support, others can mobilize volunteer labor.

Lessons from NYCCELP for Coalitions around Public Health Concerns

Several lessons can be drawn from the history of the New York City Coalition to End Lead Poisoning that are relevant to broader public health efforts. As noted in chapter 16, those seeking to change policy must define issues broadly so as to invite participation by constituencies sufficiently diverse to have a political impact. If broad support for policy changes is lacking, policymakers tend to dismiss the problem as insignificant. Because NYCCELP organized around an understanding that lead poisoning is a symptom of poor housing, it was able to attract the participation of community development groups, tenant organizations, housing organizers, and legal advocates. By recognizing the connection between lead poisoning and the broader vulnerability of low-income children to other negative health outcomes, NYCCELP has been able to draw the membership and support of child welfare organizations and advocates. And by recognizing that the solutions to lead poisoning must include community education and mobilization, NYCCELP has invited the participation of talented educators and organizers.

The range of skills and "capacity to participate" that the previous chapter identified as crucial to the effective implementation and survival of coalitions has been ensured within NYCCELP through this recruitment strategy. Table 17.1 illustrates

Table 17.1
Framework for Coalition Building on Lead Poisoning

Dimension of Lead Poisoning Problem	Constituencies Involved
Poor housing	Housing and tenant groups
Neighborhood deterioration	Neighborhood associations and community development groups
Child health	Child health advocacy groups, parents, health care providers
Education	Parents, school officials
Public health and primary prevention issues	Public health professionals and advocacy groups
Political issues	Elected officials, political parties, political aspirants
Environmental issues	Environmental organizations
Legal problems and liabilities	Law organizations, public service law groups, private attorneys
Employment issues	Trade unions, community development agencies, private environmental consulting firms
Minority issues	Civil rights groups, environmental justice groups

Reprinted from "Health Education, Public Policy, and Disease Prevention: A Case History of the New York City Coalition to End Lead Poisoning," by N. Freudenberg and M. Golub, *Health Education Quarterly* 14 (4) (1987):387–401, by permission of Sage Publications, Inc.
Copyright © 1987 by Sage Publications, Inc.

the dimensions of lead poisoning and the potential constituencies affected and there-fore involved in a coalition effort. This conceptualization of the problem helped the coalition to engage a wide variety of groups not previously involved in lead poisoning prevention. If public health advocates are to reach beyond those groups already concerned about an identified problem, they must learn how to describe the issue in terms that appeal to new constituencies' self-interests (see chapters 7 and 11).

Public health advocates working with coalition partners are able to multiply the impact of their work. When policymaking is not the principal role that one fills, policy-oriented coalitions offer opportunities to broaden the goals of one's pro-grams. Coalition members have enlightened one another on important social deter-minants of health and illness that can then influence programming. Members of the coalition enjoined from political activity (such as city employees) are able to work under the cloak of NYCCELP to advocate, testify, draft legislation and regulations, and campaign.

NYCCELP has been instrumental in helping to raise other health and wel-fare issues related to housing conditions. Asthma, for example, has been linked to the presence of cockroaches, animal proteins, and other indoor air pollutants, all of which are more likely to be found in deteriorating housing. The rising mor-bidity and mortality from asthma in New York City have prompted NYCCELP members to educate themselves on asthma and have helped to secure resources to begin addressing this condition in New York City communities.

Public health advocates must also understand how different groups influence the policy process. City Council members, for example, respond to pressure that emanates from their own districts. City agency personnel may be responsive to data and persuasion but are just as influenced by their agency heads, who in turn must respond to the Mayor's Office. The mayor's attention is captured by the media. The coalition has worked to effect policy change through each of these avenues, mindful of their interconnections (Freudenberg and Golub 1987).

Coalitions must also be able to respond to changes in the policy arena with appropriate internal redirection of resources, modifications of strategies, and, when necessary, modification of the public perception of the coalition and its mem-bers. NYCCELP has effectively balanced its role as plaintiff in advocacy lawsuits against New York City with its more unifying role as an educational body.

Another lesson is that adversarial strategies sometimes are necessary to achieve meaningful change in public health policy. Though most public health workers are more practiced in consensus building methods, the refusal to consider confrontational approaches can limit the effectiveness of the best-intentioned inter-ventions. Though we are familiar with the efforts of powerful organizations to influ-ence or silence national dialogue on major health issues (for example, the tobacco industry on smoking, the chemical industry on environmental risks), it is important that public health advocates evaluate whether similar interests are aligned against public health efforts more locally. In New York City, efforts to improve policy and increase public resources to prevent lead poisoning have been opposed by powerful real estate interests. NYCCELP's adversarial legal strategies strived to minimize the influence of these interests by moving the debate to the courts, presumably less susceptible to real estate lobbying.

In the twelve years of NYCCELP's existence, a great deal of progress has been made in the city, and indeed nationally, in addressing the risks of childhood lead poisoning. New York State now requires that an initial blood lead test be performed on all children older than six months during a routine medical visit. The New York City Department of Health more effectively targets education, screening, and inspection to neighborhoods and populations most at risk. Neighborhood institutions have emerged that educate and organize around lead paint hazards. The New York City school system has begun to assess and correct peeling paint hazards in kindergarten classrooms. New national regulations require that building owners divulge knowledge of the presence of lead paint prior to property transfers ("Lead" 1996). Public awareness in New York City of the problem of lead poisoning has never been greater. Some of these advances are directly attributable to the work of NYCCELP. Others occurred at least in part because of the influence of similar organizations in other major cities. Perhaps, then, the most important lesson from the experience of NYCCELP is that without forceful, sustainable, broad-based coalition efforts that help to frame the content and tenor of the dialogue on this and other public health issues, such progress would have been slower in coming and less effective on arrival.

Acknowledgments

We wish to acknowledge the assistance of several people who contributed to our understanding of the role of NYCCELP in addressing lead poisoning in New York City. They are Maxine Golub, Institute for Urban Family Health; Lucy Billings and Matthew Cachere, Bronx Legal Services; Diana Silver, New York University; and Megan Charlop, Montefiore Medical Center Lead Safe House. The opinions expressed in this chapter are not necessarily shared by those just named.

References

Freudenberg, N., and M. Golub. 1987. Health education, public policy, and disease prevention: A case history of the New York City Coalition to End Lead Poisoning. *Health Education Quarterly* 14 (4):387–401.

Goyer, R. A. 1993. Lead toxicity: Current concerns. *Environmental Health Perspectives* 100:177–187.

Lead: Requirements for disclosure of lead-based paint and/or lead-based paint hazards in housing; final rule. 1996. *Federal Register* 61 (45) (March 6):9063–9088.

Lead-based Paint Hazard Reduction and Financing Task Force. 1995. Putting the pieces together: Controlling lead hazards in the nation's housing. *HUD-1547-LBP* (July).

Needleman, H., C. Gunnoe, A. Leviton et al. 1979. Deficits in psychological and classroom performance of children with elevated dentive lead levels. *New England Journal of Medicine* 300:689–695.

Needleman, H., J. Riess, M. Tobin, G. Biesecker, and J. Greenhouse. 1996. Bone lead levels and delinquent behavior. *Journal of the American Medical Association* 275:363–369.

National Center for Health Statistics. 1991. NHANES III: Blood lead levels for persons ages six months to seventy-four years: United States, 1988–1991. Washington, D.C.: Department of Health and Human Services.

New York City Department of Health, Bureau of Lead Poisoning Prevention. 1994. *Annual report on lead poisoning statistics.* New York: Department of Health.

Office of the Controller. 1986. *A silent epidemic: Childhood lead poisoning.* New York: Office of Policy Management.

Provenzano, G. 1980. The social costs of excessive lead exposure during childhood. In *Low-level lead exposure: The clinical implications of current research*, ed. H. L. Needleman. New York: Raven Press.

Schwartz, J. 1994. Societal benefits of reducing lead exposure. *Environmental Research* 66:105–124.

U.S. Department of Health and Human Services, Centers for Disease Control. 1991. *Strategic plan for the elimination of childhood lead poisoning.* Washington, D.C.: Department of Health and Human Services.

U.S. Department of Housing and Urban Development. 1990. *Comprehensive and workable plan for the abatement of lead-based paint in privately owned housing.* Report to Congress. Washington, D.C.: Office of Policy Development and Research, December 7.

Part VIII

Measuring Community Empowerment

As NOTED IN CHAPTER 3, one of the biggest gaps in community organizing and community building practice lies in their frequent failure to adequately address issues of measurement and evaluation. The complex environments in which organizing typically takes place, the fact that community building and community organizing are by definition continually evolving, and the multiple levels on which change is sought all appear to conspire against effective evaluative research. When one adds to this mix severe funding constraints, lack of knowledge about evaluative processes and methods, and the fact that many traditional evaluative techniques are ill-suited to measuring the outcomes of community building and organizing, the forces mitigating against evaluating our efforts appear even more formidable. Yet without adequate evaluations of community organizing and community building projects, we will continue to be hampered in our attempts to assess our strengths and weaknesses, learn from our mistakes, and demonstrate to funders and others the worth of these community practice efforts.

If we are to see improvements in both the quantity and the quality of evaluative research on community organizing and community building in the years ahead, special evaluative techniques and approaches are needed. In particular, evaluative methods must be used that empower, rather than disempower, the community being studied. Additionally, moreover, the methods used should meaningfully involve the community itself in the design and conduct of the evaluation process. A potent new tool in this regard can be found in the philosophy and methodology of "empowerment evaluation," which Stephen Fawcett et al. (1996) define as an interactive process through which communities work with a support team in identifying their concerns, determining how to address them, measuring their progress toward the goals they have set, and using the information gained to increase the viability and success of their efforts.

In chapter 18, Chris Coombe examines the limitations of traditional research approaches for the evaluation of community change efforts and lays out a strong rationale for an alternative approach. That alternative—empowerment evaluation—is described in some detail, with attention to its rootedness in earlier research traditions (e.g., participatory action research) that legitimize community members' experiential knowledge and democratize the research process.

Empowerment evaluation is rightly described in this chapter as an *emerging* practice, yet one whose early tenets and applications suggest its considerable promise for community organizing. Borrowing and adapting Fawcett et al.'s six-element process for empowerment evaluation, Coombe then describes in more detail how similar steps might be followed in the application of an empowerment evaluation approach in the context of community organizing. The benefits and the challenges of using this approach are emphasized, and a strong case is made for its increased application in community organizing and community building efforts.

For Kathleen Roe, Cindy Berenstein, Christina Goette, and Kevin Roe, who faced the challenge of evaluating five HIV Prevention Community Planning efforts, empowerment evaluation was not consciously selected as a strategy but rather was "backed into." Desiring an evaluative methodology that would stimulate and nurture community and respect and empower participants, they evolved an approach that, in retrospect, shared many principles, commitments, and processes with empowerment evaluation.

In chapter 19, Roe and her colleagues begin with a description of HIV Prevention Community Planning as an example of a process with the potential to stimulate community organizing and community building through social planning. They then use four of the steps or stages in empowerment evaluation described in the preceding chapter to demonstrate their applicability in this difficult and challenging evaluation effort. In keeping with the spirit of evaluation that is empowering and respectful of community members, Roe et al. draw on the words, stories, and perceptions of community members to enrich our understanding of what transpired in this unique social planning experiment. Although not a "pure" application of David Fetterman, Shakeh Kaftarian, and Abraham Wandersman's (1996) empowerment evaluation, this fascinating case study demonstrates the utility, for our organizing efforts, of evaluative approaches grounded in a commitment to individual and community empowerment.

References

Fawcett, S. B. et al. 1996. Empowering community health initiatives through evaluation. In *Empowerment evaluation: Knowledge and tools for self-assessment and accountability*, ed. D. M. Fetterman, S. J. Kaftarian, and A. Wandersman. Thousand Oaks, Calif.: Sage.
Fetterman, D. M., S. J. Kaftarian, and A. Wandersman. 1996. *Empowerment evaluation: Knowledge and tools for self-assessment and accountability*. Thousand Oaks, Calif.: Sage.

Using Empowerment Evaluation in Community Organizing and Community-based Health Initiatives

Chapter 18

CHRIS M. COOMBE

EVALUATION IS OFTEN perceived by grassroots community groups as mysterious, irrelevant, or even threatening. It typically occurs only when mandated by a funder, and few participants in community-based efforts have the skills, knowledge, or tools needed to make powerful use of evaluation in service to the community. This chapter examines how the process of evaluation can be used not only for assessing the value and effectiveness of community-based programs and campaigns but also for building organizational and community capacity.

When evaluation is built into a community's process of planning and action, it can help build consensus, set priorities, and validate choices of goals. Information from members, funders, and inside and outside experts can provide valuable input on the feasibility and importance of an organization's action plan. By contributing to our knowledge of what works, what does not and why, evaluation can be a powerful planning and management tool for making programs, organizations, and communities more effective. Scarce resources can be targeted or redirected to strategies that work best. Evaluation helps local people get the knowledge and skills they need to build healthier communities.

Empowerment evaluation was developed mainly for evaluating specific programs and community-based initiatives (Fetterman, Kaftarian, and Wandersman 1996). However, it also has an important and largely unexplored role to play in community organizing, which is often ill-suited to traditional evaluation methods and approaches. Many community organizing efforts consist of a series of short-term campaigns rather than ongoing programs. Evaluation is typically an internal process in which direct-action organizers engage key leaders in postaction debriefings to discuss results—such as how many people turned out for an action, how many new members were gained, how many votes or signatures were gathered, what

amount and type of press coverage were garnered, and what the strengths and weaknesses of specific tactics were. More in-depth analyses that examine longer-term
impacts on the community are much less common.

In contrast to traditional external evaluation, empowerment evaluation is
explicitly designed to become an ongoing, sustainable part of the community's planning and action. The process and findings of evaluation are used to empower the
community. By participating in the actual evaluation as information providers, gath-
erers, and interpreters, members gain personal skills, insights, investment in the
organization, and better understanding of community resources and needs. In addition to increasing the competence of individuals, empowering evaluation can build
the community's capacity across a spectrum of levels ranging from individual to
organizational to interorganizational to community and society (Eng and Parker
1994). This is a tall order for any one component of community organization and
mobilization. However, funders, researchers, and community practitioners alike
are increasingly realizing the largely untapped potential—and the necessity—of
expanding the uses and ownership of evaluation (Fetterman et al. 1996; Connell
et al. 1995).

This chapter presents a broad overview of empowerment evaluation. First, some
limitations of traditional evaluation are discussed to establish the rationale for a
more empowering approach. Next, the theoretical foundation of empowerment
evaluation is described, including its roots in participatory research traditions from
several disciplines. A step-by-step framework that builds upon the work of Stephen
Fawcett et al. (1996) is suggested for using this methodology effectively. The final
sections show the relevance of empowerment evaluation to communitywide
health initiatives and community organizing and discuss some of the benefits as
well as challenges of this approach.

Limitations of Traditional Evaluation:
A Rationale for Empowerment Evaluation

Most evaluations of community-based programs and public health initiatives use
traditional evaluation approaches based primarily on quantitative methods, perhaps supplemented with qualitative interviews or case studies. Evaluation is often
designed and carried out by professional evaluators from outside the organization
and community; they determine what is to be studied, what methods are to be used,
and what conclusions may be drawn from the findings. Intended beneficiaries are
involved in the evaluation process minimally, if at all, and evaluators are careful
to maintain a stance of neutrality and objectivity.

Although such a sharp distinction between evaluator and study subject is the
extreme end of a continuum, it does represent the classic research and evaluation
paradigm. Many authors have been critical of this approach, arguing that it pro-

motes the myth of objectivity, oversimplifies social reality, is not conducive to subsequent action to solve social problems, and is elitist in nature (Fals-Borda and Rahman 1991; Hall, Gillette, and Tandon 1982). I contend that using only traditional research approaches to evaluate community change efforts may not only miss an opportunity for empowerment but also be counterproductive to promoting community health in at least three ways:

1. The knowledge produced may be irrelevant or invalid.
2. The methods used may reinforce the powerlessness of community members and the power imbalance between experts/professionals and "the people."
3. Results often are not applied to solving underlying problems and may indeed be used in ways that are harmful to the community.

IRRELEVANT OR INVALID KNOWLEDGE

Quantitative methodologies borrowed from biomedical research have been adapted to community settings. Expert evaluators quantitatively separate, measure, and score variables to scientifically test a priori hypotheses derived from outside the community. Although the scientific method works best for measuring only a few variables under controlled conditions and with a comparison group for interpreting results, it continues to be viewed as the "gold standard" for producing knowledge.

Community empowerment projects, however, do not take place in a laboratory. Many sectors are involved in solving complex problems with multiple causes, the unit of study is a population or group rather than an individual, and evaluators are seldom involved in initially defining the problem and designing the intervention. The project uses different strategies in different settings over varying time periods, making it difficult to track actions and outcomes, let alone establish links between the two. As a result, it is not uncommon for evaluation results to miss the mark or to be irrelevant.

Who owns the development of knowledge is another concern. As noted in earlier chapters, knowledge has become the single most important basis of power and control in our society (Maguire 1987) and is increasingly concentrated in the hands of "experts" and the elite. Rather than democratize knowledge, the information superhighway is widening the chasm between those who are poor and those who are not by escalating the accumulation of knowledge at the privileged end. In modern Western society, the most legitimate form of "knowing" is technological or scientific knowledge, which can be "produced" only by formally certified experts such as academics, researchers, and evaluators. Ordinary knowledge of the majority of people is typically seen as invalid (Hall 1979).

Participatory research paradigms, described later in this chapter, arose in response to the continued and increasing monopoly of knowledge by the power-ful. The premises underlying these approaches are (1) that oppressed people should be involved in the analysis of and solutions to social problems (Hall 1979), (2) that social scientists must work in collaboration with the community in order to identify relevant research questions and accurately understand find-ings (Hatch 1993), and (3) that scientific knowledge must be linked with social action (Greenwood, Whyte, and Harkavy 1993). Although some conventional academic research has contributed much to our understanding of oppressed groups, as exemplified in works such as Carol Stack's classic *All Our Kin* (1974), much researcher-centered investigation has been flawed by theory rooted in the perceptions, biases, and agendas of the external observer.

Like qualitative methods that attempt to surface "popular knowledge," par-ticipatory research has often been considered by more mainstream researchers to be biased and unreliable and is only beginning to gain credibility in academic and scientific circles. C. Fletcher (1992) suggests that the knowledge that people themselves produce is "counterinformation" because it is in opposition to abstract theories about them.

REINFORCEMENT OF POWERLESSNESS

Traditional evaluation methods make a clear distinction between evaluator and program participants, with the expert evaluator/researcher typically designing, imple-menting, analyzing, and reporting the findings. The evaluator holds not only the skills but also the insight, knowledge, and objectivity for interpreting the mean-ing of the data. Program participants are objects of study who are in effect depen-dent on the outside agent for interpretation of the reality of their experience. The process of evaluation remains both mystified and external to the organization's own process of planning and development.

Although the relationship between participant and evaluator is somewhat different in qualitative methodologies, the researcher is still typically outside the system and expected to be objective. The participant has more control over what type and depth of data emerge, but the evaluator usually remains in charge of the evaluation.

The role of empowerment in health promotion and the role of powerless-ness as a broad risk factor for disease have been widely discussed (Wallerstein 1992; see also chapters 3 and 12). Central to the empowerment concept is the impor-tance of individuals and communities having influence and control over deci-sions that affect them (Israel et al. 1994). (See appendix 9.) Evaluation approaches that maintain the separate and hierarchical relationship between evaluator and community foster dependence and powerlessness and thereby mitigate against empowerment as an outcome. Participatory researchers such as M. A. Chesler (1991) are refuting the disempowering notion that an external agent is necessary for the achievement of research objectivity. Perhaps objectivity is gained not through detachment from the setting but through deep involvement in and reflection about the setting.

UNAPPLIED OR HARMFUL RESULTS

Traditionally, evaluation has aimed at assessing a program's worth and value and contributing knowledge on a topic. Program improvement or community development has fallen under the domain of other professions, and the researcher/evaluator has been trained to remain neutral and impartial. Evaluators are often neither trained nor expected to be proficient in program, policy, or organizational development.

This approach may be counterproductive to the promotion of community health in at least three ways. First, it may be a missed opportunity. Evaluators have information and insights that could help an organization translate evaluation findings into implications for action rather than solely into implications for further study. Second, it may perpetuate a condition in which reflection and analysis are activities separate from organizational planning and action rather than being necessary, sequential steps in an integrated, collaborative problem-solving process. Third, because action planning is distinct from evaluation, which is perceived as external to the organization, programs and strategies may be less effective because they are not based on all the available data.

Evaluation and research findings have been used by opponents to justify actions that are harmful to the community or specific segments of it. Zoe Clayson, Beth Weitzman, Jean McGuire, and Nicholas Freudenberg (Clayson et al. 1995) have described examples in which their research findings were used against the constituencies they intended to help—pregnant homeless women, people with HIV disease, gay and lesbian youths in public high schools, and pregnant and parenting chemically dependent women. For example, policymakers in New York dismissed or misused research findings regarding the role of housing and neighborhood conditions as risk factors for homelessness among pregnant women in favor of personal dysfunction explanations. As a result, punitive policies replaced actions that would have addressed poverty and poor housing conditions.

Many evaluators struggle with the tension of competing role demands. On the one hand, they are expected to maintain sufficient professionally prescribed distance and neutrality so that their findings will be credible to policymakers, funders, and other audiences. On the other, they want to ensure that the evaluation at least improves organization and program effectiveness and, if possible, generates action to transform the social structures and conditions that oppress communities.

Given the increasing complexity and entrenchment of our health and social problems, evaluation must adapt and evolve to become more responsive and relevant to communities. People are demanding much more of evaluation and becoming intolerant of the limited role of the outside expert who has no knowledge or vested interest in their community (Green and Frankish in press). Participation, collaboration, and empowerment are becoming requirements—not just recommendations—in many community-based evaluations. Evaluation has the potential to build a dynamic community of transformative learning, thereby contributing to the empowerment of disenfranchised communities (Fetterman 1996). In the words of the turn-of-the century social reformer Jane Addams (1907), "We slowly learn that life consists of processes as well as results, and that failure may come quite as easily from ignoring the adequacy of one's method as from selfish or ignoble aims."

What Is Empowerment Evaluation?

In recent years, the concept of empowerment evaluation has been gaining increasing interest and credibility as a legitimate approach in the field of evaluation. Indeed, the selection of this topic as the theme of the 1993 annual meeting of the American Evaluation Association was cited by the conference chair as directly responsible for the event's record attendance (Fetterman et al. 1996). David Fetterman (1996) defines empowerment evaluation as the use of evaluation concepts, techniques, and findings to foster improvement and self-determination. This evaluation approach uses both quantitative and qualitative methods in a democratic and collaborative effort to help people help themselves.

The aim of empowerment evaluation is to build community competence, optimize community outcomes, and promote adaptation, renewal, and institutionalization of community health initiatives. Fawcett et al. (1996, 169) describe empowerment evaluation as "an interactive and iterative process by which the community, in collaboration with the support team, identifies its own health issues, decides how to address them, monitors progress toward its goals, and uses the information to adapt and sustain the initiative."

As suggested throughout this book, communities are strengthened when their "capacities" are developed—when their commitment, resources, and skills are increased. If evaluation is to contribute to these outcomes, evaluators must share the responsibility of evaluating merit and developing knowledge, providing opportunities for community strengthening, and facilitating action (Eng and Parker 1994).

As noted earlier, empowerment is a core concept in fields ranging from public health (Wallerstein 1992) to community psychology (Rappaport 1984) and feminism (Chafetz 1988). Defined as the process by which individuals and communities gain mastery over their lives (Rappaport 1984), empowerment highlights the value of individual strengths and competencies such as self-efficacy (Bandura 1977), natural helping systems (Israel 1985; Pilisuk and Parks 1986), group and intergroup effectiveness (Lewin 1947), and social change (Mondros and Wilson 1994).

Empowerment evaluation arises from a number of research traditions aimed at legitimizing community members' experiential knowledge, acknowledging the role of values in research, empowering community members, democratizing research inquiry, and enhancing the relevance of evaluation data for communities. These research traditions include action research (Lewin 1946; Argyris 1983), popular education (Freire 1970), grounded theory (Glaser and Strauss 1967; Strauss and Corbin 1990), naturalistic inquiry (Lincoln and Guba 1985), participatory research (Hall 1979; Tandon 1981), participatory action research (Fals-Borda and Rahman 1991), feminist research (Maguire 1987), and popular epidemiology (Brown 1992).

Participatory action research is the approach most influential in the development of empowerment evaluation and involves a cyclical approach of diagnosing, planning, and then taking action, evaluating outcomes, and identifying the learning that has occurred (Susman and Evered 1978). Like participatory action research, empowerment evaluation involves oppressed people in studying and finding solutions to social problems. It gives the people most affected by the problems control over the evaluation, with the ultimate goal of transforming societal structures to benefit their community. Breaking up the paradigm in which participants are passive objects of study and researchers are the discoverers and creators of knowledge, empowerment evaluation establishes a spirit of collaborative inquiry in which community members and evaluators work hand in hand. Participants collect and analyze data, and evaluators actively support planning, organizational development, and action.

Empowerment evaluation democratizes evaluation by putting community members at the center of defining the evaluation agenda. Participants help determine what kinds of questions are asked and what issues are investigated. Because investigators are members of the community, they often have perspectives and experiences that can help shape the inquiry and interpret results (Hancock 1989). Like participatory action research, empowerment evaluation goes beyond collecting information and links knowing and doing through a cyclical process of *investigation*, *education*, and *action*. Once information is gathered, it is analyzed, fed back to the community, and applied to the program or organizing effort to improve effectiveness. More information is then gathered on the results of the action.

In empowerment evaluation, evaluators and program participants are on a more equal footing than in traditional evaluation (Fetterman et al. 1996). Participants control and are actively engaged in the design and execution of program evaluation and improvement. Evaluators are resources, allies, coaches, and facilitators, teaching participants how to do their own evaluation so that the community becomes more self-sufficient.

Empowerment Evaluation, Community Organizing, and Comprehensive Community Initiatives

Participatory, empowering types of evaluation are especially suited to the principles, goals, and methods of community organizing and comprehensive community initiatives, all of which include collaboration and capacity building as desired outcomes. Prudence Brown's (1995) description of parallels between the goals and theories underlying participatory research and community-based initiatives also apply to empowerment evaluation. Thus, all three of these approaches

- Articulate a strong belief in individual and collective empowerment
- Rely on an iterative process of learning and doing
- Recognize the power of participation and strive to develop vehicles to enhance and sustain that participation
- Have at their core a conception of the relationship between individual and community transformation, between personal efficacy and collective power
- View creation of knowledge as an enterprise that is both technical and includes other forms of consciousness
- Rely on the release of energy and hope that is generated by group dialogue and action

Empowerment evaluation goes beyond participatory research approaches, however, by integrating evaluation into a structured, sustainable organizational development process of assessment, planning, and decisionmaking for the future.

The Methodology of Empowerment Evaluation

Empowerment evaluation as an emerging practice uses a combination of quantitative and qualitative methods along a continuum of degrees of community participation in the design, implementation, and analysis of the evaluation. It is not mutually exclusive from traditional external evaluation and can indeed produce a rich data source for a subsequent external evaluation, particularly as empowerment methodologies develop and gain acceptance. I believe that three guiding principles are essential to empowerment evaluation. First, authority over and execution of the research is a democratic, highly collaborative process between the community participants and professional evaluators as resources/allies. Second, the process of evaluation is sustainably incorporated into the ongoing planning, action, and reflection of the organization and community. Third, the ultimate goal is to help communities use self-evaluation and research to become stronger, more effective, and more self-determined.

Because of the paradigm shift that empowerment evaluation involves, it can be challenging for traditional evaluators. As a process of codiscovery (Mayer 1996), it models the learning process and is quite fluid. Investigators must continually sample a changing environment and evaluate situations by degrees rather than as absolutes. Like grounded theory in qualitative methods (Glaser and Strauss 1967; Strauss and Corbin 1990), the logic is often drawn directly from the data.

Fawcett et al. (1996) have laid out a six-element process for empowerment evaluation that parallels a model of group decisionmaking commonly used in strategic planning (Barry 1986; Burkhart and Reuss 1993). These six steps provide the framework for the following discussion of empowerment evaluation methodology, using the metaphor of the process as a journey. Participants determine where they are now (step one), where they would like to go (step two), and how to get there (step three). They monitor the journey to make sure that they are on track and making progress (step four). They collect and analyze new information along the way so that the project can adjust its course, if necessary, in response to changing conditions or unexpected results (step five). Finally, they apply what they have learned to strengthen the organization and prepare for the next journey (step six). The "participants" referred to here include volunteers, staff, organizers, members of the community active in the project, and intended beneficiaries. "Support team" refers to the professional evaluators and related staff.

STEP 1: ASSESSING COMMUNITY CONCERNS AND RESOURCES

Where are we now? The support team assists local participants in doing an inventory of community assets and needs, program strengths and weaknesses—often called environmental analysis or scanning by those in the field of organizational development. Fetterman (1996) refers to this step as taking stock of where the program or organizing effort stands, which includes assessing performance to date.

It is critical that the local community become involved and gain trust and ownership of the evaluation process during this initial stage. This phase helps participants understand the necessity of collecting data to support assessments and creates a baseline against which to measure future progress. Methods may include community meetings, focus groups, interviews, surveys, community mapping, or participant rating systems for assessing and ranking components of the initiative or organizing project (Fawcett et al. 1996).

STEP 2: SETTING A MISSION AND OBJECTIVES

Where do we want to go? Typically the mission will have already been established prior to this point, either by the lead agency, the funder, or the initial organizing members. Community participants revisit the initial mission and objectives and modify them, if necessary, to ensure consistency with current local needs and circumstances. The evaluation support team plays a critical facilitative role in

helping participants use information gathered in the assessment phase to inform
and guide decisions about future directions and desired outcomes.

Community members lay the foundation for evaluation by establishing
realistic criteria for success and improvement. Objectives and evaluation criteria
emerge from answering such questions as, What results would we like to see? How
would we know if we achieved them? What level of improvement is desirable? What
level is acceptable? How will we know if we are making progress? What changes
(intermediate outcomes) could serve as benchmarks or early markers of movement
toward our goals? How will we assess our process and our performance? The
principal activity of this step is a facilitated group meeting that includes creative
brainstorming, sorting and categorizing of ideas, critical discussion and prioritiz-
ing based on agreed-upon criteria, and reaching of consensus.

STEP 3: DEVELOPING STRATEGIES AND ACTION PLANS

How will we get there? Community members develop a set of strategies for accomplishing project goals and objectives. Strategies are broad approaches or methods
for achieving results, such as advocacy or coalition building. The process for
strategy development is similar to that used in setting goals—a facilitated meeting in which participants brainstorm and assess options, taking into consideration
community resources and needs surfaced in the initial assessment step, and then
build consensus.

Action plans lay out specific steps for achieving results, including who will
do what by when. The specificity of action plans contributes to greater accountability and monitoring to ensure that the project is on track and enables
process evaluation to take place. The outline of action plans can be sketched
out in the strategy development meeting, with details determined later by
smaller subgroups.

STEP 4: MONITORING PROCESS AND OUTCOMES

How do we know we are on track? Evaluators help participants determine what
type of evidence is needed to document progress toward their goals and how that
documentation will take place. The team must develop monitoring systems that
are realistic and make the best use of community resources, while ensuring
that results are valid and methods are free enough from bias to be credible to
interested audiences.

Evaluators and community participants work collaboratively to define measures, collect process and outcome data, and interpret findings. Regular collection,
feedback, and interpretation of information throughout the organizing or initiative process enable participants to keep on track, adjust their course, see evidence
of their progress, and report to funders and the community. Documentation
methods include periodic written activity logs or reports, journals, tracking of key

events, portfolios, interviews, surveys, observations, and review of community-level data for changes, such as in the rates of injury or disease.

STEP 5: COMMUNICATING INFORMATION
TO RELEVANT AUDIENCES

Who needs to be notified along the way? Unlike more conventional approaches, empowerment evaluation communicates findings to key stakeholders as information emerges. Participants and the community at large can be engaged in reflection, interpretation of meaning, and problem-solving, based on evaluation data, to improve the project or take advantage of new opportunities. The sharing of achievements as they occur can energize the community and build trust and commitment to the project. Support can be garnered from prospective funders, new constituencies, and neighboring communities.

Teamwork and mutual learning are critical. Evaluators share expertise in compiling and presenting data in both written and graphic form, while community leaders contribute expertise in communicating with diverse constituencies in understandable and meaningful ways. Both should convey project outcomes to interested parties outside the community, thereby contributing to other empowerment efforts, building networks beyond the local level, and setting the agenda for future research and action. By taking a more active role in helping participants effect social change, evaluators become advocates for the community. Communication methods can include written reports, community meetings, newsletter articles, media coverage, journal articles, and presentations at meetings and conferences of professional associations, labor or business groups, coalitions, and other forums.

STEP 6. PROMOTING ADAPTATION, RENEWAL,
AND INSTITUTIONALIZATION

How can we use what we have learned to prepare for the next journey? Evaluation findings must be acted upon to be useful to the community. Evaluators help participants use the lessons learned to strengthen future actions. Valuable information about how the process worked in relation to outcomes may lead the project to redefine objectives, adjust strategies, redirect scarce resources, or modify methods.

The support team uses organizational development, facilitation, and training skills to help the project strengthen its leadership and structure, integrate evaluation into ongoing operations, and seek out new funding resources. Building capacity includes striving for sustainability of hard-won improvements.

Two hands-on resources that include comprehensive evaluation frameworks and sample instruments may be particularly useful for communities designing and implementing empowerment evaluation projects. *The Work Group Evaluation Handbook: Evaluating and Supporting Community Initiatives for Health and Development*

(Fawcett 1993) documents a comprehensive system for supporting and evaluating community initiatives to promote health. This user-friendly handbook is intended for use by community leaders, evaluators, and grantmakers and includes detailed instructions, advice, and examples for each step. *Assessment and Evaluation That Empower* is a four-session training workshop with accompanying materials (Community Network for Youth Development 1995). Designed to build the capacity of youth-serving organizations to conduct authentic, youth-centered evaluations, the workshop includes participatory instruction on planning concepts, identification of indicators, assessment methods and instruments, and analysis of data and report of results.

Benefits of Empowerment Evaluation

In addition to the benefits described earlier, empowerment evaluation has the potential to advance the field of evaluation and increase its effectiveness. Empowerment evaluation can have several benefits. First, it can help overcome resistance to and suspicion of evaluation, demystify the process, and institutionalize evaluation methods within communities. When the community shares ownership of goals, process, and skills, evaluation becomes an integral part of organizing for change.

Second, empowerment evaluation can enhance the integration of qualitative and quantitative methods (Fawcett et al. 1996). Such complex interventions as community organizing efforts and broad-based health initiatives involve the operation of multiple variables. Integration of qualitative information with quantitative data on accomplishments can increase understanding of which factors contribute to the functioning of the initiative or organizing effort and in what ways.

Third, such evaluation can adapt, evolve, and invent evaluation methods, indicators, and instruments. Community participation in evaluation can be a rich source of innovation in the development of methods. For example, because associational networks play such a crucial role in community organizing and other community-wide change efforts, empowerment evaluation teams may develop better methods for measuring social networks and identifying both informal and formal community institutions and linkages (Hollister and Hill 1995).

Fourth, empowerment evaluation can enhance the ability of communities to do systematic data collection (Hollister and Hill 1995). Empowerment evaluation can provide an incentive for local organizations to maintain their records in relatively common formats so that records data can be pulled together to create a community database. Local participant/researchers can gather new data of their own to give clout and credibility to advocacy efforts, using methods ranging from mapping conditions of the physical environment to conducting household surveys.

Fifth, empowerment evaluation can creatively link community participants and evaluators in a mutual learning partnership (Fawcett et al. 1996). Training, facilitation, and technical assistance enable community stakeholders to understand and apply evaluation methods within the field's standards for validity and rigor. The experiential wisdom of community leadership can ensure that evaluation questions are important, data collection methods realistic, and findings relevant and applicable within the local cultural context. Evaluators can help make sure that community voices are heard by policymakers and other audiences.

Challenges of Using Empowerment Evaluation

There are a number of philosophical and practical challenges to the newly emerging practice of empowerment evaluation. First, as noted earlier, empowerment evaluation frameworks may conflict with traditional assumptions about objectivity and distance. Charges of bias, conflict of interest, and misuse can undermine the credibility of the evaluation, thereby lessening its clout. This may be particularly critical in policy and funding arenas. Yet even though the goal of any evaluation is usually improvement, what is not always clear is improvement for whom and at what price. Evaluation has never been neutral, and empowerment evaluation simply makes explicit the importance of community self-determination.

Empowerment evaluation must meet the field's standards for propriety and accuracy. Evaluators can increase validity and credibility by exploring ways to minimize participant bias and including multiple methods, measures, and data sources in the evaluation design. Qualitative researchers have developed a number of strategies for addressing these concerns (cf. Fawcett et al. 1996; Hollister and Hill 1995; Brown 1995; Lincoln and Guba 1985).

A second key challenge in empowerment evaluation is that both professional evaluators and community participants have to develop new skills and understanding in order for empowerment to occur. Evaluators must be able to work hands-on with participants in areas such as organizational development, program planning, implementation, and even grant writing. Community members will need training in evaluation methods in order to ensure rigor. Group process skills such as team building, collaborative problem-solving, negotiation, and consensus building may not be part of the everyday repertoire of many community members or evaluators and must be learned.

As outsiders, evaluators must be particularly sensitive to the history of the community, the local ethnic and political culture, and the aims of the project. They must understand empowerment and collaboration as outcomes, as well as processes, and talk with, not down to, the community. Above all, diverse players must operate under principles of ongoing mutual learning, collaboration, and respect.

A third challenge of empowerment evaluation is that it takes a great deal of

time, effort, and personal commitment, which both evaluators and community members may find difficult to make. They may feel that the process is diverting precious resources away from the "real work"—be it the evaluation or the program.
What may seem like an opportunity for capacity building to enthusiastic researchers
may seem like yet another "unfunded mandate" to participants, placing too much
responsibility on the community for fixing "its" problem (Fetterman 1996). Evaluation must be feasible and practical, balancing the interests of both evaluators
and community members.

A fourth challenge is that the greatest strength of this emerging approach is
also one of its greatest hurdles—being responsive to rapid and unexpected shifts
in program design and operation. To be effective, community organizing and
community-based health initiatives must be flexible, developmental, and responsive to changing local needs and conditions (Brown 1995). This requires continual
collection, description, reflection, and feedback of information about a group or
organization in all its complexity (and, not uncommonly, chaos). Besides being
time consuming, such a process conflicts with conventional notions of scientific
rigor, which preclude continual tampering with the intervention.

A fifth challenge posed by empowerment evaluation is that communitywide
initiatives and community organizing efforts typically address complex problems
with multiple interrelated causes affecting multiple constituencies in multiple ways.
Although there will be short-term objectives, most efforts have broad longer-term
goals, such as social and economic change or community empowerment, that go
beyond project time frames and are difficult to assess.

In addition to these challenges, Fawcett et al. (1996) suggest that the concept of empowerment remains problematic. In spite of many efforts currently
under way to elucidate empowerment both as a process and a goal, it remains
a vague concept. Some of the most promising work being done to identify indicators of community competence and capacity building, which are conceptually
close to empowerment, are being developed through the use of participatory
action research. The work of Barbara Israel (Israel et al. 1994) and Eugenia
Eng (Eng and Parker 1994) are prominent examples. (See appendix 9.)
Nevertheless, little is understood about the relationship between individual
and community empowerment, and it may be difficult to attribute empowerment outcomes to specific interventions, including empowerment evaluation
itself.

Conclusion

Empowerment evaluation can be a powerful tool for public health programs,
community organizing efforts, and community-based initiatives that have capacity building and social change as goals. The evaluation process itself can strengthen

participation and ownership, build community competence, and reveal important outcomes that might be overlooked in conventional evaluations.

Empowerment evaluation pays attention to the real voices of real people, demystifying and democratizing the process of developing knowledge. Working as a team, evaluators and community members learn from each other and increase their abilities to have an impact on conditions affecting the community.

Empowerment evaluation requires changes in philosophy and practice by evaluators, community members, and funders. It requires new skills, new relationships, and a fair amount of faith. Given the enormity of the problems facing poor and disenfranchised communities, it is an investment we need to make. Empowerment evaluation can make an important contribution to building healthy, competent, and self-determined communities.

References

Addams, J. 1907. *Social Ethics*. Cambridge, Mass.: Belknap Press.

Argyris, C. 1983. Action science and intervention. *Journal of Applied Behavioral Science* 19:115–140.

Bandura, A. 1977. Self-efficacy: Toward a unifying theory of behavioral change. *Psychological Review* 84 (2):191–215.

Barry, B. 1986. *Strategic planning workbook for nonprofit organizations*. Saint Paul, Minn.: Amherst H. Wilder Foundation.

Brown, Philip. 1992. Popular epidemiology and toxic waste contamination: Lay and professional ways of knowing. *Journal of Health and Social Behavior* 33:267–281.

Brown, Prudence. 1995. The role of the evaluator in comprehensive community initiatives. In *New approaches to evaluating community initiatives: Concepts, methods, and contexts*, ed. J. P. Connell, A. C. Kubisch, L. B. Schorr, and C. J. Weiss. Washington, D.C.: Aspen Institute.

Burkhart, P. J., and S. Reuss. 1993. *Successful strategic planning: A guide for nonprofit agencies and organizations*. Thousand Oaks, Calif.: Sage.

Chafetz, J. S. 1988. *Feminist sociology: An overview of contemporary theories*. Itasca, Ill.: Peacock.

Chesler, M. A. 1991. Participatory action research with self-help groups: an alternative paradigm for inquiry and action. *American Journal of Community Psychology* 19 (5):757–768.

Clayson, Z., B. Weitzman, J. McGuire, and N. Freudenberg. 1995. Politics of community-based research: Accountability and action. Workshop presented at the annual meeting of the American Public Health Association, San Diego, California, November.

Community Network for Youth Development. 1995. *Assessment and evaluation that empower*. Redwood City, Calif.: Community Network for Youth Development.

Connell, J. P., A. C. Kubisch, L. B. Schorr, and C. H. Weiss, eds. 1995. *New approaches to evaluating community initiatives: Concepts, methods, and contexts*. Washington, D.C.: Aspen Institute.

Eng, E., and E. Parker. 1994. Measuring community competence in the Mississippi Delta. *Health Education Quarterly* 21(2):199–220.

Fals-Borda, O., and M. A. Rahman, eds. 1991. *Action and knowledge: Breaking the monopoly with participatory action research*. New York: Apex Press.

Fawcett, S. B. 1993. *Work group evaluation handbook: Evaluating and supporting community initiatives for health and development*. Lawrence, Kans.: Work Group on Health Promotion and Community Development.

Fawcett, S. B., A. Paine-Andrews, V. T. Francisco et al. 1996. Empowering community health initiatives through evaluation. In *Empowerment evaluation: Knowledge and tools for self-assessment and accountability*, ed. D. M. Fetterman, S. J. Kaftarian, and A. Wandersman. Thousand Oaks, Calif.: Sage.

Fetterman, D. M. 1996. Empowerment evaluation: An introduction to theory and practice. In *Empowerment evaluation: Knowledge and tools for self-assessment and accountability*, ed. D. M. Fetterman, S. J. Kaftarian, and A. Wandersman. Thousand Oaks, Calif.: Sage.

Fetterman, D. M., S. J. Kaftarian, and A. Wandersman, eds. 1996. *Empowerment evaluation: Knowledge and tools for self-assessment and accountability*. Thousand Oaks, Calif.: Sage.

Fletcher, C. 1992. Issues for participatory research in Europe. In Van Vlaederen H. *Participatory research for community development: An annotated bibliography*. Grahamstown, South Africa: Institute of Social and Economic Research, Rhodes University.

Freire, P. 1970. *Pedagogy of the oppressed*. New York: Seabury Press.

Glaser, B. G., and A. L. Strauss. 1967. *The discovery of grounded theory: Strategies for qualitative research*. Chicago: Aldine.

Green, L. W., and C. J. Frankish. In press. Finding the right mix of personal, organizational, decentralized, and centralized planning for health promotion. In *Community health promotion*, ed. B. Beerly, E. Wagner, and A. Cheadle. Seattle: University of Washington Press.

Greenwood D. J., W. F. Whyte, and I. Harkavy. 1993. Participatory action research as a process and as a goal. *Human Relations* 46 (2):175–191.

Hall, B. L. 1979. Knowledge as a commodity and participatory research. *Prospects* 9 (4):4–20.

Hall, B., A. Gillette, and R. Tandon, eds. 1982. *Creating knowledge: A monopoly? Participatory research in development*. New Delhi: Society for Participatory Research in Asia.

Hancock, T. 1989. Information for health at the local level: Community stories and healthy city indicators. Unpublished manuscript.

Hatch, J. 1993. Community research: Partnership in black communities. *American Journal of Preventive Medicine* 9 (6):27–31.

Hollister, R. G., and J. Hill. 1995. Problems in the evaluation of communitywide initiatives. In *New approaches to evaluating community initiatives: Concepts, methods, and contexts*, ed. J. P. Connell, A. C. Kubisch, L. B. Schorr, and C. H. Weiss. Washington, D.C.: Aspen Institute.

Israel, B. 1985. Social networks and social support: Implications for natural helper and community-level interventions. *Health Education Quarterly* 12 (1):65–80.

Israel, B. A., B. Checkoway, A. Schultz, and M. Zimmerman. 1994. Health education and community empowerment: Conceptualizing and measuring perceptions of individual, organizational, and community control. *Health Education Quarterly* 21 (2):149–170.

Lewin, K. 1946. Action research and minority problems. *Journal of Social Issues* 2 (4):34–46.

———. 1947. Frontiers in group dynamics. *Human Relations* 1(a):5–41 and 1(b):143–153.

Lincoln, Y., and E. Guba. 1985. *Naturalistic inquiry*. Beverly Hills, Calif.: Sage.

Maguire, P. 1987. *Doing participatory research: A feminist approach*. Amherst: Center for International Education, University of Massachusetts.

Mayer, S. E. 1996. Building community capacity with evaluation activities that empower. In *Empowerment evaluation: Knowledge and tools for self-assessment and accountability*, ed. D. M. Fetterman, S. J. Kaftarian, and A. Wandersman. Thousand Oaks, Calif.: Sage.

Mondros, J. B., and S. M. Wilson. 1994. *Organizing for power*. New York: Columbia University Press.

Pilisuk, M., and S. Parks. 1986. *The healing web: Social networks and human survival*. Hanover, N.H.: University Press of New England.

Rappaport, J. 1984. Studies in empowerment: Introduction to the issue. *Prevention in Human Services* 3:1–7.

Stack, C. B. 1974. *All our kin: Strategies for survival in a black community.* New York: Harper and Row.

Strauss, A. L., and J. Corbin. 1990. *Basics of qualitative research: Grounded theory procedures and techniques.* Newbury Park, Calif.: Sage.

Susman, G. F., and R. D. Evered. 1978. An assessment of the scientific merits of action research. *Administrative Science Quarterly* 23:582–603.

Tandon, R. 1981. Participatory research in the empowerment of people. *Convergence* 24 (3):20–29.

Wallerstein, N. 1992. Powerlessness, empowerment, and health: Implications for health promotion programs. *American Journal of Health Promotion* 6 (3):197–205.

Community Building through Empowering Evaluation

Chapter 19

A Case Study of HIV Prevention Community Planning

KATHLEEN M. ROE
CINDY BERENSTEIN
CHRISTINA GOETTE
KEVIN ROE

OVER FIFTY YEARS AGO, Edna St. Vincent Millay wrote of the "dark hour" of her "gifted age." For so many of us, the AIDS epidemic is the dark hour of this gifted age. Nearly two decades of loss, education, remembrance, research, and politics have been like a meteoric shower, leaving meager resources, powerful interests, and diverse opinions, highly vested and uncombined, regarding who should receive prevention dollars for which types of interventions. The search to respond to the epidemic in meaningful ways at local, state, and national levels led the Centers for Disease Control and Prevention in 1994 to create a new loom—the HIV Prevention Community Planning Process. This social planning initiative was a bold and innovative attempt to require communities to work together to weave the fabric of a comprehensive, community-based approach to HIV prevention.

This chapter describes this planning-based method of community organizing and demonstrates the ways in which an empowering approach to evaluation was used to enhance the model's community and capacity building potential. Specific examples are drawn from our evaluations of five HIV Prevention Community Planning efforts. The chapter concludes with a discussion of the difficulties of stretching a social planning process to serve organizing goals and some of the skills we have drawn upon as we used evaluation as a community building tool.

HIV Prevention Community Planning:
Community Organization through Social Planning

In January 1994, the CDC awarded sixty-five grants across the United States for the specific purpose of creating communitywide planning processes for HIV prevention. The grants specified that recipients were to seek significant and meaningful involvement of their communities in developing comprehensive HIV prevention plans. The community plans would then form the basis of applications for future cooperative agreement prevention funding from the CDC.

The planning initiative was based on the conviction that a participatory process would offer the best means for making decisions about HIV prevention programming. As defined in CDC's 1995 guidance to planning grantees, community planning was to be an ongoing process in which public health agencies would share responsibility with community representatives, nongovernmental organizations, and other state/local agencies for identifying needs, determining priorities, and developing comprehensive HIV prevention plans. Community planning was envisioned as a new, ongoing process catalyzed by the 1994 planning grants and continuing in local areas as the prevention plans were implemented.

Grantees were allowed considerable flexibility in the design and operation of their planning groups. However, the CDC did specify that all community planning efforts were to be evidence based and encompass six core elements: (1) an epidemiological profile of HIV in the relevant service area, (2) an assessment of HIV prevention service needs, (3) identification and prioritization of groups to be served, (4) development of criteria for selecting prevention strategies, (5) identification of technical assistance needs of prevention providers, and (6) evaluation of the community planning process. Some planning groups extended their mandate to include developing protocols for resource allocation and monitoring of the implementation of the prevention plans. Draft plans were due nine months after funding began, with final plans due three months later.

In an effort to guarantee meaningful community participation, the CDC extended the traditional social planning framework by establishing requirements for the design and dynamics of the planning group. Local efforts were to be organized around the principles of parity, inclusion, and representation. Parity was defined as an equal opportunity for input and participation and an equal vote in decision-making among all planning body members. Inclusion was defined as meaningful representation and involvement of all affected communities. Representation required that those nominated and selected to represent a specific affected community had to truly reflect that community's values, norms, and behaviors. These terms were specified in the guidance and described in detail in a user-friendly community planning handbook (Academy for Educational Development 1995) made available to all grantees.

The specification of parity, inclusion, and representation mobilized subcommunity organizing in several ways. Many communities organized internally to nominate members for the local planning body and sent additional members to observe the open planning meetings. Key subcommunities were contacted by the planning groups and asked for input and assistance at various other points in the planning process. In addition, many affected communities and stakeholder groups organized for public comment and participation in hearings, focus groups, and sub-committees as local plans and planning needs emerged. Once preliminary priorities and resource allocations were established, communities organized to register their reactions and, if necessary, lobby for changes in the plans, priorities, or resource allocation recommendations.

In the midst of this flurry of often overlapping and reactive community organizing were the planning participants—typically a core council representing the epidemic and key stakeholders, an advisory group of additional leaders in affected communities, a group of consultants to handle facilitation or writing, and lead agency personnel (often health educators) who staffed the process. The centrality of parity, inclusion, and representation to the planning effort brought these players into unprecedented partnership. It also created unprecedented opportunity in many local areas for development of a new community of HIV prevention leaders with roots and influence in innumerable other communities.

The stakes for local areas were very high. Community planning could be disastrous, bringing unequal players to an uneven table to participate in difficult, pre-determined decisionmaking about still inadequate resources, thereby furthering the divide among stakeholders. Or community planning could break new ground, stimulating community building and broader organizing and capacity development based on the unique intersection of camaraderie, new understanding, heightened respect, skill building, broader networks, and sound decisions that could come from these historic working groups. The CDC knew that the process was volatile and therefore assigned high priority to a collaborative process evaluation.

Evaluation as a Tool for Community Building

Our experience with community planning evaluation began with an invitation to serve as the evaluators of one very large planning effort. We immediately saw the opportunity for community impact and were intrigued by the challenge of finding an evaluation approach that would meet the core objectives while also enhancing the community organizing and capacity building potential of the community planning initiative. Although standard social planning evaluation methods would have been sufficient to meet the contract requirements, we were committed to using the evaluation process to enhance and facilitate individual and community empowerment. Our health education training and a commitment to doing our part in the fight against AIDS led us to the approach now formally known as empowerment evaluation (Fetterman, Kaftarian, and Wandersman 1996).

We actually "backed into" empowerment evaluation through our embrace of working principles and methods based on respect, practical utility, and empowerment. We defined evaluation as a continual, emergent process that creates reality (Guba and Lincoln 1989). While we endorsed the notion that evaluation can be a joyful and exhilarating process for all involved (Patton 1990), we were ever mindful of other ways in which evaluation has been experienced, including victimization (Butler 1992) and intellectual theft (Fleming 1992). If evaluation could create reality, then evaluation could certainly stimulate and nurture community. In this context, the ability of the evaluation process to foster community development and capacity was dependent upon the process's empowering characteristics.

We used these working definitions and our shared values as health educators to articulate a set of assumptions about evaluating community planning. First, evaluation should enhance the group's capacity for planning. Second, it would be done with people and not to them. Third, evaluation would never be mysterious. Fourth, goals, methods, and emerging findings would always be available to everyone involved. Fifth, our work would bring forward the voices of every person involved in community planning. Sixth, the methods and findings would be based on respect for the dignity and validity of multiple perspectives. We also agreed that one of the ways in which we could contribute to stopping the spread of AIDS, the ultimate goal of our evaluation, was through contributing to the development of a community of planning participants who would take their new insights and experiences back to the communities they represented, thus extending the impact of community building and capacity development achieved during the planning process.

Unaware as yet of the emerging model of empowerment evaluation, we drew upon an eclectic and ever-expanding tool kit of approaches and techniques for what we called "empowering evaluations" of community planning. We used traditional evaluation methods, including triangulation of data, pre- and posttesting, surveys, archival review, key informant interviews, and process monitoring. Many of our less traditional methods are mentioned in the previous chapter on empowerment evaluation, including participant observation, training, coaching, and facilitating. We also imported methods from the principles of applied anthropology and qualitative research, as well as from Rapid Rural Appraisal (Schoonmaker-Freudenberger 1993), including offsetting of biases, triangulation of investigators, appropriate imprecision, and self-critical awareness and responsibility.

Together, these assumptions, principles, goals, and methods provided a fertile base from which to craft an empowering evaluation process, which we eventually applied to three different planning groups across a combined total of five community planning years. Our designs were able to incorporate new developments and emerging group dynamics. They were capable of identifying and illuminating significant moments and unanticipated outcomes of HIV Prevention Community Planning. In doing so, we watched evaluation stimulate and nurture community building among those at the planning table, thereby enhancing their individual and collective capacities for the tasks at hand as well as their broader community organizing goals.

Empowering Evaluation in Action

Our approach to empowering evaluation strategies fits nicely with the recent articulation of the empowerment evaluation model (Fetterman 1996). We can use the four stages of this new model to discuss some of the specific methods we used to stimulate community development through evaluation.

STEP 1: TAKING STOCK

In the first step of empowerment evaluation, the evaluator helps program participants take stock of the status, resources, capacities, and challenges of the community, staff, and/or the program itself. This type of preliminary analysis is familiar territory to social planning evaluators, whose traditional methods include review of an array of documents, including budgets, organizational charts, annual reports, earlier assessments or plans, reports of previous planning efforts, and the requirements of the new planning initiative. As noted in chapter 18, these archival methods, possibly supplemented with observations or key informant interviews, provide useful, fact-based snapshots of the planning task at given points in time. Implications for community building or organizing can be drawn from these methods, but they are likely to provide little insight into the development of community identity or the nuances of emerging community capacity.

From an empowering perspective, taking stock is a process full of possibility. We saw an opportunity to take stock repeatedly in HIV Prevention Community Planning evaluations and to use both the process and the results to facilitate a sense of community among planning participants. Defining community as a group with shared identity and collective resources, our evaluation team looked for opportunities to expand the ways in which planning participants knew and thought about each other. Our goal was to enhance participants' immediate capacity for sound planning and their long-term enthusiasm for future community organization.

Each of the sites we evaluated was fortunate to have facilitators who included getting acquainted activities in early group sessions. Through survey and interview questions, we expanded our process evaluation to engage participants in additional ways of taking stock, including sharing their greatest personal challenges during community planning and their own contributions to the process, articulating their own experience of community planning, and monitoring their own commitments to the planning process. The resulting data, re-presented to the group both verbatim and organized by themes, invariably stimulated reflection and group discussion. One of the most empowering ways of taking stock was through assessing background experiences.

Process evaluators often use surveys of background experiences to take stock of the resources and potential needs of a planning group. When constructed and implemented with an eye to empowerment potential, these assessments can identify and validate an astonishingly wide range of assets and often surprising similarities, and important differences, among participants. The resulting data provide a particularly valuable resource for stimulating, fostering, or reinforcing community ties.

For example, early in the first planning year, one group bifurcated along lines separating researchers and community service providers, with a deepening gulf of misunderstanding and resentment between them. A sense of community among planning participants had never taken hold in this group. Indeed, participants were increasingly vested in and bitter about the differences they perceived among themselves. Some stopped attending, others attended in increasingly bitter silence, and still others were frustrated and angry that all council members were "not actively participating" or "holding up their end."

The linear and incremental nature of planning enabled the divided group to continue making progress despite these dynamics. However, our evaluation team was concerned about the extended impact on future community building and organizing efforts that might result from entrenched alienation among people involved in HIV prevention in a relatively small geographic area. Although looking for the community building potential in our evaluation methods was not required, we did so even though this particular evaluation was done after the first planning year.

Strategic selection of questions to be included in an otherwise standard background experiences inventory enabled our team to show members of the group that, despite articulated differences in education, professional experience, status, recognition, agendas, culture, and values, and despite the broader dynamics of racism and sexism they felt entrapping their interactions, they shared something that had profound implications for each member's lifecourse. What they shared was the experience of deep and personal losses to AIDS. In this particular planning group, everyone had lost someone to the epidemic. But of far greater significance was the revelation that over two-thirds reported "a lot" or "a great deal" of experience losing not only acquaintances to AIDS but also colleagues, friends, and people they loved. Only three of the twenty-three who were interviewed reported few of these experiences to date, including the youngest member, who qualified all of his responses with a somber "not yet."

Strong communities know their history, understand how they are different from others, and find ways to honor their shared paths. Eliciting and sharing this type of evaluation data during planning or program work are uniquely valuable ways of helping group members step back from the intensity of the tasks at hand and take stock of who they are and what they share. In the HIV Prevention Community Planning groups with which we took stock of background experiences, the exercise inevitably revealed previously unrecognized common history, which, in turn, fostered a positive identity grounded in broader shared experiences. Hard decisions with enormous implications still had to be made, but the groups were better able to approach the tasks, or reflect on the experience, with the added asset of shared and respected history.

STEP 2: SETTING GOALS

In the second step of empowerment evaluation, the evaluator helps group members identify where they want to go and the kind of evaluation they want to create. This step represents a bit of a departure for traditional social planning evaluators, who most often inherit explicit, objective-driven evaluation requirements. Evaluators may request group discussion of core evaluation questions or the parameters of the inquiry, provide in-progress reports, or invite periodic feedback as ways of ensuring that at least key stakeholders are getting the kind of evaluation they want.

The community planning guidance provided by the CDC established core objectives and final outcomes for both planning and evaluation but left unspecified the task of identifying broader goals for local planning efforts. Although articulating goals or establishing common vision was not incorporated into the work plans of the groups we evaluated, our team saw either activity as an empowering opportunity for planning participants. Setting program and evaluation goals is inherently political; thus, participation in the process would be empowering and exclusion disempowering.

Our evaluation team was committed to listening for common vision and broad goals and making them explicit whenever possible. We felt strongly that hopeful communities are able to dream, willing to share their visions, and articulate what they want and what they do not want. The intense time pressures of the community planning assignment precluded our team from facilitating lengthy group discussions of potential planning or evaluation goals. However, we stretched our process evaluation to encompass an assessment of what people wanted and why, and we routinely re-presented the results to the group. Specific evaluation questions included asking individual members about their visions of an effective planning process, their understanding of the ultimate goals of community planning, and what they hoped to get from participation for themselves, their organizations, and the communities they represented. We also continually revisited our own evaluation goals, as a team and with planning participants, adjusting our activities as needed to better serve emerging group goals.

One of the most fruitful ways of eliciting unspoken goals was listening carefully for the personal dreams and perspectives that were shared during other evaluation moments. The empowering visions that brought individuals to the planning table and the dreams that kept them there were eloquent testimony to the commitment of community planning participants and their individual goals for the process. When combined across common themes and re-presented to the group, the resonance among visions began to merge into the beginnings of group goals. In each case, this was a seminal moment in community building.

This is not to suggest that common goals emerged easily. Indeed, each of the planning groups we evaluated experienced a tension between at least two competing visions of the community planning process. One vision, grounded in the assumptions and culture of service delivery (see chapter 2), assumed that the primary task of community planning was to divide resources in the most rational, cost-effective manner. From this perspective, planning should proceed through objective, sequential deliberations governed by rules of order, time, and procedure. The short-term goal was sound decisions; the long-term goal, stopping the spread of AIDS within the existing service delivery structure. Participants from this perspective dreamed of "finding a framework that will remove the politics and enable sound planning to proceed."

The other vision, grounded in advocacy, assumed that the primary task of community planning could be to radically change the way in which AIDS prevention is conceptualized. From this perspective, existing data were too weak to count on, old paradigms too narrow, and standard rules of time and order too controlling to address the urgency of the epidemic and to draw out the diversity of voices and wisdom that must be brought into any discussion of truly stopping the spread of AIDS. Community planning was seen as calling upon both heart and mind, and explicit, passionate values were an asset rather than a liability. "Getting professionals to act like advocates, with urgency and passion" was a typical dream from this perspective.

Although the conflict/encounter between the two cultures was never addressed directly by planning group facilitators, it was easy as evaluators to observe these two cultures as they met each other in the context of community planning. Standard evaluation protocol would require only that we monitor the influence of each in the unfolding process and outcome of the planning effort. However, we felt that the unacknowledged coexistence of two compelling and competing perspectives created faultlines within the planning group that precluded the trust so necessary for the emergence of collective vision beyond the required core objectives. The group's ability to understand its internal differences and respectfully work with them was, to us, an important indicator of short- and long-term community capacity.

Careful participant observation enabled our evaluation team to sound out the depth and strength of the competing perspectives. Once we had a sense of the situated details of each, we were able to present the scenario to the planning group as a potential explanation for the recurring frustrations among members. We knew we had accurately captured the passions, motivations, and visions of each perspective when members saw themselves in one depiction ("They got that from me," members could be heard to say) and saw colleagues in a new light in the other ("Oh, now I understand why they feel that way!"). The illumination of these previously obscured perspectives led to group commitment to a broader goal of *respectful engagement,* a term introduced by a planning group member. This vision, shared by members from both perspectives, became the compass that would help group members navigate the turbulent waters just ahead.

STEP 3: DEVELOPING STRATEGIES

In the third step of empowerment evaluation, the evaluator works with the program group or staff to help them develop strategies to meet their goals based on information gathered through the evaluation. Again, this is familiar terrain for collaborative process evaluators, who might systematically monitor program objectives, administer formative surveys, analyze special initiatives, and provide in-progress reports and consultation to assist in the success of social planning efforts.

Involvement in strategy development is essential for evaluators working from an empowering perspective because it provides an opportunity to constantly infuse the effort with community and capacity building possibilities. A resilient community is one that develops strategies, takes action, gauges reactions, and makes modifications in a constantly reflexive cycle. Empowered members know that their ideas are important and their experiences are valid, and they can see their contributions in the next round of innovation. As a result, we tailored all of our process evaluation queries to include opportunities for feedback and suggestions for change and made certain to appropriately attribute innovations and insight that led to new ways of thinking or working together.

One of the planning efforts we evaluated struggled with difficult group dynamics exacerbated by uneven facilitation and inexperienced and unstable staffing. The project was underfunded to begin with and quickly overbudget, and staff, consultants, and planning council members were chronically frustrated and behind. Our evaluation strategies stretched to include considerable staff and consultant coaching.

With a change of this magnitude in our role and influence, we had to constantly ground our strategy recommendations in the experience of planning participants. A group that is floundering still has insight and ideas, but they emerge with less frequency as the collective spirit falters. Thus, one of our tasks became to look for, nurture, and sustain the group's wisdom and then to anchor the eventual resolution of its processual problems in its own recommendations and capabilities.

This group's structural problems were so obvious and seemingly intractable that it was easy for group members to slide into a passive, resentful relationship with staff, consultants, and, eventually, each other. Our evaluation team addressed the structural issues through intensive individual coaching but also felt it important to help shift the group's focus from complaining about the problems and personalities to actively proposing and participating in realistic solutions. Toward that end, and in an effort to draw out the insight of individual participants, we added strategically selected and sequenced questions to the standard meeting evaluation survey. The new questions were designed to bring forward the broadest possible view of what was going wrong and to generate a varied and grounded list of suggestions for change.

For example, our team actively worked against the trend of disengagement and disempowerment by asking participants to name the biggest hassle of community planning ("people that complain," "people who don't listen," "uneven workload") and to identify what they particularly appreciated in each of the other players ("commitment," "hard work," "respect for differences"). We also invited each participant to specify something that he or she would like the other key players (council colleagues, consultants, staff, evaluators) to try ("Be there when you say you're going to be there," "Take care of more of the details before the meetings," "Smile," "Stop bickering," "Stay focused"). Finally, we asked each participant to identify something he or she could do to help the group function more smoothly ("I'll be more understanding," "Listen," "Be better prepared for meetings," "Remember we're here to fight AIDS, not each other"). Our team collected and organized the written responses, forwarding the relevant set of uplifts and requests to each of the key players within a few days and presenting the full set of responses at the next council meeting. We also facilitated a lively and productive group discussion among meeting participants of hassles, uplifts, and ways of changing course.

This simple approach to diagnosing process problems and developing strategies provided a role for everyone and generated insight and ideas within the vocabulary and priorities of group members. Our team may have been able to help solve the worst of the organizational problems through coaching alone. However, we felt that an empowering opportunity would be lost if we did not honor and amplify the self-correcting capacity of even this fragile and troubled community. Indeed, by the end of the planning period, new and more productive group norms and relationships had emerged, with clear roots in the things that participants had offered to do and asked each other to try.

STEP 4: DOCUMENTING THE PROCESS

The final step in David Fetterman's model of empowerment evaluation is documenting the process. In this step, the evaluators have the responsibility of keeping the written record of what occurred and why in a format accessible to all interested parties. Evaluators of social planning projects invariably produce written documents, often supplemented by executive summaries and other abridged versions of key findings.

Documenting of the process takes on additional dimensions when viewed from an empowering perspective. Our evaluation team found many ways in which the responsibility for documentation gave us opportunities for community building beyond the initial evaluation mandate. Based on our belief that evaluation should never be mysterious, for example, we regularly shared our methods, data, framework, and interpretations so that participants would know what we were doing, how, and why. We consciously modeled enthusiasm for evaluation, enjoyment of the many tasks it involved, and appreciation for the lessons in the data. We hoped that our love of what we do would encourage others to embrace and enjoy evaluation as well. We further hoped that our skills would be assumed and extended by those we worked with in their own community-based efforts beyond the community planning process.

In addition to generating required reports, our team regularly produced written summaries of evaluation feedback, which we distributed to all participants. We searched for a presentation style and narrative voice that were both professional and accessible, adjusting fonts, titles, and layout to fit the tone of the different planning groups we worked with. All of our reports contained verbatim quotes from respondents, and we privately checked to make sure that something from every single participant was included. If knowledge is power, then reading should be empowering. Our goal was that our written documents be inviting, interesting to read, validate lived experience, and inspire continued community work.

An empowering approach to evaluation led our team to help groups monitor their own progress through the rocky road and predictable challenges of community-based planning. Whenever possible, we charted progress through the goals and symbols indigenous to each individual planning group. Since much of the community planning vocabulary, time lines, and specific assignments was imposed on planning groups from outside, we designed exercises and facilitated discussions in which participants identified or recalled their own "fixed stars" and milestones. This native wisdom could then be used to reinvigorate a struggling process or document progress against landmarks familiar and meaningful to planning participants.

One of the most affirming examples of the empowering potential of collaborative evaluation occurred during one of the darkest moments of a community planning process. After working together for nearly a year, the planning group, on a three-day retreat, faced a crucial set of decisions. Behind-the-scenes maneuvering and miscommunication since the last meeting, combined with recent fracturing of long-standing alliances, had left group members suddenly wary, suspicious, and very angry with each other and the staff as they approached this watershed moment. As evaluators, we knew that a vote could proceed, but as community organizers, we knew that the conditions under which the decisions were about to be made were disempowering and dangerous to broader community building.

Using our mandate to document the process, we asked the facilitators for time on the agenda before the vote was to be taken. Quickly searching through our by-now-voluminous files, we found some data that we had collected after an ice-breaker exercise nearly a year before. In this exercise, the facilitators had asked participants to write down and then share their personal mottoes or messages to the world. We had retrieved these data after they had been used and discarded, sensing that they might be important later. Using a laptop computer and a local copy store, we quickly compiled and organized these messages, printed them up, and had them ready to distribute within an hour.

We used our time on the agenda to remind planning group members of the importance of the vote they were about to take and the historic progress they had made up to this moment. We then passed out the list of personal mottoes and messages and asked each participant to read aloud from the list as we went around the table:

> My friends are dying. . . . If we don't, who will? . . . One second at a
> time . . . Enjoy yourself; it's later than you think. . . . Be compassionate
> and kind towards each other. . . . Never lose your self-confidence. . . .
> Share your wealth. . . . Where will you be when they come for you? . . .
> Live in peace and be good to the earth. . . . Do something you'll be
> proud of. . . . It all pays the same. . . . Speak up; I can't hear you! . . .
> Never take a day for granted. . . . Never grow up. . . . Be kind, be
> flexible, be understanding. . . . Life is complex; being alive is simple. . . .
> Show up; tell the truth. . . . Faith is stepping out on nothing and
> believing until something is there. . . . Give back. . . . ¡Si, se puede! . . .
> Get over it; life goes on. . . . Protect our children. . . . Do what you can
> with where you are and what you have. . . . Live life like you mean it. . . .
> Never give up hope. . . . We've got to stop throwing each other
> away—each and every human being is valuable. . . . Adelante
> caminante. . . . If not now, when? . . . Keep moving forward. . . . We are
> one. . . . T-minus 50 cells and counting down. Kindly cooperate in
> stopping this disease.

The group was silent, stunned and sobered, by the end of the reading. Although names were not attributed to individual members, everyone knew that the last message read had been written by a well-respected member who had died of AIDS just a few months before. Hearing his words and their own firmly rerooted this planning group in its collective wisdom. Once again mindful of shared commitments, group members were ready to vote with a unified spirit.

This example demonstrates what happened repeatedly in our community planning evaluations. An empowering approach to our evaluation tasks gave us insight and called us to action. Holding the group's records, caring about its progress, and watching for the empowering moment in every turn in the road enabled us to transform the potentially dry task of documenting the progress of social planning into a vibrant moment of community reconciliation and renewal.

Combining Evaluation, Empowerment, and Community Building with Planning

Social planning projects and empowerment evaluation are not natural partners. Planning initiatives invariably struggle with rigorous time lines for needs assessment, data collection, strategy development, priority setting, and decisionmaking. Traditional assumptions about sound planning further contribute to an environment of very focused and linear deliberations. In most cases, evaluation is to be unobtrusive and to follow the planning process rather than actively contribute to its direction, tone, and dynamics. Staff, other planning participants, and funders may be suspicious or resistant to evaluation methods that clearly have an expanded agenda.

DEALING WITH SKEPTICS

We were extremely fortunate to work with staff who endorsed our approach to evaluation and trusted us enough to let us actively participate in a process so complex and important to them all. Empowering evaluation might not be possible under different circumstances. Some planning participants were skeptical of our approach and openly challenged our ability to rigorously evaluate planning given our methodological assumptions and community-based goals. But although they were skeptical, we never were. We believed in the integrity of people involved in HIV prevention. And we had an unshakeable trust in the power and potential of community. Although we sometimes had to double our efforts early on to prove that we could collect traditional evaluation data when it was useful and appropriate, even the most cynical skeptics eventually admitted to insight and understanding from the empowerment-based data.

THE EMPOWERING EVALUATORS' SKILL SET

Our experience with the three very different community planning groups has led us to appreciate the specific skills and talents necessary for evaluating social planning from an empowering perspective. We close by offering our own priority list, knowing that other evaluators might draw on different skills or strategies to foster community empowerment through evaluation.

Evaluators who facilitate empowerment must have excellent traditional evaluation skills. Even though the underlying assumptions may be quite different from those of empowerment evaluation, traditional methods provide a kind of data and point of observation that can be usefully triangulated with other data and perspectives. Additionally, solid traditional skills enhance the credibility of evaluators who are about to stretch the purpose and scope of a planning evaluation.

We have also found that teamwork is best when planning is evaluated from an empowerment perspective. Although the lead evaluator remained the same on all five projects, a team was created for each site that reflected the diversity of planning participants. The CDC guidance required that planning groups represent the diversity of the epidemic in the local area. We extended that requirement to our own team. As a result, our evaluators reflected the diversity of gender, race/ethnicity, sexual orientation, and HIV status of each group with which we worked. The multiple perspectives that we brought to our work greatly enhanced our ability to elicit sound data from participants and to interpret what they offered.

Most important, empowering evaluation requires an additional set of professional skills. Evaluators must be flexible, quick thinking, self-critical, optimistic, and truly interested in the groups they work with and the potential of community. Collecting this type of data requires the ability to engender trust, coax out stories, process qualitative information, and re-present heartfelt experiences. This takes time, energy, and a keen eye for the phrase or the moment that may move a group forward. Evaluators must have affection for the communities they work with while always maintaining an internal distance from which to observe process and explore empowering strategies.

Our community planning evaluations have validated our belief in the potential of collaborative evaluation to stimulate community development and capacity building. The recent formulation of the empowerment evaluation model provides a welcome structure and rationale for this kind of work. A product of this gifted age, empowerment evaluation offers a sensitive and resonant framework within which evaluation can not only document but also stimulate and reinforce community building and community organization.

Acknowledgments

We wish to thank the community planning participants we worked with on the evaluations referenced in this chapter. Special acknowledgment is made to Charles Smith, Patrick Hogan, Delfina Perkins, Tiffani Brown, and Nina Grossman and to Chuck Darrah for the beginning of our evaluation assumptions.

References

Academy for Educational Development. 1995. *Handbook for HIV prevention community planning*. Washington, D.C.: Academy for Educational Development.

Butler, J. 1992. Of kindred minds: The ties that bind. In *Cultural competence for evaluators*, ed. M. I. Orlandi. Rockville, Md.: U.S. Department of Health and Human Services.

Fetterman, D. M. 1996. Empowerment evaluation: An introduction to theory and practice. In *Empowerment evaluation: Knowledge and tools for self-assessment and accountability*, ed. D. M. Fetterman, S. J. Kaftarian, and A. Wandersman. Thousand Oaks, Calif.: Sage.

Fetterman, D. M. , S. J. Kaftarian, and A. Wandersman, eds. 1996. *Empowerment evaluation: Knowledge and tools for self-assessment and accountability*. Thousand Oaks, Calif.: Sage.

Fleming, C. M. 1992. American Indians and Alaska Natives: Changing societies past and present. In *Cultural competence for evaluators*, ed. M. I. Orlandi. Rockville, Md.: U.S. Department of Health and Human Services.

Guba, E. G., and Y. S. Lincoln. 1989. *Fourth-generation evaluation*. Newbury Park, Calif.: Sage.

Millay, E.S.V. 1988. *Collected sonnets of Edna St. Vincent Millay*. Rev. and exp. New York: Harper and Row.

Patton, M. Q. 1990. *Qualitative evaluation and research methods*. 2d ed. Newbury Park, Calif.: Sage.

Schoonmaker-Freudenberger, K. 1993. Rapid rural appraisal. Minneapolis. Unpublished manuscript.

Part IX

New Tools for Community Organizing and Community Building into the Twenty-first Century

What will community organizing look like in the next century? What communities are people most likely to identify with, and what new strategies and approaches will prove the most promising in building caring communities? Although it is far too early to answer such questions with any certainty, it is important to begin asking them and to consider the new and emerging tools that are likely to play an increasing role in community organizing and community building in the years ahead.

Although numerous tools and techniques could be described in the latter regard, two have been selected for special attention in this part. Online computer networks, which are profoundly transforming many aspects of our lives, will also increasingly transform the ways in which we define and build communities and engage in grassroots organizing for health and social change. In chapter 20, Courtney Uhler Cart examines the current and potential uses of electronic communication as a potent avenue for both community building and community organizing. Using current examples of online networks as "virtual communities" and illustrations of online social action organizing on the local and national levels, she demonstrates the tremendous potential of electronic communication for building communities based on common interest and for effecting social change.

But as she also points out, the online revolution has largely missed low-income communities and indeed may serve to further disfranchise these and other groups that lack access to this technology. The potential for online networks to substitute for face-to-face communication and organizing and the potential for virtual communities to supplant our connections with geographic and other physical communities are dangers that must be addressed. Finally, as Uhler Cart notes, the potential for prejudice and domination online and the use of this powerful technology to communicate racism, sexism, homophobia, and the like represent very real problems that we are only beginning to recognize and address. As this chapter makes clear, social change professionals have important roles to play not only in furthering the use of online networks for community building and organizing into a new century, but also in preventing their misuse.

The final chapter of this volume describes and vividly demonstrates a second tool with tremendous potential for community organizing into the twenty-first century: media advocacy. Written by Lawrence Wallack, who is widely regarded as the foremost architect of this approach, chapter 21 views media advocacy as rooted in the broader area of community advocacy. It defines media advocacy as "the strategic use of mass media to advance a social or public policy initiative." Whereas traditional media approaches try to fill the "knowledge gap," media advocacy is concerned instead with filling the "power gap" by highlighting alternative definitions of problems and policy-level approaches to their solution. Its strategies include working with community groups to harness the power of the media for changing the environment in which a problem occurs.

As Wallack suggests, media advocacy is increasingly being used by communities of color and other groups to transform the ways in which their issues and concerns are portrayed and handled by the mass media. By shifting the focus from the personal to the social, and from individual behavior to the broader policy and environmental contexts that heavily shape individual behavior, media advocacy represents a major new tool whose potential for community organizing and social change has only begun to unfold.

Chapter 20

Online Computer Networks

COURTNEY UHLER CART

Potential and Challenges for Community Organizing and Community Building Now and in the Future

Oɴʟɪɴᴇ ᴄᴏᴍᴘᴜᴛᴇʀ ɴᴇᴛᴡᴏʀᴋs are beginning to redefine personal relationships, political organizing, and even democracy itself. These networks allow individuals to engage with one another in what was originally termed *computer-mediated communication* and is now known as *electronic* or *online communication*. With access to the seemingly ubiquitous information superhighway or the Internet, online networks are playing an increasing role in the lives of individuals and communities concerned with social change.

This chapter examines the current and potential uses of online networks as potent avenues for community building and community organizing to address health and social issues and improve quality of life for communities. After a brief look at the conceptual basis for this discussion, the chapter describes the uses of online networks in community organizing and community building. Both early and contemporary examples of organizing and community building online are provided, as is a discussion of the ethical challenges and related concerns that need to be addressed as we move with this technology into the twenty-first century.

A caveat is appropriate here. With the explosion of the Internet and its endless applications, it is obvious that traditional hard-copy publishing is outpaced by the innovation that is occurring online. This chapter is intended to provide a conceptual framework, some illustrations, and critical questions for consideration in the use of online communication for community organizing. The chapter is not intended as a guide for using electronic communication and online resources for community organizing efforts. No online resources have been listed since these are likely to be outdated by the time this book is published. The best advice for anyone not yet on the information superhighway and familiar with the Internet is to get plugged in.

Use of Online Networks

There are several ways in which online networks may be used as tools for community building and community organizing. First, local communities can organize online to jointly identify community problems and resources, engage in dialogue, and actively participate in their solutions. This entails more local participation, whether in public policy or other community affairs. Second, new community groups can evolve around common interests, whether these are a specific disease or health condition or a concern with government tobacco policies or health care reform. Groups that are concerned primarily with the giving and receiving of social support for members constitute good examples of community building in action. In contrast, as Ronald Labonte points out in chapter 6, groups that are concerned mainly with effecting change in broader socioeconomic conditions could be said to be engaged in community organizing or community development. This third application, community organizing, involves the growing use of online networks by health educators, social workers, and other professionals to share strategies with colleagues, across town or around the world, that may be effective in mobilizing to address health and social problems.

Conceptual Framework

Several conceptual approaches help create a context for understanding the reality and potential of online computer networks for community building and community organizing. Alexis de Tocqueville's ([1840] 1953) notion of community association, for example, is germane to an examination of online networks and social change. As discussed in chapter 3, the uniquely American community association was described by Tocqueville in the early nineteenth century as a self-generated gathering of citizens who assume the power to decide what is a problem and how it should be solved. Tocqueville purported that this self-defining assembly of nonexpert citizens and the creation of such citizen power would lead to a powerful form of democracy.

In light of his emphasis on community association, Tocqueville might well be pleased to see the efforts of online community networks to increase citizen participation. The phrase *electronic democracy* indeed evokes Tocqueville's concept of democracy as a "self-interest rightly understood" (122). As one of the fathers of the online activist movement, Howard Rheingold (1993) suggests, online networks allow for an "electronic democracy" because of the coexistence of up-to-date factual information online and the forum for discussion and debate. Rheingold explains that "the ability of groups of citizens to debate political issues is amplified enormously by instant, widespread access to facts that could support or refute assertions made in those debates" (91).

John McKnight's conceptualizations of community building are, of course, heavily grounded in those of Tocqueville (see chapter 2). McKnight (1987, 58) emphasizes that "as institutions have grown in power, we have become too impotent to be called real citizens and too disconnected to be effective members of community." In a similar vein to Tocqueville, McKnight argues in chapter 2 that "the basic source of health is powerful citizens and vigorous associations."

John McKnight and John Kretzmann (1984) suggest that traditional community organizing approaches need to be adapted to the contemporary context. Online community networks could offer such adaptations, for example, in their capacity to engage people as meaningful participants in our health systems rather than as mere patients or consumers. Yet McKnight (1996) remains cautious about this approach since computers may distance people from communities rather than contribute to community building. In this respect, McKnight appears to agree with Sherry Turkle (1996, 57) that "it is sobering that the personal computer revolution, once conceptualized as a tool to rebuild community, now tends to concentrate on building community inside a machine."

Saul Alinsky (1972) would likely hold far fewer reservations about online networks as tools for organizing. With McKnight, he believed that participatory democracy and local interest could best be maintained and preserved by active, local associations. Alinsky's social action strategies were based on his belief that communitywide ties and community participation in the political process could effect social change. He put great emphasis on power in numbers and sought to organize a democratic "people's movement" at the grassroots level. Alinsky (1969) argued that expanded citizen participation by people not otherwise represented by interest groups aided in making the political process more equitable and closer to the goal of pluralist democracy. He wanted to establish the local community as a legitimate and recognized party in such pluralist decisionmaking.

A consistent theme of Alinsky's community organizing is the notion of power as a means to broaden citizen participation and open access to the political arena. Donald Reitzes and Dietrich Reitzes (1982) maintain that Alinsky's special skill was his ability to translate the numerical strength of a community into viable forms of influence. His efforts were to construct instrumental, communitywide, and locally controlled organizations to achieve the goals of community cohesion and greater political influence. Toward this end, Alinsky's social action strategy included educating local citizens about the shared nature of their concerns in order to work toward communitywide solution. The efforts of modern day online activists are often reminiscent of Alinsky's approach to community organizing.

Current Uses of Online Networks

ONLINE NETWORKS AS VIRTUAL COMMUNITIES

Phil Catalfo (1993, 165) has described online networks as having the potential to bring back "communities that disappeared with front porches." Many online networks are defined by their participants as virtual communities or communities with communication among members occurring online rather than in the physical, face-to-face sense. The technology that makes virtual communities possible could bring enormous leverage to ordinary people at relatively little cost: intellectual leverage, social leverage, and political leverage (Rheingold 1993). Although there has been much hype about getting online, and although unequal access and opportunity for getting online remain serious problems, the concept of community networks as the local "commons" is a practical application of the technology that is now occurring in communities around the world.

Local community networks are developed for local community residents to jointly identify community problems and resources, engage in local dialogue, and increase communication between government and citizens on various community issues. Such networks provide access to community information and bring Internet access to residents and nonprofit organizations by offering a less expensive alternative to commercial vendors. Community networks are being established through partnerships of local businesses, libraries, educational institutions, local governments, social and health organizations, and community members. The philosophy and goals of a community network are dictated largely by the community (Wilson 1994). To ensure online access to as many individuals as possible, many localities have developed low- or no-cost "freenets." Cleveland FreeNet was the first to be developed in 1986, and there are now thousands of freenets across the world, including Santa Monica's Public Electronic Network (PEN).

In addition to the role as a public commons, many virtual communities take the form of support groups for people sharing similar concerns and enable community building around these issues. Whether they are communities of caregivers for people with Alzheimers's disease or for individuals around the world who share a rare and baffling illness, many potent new communities are forming online. Participants in America speak of going online at 2:00 A.M. and receiving emotional support or advice on a new treatment from community members in Hong Kong or Portugal. One university has established a Web site that provides interactive tutorials for parents of children who have asthma or cerebral palsy. While this site provides much needed information for these parents, it also serves as a mechanism for these parents to connect with other parents to serve as an online support system for one another. Another powerful illustration of online information exchange is occurring as a result of the efforts of the Midwest AIDS and HIV Information Exchange in Chicago. This is a free online network for people living with

HIV/AIDS. It provides information on service providers, agencies, an AIDS daily new summary, news from the Centers for Disease Control and Prevention and the National Institutes of Health, newsletters, and "Ask the Doctor" and "Ask the Nurse" services.

Some nonprofit organizations have been developed solely to harness the resources of the online world. Impact Online is a national organization that was established online to connect people and organizations. As its home page states, "It's a place where you can reach people who share your other concerns . . . and begin to use the Web as a tool for social change." For example, Stop Prisoner Rape is a nonprofit organization dedicated to combating the rape of male and female prisoners and providing assistance to survivors of prison rape. This organization is utilizing Impact Online's web site to network with similar groups and recruit volunteers.

Clearly, such virtual communities are very real sources of support for their members. The popularity of such online communities, moreover, can be irrepressible. This fact was illustrated recently in the fate of a large randomized clinical trial for a new drug for patients with Lou Gehrig's Disease. Large numbers of the participants in the trial were part of an online support group for people with the disease, and they freely shared information about the drug's apparent side effects and figured out who among them were controls and who were in the treatment group. Members of the control groups began demanding that they, too, be given the experimental drug, so the trial ultimately had to be canceled (Tuckson 1996).

ONLINE NETWORKS AS TOOLS FOR COMMUNITY ORGANIZING
In addition to contributions to community building as virtual communities and support groups, online networks can be powerful tools for community organizing around health and social issues at both the national and the local levels. Professionals and community activists can use online networks to facilitate communication between one another and share timely information on community organizing strategies, public policy, and advocacy efforts. Although academicians have been taking advantage of their usually free access to e-mail (electronic mail) and Internet resources for years, other professionals and community activists are more recent converts to the online world. As computers and online access become less expensive, more and more community-based groups will be able to get online and may even find that they cannot "afford" to be offline. At this point, however, many of the social change organizations that are online are the larger nonprofits that serve as support systems for local community building efforts.

Increased access to online communication networks will enable local, community-based organizations to draw upon resources that otherwise are often unavailable to them. Beyond a role in supplementing more conventional means of sharing information on research and professional practice with colleagues across the country, larger online networks enable individuals of formal and informal statewide and nationwide constituencies to interact, organize, and influence health and social services and policy.

NATIONWIDE EFFORTS. Online networks are being used as tools to help bridge policy and practice since health and social service organizations can more efficiently create and maintain dialogue with one another. Those organizations and agencies that are creating policy can easily communicate not only with health and social service providers but also with those people who would be most affected by these policies. Frontline workers can immediately post their observations about the effects of new policies, programs, or the behavior of adversaries. For example, when a national tobacco manufacturer recently initiated an aggressive new advertising campaign, smoking control groups used a computer network to keep members informed and to mobilize opposition at every stop of the company's promotional tour (Lambert 1994). In a similar vein, antitobacco activists were armed with powerful information when a medical school library put on the World Wide Web full-text medical research reports from a major tobacco company that had not been willing to disclose this information to the public (Caruso 1996).

In another instance, a national nonprofit organization is utilizing online networks to fulfill its mission for community renewal. The Alliance for National Renewal, based in Denver, Colorado, is intended to "serve as a catalyst for inspiring diverse people to work collectively in revitalizing their communities and societies." This organization grew out of the efforts and vision of the National Civic League. Although this national organization, representing nearly two hundred local and national organizations, does not exist solely online, its online presence allows organizers a better means of networking with one another. The alliance's growing Web site provides a wealth of tools for community organizers and nonprofits, including a community stories index, a community renewal resource listing, and a newsletter, "The Kitchen Table." Alinsky and other community organizing leaders would likely applaud the efforts of the alliance's work to encourage and nourish an engaged citizenry.

National-level organizing around health care reform and health care access is taking place online. For example, Project Sound Off was launched in 1996 by a coalition of more than fifty health care consumer and provider organizations. Using a World Wide Web site to showcase managed care "horror stories," the Coalition for Health Care Choice and Accountability encouraged users to help document cases of managed care abuse. The stories collected were subsequently used in efforts to agitate for national legislation to protect consumer rights in the rapidly growing and largely for profit managed care arena (Jackson 1996).

LOCAL EFFORTS. Online networks can also be used by professionals and community activists to enhance communication at the local level to facilitate community change. Such networks are a flexible, relatively inexpensive, and very quick medium for organizing real-world events and activities since they provide community groups and citizens with timely information. Online networks can enhance the work of local coalitions and develop program-to-program links. For example, Nancy Milio (1991) expresses a vision for the nursing profession. She suggests that online communication can support community action in addressing such complex problems as AIDS and substance abuse. Milio argues that online communication is most effective when it is used to "bring people in the community together to support them in solving what are essentially community-wide problems, and to support their advocacy and development of needed services and health-promoting policies" (146).

The Alliance for Community Renewal's online presence has allowed local community-based organizers to share their successes and the lessons they have learned with others across the country. Residents of Tillery, North Carolina, a small farming community, provided online information about their experience in broadening their access to health care. Their online story tells of residents enlisting medical students from Duke University to establish a medical clinic for their isolated community. Another Tillery story describes an innovative project, the Community Health Advocacy Program, that provides practical training to grassroots health advocates for local groups ranging from Open-Minded Seniors to the Area-Wide Health Committee.

Another nonprofit organization benefiting from the alliance's online networking is the Area Health Education Center of Amherst, Massachusetts. This organization serves as the support system for community coalitions and community development operations in New England. The organization's most recent work has focused on building citizen leaders through neighborhood organizations, community organizing, and parent leadership development.

Still another application for sharing local community information has been delineated by Milio (1996). She suggests that this technology can "help outsiders connect with local, less advantaged communities, and could help communities become advocates and not just recipients of uncertain and diminishing generosity by advantaged Americans" (vii). Milio proposes that community-based organizations serve as the intermediaries, empowering local people, encouraging dialogue among local groups, and fostering informed agreement on local issues.

Although not primarily an online application, the Health Care Forum's Community Builder computer simulation program, developed in collaboration with twelve communities around the world, is illustrative of how computer software can initiate a local collaborative process that can later be maintained through online communication. Through this interactive program, a wide variety of community members, from homeless persons to government officials, have worked together to share a community vision, explore and better understand their community's assets, decide on actions to be taken, and select measures for evaluating progress. In the words of Bette Gardner (1996), this gamelike simulator "provides an opportunity for participants to 'step back' and see how different actions and different ways of working together can influence community members. Participants come away with an appreciation for the value of building both the physical assets of their community (e.g., jobs and education systems) and its social assets (e.g., leadership and trust)."

A strength of the Community Builder, and one that addresses concerns raised by Sherry Turkle and John McKnight, among others, is that it combines face-to-face interaction with computer simulation. People in small groups talk about each step and make decisions together, and a member of the group then enters their decisions into the computer. The computer projects ahead for a year to show the group the results, which in turn can be evaluated by participants. Although this software can be expensive, the massive shift to managed care may prompt agencies to purchase such programs as a tool for better working with their local communities toward the end of improving community health and well being.

Early Online Community Networks: The Public Electronic Network

Before the Internet became something a household word, the forerunners of the online activism movement were using local online networks to address social and health concerns. One of these early networks, the Public Electronic Network of Santa Monica, California, with its share of early successes, ethical and practical dilemmas, and lessons learned, offers an appropriate case study for organizing online.

PEN was the first free, government-sponsored online community network in the country. Owned and operated by the city government, PEN was developed in 1989 to increase public participation in local government. PEN electronically links residents to city hall, giving them a chance to ask questions and express their opinions. For those who do not own computers, the city provided twenty free "walk-up" terminals in libraries, recreation centers, and other public buildings. The city also provided free training and user support materials. Since PEN went online in 1989, thousands of residents have signed onto the network.

PEN has proved to be useful in handling various communication and information tasks for residents. PEN users can read city information, send e-mail messages to their representatives in city hall or to one another, and join online conferences to debate issues. For instance, PEN can help residents in locating local health and social service agencies or in identifying affordable housing. Residents can find out what issues are on the next City Council agenda and send e-mail messages to city hall. The online conferences for debating issues enable users to come and go as their schedules allow, while never missing any comments since they are automatically saved for everyone to read. Online conferences on local topics include youth concerns, City Council Watch, environment, crime, and homelessness. Some of the debates in these conferences serve to bridge the communication gap between people on opposing sides of issues, as when the city attorney and a landlord attorney argue in public view about rent control.

PEN has had its share of successes that indicate the potential for local community networks to be catalysts for political action (Wittig 1991). For example, when PEN was launched in 1989, homelessness was a high-profile online conference. Substantive online discussions took place between housed and homeless residents, which resulted in the creation of several human services. The homeless suggested that to find and keep a job, they most needed access to morning showers, clean clothes, and secure storage for their belongings. The newly formed PEN Action Group took up this issue as its first project, with group members meeting online and face to face with the homeless. The Action Group decided to lobby the city to create a program, which was dubbed SHWASHLOCK, for the showers, washing machines, and lockers that the homeless needed. The city responded by allocating $150,000 for the addition of showers and lockers to an existing facility and by providing vouchers redeemable at local laundromats. PEN put some dignity back into the lives of some homeless persons by allowing them to define their needs and solutions. As one homeless man explained:

> We without shelter are looked on with disdain, fear, loathing, pity and hatred. . . . In the minds of many, we must be avoided. This is why Santa Monica's PEN system is so special to me. No one on PEN knew that I was homeless until I told them. . . . To me, the most remarkable thing about the PEN community is that a city council member and a pauper can coexist . . . on an equal basis. . . . Pen is a great equalizer. . . . On any one topic, one can never accuse PENers of agreeing fully. But we are communicating, and that is a start.   (Wittig 1991, 26)

This man's comments reveal much about PEN and how the system brings together disparate social elements and promotes communication and community building among residents.

PEN has had its share of successes, but it has also learned that the network can attract unwanted attention. A few males on PEN (most of them adolescents) began writing scenarios online in which various PEN women were subjected to sexual domination and other degrading behavior. In response, women on PEN organized a women's support group known as PENfemme. The group met face to face, decided to ignore the attackers, and sent calming messages to one another by personal e-mail. Even though this particular problem was addressed, there continues to be overzealous users on PEN (Maher 1994). These "flamers" drive some moderate users away from the system with their virulent language and personal attacks on other users and city officials. In response, the city has decided to have a moderator who can edit messages on city government topics for length and who can block users who send messages too frequently on the same subject.

Even though the problem with the flamers is being addressed, and even though PEN clearly has had some successes, some creators of the project indicate that PEN is not what they intended. The founders acknowledge that people can get on the system and abuse free speech by treating PEN like a soap box (Maher 1994). Yet although PEN sometimes may be dominated by a few strong-minded participants, and although broad-based dialogue may have decreased, many still suggest that PEN has made local government more inclusive. In the words of one user, "It's made people more government literate; you can get facts and participate in an informed way—and that's empowering" (4). Local online networks such as PEN may play a role in helping to change the modern trend toward voter apathy and alienation. As one PEN user suggests: "If I had to pick a simple word to characterize PEN, it would be empowerment. When traditional social cues are lacking, individuals become equals, judged on the strength of their ideas" (Schaffer and Anundsen 1993, 42).

Ethical and Practical Challenges of Online Networking

There are obviously many unanswered questions about the future of online networking for social change. As electronic communication becomes an ever-larger part of our lives and our professional practice, a number of ethical and practical challenges call out for our immediate attention. As a supplement to the broad outline of issues presented here, Nancy Milio's *The Engines of Empowerment: Using Information Technology to Create Healthy Communities and Challenge Public Policy* (1996) provides an excellent in-depth look at these issues. A new publication, Douglas Schuler's *New Community Networks: Wired for Change* (1996), is a good source of information and thoughtful commentary in this regard.

ACCESS TO ONLINE NETWORKS

Probably the most critical issue for community organizers and activists in the use of online networks is the very real possibility of the further disfranchisement of low-income people and communities and other groups that lack access to computers. This issue, known as "information redlining," has become a major concern among advocates in building the information superhighway. For as Turkle (1996, 57) notes, "Although some inner city communities have computer mediated communication as a tool for real community building, the overall trend seems to be the creation of an information elite."

Although organizations and activists may speak for and about low-income and other disfranchised persons, there needs to be far more engagement of these individuals. Unfortunately, community-based organizations working with the disfranchised often lack their own affordable access to the Internet, as well as a voice in the development of its online content (Working Group Against Information Redlining 1995).

It will be the role of public policy makers, spurred by community organizers and others, to ensure that access to the online world is made more equitable. As Milio (1996) explains, the commercial world of telecommunications could jeopardize universal access without appropriate policies in place. Efforts by policy leaders such as the RAND Corporation, which recently published *Universal Access to E-Mail: Feasibility and Societal Implications* (Anderson et al. 1995), can guide policies and legislation that ensure the existence of "public space" online. Members of the Working Group Against Information Redlining, which range from the Rural Coalition to the Nation Council of Nonprofit Associations, offer a breadth of skills and resources that could help to address this problem. If the importance of universal online access continues to be emphasized at decisionmaking levels, government, foundations, and businesses may be more willing to provide needed support and resources.

Increasingly, freenets or community-based networks are providing free access by setting up public online terminals. Such kiosks can be located in libraries, schools, community centers, city halls, and shopping malls. This approach is currently being demonstrated in a variety of locations, such as Ohio's culturally and linguistically diverse Franklin County. The county's "Together 2000" initiative has as its goal to "close the gap between the information rich and the information poor" by placing computer equipment and training instructors not only in schools and libraries but also in churches, public housing developments, and homeless and domestic violence shelters.

In addition, community-based networks are attempting to ensure online access for community-based nonprofits and their consumers by offering them free or reduced-price access to their local network and, in many cases, the Internet. Unfortunately, when reduced rates of access to the Internet have been offered by community networks, the commercial vendors in some local markets have used their local political ties to prevent this from happening. In Knoxville, Tennessee, for example, the local community network, KORR-Net, finally had to agree to the terms of the main local Internet service provider: that KORR-Net would provide only text-based accounts to cash-strapped nonprofits rather than the more user-friendly graphical interfaces that were also available. Community organizers and other social change professionals may have an increasing role to play in fighting such efforts at limiting access.

The barrier of start-up and maintenance expenses of online networks remains overwhelming, however, for many low-income individuals and community groups. User-friendly computer interfaces and Internet connectivity are not inexpensive. Grant support from businesses, government, and foundations and in-kind support, including technical assistance, from larger institutions such as local universities and technology-related companies must increasingly be made available.

In addition to policy efforts, national organizations have emerged that focus on the actual provision of broad access to computer technology and the Internet. For example, Community Technology Centers' Network (CTCNet) of Newton, Massachusetts, is a nonprofit organization representing a nationwide coalition of community-based computing centers whose common mission is to ensure access to computer technology, and the Internet when affordable, for disfranchised populations. This organization recognizes in its mission statement that "people who are socially and/or economically disadvantaged will become further disadvantaged if they lack access to computers and computer-related technologies" (Community Technology Centers' Network 1996, 1). CTCNet brings together agencies and programs that provide training for those who do not have skills on computers and related technologies. Through such organized efforts, the goal of involving of a diverse array of community residents in local online networks one day could be realized.

THE SUBSTITUTION EFFECT

In addition to the problem of unequal access, many organizers have objected to the appropriateness of online networks as a substitute for face-to-face communication. This concern is legitimate, for as Turkle (1996, 57) points out, some cyberspace users substitute "life on the screen for life in our bodies and physical communities." To counter such developments, online networks should be considered as a supplement to face-to-face communication. Online communication can be used in between face-to-face meetings for people to maintain contact and keep up-to-date on issues. Similarly, as suggested in the Community Builder example, computer simulations should increasingly be developed that encourage local groups to work together in person on creating a shared vision, identifying resources, and developing action plans and only then turning to the computer to "try out" actions and scenarios and project their longer-term consequences for the community. Although exciting progress is being made in this regard, much more creative effort is needed.

PREJUDICE AND DOMINATION ONLINE

Another challenge for organizers is that of being alert to and working to prevent sexism, racism, homophobia, and other forms of prejudice and domination online. Many networks are male dominated, thereby raising gender issues of access for women and possible sexual harassment. To the extent possible, we must create online norms about appropriate behavior; provide training and outreach to women-focused, community-based programs such as domestic violence shelters; and develop safe places or women-only spaces.

In the latter regard, some of the first online activists interested in women's issues belong to an online network called WomensNet. This network was particularly active in publishing information online regarding women's issues for the U.N. Women's Conference held in Beijing, China, in 1995. The network enabled community-based organizations across the world to have access to up-to-date information regarding issues of concern and provided them with a vehicle for sharing information on their community's issues and solutions. Less issue-oriented Web sites targeted to women and girls are sprouting up, such as Femina and Webgrlls. These sites maintain current links to other women-related sites, and they also list classes, face-to-face meeting times and places, and job opportunities. Such sites may provide important vehicles for community building among groups that not infrequently confront prejudice and domination based on gender, race, sexual orientation, or other factors.

Much of the effort to organize virtual communities online has in fact occurred because different groups faced with prejudice have realized the power in articulating their cause, with no sensors, filters, publishers, or agents, to millions of people. Different groups are using the online world to try to shape their reality in the real world. Unfortunately, this boundlessness can just as easily serve as a breeding ground for those who are trying to spread their own prejudices. It is critical, therefore, that activists and concerned social change professionals be vigilant to instances of online racism, sexism, homophobia, and the like and work with concerned constituencies to demonstrate a policy of zero tolerance for the expression of such prejudices.

Conclusion

Although there are valid concerns stemming from the ethical and practical challenges of online activism, individuals who have used electronic communication to further their social change efforts suggest that the use of this technology is certainly worth exploring. We need to embrace the technology so that we can learn how to refine its uses and address its shortcomings in order to have an increased impact on pressing health and social problems that require community effort. Whether the technology is used to bring support to home care-givers of chronically ill family members or to foster communication and networking among AIDS activists across the country, these online applications of community building and community organizing are increasing at a remarkable pace. As Turkle (1996, 57) suggests: "Having literally written our online worlds into existence, we can use the communities we build inside our machines to improve the ones outside of them. Like the anthropologist returning home from a foreign culture, the voyager in virtuality can return to the real world better able to understand what about it is arbitrary and what can be changed."

Online Resources

Given the ever-changing nature of online resources, the best approach to finding information online is to use one of the Internet search engines. On the World Wide Web, these search tools include Alta Vista, Yahoo, Lycos, and Webcrawler. If you have only text-based access to the Internet, you can use the search tools Archie or Veronica to find appropriate Gopher sites.

References

Alinsky, S. D. 1969. *Reveille for radicals*. Chicago: University of Chicago Press.
———. 1972. *Rules for radicals*. New York: Random House.
Anderson, R. H., T. K. Bikson, S. A. Law, and B. Mitchell. 1995. *Universal access to e-mail: Feasibility and societal implications*. Santa Monica, Calif.: RAND.
Caruso, D. 1996. The Net nobody knows. *Utne Reader* (May-June):41–48.
Catalfo, P. 1993. America, online. In *The Graywolf annual ten: Changing community*. Saint Paul, Minn.: Graywolf Press.
Community Technology Centers' Network. 1996. Mission statement. Newton, Mass.: Community Technology Centers' Network.
Gardner, B. 1996. *Community builder workbook*. San Francisco: Health Care Forum.
Jackson, V. 1996. Managed care "horror stories" find home on World Wide Web. *Healthcare Management Solutions* 11 (3):25.
Lambert, M. H. 1994. Technology: Armchair conferencing. *Foundation News and Commentary* (March-April):1–3.
Maher, A. 1994. Traffic cops on the information superhighway. *Los Angeles Times*, May 19.
McKnight, J. L. 1987. Regenerating communities. *Social Policy* (Winter):54–58.
———. 1996. Personal communication, April 23.
McKnight, J. L., and J. P. Kretzmann. 1984. Community organizing in the 80s: Toward a post-Alinksy agenda. *Social Policy* (Winter):15–17.
Milio, N. 1991. Information technology and community health: Invitation to innovation. *Journal of Professional Nursing* 7 (3):146.
———. 1996. *The engines of empowerment: Using information technology to create healthy communities and challenge public policy*. Chicago: Health Administration Press.
Reitzes, D. C., and Reitzes, D. C. 1982. Saul D. Alinsky: A neglected but promising resource. *American Sociologist* 17:47–56.
Rheingold, H. 1993. *The virtual community: Homesteading on the electronic frontier*. Reading, Mass.: Addison-Wesley.
Schaffer, C. R., and K. Anundsen, K. 1993. *Creating community anywhere: Finding support and connection in a fragmented world*. New York: Putnam.
Schuler, D. 1996. *New community networks: Wired for change*. Reading, Mass.: Addison-Wesley.
Tocqueville, A. de. [1840] 1953. *Democracy in America*. New York: Knopf.
Tuckson, R. 1996. Making a commitment to life. Paper presented at the annual meeting of the Health Care Forum, San Francisco, California, April 21.
Turkle, S. 1996. Virtuality and its discontents. *American Prospect* 24 (Winter):50–57.
Wilson, D. L. 1994. Putting citizens online. *Chronicle of Higher Education*, July 27, A17–A19.
Wittig, M. 1991. Electronic city hall. *Whole Earth Review* (Summer):24–27.
Working Group Against Information Redlining. 1995. *"Redlining" on the information superhighway*. Washington, D.C.: Working Group Against Information Redlining.

Chapter 21   Media Advocacy

LAWRENCE WALLACK   *A Strategy for Empowering*
People and Communities

If you don't exist in the media,
for all practical purposes, you don't exist.
DANIEL SCHORR

Introduction

AN EIGHTH GRADE GIRL in Pojoaque, New Mexico; a family physician in Davis, California; and a network of tobacco control advocates around the country all share a strong belief in the power of the media to promote public health goals. Each took on powerful "manufacturers of illness" (McKinlay 1986), and each, with creative use of mass media, was able to achieve their objectives. In Pojoaque, a school substance abuse project turned into a battle to remove alcohol billboards from the immediate area of the school. The combination of community organizing and the power of the press made a young girl into a giant-killer and brought the billboards down. In Davis, a physician concerned about children inadvertently killing other children with easily available handguns that often were mistaken for toy guns combined scientific research with a topic the media could not resist to focus attention on the need for policy change. One short-term outcome is the difficulty of finding certain kinds of toy guns in California stores. Tobacco control advocates successfully developed a media strategy to counter the Philip Morris "Bill of Rights Tour." The cigarette maker's public relations dream turned into a nightmare when advocates successfully reframed the issue in the media and made it a health story.

The experience of these people is part of the foundation of a creative and innovative approach to use mass media as an advocacy tool. What they learned, and what people are learning in communities across the country, is that the power of the press can be claimed by advocacy groups and used to promote changes in the social environment. In breaking from traditional public education campaigns

Reprinted from *Journal of Public Health Policy* 15 (4) (1994):420–436, by permission of the publisher.

that convey health messages, they developed a "voice" to wield power. Media advocacy can be a significant force for influencing public debate, speaking directly to those with influence, and putting pressure on decisionmakers. Media advocacy is a tactic for community groups to communicate their own story in their own words to promote social change. It is a hybrid tool combining advocacy approaches with the strategic and innovative use of media to better *pressure* decisionmakers to support changes for healthy public policies.

Historically, the mass media have tended to present health issues in medical terms, with a focus on personal health habits, medical miracles, physician heroics, or technological breakthroughs (Turow and Coe 1985; Gerbner, Morgan, and Signorielli 1981; Wallack et al. 1993; Turow 1989; Wallack and Dorfman 1992). High tech curative treatment and low tech preventive behavior change have been the primary focus. Social, economic, and political determinants of health have been largely ignored by the most pervasive media. Media advocacy tries to change this by emphasizing the social and economic, rather than individual and behavioral, roots of the problem.

The research base in public health strongly suggests, while a balance of initiatives are necessary, policy change is a key factor in promoting public health goals. Current research in public health and mass communication clearly indicates that it is time to shift the balance of our efforts in using the mass media from individual change to social change, from promoting health information to promoting health policies, from giving people a message about their personal health to giving communities a voice in defining and acting on public health issues. Certainly the provision of clear, accurate information about risk factors and personal behavior change through public information campaigns must be a constant part of the media environment. However, the research indicates that it is appropriate and necessary for public health to move from the public affairs desk to the news and opinion desks.

Health advocates are attracting news attention more and more frequently on issues such as violence, alcohol, tobacco, and HIV infection (Wallack et al. 1993). Public health issues are newsworthy because they can link personal stories with broader social and political concerns. Community initiatives have provided solid evidence that local groups can gain access to media, reframe issues to focus on policy, and advance community initiatives for policy change.

The Information Gap versus the Power Gap

Traditional forms of mass media interventions emphasize the "information gap," which suggests health problems are caused by a lack of information in individuals with the problem or at risk for the problem. Public education campaigns provide information to fill that gap. Media advocacy, on the other hand, focuses on the "power gap," where health problems are viewed as a lack of power to define the problem and create social change. The target of media advocacy is the power gap. It attempts to motivate broad social and political involvement rather than changes in personal health behavior.

The mass media regularly reinforce the view that health matters are personal problems rather than social or community concerns (Wallack 1990; Iyengar 1991). The definition of the problem at the personal level leads to solutions designed for and directed to the individual. In this "information gap" model the person is seen as lacking some key information, and it is this lack of information which is the problem. When people have the information and "know the facts," it is assumed they will then act accordingly and the problem will be solved. If every individual gets the right information and makes the right decision, then the community's problem will be eliminated. The role of the media is to deliver the solution (knowledge) to the millions of individuals who need it.

The information gap model sees the context in which the problem exists only as a place to deliver a message. It accounts for the pressures and demands of daily life only in determining how to deliver the message. It assumes people have adequate available resources for meeting those demands. Family, school, community, and social variables are seen as less important than having the "right information."

A classic example of using the media to fill the information gap is the Partnership for a Drug Free America. This program is based on the idea that "if only people really knew how bad and uncool drugs were, they wouldn't use them." Many of these ads are memorable, but their strong statements generally do not take a public health approach. Instead, they focus almost exclusively on individual behavior and personal responsibility. The partnership ads insist that "the drug problem is *your* problem, not the government's. The ads never question budget allocations or the administration's emphasis of [law] enforcement over treatment. . . . If there are mitigating reasons for drug use—poverty, family turmoil, self-medication, curiosity—you'd never know it from the Partnership ads" (Blow 1991, 31–32). The partnership ads laud volunteerism, self-discipline, and individualism (Miller 1988, 34), precisely the values that resonate with the American people. And the partnership strategies meet with little political resistance because they are consistent with a victim-blaming orientation toward public health (Ryan 1976).

The partnership campaigns, like virtually all public information efforts, assume that information is the magic bullet which inoculates people against drugs. Social conditions that form the context of the problem, such as alienation, poor housing, poor education, and lack of economic opportunity, are ignored. Because the context of the problem is part of the problem, any solution that does not take the context into account inevitably will be inadequate. In fact, the partnership's public service advertisements, despite their intent to improve the public's health, ultimately may do more harm than good by undermining support for more effective health promotion efforts that focus upstream on power relationships and social conditions. The ads occupy valuable media time with compelling messages that reinforce a downstream, victim-blaming approach.

Media advocacy emphasizes the power gap by highlighting alternative definitions of problems and policy level approaches to addressing the problem. In the tradition of sociologist C. Wright Mills (1959), media advocacy takes personal problems and translates them into social issues. A primary strategy of media advocacy is to work with individuals and groups to claim power from the media to change the context or environment in which the problem occurs.

The focus on policy addresses determinants of health which are external to the individual. These determinants include variables such as basic housing, employment, education, health care, and personal security and might be considered under the general rubric of social justice issues. A second set of determinants focus more closely on immediate marketing variables associated with health-compromising products such as alcohol, tobacco, high fat foods, and other dangerous products. These marketing variables include advertising and promotion, pricing, product development, and product availability. For example, alcohol activists are concerned about advertising and promotion of alcohol at events or in media which attract large youth audiences. In addition, the pricing of alcohol so that it is competitive with soft drinks coupled with its easy availability contributes to an environment that is conducive to problematic use of the product. Store owners who indiscriminately sell malt liquor to children or companies that develop new products such as wine coolers which target youth further contribute to the seductive environment. These are all potential focal points for media advocates.

The Practice of Media Advocacy

Media advocacy is the strategic use of mass media to advance a social or public policy initiative (U.S. Department of Health and Human Services 1989). It uses a range of media and advocacy strategies to define the problem and stimulate broad-based coverage. Media advocacy attempts to reframe and shape pubic discussion to increase support for and advance healthy public policies. Fundamental to media advocacy is knowing what policy goals you want to accomplish. Thus, the first step is to establish what your group's policy goal is—what do you want to happen? The second step is to decide who your target is—to whom do you want to speak? Does this person, group, or organization have the power to make the change you want to see happen? The third step is to frame your issue and construct your message. The fourth step is to construct an overall media advocacy plan for delivering your message and creating pressure for change. Finally, you want to evaluate how well you have done what you set out to do.

To illustrate the planning process, consider a coalition that is seeking to reduce deadly violence among youth. They decide on three local policy goals: limit handgun availability, limit alcohol availability, and, increase employment opportunities for youth. They decide their primary audience is the city council, with community opinion leaders as a secondary audience. The general message they decide to use is that violence is a public health issue, is predictable, and can be prevented. They frame their message to emphasize the social and economic aspects of violence among youth. They develop a media strategy to reach their audience with the message and to promote their policy initiatives. In their media strategy they consider methods for creating news, taking advantage of existing news opportunities (e.g., localizing a national story), and buying media time and space to speak directly to their audience. All through the process they institute feedback mechanisms to get a sense of how they are doing.

The process and success of media advocacy, however, are linked to how well the advocacy is rooted in the community. Local media outlets feel a legal and civic responsibility to their communities. They are concerned about what the community wants. The more support and participation at the local level for media initiatives, the more likely journalists will define the issue as relevant and newsworthy. As Tuchman (1978, 92) notes, "The more members, the more legitimate their spokesperson." Media advocacy, then, really combines the separate functions of mass communication with community advocacy.

Traditional public health communication strategies tend to see individuals and groups as part of an audience to be addressed in a one-way communication. At best if the "audience" is included in the planning, it is after major boundaries of the issue have been set. Media advocacy treats the individual or group as potential advocates who can use their energy, skills, and other resources to influence what issue is addressed and what solutions are put forth. While traditional campaigns seek to convince individuals to change their health habits, media advocacy initiatives create pressure to change the environment which, in large part, determines these habits.

The Functions of Media Advocacy

Mass media are like the beam of a searchlight that moves
restlessly about, bringing one episode and then another out
of darkness into vision.   WALTER LIPPMANN (1922)

The three functions of media advocacy can be thought of in terms of Lippmann's classic image of the mass media. First, media advocacy uses the media to place attention on an issue by bringing it to light. This is the process of agenda setting.

Substantial evidence suggests that the media agenda determines the public agenda: what's on people's minds reflects what is in the media (e.g., McCombs and Shaw 1972; Rogers and Dearing 1988; Dearing and Rogers 1992). Second, media advocacy holds the spotlight on the issue and focuses in on "upstream" causes. This is the process of framing. Recent research from the political science field suggests that the way that social issues are framed in the news media is associated with who or what is seen as primarily responsible for addressing the problem (Iyengar 1991). Third, media advocacy seeks to advance a social or public policy initiative(s) as a primary approach to the problem. Changes in the social environment through the development of healthy public polices are viewed as the means for improving public health.

SETTING THE AGENDA: FRAMING FOR ACCESS
A local news program in the San Francisco Bay Area used billboards and television commercials to tell people, "If it goes on here, it goes on [Channel] 4 at 10." The implication was that if you do not see it on the news, then an event has not happened. When AIDS was not covered by the *New York Times*, it did not make it on the nation's policy agenda either. If the press does not cover your demonstration to highlight a contradiction in health policy, it might as well as have not taken place as far as the broader community (and probably the person with the power to make the change you want) is concerned. Daniel Schorr, National Public Radio commentator and longtime journalist, says, "If you don't exist in the media, for all practical purposes, you don't exist." Gaining access to the media is the first step for media advocates who want to set the agenda.

Gaining access is important for two reasons. First, the public agenda setting process is linked to the level of media coverage and thus the broad visibility of an issue. The media alert people about what to think about, and the more coverage a topic receives in the media, the more likely it is to be a concern of the general public (Cohen 1963; Iyengar and Kinder 1987; McCombs and Shaw 1972; Rogers and Dearing 1988). Second, media are a vehicle for gaining access to specific opinion leaders. Politicians, government regulators, community leaders, and corporate executives are people you might want to reach specifically. In successful media advocacy both objectives will be met. For example, recent efforts to remove PowerMaster malt liquor from the market were able to get the problem out in the media, which helped to make it a public issue (Wallack et al. 1993). At the same time, specific politicians and government regulators at the Bureau of Alcohol, Tobacco, and Firearms were exposed to media reports which gave them a greater sensitivity to the issue and a greater expectancy that others around them would be aware of the issue. Journalists themselves put pressure on bureaucrats just by doing the story, apart from what might happen with public opinion after the story is broadcast. With tape rolling, officials had to answer for their actions. Consequently, advocates were able to muster enough public and regulatory pressure to prevent the product from staying on the market.

NEWSWORTHINESS. None of us is the president of the United States or an editor for the *New York Times*, so how can we get access to the media? Media advocates gain access by interpreting their issue in terms of newsworthiness. In a variety of ways, media advocates take advantage of how news is constructed and what its objectives are. Their issue will be covered only to the extent that it is timely, relevant, defined to be in the public's interest, and/or meets a number of other news criteria. Shoemaker with Mayfield (1987) presents an extensive list of factors that go into determining newsworthiness. Criteria for selecting news "include sensation, conflict, mystery, celebrity, deviance, tragedy, and proximity." To that list Dearing and Rogers (1992, 174) add "the 'breaking quality' of a news issue, how new information can be molded to recast old issues in a new way, and the degree to which new information can be fit into existing constructs." "Human interest," which focuses on people overcoming difficult odds; or helping others; or unusualness is also an important variable.

Very few social problems are new. Alcohol problems, teen pregnancy, drugs, and poverty have been around for a long time and are periodically rediscovered. Gaining access for a particular issue may depend on where it falls in a cyclic media attention span. Anthony Downs (1972) has identified a well ordered "issue-attention cycle" for many domestic problems. His first stage is the preproblem stage. At this stage the problem fully exists and can be quite bad, but it is yet to be discovered and seen as a problem by the broad public. The April 1992 civil unrest in Los Angeles brought to light basic problems of racism, poverty, and alienation that have long existed but were below the threshold of mainstream public attention. The uprising provided the basis for the second stage of the cycle: "alarmed discovery and euphoric enthusiasm" by the media and the mainstream public. Many thought that racism was no longer a problem in our society; the uprising brought home the fact that conditions remained, in fact, quite bad. Fundamental to the American character is a basic optimism that even the most intractable problems can be solved. Soon the media enthusiasm moved from the horrors of the violent disturbances to the "road to recovery," highlighting how volunteers from many different areas were pitching in to clean up the devastation. The media pictures and descriptions of people joining together to clean up reinforced the idea that through diverse people working together, the problem can be solved.

Downs's third stage involves a realization of the cost of making significant progress. Most important here is the awareness that change will require sacrifice and that better off groups may have to bear a burden to help those who are less well off. However, from this stage it is a short trip to a decline in public interest and pessimism about whether change can take place at all. Next is the postproblem stage, which is a kind of twilight where the problem continues to exist but gets little public or media attention. The trail in Los Angeles from Watts of 1965 to South Central of 1992 illustrates two complete cycles of the media attention process.

When the media spotlight fades, attention recedes, and often we return to prior arrangements and prior levels of concern. The shift of the media away from a problem is a curious form of both cause and effect of public perceptions. It is a cause of attention fading because without the media spotlight, issues will gradually fall out of public discussion and will lose a sense of legitimacy as a problem and urgency as a concern. It is an effect because the media will shift only after they sense that people are bored with the issue or that some new, more pressing problem has emerged. The media, after all, are in the business of attracting large audiences, and if they bore or threaten people because the solutions are complex or call for personal sacrifice, they will lose their audience and diminish their economic base (i.e., audience for advertisers).

SHAPING THE DEBATE: FRAMING FOR CONTENT

Gaining access to the media is an important first step, but it is only a first step in influencing the public and policy agenda. After access, the next barrier that media advocacy seeks to overcome is the definition of health issues in the media as primarily individual problems. As Henrik Blum (1980, 49), a well-known health planner, notes, "There is little doubt that how a society views major problems . . . will be critical in how it acts on the problems." If we alter the definition of problems, then the response also changes (Powles 1979; Watzlawick, Weakland, and Fisch 1974). Problem definition is a battle to determine which group and which perspective will gain primary "ownership" of the solution to the problem.

The tendency in the U.S. is to attempt to develop clear and concise definitions of problems to facilitate concrete, commonsense-type solutions. This is a very pragmatic approach with strong appeal. Oftentimes, however, problems of health and social well-being are difficult to define, much less solve, and increasing levels of problem complexity are highly correlated with rising degrees of disagreement in definition. Our tendency is to simplify the problem by breaking it down into basic elements which are easier to manage. In most cases this is either a biological unit and the solution is medical or an information unit where the solution is education.

This misguided pragmatism about problem-solving reduces society's drug problem, an enormously complex issue that involves every level of society, to an inability of the individual to "just say no" and resist the temptation to take drugs. Generally diseases are reduced to cognitive, behavioral, or genetic elements. Public and private institutions end up allocating significant resources to identifying the gene for alcoholism while leaving the activities of the alcoholic beverage industry largely unexamined. Even though 30 percent of all cancer deaths and 87 percent of lung cancer deaths are attributed to tobacco use, the main focus of cancer research is not on the behavior of the tobacco industry but on the biochemical and genetic interactions of cells.

The alternative is to see problems as part of a larger context. Tobacco use, for example, rather than being seen as a bad habit or a stupid thing to do, can be seen as a function of a corporate enterprise which actively promotes the use of a health-compromising product. Decisions at the individual level about whether to smoke could be seen as inextricably linked to decisions of a relatively few people at the corporate level regarding production, marketing, and widespread promotion. Smoking, in this larger context, is seen as a property of a larger system in which a smoker or potential smoker is one part, rather than simply as a property of individual decisions. The same could be applied to automobile safety, nutrition, alcohol, and other issues. This type of analysis takes the problem definition upstream. The key for media advocates is to frame their issue in terms of upstream problem definitions.

THE ENVIRONMENTAL PERSPECTIVE. In public health a new environmental perspective has evolved that directs attention to the role of policy and community-level factors in health promotion. This environmental perspective includes both a physical and a social element. For example, policies and practices that support product availability and marketing of alcohol and tobacco, both of which help cultivate positive social perceptions about these products, are primary targets for change. Thus, tobacco control advocates have shifted the focus from the behavior of the smoker to the behavior of the tobacco industry and to the policies that support advertising and general marketing activities contributing to excess mortality. Limiting billboard advertising, vending machines, and sponsorship of community activities while also promoting clean indoor air legislation are key targets of the tobacco control movement.

The focus on the immediate marketing and community-level environment is important but still fails to address the most significant variable regarding health status. An extensive body of literature clearly indicates that social class is the single most important determinant of health (Haan, Kaplan, and Syme 1989). Virtually every disease shows an association with measures of social class (Marmot, Koqevinas, and Elston 1987). This is not the result of a simple rich-poor dichotomy but a *graded* response that can be seen even in the upper quadrant of society (e.g., Haan, Kaplan, and Camacho 1987; Smith and Egger 1992; Kitagawa and Hauser 1973). Recent work suggests that the most important factor within the social class construction may be level of education (Winkleby et al. 1992). Also, in cross-cultural comparisons, it appears that a society's health status is not linked solely to per capita income, but to income variability and therefore the extent of relative deprivation and discrepancy within a society (Wilkinson 1992). The United States, for example, fares poorly on a number of key health indicators when compared to some countries that are less afflu-ent but also show less variability in income across social strata. Successful health promotion thus relies less on our ability to disseminate health information and more on our efforts to establish a fairer and more just society.

There are two important reasons for emphasizing the environment. First, as the history of public heath amply demonstrates, prevention that is population-based and focused on social conditions is more effective than efforts aimed primarily at treating individuals (e.g., McKinlay, McKinlay, and Beaglehole 1989; Dubos 1959; McKeown 1978). It is the policies that define the environment in which people make choices about health that appear to have the greatest potential to improve health. Second, public health research points to the importance of equality and social justice as the foundation for action. Environmentally ori-ented solutions try to address the underlying conditions that give rise to and sus-tain disease and thus promise long term change.

ADVANCING THE POLICY

The ultimate goal of media advocacy is to create changes in policies that improve health chances for communities. This requires clarity about the policy being advanced, appropriate framing of the issue and consistency in the messages about the policy, and the ability to capitalize on opportunities in the media to advance the policy. Mass media can be used to put pressure on policymakers and influentials, but the pressure is not automatic. The media coverage must be carefully crafted and reflect broad-based support. There are many examples of how this can work, and a series of ten brief case studies have been presented by Wallack and his colleagues (1993).

In many cases media access is relatively easy, but shaping the story and focusing it on policy goals can be quite difficult. Consider a typical, and tragic, example from a major city in California. Early in the evening, on her way home from work, a young woman was kidnapped on the way to her car from public trans-portation. Her abductors put her in the trunk of her own car, robbed, raped, and murdered her.

The tragedy received tremendous coverage on television and in the local papers. Community members were horrified, frightened, and desperate to do something about public safety. A local church held a candlelight vigil for the woman, and more than five hundred community members attended her funeral.

Several community-based organizations (CBOs) were involved in orga-nizing the vigil, which they anticipated would attract significant media atten-tion. It did. Nevertheless, members of the CBOs were frustrated with the type of coverage the woman's death and the vigil received. They blamed the reporters for focusing too much attention on the drama of the event rather than on the issues of importance for safety and well-being in the community.

Indeed, news reports that discussed safety emphasized what individuals should do to protect themselves. Articles quoted mass transit officials giving advice such as:

- Observe all posted parking regulations and park in designated areas.
- Before leaving, check your headlights, lock your car, and do not leave valuables or packages where they can be seen.
- Carry your keys in your hands.
- When at stations at night, be aware of your surroundings, and stand in the center of the platform. If you need help, call station police.
- If you do not feel safe walking to your parked car, go back to the station.

While all of this is good advice, it places almost total responsibility for safety on the rider. This is important. However, who is asking the question "What would it take to make the environment safe, regardless of what various individual passengers do?" The stories did not focus on environmental factors such as lighting in the station area, cutbacks in station security personnel, or the much larger issue of violence against women.

The responsibility for news coverage does not rest solely with journalists. While members of the CBOs were unsatisfied with the coverage, they also had not clearly articulated the solutions they desired in terms the media could easily use. Access, in this case, was abundant. The work, from the media advocacy perspective, needed to be done to frame for content in order to articulate the solution and move a policy forward.

One of the key goals of media advocacy is to advance a policy or approach to address the problem. Getting the media's attention and having stories air or appear in print are often the easy part of the job. The difficult part occurs when advocates have to put their issues and approaches in the media and in front of the people they want to reach.

The important work of media advocacy is really done in the planning stage before calling the media. Advocates need to know how they will advance their approach, what symbols to use, what issues to link it with, what voices to provide, and what messages to communicate. The issue can be reexplored in terms of media opportunities. Strategies can then be developed to frame for access and frame for content. Framing for access and framing for content force advocates to think in terms of the media and its needs.

In reality, most CBOs do not have the resources or training to use mass media effectively. In this example, the CBOs were in a reactive position. Community groups can anticipate similar situations and prepare their policy solutions and how they want them framed in media coverage. Articulating this vision is the hard work of media advocacy. Media advocacy can then effectively be used to help communities claim the power and confidence they need to better tell their story.

Conclusion

For advocates, the press is a grand piano waiting for a
player. Strike the chords through a news story, a guest
column, or an editorial and thousands will hear. Working in
concert, unbiased reporters and smart advocates can make
music together.   SUSAN WILSON, NEW JERSEY
                        NETWORK FOR FAMILY LIFE

Since the late 1980s media advocacy has become an increasingly popular approach to using mass media to promote public health goals. This approach seeks to enhance the visibility, legitimacy, and power of community groups. Media advocacy represents more than just a different way of using mass media to promote health. It is an effort to fundamentally shift power back to the community by cultivating skills that can enhance and amplify the community's voice. Instead of giving individuals a message about personal health behaviors, it gives groups the ability to broadly present approaches to healthy public policy. It is based on the premise that real improvements in health status will not come so much from increases in personal health knowledge as from improvements in social conditions. It is the power gap, rather than the knowledge gap, which is the primary focus of media advocacy.

Media advocacy reflects a public health approach that explicitly recognizes the importance of the social and political environment and defines health problems as matters of public policy, not just individual behavior. Media advocacy attempts to help individuals claim power by providing knowledge and skills to better enable them to participate in efforts to change the social and political factors that contribute to the health status of all. The health of the community, not necessarily the convenience of the individual, is the primary focus. Active participation in the political process is the mechanism for health promotion.

Social and health programs generally tend to focus on giving people skills to *beat the odds* to overcome the structural barriers to successful and healthy lives. In the long run it makes more sense to *change the odds* so that more people have a wider and more accessible range of healthy choices (Schorr 1988). Media advocacy helps to emphasize the importance of changing social conditions to improve the odds. Media advocacy can be instrumental in escaping a traditional, limited focus on disease conditions and instead promote a greater understanding of the conditions that will support and improve the public's health.

References

Blow, R. 1991. How to decode the hidden agenda of the partnership's Madison Avenue propagandists. *Washington City Paper* 11:29–35.

Blum, H. 1980. Social perspective risk reduction. *Family and Community Health* 3:41–61.

Cohen, B. 1963. *The press and foreign policy.* Princeton: Princeton University Press.

Dearing, J., and E. Rogers. 1992. AIDS and the media agenda. In *AIDS: A communication perspective,* ed. T. Edgar, M. A. Fitzpatrick, and V. S. Freimuth. Hillsdale, N.J.: Lawrence Erlbaum.

Downs, A. 1972. Up and down with ecology. *Public Interest* 28:38–50.

Dubos. R. 1959. *Mirage of health.* New York: Harper and Row.

Gerbner, G., M. Morgan, and N. Signorielli. 1981. Health and medicine on television. *New England Journal of Medicine* 305:901–904.

Haan, M., G. Kaplan, and T. Camacho. 1987. Poverty and health. *American Journal of Epidemiology* 125:989–998.

Haan, M., G. Kaplan, and S. L. Syme. 1989. Socioeconomic status and health: Old observations and new thoughts. In *Pathways to health: The role of social factors,* ed. J. P. Bunker, D. S. Gomby, and B. H. Kehrer. Menlo Park, Calif.: Henry J. Kaiser Family Foundation.

Iyengar, S. 1991. *Is anyone responsible? How television frames political issues.* Chicago: University of Chicago Press.

Iyengar, S., and D. R. Kinder. 1987. *News that matters.* Chicago: University of Chicago Press.

Kitagawa, E., and P. Hauser. 1973. *Differential mortality in the United States: A study in socio-economic epidemiology.* Cambridge, Mass.: Harvard University Press.

Lippmann, W. 1922. *Public opinion.* New York: Harcourt Brace.

Marmot, M., M. Koqevinas, and M. Elston. 1987. Social/economic status and disease. *Annual Review of Public Health* 8:111–135.

McCombs, M., and D. Shaw. 1972. The agenda-setting function of mass media. *Public Opinion Quarterly* 36:176–187.

McKeown, T. 1978. Determinants of health. *Human Nature* 1:60–67.

McKinlay, J. 1986. A Case for refocusing upstream: The political economy of illness. In *The sociology of health and illness,* ed. P. Conrad and R. Kern. New York: St. Martin's Press.

McKinlay, J., S. McKinlay, and R. Beaglehole. 1989. Trends in death and disease and the contributions of medical measures. In *Handbook of medical sociology,* ed. H. Freeman and S. Levine. Englewood Cliffs, N.J.: Prentice-Hall.

Miller, M. 1988. Death grip. *Propaganda Review* (Winter):34–35.

Mills, C. 1959. *The sociological imagination.* New York: Oxford University Press.

Powles, J. 1979. On the limitations of modern medicine. In *Ways of health: Holistic approaches to ancient and contemporary medicine,* ed. D. Sobel. New York: Harcourt Brace Jovanovich.

Rogers, E., and J. Dearing. 1988. Agenda-setting research: Where has it been, and where is it going? In *Communication yearbook,* ed. J. A. Anderson. Beverly Hills, Calif.: Sage.

Ryan, W. 1976. Blaming the Victim. New York: Vintage Books.

Schorr, L. 1988. *Within our reach: Breaking the cycle of disadvantage.* Garden City, N.Y.: Anchor Press.

Shoemaker, P., and E. Mayfield. 1987. Building a theory of news content: A synthesis of current approaches. *Journalism Monographs* 103:1–36.

Smith, D., and M. Egger. 1992. Socioeconomic differences in mortality in Britain and the United States. *American Journal of Public Health* 82:1079–1081.

Tuchman, G. 1978. *Making news: A study in the construction of reality.* New York: Free Press.

Turow, J. 1989. *Playing doctor: Television, storytelling, and medical power*. New York: Oxford University Press.

Turow, J., and L. Coe. 1985. Curing television's ills: The portrayal of health care. *Journal of Communication* 34:36–51.

U.S. Department of Health and Human Services. 1989. *Media strategies for smoking control: Guidelines*. Washington, D.C.: Department of Health and Human Services.

Wallack, L. 1990. Mass communication and health promotion: A critical perspective. In *Public communication campaigns*, ed. R. Rice and C. Atkin. Newbury Park, Calif.: Sage.

Wallack, L., and L. Dorfman. 1992. Television news, hegemony, and health. *American Journal of Public Health* 82:125.

Wallack, L., L. Dorfman, D. Jernigan, and M. Themba. 1993. *Media advocacy and public health: Power for prevention*. Newbury Park, Calif.: Sage.

Watzlawick, P., J. Weakland, and R. Fisch. 1974. *Change: Principles of problem formation and problem resolution*. New York: Norton.

Wilkinson, R. 1992. National mortality rates: The impact of inequality? *American Journal of Public Health* 82:1082–1084.

Winkleby, M., D. Jatulis, E. Frank, and S. Fortmann. 1992. Socioeconomic status and health: How education, income, and occupation contribute to risk factors for cardiovascular disease. *American Journal of Public Health* 82:816–820.

Action-oriented Community Diagnosis Procedure

Appendix 1

EUGENIA ENG
LYNN BLANCHARD

Editor's note: the tool in this appendix was developed by Eugenia Eng and Lynn Blanchard over a period of several years. Its emphasis on assessing and contributing to community competence, rather than merely identifying needs, amply illustrates the perspective on community assessment described in chapter 9. Additionally, the broad range of assessment techniques incorporated in this procedure underscore the utility of triangulation, or the use of multiple methods, to provide the richest possible data base for analysis.

Action-oriented Community Diagnosis Procedure

I. Specify the target population and determine its component parts using social and demographic characteristics that may identify commonalities among groups of people.

   A. Race or ethnicity

   B. Religion

   C. Income level

   D. Occupation

   E. Age

Reprinted from "Action-oriented Community Diagnosis: A Health Education Tool," *International Quarterly of Community Health Education* 11 (2) (1990–91):96–97. Copyright © 1991 by the Baywood Publishing Company, Inc., Amityville, N.Y. All rights reserved.

II. Review secondary data sources, and identify possible subpopulations of
interest and geographic locations.
   A. County and townships
   B. Church, school, and fire districts
   C. Towns
   D. Agency service delivery areas
   E. Industries and other major employers
   F. Transportation arteries and services
   G. Health and other vital statistics

III. Conduct windshield tours of targeted areas, and note daily living
conditions, resources, and evidence of problems.
   A. Housing types and conditions
   B. Recreational and commercial facilities
   C. Private and public sector services
   D. Social and civic activities
   E. Identifiable neighborhoods or residential clusters
   F. Conditions of roads and distances people must travel
   G. Maintenance of buildings, grounds, and yards

IV. Contact and interview local agency providers serving targeted areas.
   A. What are the communities most in need, and why?
   B. Which communities have histories of meeting their own needs, and
      how?
   C. What services are being provided by agencies or other organized
      groups? Which are utilized, and which are underutilized?
   D. What, in their opinion, are the major problems still facing
      communities they serve?
   E. Where do they recommend finding additional information to
      document needs?
      — Referrals to other service providers
      — Rreferrals to leaders of community organizations
      — Referrals to informed members of communities

V. Select a community, and contact and interview community informants most frequently cited in provider interviews.

    A. What is the name their community is most commonly known as?

    B. Describe a time when there was a problem in their community that they tried to resolve.
   — How was the need determined?
   — How did the community organize themselves?
   — Who were the influential people involved?

    C. In their opinion, what are the present needs in their community?

    D. Who would have to be involved to get things done in their community?

    E. What outside services or resources do people in their community know and use to meet their needs?

    F. What other people like themselves who know about their community do they recommend being contacted?

    G. Would they be interested in attending a meeting to find out the results from these interviews? And what do they suggest as times and places to hold such a meeting?

VI. Tabulate the results from the secondary data, the provider interviews, and the community informant interviews, and analyze the degree of convergence among the needs identified.

    A. Determine the extent of agreement/disagreement across the three lists of needs on how each identified need is defined.

    B. Determine the extent of agreement/disagreement across the three lists of needs on the priority accorded to each identified need.

VII. Present the findings in meetings with community informants interviewed and other influential community members frequently cited by the providers and community informants.

    A. Assess the validity of the definitions for each need, and redefine them, if necessary, according to how they are manifested in this community.

    B. Determine a priority listing of needs according to interest in undertaking a solution.

C. Select a need with high priority, and determine questions that need to be answered, such as:
— Who suffers from this problem?
— When is this problem most prevalent?
— How severe are the short- and long-term consequences from this problem?
— What are the possible causes of this problem?
— What is the range of solutions for reducing or controlling this problem?
— What are the available resources and additional resources required for each possible solution?

D. Plan the next steps for finding answers to the questions.

Appendix 2   An Associational Map

JOHN L. McKNIGHT

Artistic organizations:	choral, theatrical, writing
Business organizations:	chamber of commerce, neighborhood business associations, trade groups
Charitable groups and drives:	Red Cross, Cancer Society, United Way
Church groups:	service, prayer, maintenance, stewardship, acolytes', men's, women's, youth, seniors'
Civic events:	July 4th, art fair, Halloween
Collectors' groups:	stamp collectors, flower dryers, antiques
Community support groups:	"friends" of the library, nursing home, hospital
Elderly groups:	senior citizens
Ethnic associations:	Sons of Norway, Black Heritage Club, Hibernians
Health and fitness groups:	bicycling, jogging, exercise
Interest clubs:	poodle owners, antique car owners
Local government:	town, township, electoral units, fire department, emergency units

Reprinted from *Mapping Community Capacity* (Evanston, Ill.: Center for Urban Affairs and Policy Research, Northwestern University, 1988), by permission of the author.

Local media:	radio, newspaper, local access cable TV
Men's groups:	cultural, political, social, educational, vocational
Mutual support (self-help) groups:	Alcoholics Anonymous, Epilepsy Self-Help, La Leche League
Neighborhood and block clubs:	crime watch, beautification, Christmas decorations
Outdoor groups:	garden clubs, Audubon Society, conservation clubs
Political organizations:	Democrats, Republicans, caucuses
School groups:	printing club, PTA, child care
Service clubs:	Zonta, Kiwanis, Rotary, American Association of University Women
Social cause groups:	peace, rights, advocacy, service
Sports leagues:	bowling, swimming, baseball, fishing, volleyball
Study groups:	literary clubs, bible study groups
Veteran groups:	American Legion, Amvets, Veterans of Foreign Wars, their auxiliaries
Women's groups:	cultural, political, social, educational, vocational
Youth groups:	4H, Future Farmers, Scouts, YWCA

Appendix 3   Coalition Checklist

CHERIE R. BROWN

Getting Started

1. Has at least one of these catalysts generated interest in forming a coalition:

a significantly committed individual	☐ yes	☐ no
a disturbing or dramatic event	☐ yes	☐ no
detailed, timely information about the issue	☐ yes	☐ no

2. Is there enough time to decisively affect policies related to the issue chosen by the coalition?   ☐ yes   ☐ no

3. Will a coalition help potential members achieve goals they cannot achieve alone?   ☐ yes   ☐ no

4. Is each potential member adequately organized?   ☐ yes   ☐ no

5. Are there adequate leadership links between potential coalition members?   ☐ yes   ☐ no

6. Is there adequate funding?   ☐ yes   ☐ no

Reprinted from *The Art of Coalition Building: A Guide for Community Leaders* (New York: American Jewish Center, 1984), by permission of the author.

Building a Constituency

1. Has a list been made up of who is affected by the issue? ❏ yes ❏ no

2. Has it been determined which groups have already
    done work on the issue? ❏ yes ❏ no

3. Is it known which groups will benefit from action on
    the issue? ❏ yes ❏ no

4. Is there an outline of separate strategies to attract
    each group to join the coalition? ❏ yes ❏ no

5. Does each group that is considering joining the
    coalition have an acceptable image in the community? ❏ yes ❏ no

6. Is there an outline of resources (e.g., staff time, money,
    publicity) expected from each member organization? ❏ yes ❏ no

7. Do the bylaws of each member group permit
    participation in the work of the coalition? ❏ yes ❏ no

8. Does the person representing each organization have
    the power to act on behalf of that organization? ❏ yes ❏ no

9. Will certain organizations need incentives (e.g., veto
    rights) to join the coalition? ❏ yes ❏ no

10. Has it been determined who agrees with the issue,
    who disagrees, and who might agree if more
    information were provided? ❏ yes ❏ no

Joining a Coalition: What Groups Should Consider

1. Will the member organization gain visibility? ❏ yes ❏ no

2. Will membership potential be increased? ❏ yes ❏ no

3. Will links be created with other important organizations? ❏ yes ❏ no

4. Does the potential member have the resources to contribute:

staff time	☐ yes	☐ no
money	☐ yes	☐ no
office space	☐ yes	☐ no
new allies	☐ yes	☐ no
research capabilities	☐ yes	☐ no
a better reputation in the community	☐ yes	☐ no
media and press coverage	☐ yes	☐ no
a broader constituency	☐ yes	☐ no

5. Do the individual member's decisionmaking processes fit in with the coalition's decisionmaking structure?   ☐ yes   ☐ no

6. Are the member organization's ideological principles compatible with those of the coalition?   ☐ yes   ☐ no

Mapping Out Coalition Strategy

1. Are invitations to join the coalition being extended to concerned organizations early enough for them to contribute to the formulation of strategy?   ☐ yes   ☐ no

2. Is the issue broad enough to include the larger human needs of all the member groups?   ☐ yes   ☐ no

3. Have inflammatory rhetoric and moral posturing been excluded from the coalition's statements and slogans?   ☐ yes   ☐ no

4. Have the positions of groups that may be reluctant to join the coalition been carefully checked to see if differences of opinion can be bridged?   ☐ yes   ☐ no

5. Is there an arrangement for groups that might come to the coalition with other urgent issues to find a forum for those issues?   ☐ yes   ☐ no

6. Is there an agreement to focus on the key issue around which the coalition was formed and to refrain from adding other issues that may be important to other member groups?   ☐ yes   ☐ no

7. Have controversial positions on which there is no
consensus been put into nonbinding statements rather
than trying to force an agreement?   ❏ yes   ❏ no

8. Has a special evening been arranged at which each
member organization can present its agenda and
attract new support in the community?   ❏ yes   ❏ no

Determining Coalition Goals

1. Have the following been determined:
   the ideal situation   ❏ yes   ❏ no
   the present reality   ❏ yes   ❏ no
   the differences between the ideal and the reality   ❏ yes   ❏ no

2. Have the following kinds of changes been considered?
   changes in consciousness   ❏ yes   ❏ no
   changes in policy   ❏ yes   ❏ no

Building Internal Commitment

1. Have special resources been developed for member
groups within the coalition?   ❏ yes   ❏ no

2. Have special parties, cultural events, or celebrations
been planned to help member groups feel more included? ❏ yes   ❏ no

Coalition Leadership

1. Has each person been approached by the leader in order
to build a one-to-one relationship?   ❏ yes   ❏ no

2. Has personal support been built for the leader by:
   encouraging personal responsibility   ❏ yes   ❏ no
   arranging time for self-estimation   ❏ yes   ❏ no
   arranging time for appreciations   ❏ yes   ❏ no

3. Is the leader able to elicit every member's thinking, to
consult widely among members, and then to draw the
the thinking into a concrete program?   ❏ yes   ❏ no

4. Does the leader acknowledge and correct mistakes?   ❏ yes   ❏ no

5. Can the leader help the coalition move forward after defeats and, in times of discouragement, recognize the success it has achieved?   ❏ yes   ❏ no

6. Have one or more replacements been selected for leadership training?   ❏ yes   ❏ no

7. Does the leader understand the reasons behind attacks and effectively respond to criticism?   ❏ yes   ❏ no

8. Is the leader willing to disband the coalition when it has outlived its usefulness?   ❏ yes   ❏ no

The Coalition's Internal Functions

1. Is it clear which member organizations will contribute staff or, if none, where the staff will come from?   ❏ yes   ❏ no

2. Is there an explicit agreement about the role of staff in coalition decisions?   ❏ yes   ❏ no

Decisionmaking

1. Has the coalition decided who will speak for it in public?   ❏ yes   ❏ no

2. Have any of these procedures been agreed upon for making coaltion decisions:

consensus	❏ yes	❏ no
democratic voting	❏ yes	❏ no
working consensus	❏ yes	❏ no
organizational vetoes	❏ yes	❏ no
weighted decisions	❏ yes	❏ no
other	❏ yes	❏ no

Fund-raising

1. Does the coalition have a procedure that avoids competition for funding among member organizations?   ❏ yes   ❏ no

Maintaining Commitment

1. Does the coalition leadership allow multiple levels of organization on the part of member organizations? ☐ yes ☐ no

2. Does the coalition develop resources (e.g., newspapers, position papers, etc.) to nurture coalition members? ☐ yes ☐ no

3. Have parties, cultural sharing, and coalition celebrations been planned to increase member participation? ☐ yes ☐ no

Managing Negotiations

1. Has the coalition assessed its bargaining power in dealing with a negotiating partner and made plans to increase it? ☐ yes ☐ no

2. Has the coalition determined its bottom line in negotiation? ☐ yes ☐ no

3. Has the negotiation team thoroughly studied the interests, goals, and positions of the other parties? ☐ yes ☐ no

4. Have roles been assigned to each person who will participate in the negotiation? ☐ yes ☐ no

5. Are the negotiating partners proceeding through each of the six stages of negotiations: rhetoric, issue definition, exploring positions, explorinig underlying interests, developing parameters for a settlement, and formalizing an agreement? ☐ yes ☐ no

6. Has the negotiating team taken into account cultural differences between itself and the other negotiating team(s)? ☐ yes ☐ no

7. Have the negotiating partners identified overlapping objectives? ☐ yes ☐ no

8. Has each side attempted to understand how the other perceives it? ☐ yes ☐ no

9. Have the issues that can be resolved the most easily
   been dealt with first? ☐ yes ☐ no

10. Has someone been chosen to take on the role of
    mediator? ☐ yes ☐ no

11. Has each side taken care to adopt a problem-solving
    attitude in the negotiation? ☐ yes ☐ no

Bridging Culture, Ethnicity, and Class Issues

1. Have ways been developed to reach out to diverse kinds
   of groups through
   symbols ☐ yes ☐ no
   quotations ☐ yes ☐ no
   religious teachings and rituals ☐ yes ☐ no

2. Is the coalition sensitive to the needs of religious groups
   when it establishes meeting times and locations and
   provides food? ☐ yes ☐ no

3. Are opportunities for cultural sharing built into the
   coalition's ongoing activities? ☐ yes ☐ no

4. Have members of the coalition been offered training in
   dealing with stereotypes and intergroup tensions? ☐ yes ☐ no

5. Have group caucuses been used to facilitate intergroup
   negotiations and otherwise improve meetings? ☐ yes ☐ no

Appendix 4

TOM WOLFF

Money and Coalitions

Delights and Dilemmas

Most discussions of funding and coalitions deal solely with the issue of how to find funding to sustain coalition groups. We would like to start with an earlier premise and ask the question "Is funding really needed for coalition development?" It is interesting to compare coalitions that were started by grassroots groups with no money versus coalitions that were gathered specifically around a funding source. In those coalitions that developed around a grassroots community issue, whether it is substance abuse, violence, or teen pregnancy, we see genuine community interest at the outset. Often, they have little or no money. When we contrast that with those coalitions that were started with the potential lure of dollars, we do not necessarily see a great level of community involvement. There is no question that some community coalitions have been highly successful with virtually no funding. We have also seen very-well-funded coalitions (one might suggest, over-funded) fail. The keys to success remain the core principles of coalition success, such as clear mission, organizational competence, time, and persistence. This raises fundamental questions about whether funding is always required for coalitions—and if so, how much and what that funding is used for and what are the kinds of problems, dilemmas, strengths, and resources that are created by funding?

In our experience, we have seen the full spectrum—coalitions that had virtually no money, those that had a moderate amount of resources to sustain the coalition efforts, or those with large amounts of resources to both sustain coalition efforts and develop community programming—be both successful and unsuccessful. Funding in and of itself did not guarantee success or failure, but

Reprinted from an unpublished AHEC/Community Partners tip sheet (Amherst, Mass., January 1994), by permission of the author.

the degree of funding and the way in which decisions about funding are made created very different sorts of organizations.

How Much Funding

Coalitions often need a certain amount of funding just to sustain their core, basic efforts of coordination, collaboration, and information exchange. The "basics" include money for mailings, agendas, rental of meeting space, and enough money for an annual meeting. The next increase of funding for coalitions often pays for part-time or full-time secretarial support to do the clerical work that goes along with coalitions: mailings, minutes, newsletters, etc. Many coalitions also see the need for more skilled staff to assist with coalition planning, direction, leadership, facilitation, or mediation. After funding for the basics, and potential funding for staff, the next thing that coalition funding often goes to is specific programming. The programs developed—substance abuse prevention, teen pregnancy, tobacco cessation etc.—are often determined by the availability of a particular funding source. Our experience suggests that when funding is obtained for coalitions, it is best first spent on basics, then staffing, and finally programming.

Funding for What

An important distinction should be made between coalition funding that goes to sustaining the process, the development, and the maintenance of the collaborative coalition process itself and coalition funding that goes into the development of programming. Once a coalition gets into the business of delivering programming itself, or subcontracting out dollars for programming in other agencies, it runs the risk of moving from a collaborative organization whose sole function is to promote coordination and collaboration, to becoming another community agency. This can create a conflict where the coalition is in competition with its own members. Also risky is subcontracting program dollars to other agencies by coalitions. When a coalition does this, it needs to engage in a process of awarding and then monitoring the contracts. Subsequently, the coalition as a contracting body also becomes a monitor of its own members, which creates an inordinately complex set of roles. In our experience, one set of functions often interferes with the other: it is hard to be a collaborative partner with an agency if you are also monitoring a subcontract and potentially telling them that they are not doing a good job!

Issues Created by Coalition Funding

MONEY AS MOTIVATOR

When coalitions are gathered together around the lure of external funding sources, one can never be sure that the partners at the table are not there just for the dollars. This leads to great ambiguity in the start-up of these coalitions. The best one can hope for is an open discussion of what brings people to the coalition table.

LEAD AGENCY

When a coalition gets involved with significant funds, it sometimes finds a lead agency to handle these dollars, rather than just a fiscal conduit or financial manager. The lead agency may then take on roles, responsibilities, and power that place it on an unequal basis with other coalition members. Since one of the core premises of coalitions is that all members come to the table with equal power, this can create difficulties.

DECISIONMAKING

If a coalition does have resources beyond the core functions of process and staff, questions arise about how resources get spent and who decides upon those directions and specific allocations. These money issues can highlight how democratic the overall decisionmaking process is or expose its authoritarian tendencies.

Money and Membership

If one of the major sources, or even one of the sustaining sources, of a coalition is participant fees, the money may limit membership in the coalition. We propose a membership process that has no fees attached. There should be a coalition sponsorship process that allows people to contribute on an annual basis, generally based on the size of their organization. This distinction between membership and sponsorship is helpful in making sure that dollars do not become a criteria for joining a coalition.

How Money Can Help a Coalition

In spite of the above warnings, money can help a coalition. Core funding for staffing and maintaining the process and development of the coalition is critical for the success of most coalitions. It is our belief that, although unstaffed coalitions can be successful to some degree, the capacity of coalitions to take on multiple issues over a long period of time and have a significant impact can be increased with paid, facilitative coalition staff. Thus, finding the resources to fund such staff is enormously helpful. Even a half-time staff person and secretarial support can be enough to move a coalition forward in a rapid fashion.

Where to Find the Dollars

This, of course, is the million-dollar question. The experiences of numerous coalitions across the country indicate that there are a variety of sources. Most larger coalitions have been developed around an initiative from state, federal, or private sources soliciting coalition responses to issues such as violence prevention, teen pregnancy prevention, tobacco cessation. Other sources of coalition funding include (a) sponsorship fees from members, (b) community foundations, (c) larger foundations and corporate giving programs, (d) local cities and towns—especially through Community Development Block Grants and Small Cities Grants.

In sum, money can be a key force in moving coalitions forward or can be a major barrier to coalition success. The basic instinct to seek large amounts of dollars for coalitions should be tempered by a planning process that asks, How much funding do we need? For what coalition functions? Who will decide how it is spent? Can we anticipate the benefits and problems that funding might bring? It is only after coalitions have successfully answered these question that the search for funding should begin.

How to Build Effective Multicultural Coalitions/Inclusivity Checklist

Appendix 5

BETH ROSENTHAL

CULTURAL DIFFERENCES can either enrich or impede coalition functioning. Creating multicultural coalitions challenges us to deal with differences and use them to strengthen our common work. Awareness of sensitive issues and dynamic can help you to detect potential obstacles and develop approaches to address them— either before problems arise or after they occur.

Building effective multicultural coalitions involves:

- Articulating a vision

- Conducting strategic outreach and membership development

- Setting ground rules that maintain a safe and nurturing atmosphere

- Establishing a structure and operating procedures that reinforce equity

- Practicing new modes of communication

- Creating leadership opportunities for everyone, especially people of color and women

- Engaging in activities that are culturally sensitive or that directly fight oppression

Reprinted from *From the Ground Up: A Workbook on Coalition Building and Community Development*, ed. Tom Wolff and Gillian Kaye (Amherst, Mass.: AHEC/Community Partners, 1995), 54–55, 69, by permission of the editors.

Inclusivity Checklist

Instructions:
Use this Inclusivity Checklist to measure how prepared your coalition is for multicultural work and to identify areas for improvement. Place a check mark in the box next to each statement that applies to your group. If you cannot put a check in the box, this may indicate an area for change.

☐ The leadership of our coalition is multiracial and multicultural.

☐ We make special efforts to cultivate new leaders, particularly women and people of color.

☐ Our mission, operations, and products reflect the contributions of diverse cultural and social groups.

☐ We are committed to fighting social oppression within the coalition and in our work with the community.

☐ Members of diverse cultural and social groups are full participants in all aspects of our coalition's work.

☐ Meetings are not dominated by speakers from any one group.

☐ All segments of our community are represented in decisionmaking.

☐ There are sensitivity and awareness regarding different religious and cultural holidays, customs, recreational and food preferences.

☐ We communicate clearly, and people of different cultures feel comfortable sharing their opinions and participating in meetings.

☐ We prohibit the use of stereotypes and prejudicial comments.

☐ Ethnic, racial, and sexual slurs or jokes are not welcome.

Appendix 6

The Six "R's" of
Participation

GILLIAN KAYE

THESE REASONS explain why people participate in all kinds of groups, organizations, or associations. It has been observed that we are a nation of joiners. Our neighborhood coalitions can be successful when we design organizations that seek to meet the needs of all of our members.

Recognition

People want to be recognized for their leadership to serve the members of their communities and organizations. We all want to be recognized, initially by the members of our own group and then by members of other groups, for our personal contribution to efforts to build a better quality of life.

TIP: Recognition can be given through awards and dinners, highlighting contributions and praising and naming at public events.

Respect

Everyone wants respect. By joining in community activities, we seek the respect of our peers. People often find their values, culture, or traditions are not respected in the workplace or community. People seek recognition and respect for themselves and their values by joining community organizations and coalitions.

TIPS: Don't schedule all of your planning meetings during regular working hours—this may exclude many grassroots leaders who hold other jobs. Meet in the evenings and provide dinner and child care, or at least meet late enough so that those attending can take the time to provide dinner and child care for their families.

Reprinted from *From the Ground Up: A Workbook on Coalition Building and Community Development*, ed. Tom Wolff and Gillian Kaye (Amherst, Mass.: AHEC/Community Partners, 1995), 100–102, by permission of the editors.

Translate materials and meeting agendas into languages other than English if it's necessary, and provide translators at meetings.

Role

We all need to feel needed. It is a cliché, but it's true. We want to belong to a group which gives us a prominent role and where our unique contribution can be appreciated. Not everyone searches for the same role. But groups must find a role for everyone if they expect to maintain a membership.

TIP: Grassroots leaders and members have had the experience of being "tokens" on coalitions. Create roles with real power and substance.

Relationship

Organizations are organized networks of relationships. It is often a personal invitation which convinces us to join an organization. People join organizations for personal reasons to make new friends and for the public reason to broaden a base of support and/or influence. Organizations draw us into a wider context of community relationships, which encourage accountability, mutual support, and responsibility.

TIP: Provide real opportunities for networking with other institutions and leaders.

Reward

Organizations and coalitions attract new members and maintain old members when the rewards of membership outweigh the costs. Of course, not everyone is looking for the same kind of rewards. Identify the public and private rewards which respond to the self-interests of members in order to sustain their role in the coalition.

TIP: Schedule social time and interaction into the agenda of the coalition where families can participate. Make sure there is an ongoing way to share resources and information, including funding opportunities and access to people in power.

Results

Nothing works like results! An organization which cannot "deliver the goods" will not continue to attract people and resources.

TIP: To many grassroots leaders and residents, visible projects and activities that directly impact on conditions and issues in their communities are the results they are looking for in return for their participation.

Appendix 7   Lessons from Geese

ANGELES ARRIEN

FACT 1
As each goose flaps its wings, it creates an "uplift" for the birds that follow. By flying in a "V" formation, the whole flock adds 71 percent greater flying range than if each bird flew alone.

LESSON
People who share a common direction and sense of community can get where they are going quicker and easier because they are traveling on the thrust of one another.

FACT 2
When a goose falls out of formation, it suddenly feels the drag and resistance of flying alone. It quickly moves back into formation to take advantage of the lifting power of the bird immediately in front of it.

LESSON
If we have as much sense as a goose, we stay in formation with those headed where we want to go. We are willing to accept their help and give our help to others.

Transcribed from a speech given at the 1991 Organizational Development Workshop and based on the work of Milton Olson.

FACT 3

When the lead goose tires, it rotates back into the formation, and another goose flies to the point position.

LESSON

It pays to take turns doing the hard tasks and sharing leadership. As with geese, people are interdependent on others' skills, capabilities, and unique arrangements of gifts, talents, or resources.

FACT 4

The geese flying in formation honk to encourage those up front to keep up their speed.

LESSON

We need to make sure our honking is encouraging. In groups where there is encouragement, the production is much greater. The power of encouragement (to stand by one's own heart or core values and encourage the heart and core of others) is the quality of honking we seek.

FACT 5

When a goose gets sick, wounded, or shot down, two geese drop out of formation and follow it down to help and protect it. They stay with it until it dies or is able to fly again. Then they launch out with another formation or catch up with the flock.

LESSON

If we have as much sense as geese, we will stand by each other in difficult times as well as when we are strong.

Appendix 8   Leadership Teams

MIKE MILLER

IF A MEETING is to proceed according to an agenda, complete the business before it, clarify and resolve issues that require decision, provide an opportunity for sociability, and help build an organization, it must be planned. If the meeting is only planned by the organizer, it will be the organizer's meeting. If the meeting is planned only by the chair with the assistance of the organizer, it will be the chair's meeting. If the meeting is planned by the chair and an active group with the assistance of the organizer, it will be the meeting of this group of planners. The broader the base of participation in the planning of the meeting, the more the meeting will really be "owned" by the people.

Planning Role

The people who plan the meeting are the leadership team for a meeting. If they are the people who have or are developing a following among the people coming to the meeting, their planning will anticipate and take into account the interests and aspirations of the people coming to the meeting. They will make sure there is time for everyone to get his/her "oar" in the waters, to place his/her interest before the group. They will make sure the meeting has a focus. They will make sure that the meeting has some plan for dealing with potential disagreements. Having done all this, and having reviewed a proposed agenda with meeting participants, the leadership team has done its premeeting job.

Reprinted from an unpublished training packet for the Organize Training Center, by permission of the author.

Meeting Role

During the meeting itself, the leadership team acts as a "floor team" to keep the meeting moving according to the prepared agenda. In this capacity, the leadership team might engage in various activities:

- Say something to support the chair.
- Make a motion to close debate.
- Say something that seeks to bring together people who are saying conflicting things.
- Ask the chair to keep a meeting on the agenda if the chair is losing control (because of a disruptive personality or general ineffectiveness).
- Add some humor in a meeting if things are getting tense.

The Organizer Vis-à-vis Leadership Teams

The organizer's role in relation to a leadership team is one of facilitator. During the meeting planning, s/he helps the team to build a logical, complete agenda that will lay the foundation for fulfilling all the meeting objectives and to organize preparatory assignments for the meeting.

During a meeting, the organizer "works" the flow of the meeting through the leadership team. The less the organizer says in a meeting, the better. If the organizer doesn't say anything in the meeting as a whole, it is generally because s/he has done an excellent job in planning it. If s/he observes something going astray in the meeting (for example, the chair is losing control of the meeting), the organizer might ask a member of the leadership team whether s/he thinks that the chair needs some help. Similarly, the organizer can work the floor or other problems of the meeting.

Scale for Measuring Perceptions of Individual, Organizational, and Community Control

BARBARA ISRAEL
BARRY CHECKOWAY
AMY SCHULZ
MARC ZIMMERMAN

Authors' note: the scale herein was developed by my colleagues and me at the University of Michigan and was tested with respondents from Detroit, Michigan, who were primarily of African-American or European-American descent. The scale was created to assess individual perceptions of control or influence at three levels of analysis—individual, organizational, and community. In accordance with our conceptualization of empowerment across all three levels, the intent of the items at the organizational and community levels was to assess both perceptions of individual influence within an organizational and community context and the perceived influence of the organization and community within a broader sphere. Questions measuring perceived control at the organizational level were asked regarding the organization that respondents identified as being most important to them.

The scale provides a partial measure of empowerment, examining individual perceptions of control or influence at multiple levels. However, it does not measure the development of conscientization, or critical consciousness (see chapters 3 and 12), nor does it assess the broader social, political, economic, and cultural context that affects empowerment. The scale is further limited in that it does not measure actual control or obtain a collective assessment, at the organizational and community level, of perceived or actual control. For these reasons, we strongly suggest that this survey instrument be used together with such qualitative approaches as focus groups, community observations, and in-depth semistructured interviews. Finally, concepts of community, control, and empowerment may differ across

Reprinted from "Health Education and Community Empowerment: Conceptualizing and Measuring Perceptions of Individual, Organizational, and Community Control," *Health Education Quarterly* 21 (2) (1994):149–170, by permission of Sage Publications, Inc. Copyright © 1994 by Sage Publications, Inc.

cultures and regions, and these differences should be taken into account when the scale is adapted to other areas or population groups.

Despite these limitations, the perceived control indices presented here have considerable potential use for health educators and other social change professionals engaged in empowerment interventions. (See Israel et al. 1994 for a more detailed look at the instrument's conceptual grounding and development, its strengths and limitations, and its applications in the field.)

Perceived Control Scale Items: Multiple Levels of Empowerment Indices

For the first five items, the interviewer asked the participants to "please answer the following questions thinking about the organization that you identified as most important to you. Do you agree strongly, agree somewhat, disagree somewhat, or disagree strongly?"

1. I can influence the decisions that this organization makes.
2. This organization has influence over decisions that affect my life.
3. This organization is effective in achieving its goals.
4. This organization can influence decisions that affect the community.
5. I am satisfied with the amount of influence I have over decisions that this organization makes.

The interviewer then commented that "I have been asking about your participation in specific organizations. I am also interested in how much influence you think you have in your life and in your community. I am going to read you a list of statements. For each one, please tell me how strongly you agree or disagree."

6. I have control over the decisions that affect my life.
7. My community has influence over decisions that affect my life.
8. I am satisfied with the amount of control I have over decisions that affect my life.
9. I can influence decisions that affect my community.
10. By working together, people in my community can influence decisions that affect the community.
11. People in my community work together to influence decisions on the state or national level.
12. I am satisfied with the amount of influence I have over decisions that affect my community.

INDICES

Perceived control at the individual level includes items 6 and 8 above (alpha = .66).

Perceived control at the organizational level includes items 1 through 5 above (alpha = .61).

Perceived control at the community level includes items 7, 9, 10, 11, and 12 above (alpha = .63).

Perceived control at multiple levels includes all 12 items above (alpha = .71).

References

Israel, B. A., B. Checkoway, A. Schulz, and M. Zimmerman. 1994. Health education and community empowerment: Conceptualizing and measuring perceptions of inidividual, organizational, and community control. *Health Education Quarterly* 21 (2):149–170.

Appendix 10

Ten Principles for Effective Advocacy Campaigns

HERBERT CHAO GUNTHER

1. Communicate values. Effective advocacy communication is predicated upon the strong, clear assertion of basic values, moral authority, and leadership.
2. American political discourse is fundamentally oppositional. People are more comfortable being against something than for something.
3. Most issues are decided by winning over the undecided. Typically, the percentage on one side of an issue is offset by a roughly equivalent percentage on the other side. It is the undecided or conflicted percentage left in the middle that determines the outcome.
4. More than anything else, Americans want to be on the winning side. The dominant factor influencing the undecided to choose one side or another is the perception that they're joining the winning side. So for advocacy campaigns, acting like a winner—projecting confidence, asserting the moral high ground, aggressively confronting the opposition—is a prerequisite to winning.
5. Make enemies, not friends. Identify the opposition, and attack their motives. Point your finger at them, and name names.
6. American mass culture is fundamentally alienating and disempowering. Most Americans don't feel they can make a difference or that they count, and they feel unqualified or unprepared to make important decisions about complex social questions. The key is to educate, empower, and motivate your target audiences.
7. Successful advocacy and social marketing campaigns, which generally have limited budgets, mainly utilize communications strategies based on social diffusion through opinion leaders and not on mass media. Effective social policy

Reprinted from a handout distributed by the Public Media Center by permission of the author.

movements develop through the creation of substantive messages which empower, challenge, and target a few key audiences that, in turn, influence larger constituencies.

8. Responsible extremism sets the agenda. To move the media, you must communicate as responsible extremists, not as reasonable moderates.

9. Social consensus isn't permanent and must continually be asserted and defended. Social advocacy is an ongoing process that doesn't end with the passage of a law or resolution of a specific problem.

10. In the same way that biological diversity is essential to planetary survival, strategic diversity is critical to successful social movements. Multiple, independent advocacy campaigns on a single issue should be encouraged, while centralized monocultural efforts should be avoided.

Appendix 11

LELAND BROWN

1. Thou shalt not define, design, nor commit community research without consulting the community!

2. As ye value outcomes, so shall ye value processes!

3. When faced with a choice between community objectives and the satisfaction of intellectual curiosity, thou shalt hold community objectives to be the higher good!

4. Thou shalt not covet the community's data!

5. Thou shalt not commit analysis of community data without community input!

6. Thou shalt not bear false witness to, or concerning members of the community!

7. Thou shalt not release community research findings before the community is consulted (premature exposition)!

8. Thou shalt train and hire community people to perform community research functions!

9. Thou shalt not violate confidentiality!

10. Thou shalt freely confess thyself to be biased and thine hypotheses and methodologies to be likewise!

Leland Brown, M.P.H., is Principal Consultant for the Global Bridges Group in Oakland, California.

About the Contributors

ANGELES ARRIEN is an anthropologist, author, educator, and corporate consultant. She is also the founder and president of the Foundation for Cross-Cultural Education and Research. She received an honorary Ph.D. from the California Insitute of Integral Studies. She lectures and conducts workshops worldwide showing the bridge among cultural anthropology, psychology, and comparative religions. Her books include *The Four Fold Way: Walking the Paths of the Warrior, Teacher, Healer, and Visionary*.

CINDY BERENSTEIN is a program evaluator with the Center for Health Studies at San Jose State University. She received her B.S. in community health education at San Diego State University and her M.P.H. at the Department of Health Sciences, San Jose State University.

LYNN BLANCHARD is a research assistant professor in the Department of Pediatrics at the University of North Carolina School of Medicine. She holds a joint appointment as a lecturer in health behavior and health education at the School of Public Health, where she received her M.P.H. and Dr.P.H. A former doctoral fellow at the Bush Institute for Child and Family Health Policy, her current research interests include evaluation of the efficacy of peer support for parents of young children with special needs, community attitudes toward HIV vaccine trials, and parent/professional partnerships.

CHERIE R. BROWN is founder and executive director of the National Coalition Building Institute in Washington, D.C., a leadership training organization that trains community leaders, government officials, and campus administrators. She received her Masters of Education in counseling and consulting psychology at Harvard University and has been doing training in prejudice reduction and coalition building for twenty years in the United States, Canada, Europe, and the Middle East. Her publications and videos include *The Art of Coalition Building: A Guide for Community Leaders and Working It Out: Blacks and Jews on the College Campus*.

FRANCES D. BUTTERFOSS is a public health educator and assistant professor at the Center for Pediatric Research in Norfolk, Virginia, which is run by the Eastern Virginia Medical School and Children's Hospital of the King's Daughters. She received her Ph.D. from the School of Public Health at the University of South Carolina at Columbia. Butterfoss coordinates local and statewide immunization coalitions and directs the national Coalition Training Institute in Norfolk. Her research focuses on evaluating the effectiveness of community coalitions for health promotion.

COURTNEY UHLER CART has been active in research, coalition building, professional education, and grant writing in areas including women and children's issues, family welfare, social epidemiology, homelessness, substance abuse, and philanthropy. She holds an M.S.W. from the University of California at Berkeley, School of Social Welfare, and is currently completing her M.P.H. Uhler Cart has worked as a staff member with organizations including the Fort Sanders Health System Foundation in Knoxville, Tennessee; the Center for Substance Abuse Prevention Resource Center in Fairfax, Virginia; and the Vanderbilt Institute for Public Policy in Nashville, Tennessee.

BARRY CHECKOWAY is professor of social work and urban planning and director of the Center for Learning Through Community Service at the University of Michigan, Ann Arbor. He received his Ph.D. in urban planning at the University of Pennsylvania. His research interests include community organization, social planning, and neighborhood development.

CHRIS M. COOMBE is an independent consultant and trainer to public and nonprofit organizations in program planning, organizational development, community organizing, and fund-raising in the San Francisco Bay Area. An adjunct faculty member at the California Institute of Integral Studies in San Francisco, she holds an M.P.H. from the School of Public Health, University of California at Berkeley. With over twenty-five years of community experience, Coombe is particularly interested in designing public health interventions that empower communities to create lasting change and that seek to overturn the societal inequities that lead to ill-health.

LILY DOW is executive director and one of the founders of the Adolescent Social Action Program at the School of Medicine, University of New Mexico. She is active in Hispanic youth leadership programs and was a recent past president of the New Mexico Public Health Association. Dow holds a Master's in Public Administration from the University of New Mexico.

EUGENIA ENG is an associate professor in the Department of Health Behavior and Health Education at the School of Public Health, University of North Carolina at Chapel Hill, where she received her Dr.P.H. and M.P.H. She has served as a consultant, trainer, and expert adviser for the World Health Organization, the Pan American Health Organization, the Peace Corps, and other agencies. Eng was principal investigator at the W. K. Kellogg Foundation–funded Community-based Public Health Initiative in North Carolina. Her research interests include farmworker health, breast cancer screening, lay health worker initiatives, and community participation domestically and internationally.

ROBERT FISHER is professor and chair of political social work at the University of Houston Graduate School of Social Work. He received his Ph.D. in urban and social history from New York University and his B.A. in history from Rutgers University. He is the author of *Let the People Decide: Neighborhood Organizing in America* and co-editor of *Mobilizing the Community: Local Politics in the Era of the Global City.*

NICHOLAS FREUDENBERG is professor of community health in the Hunter College School of Health Sciences and executive director of the Hunter College Center on AIDS, Drugs, and Community Health. He received his Dr.P.H. from Columbia University School of Public Health. He has been active in the health and environmental movements for many years, with most of his recent research and activism in the areas of AIDS and violence prevention. His publications include the book *Not in Our Backyards: Community Action for Health and the Environment* and the coedited volume *AIDS Prevention in the Community: Lessons from the First Decade.*

CHRISTINA GOETTE is a program evaluator with the Center for Community Health Studies in the Department of Health Sciences at San Jose State University. She received her B.A. in sociology from the University of California at Berkeley and her M.P.H. from the Department of Health Sciences at San Jose State University.

ROBERT M. GOODMAN is an associate professor and director of the Center for Community Research at the Bowman Gray School of Medicine, Winston-Salem, North Carolina. His current research involves studies on racial harmony, multicounty-based health needs assessments, and improvement in the effectiveness of social service delivery in North Carolina communities. Goodman received his Ph.D. from the School of Public Health at the University of North Carolina at Chapel Hill.

HERBERT CHAO GUNTHER has been president and executive director of the Public Media Center, the nation's leading nonprofit, public interest advertising agency, for the past twenty-one years. The center creates media campaigns that address critical social issues for organizations including Planned Parenthood, Rainforest Action Network, Greenpeace, and two hundred other environmental, women's, and social justice organizations in the United States and Canada, Latin America, Asia, and Europe. The center also undertakes campaigns in cooperation with numerous philanthropic foundations across the United States.

LORRAINE M. GUTIERREZ is an associate professor with a joint appointment in the School of Social Work and Department of Psychology at the University of Michigan, Ann Arbor. She is also the codirector of the Detroit Initiative in Psychology. Gutierrez received her Ph.D. in social work and psychology at the University of Michigan. Her research focuses on multicultural issues in communities and organizations. Current projects include an evaluation of gender and ethnically relevant AIDS prevention interventions; identification of multicultural issues in community and organizational practice; and definition of culturally competent mental health practice. Gutierrez has published on topics such as empowerment, practice, and women of color.

TREVOR HANCOCK is a public health physician and health promotion consultant based in Toronto. Much of his work in the past decade has been in the area of healthy cities and communities, an approach he helped pioneer. He helped to design the first community health survey and health status report for the City of Toronto in the early 1980s. As an adviser to WHO Europe, he helped organize the first technical workshop on healthy city indicators in Barcelona in 1987 and has maintained his interest in the subject ever since.

BARBARA ISRAEL is professor and chair of health behavior and health education at the School of Public Health, University of Michigan, Ann Arbor. She received her M.P.H. and Dr.P.H. at the School of Public Health, University of North Carolina at Chapel Hill. Her research interests include stress and social support, community empowerment, and participatory action research.

DANIEL KASS is director of the Hunter College Center for Occupational and Environmental Health and received his M.S.P.H. from the School of Public Health at the University of California at Los Angeles. He assists community-based organizations in understanding and addressing environmental concerns and works with local coalitions and public health agencies in developing environmentally protective public health policies.

GILLIAN KAYE is an international community development consultant in the areas of organizational and leadership development, coalition building, strategic planning, community organizing, and training. Based in Brooklyn, New York, she has extensive experience providing training, consultation, and technical assistance to grassroots community organizations, coalitions, community organizers, nongovernmental organizations, law enforcement personnel, and social service providers.

JOHN P. KRETZMANN is codirector of the Asset-based Community Development Institute at Northwestern University's Center for Urban Affairs and Policy Research. A former community developer and organizer, he writes on community building themes and is coauthor of *Community Building from the Inside Out: A Path Toward Finding and Mobilizing a Community's Assets*, one of the field's most cited works.

RONALD LABONTE has worked in community health promotion for over twenty years in settings ranging from community groups to labor unions to U.N. agencies. He is currently president of Communitas Health Consulting and teaches part time in the graduate health promotion program at the University of Toronto, where he received his Ph.D.

EDITH A. LEWIS is an associate professor in the School of Social Work and Women's Studies at the University of Michigan, Ann Arbor. She received her M.S.W. in social work from the University of Minnesota and her Ph.D. in social welfare from the University of Wisconsin-Madison, where she also held an appointment as lecturer. Her current research interests include women's empowerment, community organizing with people of color, and the incorporation of African-American structures and traditional strengths into group work and other intervention approaches.

JoANN McALLISTER is the research director of *manalive* Education and Research Institute in Marin County, California, an organization that focuses on the prevention of men's violence toward their intimate partners and on the role of male socialization as an underlying factor in all forms of violence, from gang warfare to international disputes. Her research interests include the influence of beliefs on human behavior, how individual and social beliefs change, and community organizing efforts that require changes in beliefs and behaviors. McAllister is a Ph.D. student in the Human Sciences Program at the Saybrook Institute in San Francisco, California.

JOHN L. McKNIGHT is director of the Community Studies Program at the Center for Urban Affairs and Policy Research at Northwestern University, where he is a professor in both the School of Speech and the School of Education and Social Policy. He has worked with communities across the United States and Canada and is author of *The Careless Society: Community and Its Counterfeits* and coauthor of the workbook *Building Community from the Inside Out.*

MIKE MILLER is the executive director of the San Francisco–based ORGANIZE Training Center. He began organizing in 1959, working with public housing tenants on New York's Lower East Side. For five years, he served as a field secretary for the Student Nonviolent Coordinating Committee. He was associated with Saul Alinksy from 1960 to 1970, and from 1967 to 1968 he directed one of Alinsky's organizing projects. With Bay Area friends and colleagues, he strated ORGANIZE in 1972.

MEREDITH MINKLER is professor and chair of community health education in the School of Public Health at the University of California at Berkeley, where she received her Dr.P.H. For over twenty years, she has taught community organization and worked with organizing efforts in health and housing, aging and disability, intergenerational issues, and human rights in Latin America. Minkler was founding director of the UC Berkeley Center on Aging and a cofounder of the San Francisco–based Tenderloin Senior Organizing Project. Her other publications include two coedited books on the political economy of aging and a coauthored book, *Grandmothers as Caregivers: Raising Children of the Crack Cocaine Epidemic.*

CHERI PIES is associate director and adjunct professor of maternal child health in the School of Public Health, University of California at Berkeley. She received her M.S.W. from Boston University and her M.P.H. and Dr.P.H. from the School of Public Health, University of California at Berkeley. Formerly an associate professor in the Department of Health Sciences at San Jose State University, she has served as a consultant in AIDS prevention and education, women's health issues, family planning, and the development and evaluation of community-based programs. Her research interests include reproductive ethics, lesbian and gay health care concerns, and the use of qualitative methodologies in public health research.

MARC PILISUK is professor emeritus at the University of California at Davis and Berkeley. He received his doctorate at the University of Michigan in clinical and social psychology. Pilisuk combines research and activism in the areas of conflict resolution, social support, health and caring, and environmental and social justice. His most recent book is *The Healing Web: Social Networks and Human Survival* (coauthored). Pilisuk currently teaches at the Saybrook Institute in San Francisco, California.

KATHLEEN M. ROE is professor and chair of the Community Health Education Program in the Department of Health Sciences, San Jose State University, and director of the Center for Community Health Studies. She received her Dr.P.H. and her M.P.H. from the School of Public Health, University of California at Berkeley, where she also served as lecturer. Roe serves as a consultant to health education programs on the local through the national levels and to state and local health departments. Her research interests include qualitative methodologies, contemporary women's history, children's perceptions of AIDS, grandparent care-giving, and program evaluation, and her recent publications include the coauthored book *Grandmothers as Caregivers: Raising Children of the Crack Cocaine Epidemic*.

KEVIN ROE is a program evaluator with the Center for Community Health Studies at San Jose State University. He received his B.A. in Health Education from San Francisco State University.

BETH ROSENTHAL is a consultant, researcher, and trainer in organizational community and coalition development and management for nonprofits, government agencies, and foundations. Based in New York City, she received her M.S. from Columbia University. Rosenthal has organized numerous coalitions and task forces, and her research and practice interests include new immigrants, homelessness, neighborhood and housing development, and intergroups relations. Her publications include a workbook entitled *Strategic Partnerships: How to Create and Maintain Interorganizational Collaborations and Coalitions*.

JACK ROTHMAN is professor emeritus at the University of California at Los Angeles, Department of Social Welfare, School of Public Policy and Social Research. He received his doctorate from Columbia University and taught for many years at the University of Michigan in the School of Social Work. Rothman's areas of research are community organizing, social planning research utilization, and intervention research. His latest publications are *Intervention Research: Design and Development for Human Service* and *Practice with Highly Vulnerable Clients: Case Management and Community-based Service*.

VICTORIA SANCHEZ-MERKI is a doctoral candidate in the School of Public Health at the University of North Carolina, Chapel Hill, and received her M.P.H. from the School of Public Health, University of California at Berkeley. She has held numerous positions in community-based organizations and health departments, including that of program coordinator for the Adolescent Social Action Program dissemination grant in northern New Mexico.

AMY SCHULZ is a Robert Wood Johnson Post Doctoral Scholar in Health Policy Research at Yale University. She received her M.P.H. and her Ph.D. from the University of Michigan in the School of Public Health and the Department of Sociology, respectively. Her research interests include social inequality and health, women's health and women's activism around health-related issues, and community organizing to address inequalities in health. Her current involvments include a community-based effort to address women's and children's health in an urban community, using community organizing strategies to create change at the organizational and community levels.

LEE STAPLES is a an associate clinical professor at Boston University School of Social Work, where he teaches community organizing and macro social work practice. He also serves on the faculty of the Center for Community Responsive Care, a multidisciplinary training program that helps prepare health professionals to work in respectful partnership with community members and consumers. Staples received his Ph.D. in sociology/social work from Boston University. Since the late 1960s, he has been involved in numerous social change efforts as an organizer, supervisor, staff director, trainer, consultant, and educator. His work has included welfare rights, housing, child care, mental health consumers, labor, neighborhood, and public health organizing.

LAWRENCE WALLACK is professor of community health education at the School of Public Health, University of California at Berkeley, and codirector of the Berkeley Media Studies Group. He is primary author of the book *Media Advocacy and Public Health: Power for Prevention* and a coeditor of *Mass Communication and Public Health: Complexities and Conflicts*. Wallack received his M.P.H. and Dr.P.H. degrees from the School of Public Health, University of California at Berkeley, and has been a consultant with the World Health Organization and with numerous other community, philanthropic, and government organizations.

NINA WALLERSTEIN is faculty director of the Adolescent Social Action Program, director of the Masters in Public Health Program, and associate professor in the Department of Family and Community Medicine at the University of New Mexico. She received her Dr.P.H. and M.P.H. from the School of Public Health, University of California at Berkeley. For the past twenty years, she has been involved in empowerment/popular education and community organizing efforts, and recently she was engaged in a healthier community initiative in New Mexico. She was senior editor of the two-volume special issue of *Health Education Quarterly* on community empowerment, participatory education, and health in 1994.

CHERYL L. WALTER is a doctoral student at the School of Social Welfare, University of California at Berkeley, where she also received her M.S.W. and her M.P.H. Formerly a consultant to the Alameda County Health Care Services Agency, Walter was principal author of the overall design of the county's MediCal Managed Care Plan. She also served as a board member and development director of the Women's Cancer Resource Center in Berkeley and as executive director of the Gay and Lesbian Resource Center in Santa Barbara, California.

ABRAHAM WANDERSMAN is professor of psychology at the University of South Carolina, Columbia. He received his Ph.D. from Cornell University, with specialization in social psychology, environmental psychology, and social organization and change. Wandersman was interim codirector of the Institute for Families and Society at the University of South Carolina. His research interests include environmental issues and community responses, citizen participation in community organizations and coalitions, and interagency collaboration. His publications include the coauthored book *Prevention Plus III* and and the coedited book *Empowerment Evaluation: Knowledge and Tools for Self-assessment and Accountability.*

DAN WOHLFEILER has been education director of the San Francisco-based STOP AIDS Project since 1990. He has also worked at the World Health Organization's Global Programme on AIDS and the Program for the Prevention and Control of AIDS of Catalonia, Spain. Wolfheiler received his M.P.H. in Community Health Education from the School of Public Health, University of California at Berkeley.

TOM WOLFF is the director of community development for the Massachusetts Area Health Education Center of the University of Massachusetts Medical Center and the director of the center's Community Partners Program. He is an applied community psychologist who has spent the last ten years developing community coalitions across the Commonwealth. Wolff received his undergraduate degree from Clark University and his Ph.D. in psychology from the University of Rochester. Wolff currently heads Community Partners, a technical assistance and training program for those involved in community coalition building.

MARC ZIMMERMAN is an associate professor at the School of Public Health, University of Michigan at Ann Arbor. He received his Ph.D. from the University of Illinois at Champaign in the Psychology, Personality, and Social Ecology Program, with a dissertation entitled "Citizen Participation, Perceived Control, and Psychological Empowerment." His research interests include empowerment theory, health promotion, community psychology, and program development. Zimmerman is coeditor of *AIDS Prevention in the Community: Lessons from the First Decade.*

Subject Index